10⁰⁰

Calculator Navigation

Mortimer Rogoff

Calculator
Navigation

W· W· Norton & Company

New York   London

Published simultaneously in Canada by George J. McLeod Limited, Toronto. Printed in the United States of America.

Library of Congress Cataloging in Publication Data

Rogoff, Mortimer.
    Calculator navigation.

    Includes index.
    1. Navigation.   2. Calculating-machines.   I. Title.
VK587.R63   1979   623.89   79–12385
ISBN 0–393–03192–6

1 2 3 4 5 6 7 8 9 0

*Dedicated to the memory
of Harold H. Buttner*

Contents

5 Loran

Appendix

Index

Routines and Programs

For each title listed, page numbers are specified first for the routine and then for the corresponding program.

Acknowledgments

When a volume draws on a lifetime of experience and takes five years to write, inevitably the author ends up owing a large debt of appreciation to many people; that is certainly the case in this instance.

The direct inspiration for organizing these materials on navigation came from sailing with John Ackley on his huge trimaran *Oha Oha,* especially when dense fogs on Long Island Sound brought home what finding your way is really all about. When the HP-65 calculator appeared early in 1974, I realized that it was possible to join the speed and precision of the calculator to the navigator's art, and I determined to make the attempt. My hope was that I would develop a tool that could be used by anyone, on any boat, small or large.

Once the book was started, many people made direct contributions. Dr. Peter M. Winkler provided much of the programming for the chapters on loran and celestial navigation; he created the mathematical approaches to the loran problem, and devised the means for utilizing on the HP-67 the data in the new *Almanac for Computers.* Keith Cohon also contributed to the programming, by working on the procedures for the SR-52.

I must not overlook the assistance provided by David Julyan and his brother Mark in the early discussions that led to the work on the "Sailing" chapter. Many of the ideas in that chapter were brought to life during my sails with the Julyans on the Chesapeake. As the work continued and the programs and routines progressed from concept to reality, Dr. Bernard Nathanson generously provided opportunities to try them on board his vessel. Along the way, Richard McCurdy of Kenyon Marine was graciously helpful with ideas and support, especially in the portion of the work involving polar performance curves.

I have tried to use each program and routine in as many as possible of the circumstances that may be encountered on board various types of vessels on various kinds of seas. A number of individuals have helped me in this effort. Robert Benson had me navigate in a drenching rainstorm off Oyster Bay, in Long Island Sound; and Sue Barrie, on her yacht *Sunbird,* provided the opportunity to navigate in heavy seas off St. Thomas. Both times the results were good. I was able to demonstrate conclusively the increases in accuracy that result from using regression methods—in coastwise and in celestial navi-

gation—when the deck is hardly a stable platform. Special thanks are due Captains Peterson, McGovern, Canvin, and O'Donnell of the New York and New Jersey Sandy Hook Pilots' Association, who spent hours with me as we made loran surveys of New York Harbor. With their assistance, I was able to use the loran programs and routines to test, and demonstrate, the accuracy and stability of Loran C, in waters for which loran charts have never been published by the government. Murray Buttner provided additional opportunities to test Loran C, and the bottom of his yacht has a few new scratches, where we found rocks for calibration points!

The United States Coast Guard has been extremely helpful during the development of the loran section of this book. In particular, Commander William Walker has been of great assistance, first by arranging for a test voyage on the cutter *Firebush* and then by making data available and reviewing the results obtained during the development of the approach to loran co-ordinate conversion.

One of the great rewards of this undertaking has been that a large number of people have become my friends through the professional association and collaboration that resulted from common interests. Kenneth Newcomer, the author of the Hewlett-Packard Navigation Pac, is such a friend. We have been sharing ideas on writing better navigation programs ever since this project began, and I have certainly benefited from his thoughts. Eric Swenson, vice chairman and executive editor of W. W. Norton & Company, has been a constant and patient supporter over the years that the book was in progress. Bill Reyman, who created the illustrations, has been especially understanding and supportive.

Actually, producing the book has been a family affair. Each of my daughters has played a role: Alice organized the early sailing days on the Chesapeake; Louisa did much of the early editing and organizing of the text; Julie typed most of the manuscript, including the intricate routines and the legends for the drawings. The ability of Louisa and Julie to make sense of a rough navigation manuscript was essential for the realization of the book. Judy Gies—not in the family—also helped considerably in this connection.

The understanding of my family and friends during the long period from the start of the book to its ultimate completion is most gratefully acknowledged. My wife, Sheila, has been patient, long-suffering, and still encouraging in spite of the fact that this work has been unrelenting in its demand for time and attention. Friends have had to put up with this weekend guest who comes burdened with papers, calculators, charts, and research material, and then appears only for meals. Ralph and France-Hélène Weindling have had more than their share of such strange behavior.

Finally, I would like to acknowledge Esther Jacobson's contributions to the order, accuracy, consistency, and simplicity that this volume may possess. As copy editor, she insisted that it come out right, and she deserves the credit for these qualities in the book.   *New York City, February 1979*

1

Calculators and Navigation

1.1 The Objectives of This Volume

This book was begun in 1974, when it became apparent that there were hand-held scientific calculators available, at reasonable prices, which could be used to solve virtually every problem that might arise in navigating at sea. Particularly suitable was the Hewlett-Packard 65, the first calculator which was not only programmable but permitted the permanent storage of any number of programs, on small magnetic cards.

The advent of the external memory in the form of magnetic cards made possible a *breadth* of application not obtainable with programmable calculators lacking the external memory. The latter can be programmed to do many things, but when the next application comes along and fills the program memory, the first program is lost. To be used again, the first program must be re-entered, keystroke by keystroke. By contrast, on a calculator with external memory, a program—once stored on a magnetic card—can be used over and over. When needed, it is simply read into the memory, in a process which takes one or two steps, and it is as easily replaced when the next program is to be used.

The capacity of the HP-65's program and data memories was large enough so that the calculator could cope with all of the problems in coastwise navigation, and could provide a useful approach to celestial navigation. The calculator was powerful enough to make unnecessary the use of the sight-reduction tables (such as H.O. 214, 229, and 249), thereby removing much of the pain associated with the conversion of sextant angles to fixes. In particular, it eliminated the need to interpolate between the values provided by the tables in order to obtain those required by the observations. To enable the navigator to take advantage of this new convenience is one of the fundamental purposes of this book.

Today, external memories take two forms: magnetic cards and solid-state transistor arrays. The form of external memory introduced in the HP-65, incorporating a miniature magnetic-card reader/writer, was later utilized in the Texas Instruments SR-52 and in the next-generation HP-67 and HP-97. It is provided also in the TI-59, in which, in addition, Texas Instruments has introduced solid-state memory modules (small, plastic-enclosed units, less than 1 inch square by 1/8 of an inch thick, which contain the equivalent of approximately twenty magnetic cards of the Hewlett-Packard type). The disadvantage of these solid-state memory modules is that they cannot be reprogrammed. If new programs are written, they must be designed into the

arrays, at considerable expense. These modules are consequently not suited to the custom programmer; they must be made and sold in large volume if their price is to be competitive with that of magnetic cards. Therefore, future calculators, while doubtless possessing interchangeable solid-state memories even more compact, and with larger capacities, than those now available, will also most probably continue to include some form of magnetic memory, such as cards or cassettes.

When the HP-67 calculator was introduced, along with its integral-printer counterpart, the HP-97, the increase in its memory capacity over that of the HP-65—and its ability to store data and programs separately, each on their own magnetic cards—made possible two important new developments in methods of calculator navigation: loran navigation, and celestial navigation without the need for any form of nautical almanac.

The convenience of calculator navigation thus arises from the extensive memory capacity of the models now available, and from the possibility of using unlimited numbers of external memory cards or modules. For example, once the locations of objects to be observed have been prerecorded on the magnetic cards, it is only necessary, when taking bearings on a light or buoy, to load the appropriate data card into the calculator and select the object by keying in a few identifying digits, instead of entering its whole latitude and longitude. In effect, a magnetic-card "light list" is employed which turns the whole process into a button-pushing exercise. Similarly, in celestial navigation, once the requisite data cards have been prerecorded, the user need only enter the date, Greenwich time, dead-reckoning position, sextant altitude, and height of eye for a particular observation to obtain the altitude intercept and azimuth of a celestial line of position. Indeed, if two observations are handled in this manner, manual plotting becomes unnecessary, since the calculator displays the actual latitude and longitude of the fix.

The fact that chart plotting can be eliminated—or at least kept to a mini-mum—is especially helpful on small yachts, where folding and unfolding charts on the knees of the navigator can be particularly awkward. In coastwise navigation, this convenience is available even when prerecorded data is not used. The calculator accepts the appropriate input concerning the bearings to observed objects, time, current, and vessel course and speed, and then displays the vessel's position with respect to one of the objects. The calculated position can then be spotted on the chart, without the need to lay out lines of position that radiate from charted objects or positions.

Another significant convenience in coastwise navigation results from the fact that the calculator programs embody the rules for taking into account the variation and deviation of the compass. This is important where the magnetic compass is the principal steering and bearing measuring reference. All the user need know is the amount and direction of variation and deviation. When these are entered, the calculator corrects or uncorrects the compass readings as necessary. One no longer has to remember that "True Virgins Make Dull

4

Companions Add Whiskey"* in order to use the compass correctly.

A second objective of this volume is to present methods which result in improved accuracy. Whenever input data contains random fluctuations— as in visual bearings taken from a hand-bearing compass or sextant readings made on board a vessel in rough seas—statistical methods can substantially increase the accuracy of the results. These methods use as the basis for an answer a series of observations, each consisting of a bearing or a sextant altitude and the time at which it was taken. Regression, which is more powerful and useful than simple averaging, requires numerous, involved manipulations of the values of each of these angle–time pairs—just the sort of mathematical operations that most navigators shun. The hand-held calculator performs them with ease, usually upon entry of a reading; the navigator is unaware of the process, which is accomplished in far less time than is required to take the next reading. These operations make possible the identification of the smooth, underlying trend of the data, from which can be obtained results much more accurate than those based on any single observation made under difficult conditions. The trend provides, first of all, a best estimate of the actual bearing or sextant angle being observed, minimizing the effects of an unsteady hand or rough seas. Second, the trend reflects the vessel's motion; a value of bearing or sextant altitude calculated for any time within the interval covered will incorporate the effect of this motion.

The convenience and accuracy obtainable with the hand-held calculator are also exemplified by the procedures involving loran. The programs and routines for the HP-67 and HP-97 enable one to use loran to obtain positions even in the absence of charts showing the loran lines of position. This material should be especially helpful during these years of transition from Loran A to Loran C, when new Loran C transmitter chains are put into operation even before the appropriate loran charts are available. High accuracy is served by the programs' ability to utilize local calibrating data, obtained by the user himself.

Convenience and accuracy, then, are the advantages of calculator navigation. The calculators already developed provide these in good measure; future generations of these electronic tools will surely offer even more.

1.2 The Intended User

This volume will be of service to several different types of readers, among them the yachtsman-navigator, the commercial mariner, the navigation officer on a large vessel, and the naval officer.

The yachtsman who is often his own navigator will welcome the convenience of methods that permit position fixing and planning of courses free of

---

*A typical device for recalling the rules for applying variation and deviation to compass or chart angles, quoted (along with others) by S. T. Simonsen, *Simonsen's Navigation* (Englewood Cliffs, N.J.: Prentice-Hall, 1973), pp. 24–25.

cumbersome chart constrictions. The tracking routines, which yield a "plot" of position, will be especially helpful.

All small-boat navigators, who work on an extremely unstable platform —the heaving deck—will find that use of the regression routines results in a substantial increase in accuracy.

The racing sailor should discover that the sailing routines make it easier to select tack courses and to make tactical decisions. If he is willing to invest the time required to determine the polar performance curves of his boat, the calculator can show him when he is sailing the optimum course under any given conditions.

The commercial boat operator—for example, the fisherman—will find that the routines make possible better use of his loran: he will be able to convert his "hang" co-ordinates and fishing locations from Loran A to Loran C readings; he will be able to steer accurate courses to reach his fishing grounds; he will have the advantages of loran navigation even in waters for which loran charts don't yet exist.

The navigator of a large vessel will make good use of the celestial routines while sailing the oceans; the improved accuracy obtainable from regression methods, including the elimination of steaming errors, will enable him to add a fix based on observations of the noonday sun to the daily routine at sea. When the vessel reaches a shoreline or enters a harbor, the precision of presurveyed loran will add to the ease of safely completing a journey.

The naval officer, exposed to a large variety of conditions and locations, can benefit from all of the foregoing; prerecorded cards of objects likely to be used for position fixing will yield extremely rapid calculations of his vessel's track. Regression methods used during heavy seas will improve accuracy. Planning of new courses while maneuvering will be facilitated. The programmed calculator will take its place as a useful tool in the hands of a navy navigator.

Indeed, in view of the advantages of calculator navigation, many individuals who enjoy programming will doubtless use the material in this volume as a point of departure for applications of their own.

1.3   Arrangement of the Material

Two types of material are needed for the use of the calculator—programs and routines. A program consists of the instructions which cause the calculator to carry out a particular sequence of operations. The programs for the procedures covered in this volume are presented in the Appendix. The content of these is fixed, so the user can record on magnetic cards those that will be employed repeatedly.

A routine consists of the step-by-step instructions for entering data and obtaining answers to a particular navigation problem once the appropriate program has been loaded into the calculator. The routines for various types of applications are presented in the several chapters of the book. The accompanying text explains the principles that are involved in each routine and pro-

6

gram. An illustrative example is normally provided. Performing the routine with the data in the example as input can serve two important purposes. First, it provides a test of the accuracy with which the program has been copied onto its magnetic card. It is virtually impossible to obtain correct answers with a program that has even a single error; therefore, if the answers displayed are those given in the example, the chances are that the program is correct.

Second, running through the routine in this manner is a way of gaining familiarity with the sequence in which the data is entered and the resulting answers are displayed. The program card prepared by the user is labeled to identify the function of each of the lettered keys. This labeling on the card serves as a built-in set of abbreviated instructions, which can guide the user in entering the required data. With practice, he will find it less and less necessary to refer to a routine while entering data; a glance at the label may be sufficient. The examples in the text can be employed to speed up this process of familiarization.

1.4   The Selection of Navigation Applications

Applications have been selected for this volume first of all on the basis of their general usefulness in navigation. A special effort has been made to include those not available—or readily available—elsewhere. Indeed, a number of completely innovative applications of the calculator to navigation problems are presented.

For example, in the "Coastwise Navigation" chapter are to be found routines utilizing the statistical method of linear regression to obtain fixes from bearings on one or two objects. As was pointed out earlier, under conditions where any single reading is likely to be unreliable, perhaps because of an unsteady deck in rough seas, accuracy can be substantially increased by utilization of this method. Thus the calculator makes it possible to improve the over-all result in a way heretofore unavailable to the practising navigator.

A second innovative application of the calculator in coastwise navigation is exemplified by the tracking routines. The programmable calculator can make repeated calculations of position, displaying the result at the end of each sequence. Since time is required for each calculation (twenty-four seconds in the HP-67, thirteen seconds in the HP-97), the program is arranged so that the calculator determines the advance in the vessel's position during the calculation interval, and displays the updated position at the end of each cycle. The result is a continuing display of updated position in real time—as if a plot were being made of the vessel's movement.

Another group of routines in the chapter on coastwise navigation takes advantage of the extensive data memory of the calculator by utilizing prerecorded object co-ordinates. For these routines, the latitude and longitude of each object likely to be used for visual bearings is recorded on a magnetic card. This need be done only once, unless the position in question subsequently changes (as it may, for example, in the case of a buoy), Thereafter, the position

can be recalled by a simple one- or two-digit keyboard entry. When using these cards, one can obtain a fix on two objects by entering little more than two bearings and the identifying digits of the two objects.

The routines in the "Sailing" chapter incorporate a number of procedures that should make them useful in solving the special problems of the cruising or racing sailor. For example, it is possible to take into account the combined effects of wind and current on a sailing vessel, in order to calculate the course to steer on each tack to reach a predetermined mark.

The chapter also describes a method of calculating *optimum* courses to steer, to reach a mark in the minimum time. Use of this method requires prior determination of the individual vessel's sailing characteristics: a plotting of the polar performance curves that define the vessel's speed through the water in various relative directions at various wind speeds. Specific instructions are included for constructing these curves, using data concerning wind and vessel speed as measured by the vessel's own instruments. When one of the routines for optimum course is used, the calculator displays the wind speed, wind direction, and vessel speed that *should* be observed on the vessel's instruments to indicate that it is optimally trimmed and steering the course for best performance.

The polar performance curves are also used in programming routines which enable one to determine and compare the speed made good that a vessel would achieve by sailing directly toward a downwind mark and by tacking toward that mark, under the same conditions. An explicit calculation of elapsed time to the mark is made for each method of sailing. The anticipated current is taken into account, and is shown to be of major significance in selecting the correct tactic.

The "Celestial Navigation" chapter contains routines utilizing the material in the *Almanac for Computers,* published yearly by the Nautical Almanac Office of the U.S. Naval Observatory. At this writing, there is no other published set of calculator programs and routines that utilizes this material. Its great advantage is that *all* of the celestial bodies, including the moon and the planets, are covered. The typical calculator procedures, as in the Hewlett-Packard Navigation Pac 1, and the self-contained, preprogrammed Tamaya NC-77 calculator, include algorithms for calculating the Greenwich hour angle and declination of the sun, and the Greenwich hour angle of Aries. Data on the sidereal hour angles of stars is also stored, so sight reduction of sun and star data is possible. But if observations of the moon or planets have been made, the nautical almanac must be used to obtain the Greenwich hour angle and declination of these bodies. By contrast, the method presented in this volume makes any reference to the nautical almanac completely unnecessary. The data covering all bodies for one year, as provided by the *Almanac for Computers,* is recorded on a set of magnetic data cards. Using the moon is then no different than using the sun; the extra corrections for moon position required in manual methods are eliminated. To calculate a line of position from an observation on the moon—or any other body—little data input beyond sextant altitude, time, and height of eye is required. The moon is the only body

other than the sun that is visible to the naked eye during the day, at a time when the sea horizon can be seen; there are days when the sun and moon can be observed for a two-body fix. It is to be hoped, therefore, that the ease of this method will encourage more use of the moon in celestial navigation.

A useful dividend in the sight-reduction routines is provided by the particular method that is employed to calculate the azimuth and altitude of the celestial object. The initial data entries include date, time, and dead-reckoning or estimated position. The azimuth of the body as it would be observed at that time and place is then displayed. This result can be used to check the errors of the magnetic compass (the combined effects of variation and deviation) or gyro error. For example, if a hand-bearing compass is employed, the first step in this checking process will be to obtain with the compass a reading for the sun's azimuth, taken from the exact spot on deck from which bearings are normally taken. The sun's azimuth is shown by the place on the compass card where the shadow of the lubber line falls. The time is then noted, and the result is compared with the azimuth obtained for this time, date, and position in the sight-reduction routine. For this purpose, the time entered need be accurate only to the nearest minute or two, and the dead-reckoning position to within a few minutes of latitude and longitude.

As in coastwise navigation, regression techniques can increase accuracy, and they are emphasized in the chapter on celestial navigation. I have tried them on both small craft and stable platforms; they clearly work, yielding much more accurate angles than could be obtained from individual readings under conditions where there are severe fluctuations.

As the sun approaches and crosses the local meridian, the successive readings of its altitude take the form of a parabolic curve. The chapter presents methods—equivalent to the linear-regression procedures used for coastwise navigation and for celestial observations at times other than meridian passage —for calculating the smooth trend underlying fluctuating observations of these altitudes. In addition, there is a detailed discussion of the effect on these observations of the vessel's own motion, which distorts the perception of *when* the meridian passage actually occurs. A routine incorporating a correction factor to compensate for vessel motion in determining the time of local apparent noon is one of the innovative features of this chapter. The results can then be used for the calculation of latitude and—under certain specified conditions —longitude as well.

The "Loran" chapter presents completely new material, specifically developed for this volume. The great value of loran, especially the new Loran C system, lies in its potential accuracy, stability, and range. The ability to use a hand-held calculator to determine position in terms of latitude and longitude, or distance and bearing, *with all of the precision inherent in the transmitted signals,* should extend the popularity of this method of electronic navigation.

The chapter includes instructions for making local calibrations, which are needed for the methods of high-accuracy position fixing which are described. Using these methods (in surveys in New York Harbor made jointly with the New York and New Jersey Sandy Hook Pilots' Association), I have obtained

repeatable results with an average accuracy of 30 yards. Even better accuracy can be expected from the 9960 Loran C chain.

The loran calculations can be made in two ways: given time differences, the corresponding position will be displayed; given latitude and longitude, the time differences observed at that location will be displayed. The latter procedure allows the user to predict the loran co-ordinates of a destination or rendezvous. Also, performed in sequence, these two operations can be used to convert Loran A time differences to the Loran C values for the same location. The routine embodying this process will be useful during the present transition from the old to the new system.

Most important is the fact that the calculator makes it possible to employ loran without being limited to loran charts, which are at present available only in relatively small-scale (large-area) versions. Instead, one can use charts of larger scale (such as 1 to 40,000 or 1 to 20,000), which are particularly desirable for navigating in confined areas. The loran time differences are utilized in the calculator routine, and the resulting position—which can be displayed in terms of the vessel's distance and bearing to a fixed point or in terms of latitude and longitude—can then be plotted on any chart of the area.

Also included in the chapter are routines in which successive loran fixes provide the basis for calculating the "current" (i.e., the actual current along with such factors as unrecognized leeway and compass or steering errors) which may be deflecting the vessel. This result is then taken into account in the subsequent calculation of the course to be steered to reach a destination or way point.

A number of important topics have *not* been discussed in this volume. Among them are the use of the calculator in radar maneuvering problems, calculations of distance to the horizon, and great-circle calculations. These subjects have been omitted because they are covered in the navigation program packages published by Hewlett-Packard and Texas Instruments, which provide the necessary programs for the HP-67 and HP-97 and the SR-52, respectively. Since most navigators will have access to these programs, repeating them appeared unnecessary.

1.5 Calculators Chosen for Navigation Applications

This volume presents programs and routines for the Hewlett-Packard models 67 and 97 and the Texas Instruments SR-52.

The HP-67 (figure 1.1) and HP-97 (figure 1.2) are identical except in two respects. One of the differences, important to the small-boat navigator, is that for the model 67, Hewlett-Packard offers a 12-volt recharging power supply that permits long-term operation on board. (However, it is also possible to acquire a small solid-state inverter that will convert the vessel's 12-volt DC power into 115-volt AC that can drive the model 97, so actually both can be

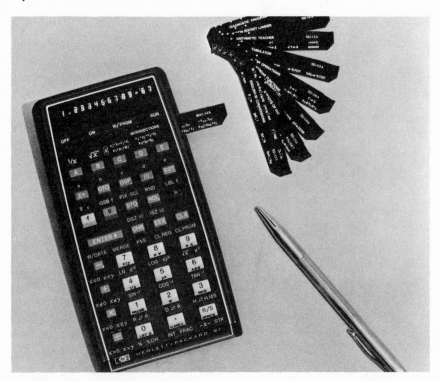

1.1. The HP-67 Calculator

1.2. The HP-97 Calculator

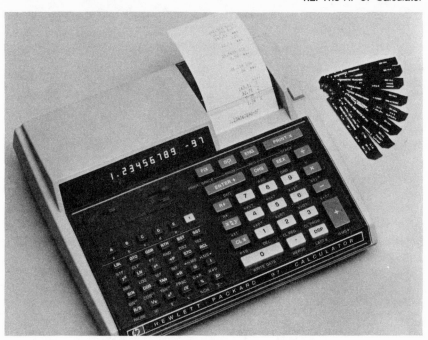

11

1.3. The SR-52 Calculator

used with 12-volt DC power.) Since both models are battery-operated, one can also solve the power-supply problem by simply keeping on hand enough fully charged batteries to last until recharging will be possible.

The other difference between the two models is that the HP-97 provides a printed display. The presence of this feature is a good reason for choosing the HP-97 over the HP-67—size, weight, power requirements, and cost permitting. For one thing, the printed record is extremely helpful in finding out what went wrong when clearly erroneous answers are displayed, since it makes it possible to check whether the correct input data has been entered in the correct sequence and the correct label keys have been pressed.

Second, the printed tape showing the successive input and output data is a form of log of a journey. In particular, if one of the tracking routines is employed, the listing of the series of values for time, distance, and bearing provides a record of the vessel's movement.

The SR-52 of Texas Instruments (figure 1.3) is powered by batteries rechargeable from a 110-volt AC power source. An accompanying printer— the PC-100A—is available, but since it too requires 110-volt AC power, an inverter to convert the vessel's 12-volt DC power is necessary. The SR-52 is

12

not the latest model; that honor belongs to the TI-59. The latter appeared on the scene too late to be included in this volume. However, there is available from Texas Instruments a solid-state program module for the TI-59 which includes virtually all of the navigation programs previously written for the SR-52. As explained elsewhere, the equations for the coastwise and sailing programs that appear in the SR-52 navigation package were written by me, and the resulting programs are included in this volume. Hence, the owner of a TI-59 who obtains the solid-state navigation module can in fact use many of the SR-52 programs discussed in the chapters on coastwise navigation and sailing.

The same cannot be said, however, for the chapters on loran and celestial navigation. These present material only for the HP-67 and HP-97. The memory capacity of the SR-52 is too limited for the operations required.

Hewlett-Packard has announced its newest calculator, the model 41C. All of the programs for the HP-67 and HP-97 that appear in this volume should function on the model 41C, provided the following conditions are fulfilled:

- Programs and data should be recorded on magnetic cards by means of the HP-67 or HP-97.
- The model 41C should be equipped with a card reader (an accessory unit that attaches to the calculator); this can properly read and use the cards recorded on the HP-67 and HP-97.
- The model 41C should be equipped with a minimum of one accessory plug-in (random access) memory module.
- The model 41C data-memory allocation should be set to twenty-six registers. Instructions for doing this are included in the manual for this calculator.
- Where program cards are customized (as in the chapter on sailing), or data cards are recorded (as for the positions of buoys, lighthouses, and the like in the chapter on coastwise navigation), certain special procedures, explained in the Appendix, are necessary.

If these requirement are met, all of the HP-67 or HP-97 program and data cards *should* function properly on a model 41C. It is probably a wise precaution to test any program to be used in this manner, preferably by comparing answers obtained on the model 41C to those obtained on the HP-67 or HP-97, or to those specified in the illustrative examples of this volume.

Notice that the program listings in the Appendix can *not* be used directly as programming steps for the model 41C, because its programming rules and structure differ in certain respects from those of the HP-67 and HP-97. However, when the preceding conditions have been fulfilled, cards made for the HP-67 or HP-97 can be used in the model 41C with the card reader.

Recognizing that many readers will want the convenience of prerecorded and prelabeled program and data cards, I have arranged for the preparation of such cards by a reputable retailer and mail-order supplier of calculators and their accessories. Details on price and delivery can be obtained from Barco-Navigation, 62 West 45th Street, New York, N.Y. 10036; for calls originating

within the continental United States, the toll-free telephone number is 800–221–2466. The prerecorded program and data cards that are available apply to routines for coastwise, sailing, celestial, and loran navigation on the HP-41C, HP-67, and HP-97. In addition, programs and data cards for loran navigation using the TI-59 calculator (based upon programs *not* included in this volume) are available from Barco-Navigation.

1.6 Using the Calculator in a Marine Environment

As a useful navigational tool, the calculator should be treated with the same care given to any other valued tool or instrument. The damp, salty marine environment can be especially harsh on electronic equipment. Keeping the calculator dry—difficult though that may sometimes be—is really the only way to insure its continued functioning. It may still work after having been dunked and dried, but one can't be certain; in particular, the motorized card-puller in the calculator is likely to be damaged by a severe wetting.

Belowdecks, keeping a calculator dry should not be much of a problem. But using it up on deck may sometimes be necessary—as when it is employed to record a series of bearing–time pairs for one of the regression routines. In these circumstances, especially in small craft, it may be wetted by seas breaking over the rail and spraying about. One way to keep the calculator dry in such a situation is to enclose it in a transparent plastic bag after the necessary magnetic cards have been loaded. The keys can be manipulated through the flexible sides of the bag, and the keys and display can be seen through the transparent plastic. Sandwich bags and those that seal with a zipperlike arrangement are available in appropriate sizes.

The calculator must also be protected from damage due to dropping. Therefore, when not in actual use it should be put out of harm's way, in a sturdy, shock-absorbing case if possible. Some cases can be worn on the belt, keeping the calculator protected and yet immediately available.

Another hazard is the loss of the magnetic program cards and data cards, which are so small that they may easily slip into unreachable crannies. This problem can be minimized by use of the small carrying cases supplied by Hewlett-Packard and Texas Instruments. In addition, cards should be made in duplicate, just to avoid the problem of loss. And spare blank magnetic cards should be carried on board, so that programs and data can be re-recorded if necessary.

2

Coastwise Navigation

ABBREVIATIONS   Used in the Routines of Chapter 2

Bc compass bearing from vessel to object

Bc1 first compass bearing from vessel to object, or compass bearing from vessel to first object

Bc2 second compass bearing from vessel to object, or compass bearing from vessel to second object

Bc3 third compass bearing from vessel to object

Bc1o1 first compass bearing from vessel to first object

Bc1o2 first compass bearing from vessel to second object

Bc2o1 second compass bearing from vessel to first object

Bc2o2 second compass bearing from vessel to second object

Bcom1 bearing from vessel to first object corresponding to common time

Bcom2 bearing from vessel to second object corresponding to common time

Bmid1 bearing corresponding to mid-time of first bearing sequence

Bmid2 bearing corresponding to mid-time of second bearing sequence

Bt true bearing from vessel to destination

Bt1 true bearing from vessel to first object

Bt2 true bearing from vessel to second object

Btdest true bearing from start to destination, or from object to destination

BtEP true bearing from start to estimated position

Bto2 true bearing from second object to vessel

Btobj true bearing between objects

Btp true bearing from vessel to object at time selected

C course

Cc compass course

Cm magnetic course

CMG true course made good

Ct true course

D distance from vessel to destination

D1 distance off first object

D2 distance off second object

DD.d, DDD.d degrees and tenths of a degree

Ddest distance from start to destination, or from object to destination

DD.MMSS degrees, minutes, and seconds

De deviation

DMG distance made good

Dn distance of nearest approach

D1o1 distance off first object at time of first set of bearings

D1o2 distance off second object at time of first set of bearings

D2o1 distance off first object at time of second set of bearings

D2o2 distance off second object at time of second set of bearings

Dobj distance between objects

Dp distance off object at time selected

Dr drift of current

E east

EP estimated position

H.hh hours and tenths of an hour

H.MS hour(s), minute(s), and second(s)

L latitude

Ldest latitude of destination

Lend latitude at end of run or leg

LEP latitude of estimated position

Lfix latitude of fix

lm chart factor

Lo longitude

Lobj latitude of object

Lodest longitude of destination

Loend longitude at end of run or leg

LoEP longitude of estimated position

Lofix longitude of fix

Lo-obj longitude of object

Lostart longitude of start

Lstart latitude of start

N north

naut. mi. nautical miles

O1 first object

O2 second object

S vessel speed; south

SMG speed made good

St set of current

ΔT time required to reach destination

T1 time of first bearing

T2 time of second bearing

T3 time of third bearing

Tcom common time

Tend time of end of run or leg

Tmid1 mid-time of first bearing sequence

Tmid2 mid-time of second bearing sequence

Tn time of nearest approach

ΔTn interval between time selected and time of nearest approach

Tp time selected—time for which a fix is required

Tstart time of start of run or leg

Tstop time at which calculator is stopped

Var variation

W west

→ following a data-entry item indicates that its entry initiates (without further keyboard activity) the calculation and display of one or more results.

+ indicates that the item (e.g., east variation or north latitude) is entered simply by pressing the appropriate numerical keys, on both the HP-67/97 and the SR-52.

− indicates that the item is entered on the HP-67/97 by pressing the appropriate numerical keys followed by $\boxed{\text{CHS}}$, and on the SR-52 by pressing the appropriate numerical keys followed by $\boxed{+/-}$.

2.1 Introduction

Coastwise navigation is navigation within sight of land—usually in restricted waters, where the possibility of going aground or of colliding with another vessel is ever-present. For the safety of the vessel and its occupants, knowledge of its position—actual and anticipated—is essential. In the past, the precise computation of position has been unattractively laborious, but now, with the calculator, it is readily performed. This chapter discusses the input data required and the methods used, and gives the specific calculator routines.

Certain assumptions, methods of measurement, potential sources of error, and the like are common to virtually all navigation work. These matters are examined in section 2.2, and some of the ways in which their handling is facilitated by use of the calculator are indicated.

The largest part of the chapter—sections 2.3 and 2.4—is devoted to step-by-step instructions for using representative calculators in various navigation applications. These sections by no means cover all the ways in which calculators can be used for navigation. However, the routines specified do cover most typical problems, and they are sufficiently representative to indicate the capability of the method. The following applications are included:

Planning   Determining the course to steer and the speed made good between two points when the bearing and the distance between them are known, in the presence of current.

Determining the course to steer and the speed made good between two points of known latitude and longitude, in the presence of current.

Position Fixing   Finding the distance off two objects or off one of the two objects when the bearing and the distance between them are known.

Making a fix on two objects whose latitude and longitude are known.

Finding the distance off one object.

Running fixes on one or two objects whose positions are known, in the presence of current.

Determining Estimated Position   Obtaining estimated position from knowledge of starting position, vessel course and speed, current set and drift, and elapsed time.

Current Determination   Determining the set and drift of current by comparing a position fix to a dead-reckoning position.

Position Tracking   Displaying continuously an updated estimated position, in terms of distance and bearing to a selected object.

2.1.1 Latitude and Longitude Versus Distance and Bearing The methods of coastwise navigation by calculation fall into two principal classes: those which involve latitude and longitude co-ordinates, and those which are based upon the bearing and distance between objects. Any scientific calculator with trigonometric functions can handle latitude and longitude, but the use of this data becomes truly convenient only with a programmable calculator having external storage, such as the HP-67, HP-97, and SR-52.

With a simple, nonprogrammable calculator, a separate keystroke is required for each digit of the latitude and longitude of the objects observed, for each digit of the figures for bearing, deviation, set and drift of current, and other input data, and for each step in the calculations. For example, in a case involving the latitude and longitude of two buoys, the compass variation and deviation, and a chart factor, forty-three keystrokes for input data are necessary. With programmable calculators having external storage, this data can be prerecorded on the magnetic cards, as can many of the instructions. Position fixes can then be calculated in a few seconds, with only seven or eight keystrokes.

Computation involving latitude and longitude is discussed in section 2.4; computation in terms of distance and bearing is discussed in section 2.3.

2.2 General Considerations

Before the actual procedures for employing calculators in navigation are considered systematically, a number of elements common to most of the applications will be examined. These include the plane-earth assumption, the role of smoothed or averaged bearings as input data, the methods of accounting for the effects of current and of compass variation and deviation, and two especially tricky matters—the methods of correcting for leeway, and of obtaining accuracy in "simultaneous" bearings taken from a moving vessel.

2.2.1 The Plane-Earth Assumption Consider a course or bearing extended over 10 nautical miles. In this situation, the bearing error—the difference between the angle calculated when the earth's surface is regarded as a plane and the one obtained when the earth is assumed to be a sphere—will be approximately 0.02 of a degree; the corresponding error in a calculation of the distance involved will amount to 0.02 of a nautical mile. Clearly, these are negligible errors, which can be tolerated. In coastwise navigation, where position is defined through sightings of visible objects, distances rarely exceed 10 miles, and most often are limited to a mile or less. Accordingly, in all the calculator routines in this book *not involving latitude or longitude,* the earth is assumed to be flat; when distances are this short, the errors resulting from this assumption are slight, and can be ignored.

As the distances in question increase, the possibility of error increases as well. For example, at 120 nautical miles, the difference between the results of plane-earth and of spherical-earth calculations increases to 0.5 of a degree and

18

0.7 of a nautical mile. While the course error is still relatively small, the distance error is approaching a level that might cause difficulty in achieving a safe passage. Plane-earth calculations should therefore be employed only when the distances are relatively short.

In the routines in this book involving latitude and longitude, the earth is assumed to be a sphere. There are many different methods available for making calculations of course and distance on a spherical earth; among them are great-circle sailing, Mercator sailing, and mid-latitude sailing. In the first method, spherical trigonometry is employed. In the other two, a conversion is made from a sphere to a plane surface, with certain distortions in appearance accepted for the sake of accuracy and relative ease of calculation. For example, the familiar Mercator projection widens areas near the poles, but is nevertheless extremely useful, since a straight line on its surface—a rhumb line—is a line of constant course.

The mid-latitude approximation of a sphere on a plane surface is important because it is simple, permits introduction of latitude and longitude co-ordinates into the calculation process, and is quite accurate over extended distances. Representative errors in mid-latitude calculations—which can be compared with those resulting from the plane-earth assumption, cited previously—are 0.08 of a degree and 0.003 of a nautical mile for a distance of 10 nautical miles, and 0.5 of a degree and 0.006 of a nautical mile for a distance of 120 nautical miles. Even at 120 miles, the error in distance is negligible, while the course error (compared to the initial great-circle course) remains reasonably small.

In computing the actual mid-latitude, half the difference between the start and the destination latitudes is employed. A variation of the mid-latitude method is to be found in many of the routines in this volume. Instead of the cosine of the mid-latitude, which often plays a role in mid-latitude calculations, a similar factor obtained from a nautical chart for the region in question is used. This "chart factor" (lm) is the ratio of the length (in nautical miles) of a stated interval of longitude—say 5 minutes—to the length of the same interval of latitude. At a latitude of 40°, these are 3.78 nautical miles and 5.0 nautical miles, respectively, yielding a ratio of 0.756. The cosine of the mid-latitude in this case would be 0.766; the difference between the two arises because the earth is not a perfect sphere, and the chart is distorted by this amount in order to correct for the earth's lack of sphericity. If the course in question has a large north-south component, the measurement of the mapping or chart factor directly from the chart should be limited to rather short distances (say, up to 10 nautical miles). For greater distances, normal mid-latitude calculations should be made.

2.2.2 Bearing Averaging and Regression   A major cause of inaccuracy in navigation is error in the initial observations. Particularly aboard small craft, unless the seas are calm, the unsteady platform of the vessel causes the bearings read from any type of magnetic compass to be fluctuating rather than constant.

In these circumstances, position finding is significantly more accurate when it is based on the averaging of a series of bearings rather than on a single observation. The calculator is particularly well suited to handling the sequence of figures, especially when the statistical method employed is linear regression, which not only smooths the data, but takes into account the actual change in the position of the vessel as well.

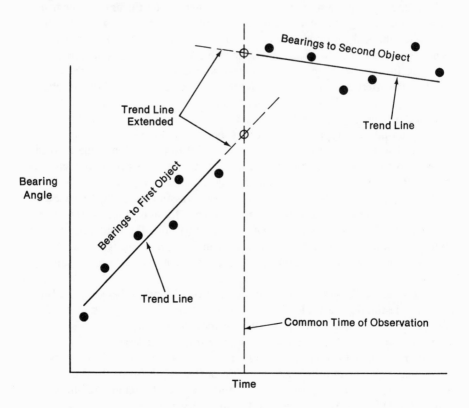

2.1. Bearing Regression

Linear regression produces a smoothed trend line from a group of fluctuating bearing observations. In general, the greater the number of observations, the more reliable and precise will be the trend that is established. Bearings taken from swinging compass references tend to have a high probability of error: each reading is made when the card has reached the end of its swing, which is generally when it is farthest from the true value. Because the card swings on both sides of the true value, errors will be reduced if a number of observations are made, so that values both above and below the correct one are accumulated. The linear-regression method results in a single, straight line which makes the best possible fit to all points in the data, lying above some of the points and below others, as illustrated in figure 2.1. Here, two series of observations are shown on the same graph. On the left is the set of bearings

20

taken earlier—on a nearby object, as evidenced by the sizable variation of bearing with time. The solid line is the calculated regression line which makes the best fit (on a least-squared-error basis) to the observed data. On the right is the regression line calculated from the second set of observations, taken a little later. These bearings exhibit a smaller average change with respect to time because the second object is farther away from the vessel. The geographical situation that gives rise to these bearing variations is shown in figure 2.2.

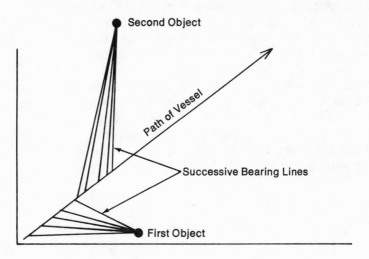

2.2. Bearings on Two Objects

The regression lines that are constructed from the observed data include the effects of the movement of the vessel during the time period in which the bearings were taken. As long as some precautions (to be specified shortly) are maintained with respect to vessel speed, nearness of the objects, and timing of the observations, the regression method eliminates the need to make a running-fix calculation when the bearings on two different objects are observed at different times. Two series of bearings are taken, the first on one object, and the second on the other; the trend line for each series is calculated, and the lines are then extended to a common time. This extrapolation process is illustrated in figure 2.1, where the first line has been extended forward in time and the second line backward. The bearings on the extensions at the common time become the input for the calculation for a fix on two objects.

Another attribute of the regression technique is that the observations need not be made at equal time intervals, clearly an advantage under the difficult conditions that prevail at sea.

A caveat: linear regression rests on the assumption that the motion is indeed linear—in other words, that bearing changes, if accurately plotted, would fall on a straight line. This assumption is valid if the vessel is not too close to the

21

object being observed, if it is not moving too fast, and if the total elapsed time, and the intervals between successive readings, are not too long.

In practical terms, these conditions will be satisfied in a boat going not faster than 8 knots, with the closest object not less than one-quarter mile away, and with about six to eight observations taken at intervals of approximately 30 seconds. Under these circumstances, the error in a position fix obtained by the linear-regression method will be under 50 yards. If the vessel speed is 18 to 20 knots, the minimum distance to the object should be increased to one-half mile. Conversely, for a vessel making 3 to 6 knots, the minimum distance to the object can be reduced to one-tenth mile, the number of observations increased, and the intervals between them lengthened.

There are two ways in which regression techniques can be used for position finding in coastwise navigation. The first of these, illustrated in figures 2.1 and 2.2, has already been discussed. A succession of bearing–time pairs is treated as numerical data, with the calculator analyzing the sequence for its underlying trend. This analysis gives rise to the regression line—always straight—which can be evaluated to yield a value of bearing for any time within the period in question.

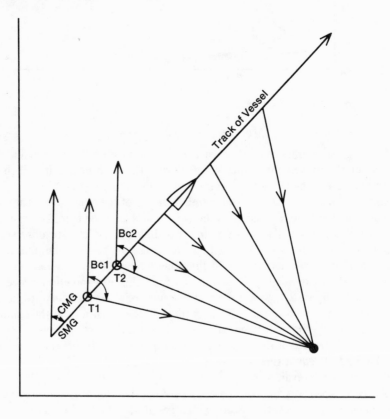

2.3. Regression Running Fix

In the second method, the values for bearing at successive times are just part of the data input, and the problem takes the form of making a running fix on one object. Figure 2.3 illustrates this case, in which bearings on a single object are taken from a moving vessel. In this instance, the calculation takes into account the actual geometry of the situation, and the regression equation which results involves not only the bearing–time pairs but also values for course and speed made good. For this method, unlike the first one, no assumption is required that the bearing–time relationship be expressible as a straight line. The calculated regression equation will produce exact values for position regardless of how close the vessel is to the object, and regardless of what speed it is making. These results are obtainable because values can be assumed for course and speed made good, based on the available figures for the vessel's speed and course, and for the set and drift of any currents that may be affecting its motion over the bottom. Consequently, obtaining accurate results with this regression technique—or indeed with any method of making a running fix —requires correct input data for vessel course and speed and the set and drift of the current.

In addition, there is a restriction attached to the use of the regression running fix which derives from the way it behaves in the presence of fluctuating data. One of the reasons for using the regression method is that it can smooth data, thereby improving the accuracy of position fixing when fluctuating bearings are utilized. If a regression *running* fix is to be made, *data should be taken only when the object under observation lies within the interval of 45 to 135 degrees or of 225 to 315 degrees of relative bearing.* Unless this precaution is taken, the answers obtained are likely to have a high level of error. This deterioration results because the regression equation includes a term involving the cotangent of the relative bearing to the object; a small change in this angle when the object observed is close to the bow or stern of the vessel is therefore magnified, and the answer is distorted accordingly. As long as this precaution is taken, the method will perform well.

A special difficulty in utilizing a calculator for regression problems may arise when the bearings in question range a few degrees to either side of 360, so that a sequence of data may contain something like the following: 353, 359, 004, 002, 357, . . . However, the programs provided in this chapter are written in such a manner that these values are properly interpreted.

Specific calculator routines that incorporate regression methods are presented in sections 2.3.5–2.3.7.

2.2.3 The Effects of Current   The motion of vessels in coastal waters is almost invariably affected by current; consequently, virtually every example given in this chapter either takes into account the set and drift of a known current, or involves calculation of the set and drift of an unknown, or imperfectly known, current.

In both cases, a vector problem is solved: the known values of vessel speed and direction are combined with those of the set and drift of the current, to yield the vessel's net motion; or they are combined with the known values of speed and course made good, to yield the set and drift of the current. This vector manipulation actually constitutes a subproblem in many navigation calculations. For example, problems involving a running fix require calculation of the motion of the vessel during the run, which in turn is affected by the current.

The routines that follow include the solution of the appropriate current subproblems wherever necessary.

2.2.4 Compass Variation and Deviation For the sake of the small-boat navigator, who in most cases has no directional reference except a magnetic compass, virtually all of the routines presented in this chapter use as input compass bearings and compass-course readings—taken at the vessel's permanently mounted or hand-bearing compass, or found by combining relative bearings with compass course. Corrections to account for variation and deviation must be made before this data can be utilized in the calculations.*

Fortunately, with the calculator it is unnecessary to remember the rules for applying variation and deviation, since the programs for the routines incorporate the corrections. In using models like the HP-67, HP-97, and SR-52, the data for courses or bearings can be entered directly as read from the compass, and once the values for variation and deviation have been introduced, the necessary adjustments are made automatically. On the HP-67 and HP-97, when latitude and longitude are prerecorded, it is possible to prerecord variation as well, thus further reducing the number of steps needed for entering data in the routines.

2.2.5 Leeway The motion of a sailing vessel to leeward of its heading is the result of a balancing of the forces on the hull (particularly the keel) and the forces on the sails; this motion, called *leeway,* is expressed as the angular difference between the heading of the vessel and the direction it actually travels through the water. The amount of leeway varies with the force of the wind, the heading of the vessel relative to the wind, the type of vessel, and other factors.

A concept useful in dealing with leeway is that of "wake course"—the course actually made good, as evidenced by the line of wake that is visible in relatively calm water.† Figure 2.4 shows the downwind drift of a vessel, its net motion seen in the line of its wake, while its bow points in an offset direction. It is evident that a statement of navigation information given in terms of a

---

*If a gyrocompass is used, corrections, if any, can be entered as deviations, and the variation set equal to zero. In this instance, all directions, both in the input data and in the results, will be true.

†The concept of wake course is clearly discussed and illustrated in Thomas John Williams, *Coastal Navigation,* Reed's Yachtsmaster Series (London, Thomas Reed Publications, 1970), pp. 90–92.

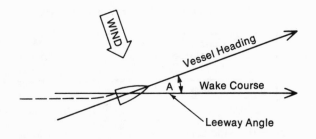

2.4. Wake Course, with Leeway

compass course or a relative bearing as measured from the direction of the bow, must be adjusted to compensate for the effect of the leeway angle *(A)*.

The navigational aspects of leeway can be summarized as follows:

1. The *speed* of the vessel through the water can be measured accurately, even though many degrees of leeway may be present, because speed meters are relatively insensitive to "crab angle" (sideways movement).

2. The actual track made through the water—the wake course—differs from the vessel's heading by the amount of the leeway angle. Though it is difficult to measure, the leeway angle can be estimated with fair accuracy.

Since the leeway angle is likely to be as large as 4 to 6 degrees, it should be taken into account when a highly accurate position fix must be obtained, and when one is steering a planned course. The leeway angles actually encountered on a particular vessel can be determined by taking many observations for a variety of wind velocities and relative directions. Once obtained, this information should be organized into a table of leeway angles for the vessel, to be used in a manner similar to that of a compass-deviation table.

The concept of *correcting* or *uncorrecting* for leeway effects has been borrowed from the handling of magnetic-compass deviation and variation. *Converting a ship's heading to a wake course is defined as correction; converting a wake course to a course to be steered is defined as uncorrection.* Table 2.1 lists the principal types of routine employed in coastwise navigation, indicates those in which the leeway angle should be taken into account, and specifies whether the course should be corrected or uncorrected.

Table 2.1   Application of Leeway

Type of Routine	Action Required
Planning	Uncorrect
Fix on two objects	None
Running fix	Correct
Estimated position	Correct
Set and drift	Correct
Course and speed made good	None

Table 2.2   Correction and Uncorrection for Leeway

Wind on:	Correct (From Heading to Wake Course)	Uncorrect (From Wake Course to Heading)
Port	ADD	SUBTRACT
Starboard	SUBTRACT	ADD

Table 2.2 indicates the wind conditions which determine whether the leeway value should be added or subtracted in making these conversions. This table assumes that all bearings and courses are measured clockwise through 360 degrees, with 000 degrees at the bow. Figure 2.5 illustrates this relationship between vessel heading, wake course, and wind direction.

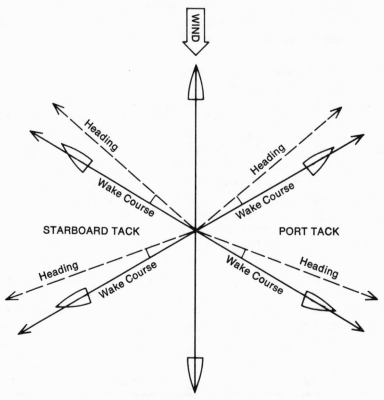

2.5. Course Shifts Due to Leeway

Since deviation tables are constructed to yield corrections based on the reading of the compass card, leeway changes should be made only after a ship's course has been corrected for deviation. Premature addition or subtraction of the leeway angle may result in an erroneous deviation value.

None of the calculator routines in this volume has labeled keys or numbered steps that call for the leeway angle as an input quantity. If leeway must be

26

taken into account, this fact is indicated in the routine by an asterisk (*) where correction is required, or a double asterisk (**) where *un*correction is required. The recommended practice is to add or subtract the leeway angle (mentally or manually) just after the amount of deviation has been determined; a combined value—"deviation $\pm$ leeway"—can be used. It is also possible to wait until the routine has been completed, and then make the necessary change in the answer that has been calculated.

2.2.6 Bearings from a Moving Vessel Fixing a vessel's position by taking a single bearing on each of two objects is a basic procedure in coastwise navigation. However, even if the bearings themselves are correct, the results may be inaccurate if the vessel is in motion while the observations are being made, since the position is then no longer defined simply by the intersection of the two bearing lines. This problem is illustrated in the two parts of figure 2.6. In part A, the vessel is stationary, and the intersection of the two lines of position determines an accurate fix. However, if—as shown in part B— the vessel is in motion, along the line *F–F'*, and successive bearings are taken at times *T1* and *T2*, the intersection of the two bearing lines will locate the fix improperly. The error in distance is the length of the line segment *e* in the figure.

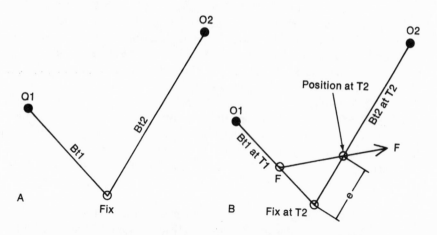

2.6. Problem of the Fix on Two Objects

Typical values of this error can amount to as much as 520 yards—for a 10-knot vessel when the two bearings are taken a minute apart, the first object is abeam, and the bearing difference between the two objects is 40 degrees. On the other hand, if the first object is dead ahead, the vessel motion between bearings results in no error at all.

Accordingly, there are several methods of minimizing the error. The navigator must exercise judgment in choosing the most suitable one. If the vessel is moving slowly, the discrepancy is likely to be so slight that it can safely be ignored. If the vessel is moving fast, the resulting error can be eliminated or reduced to reasonable proportions by the adoption of a course directly toward

or away from one of the objects. Another way to reduce the error is to keep the relative bearing of the *first* object observed as small as possible; this can usually be accomplished by viewing the objects in the proper order.

If none of these solutions is practical, the calculation should be changed to a running fix on two objects. In the running fix, the fact that the vessel is moving and the second bearing is taken from a different place than the first is accounted for in the calculation. Even assuming some uncertainty about the precise amount of motion—due, say, to an imperfect knowledge of the currents that are acting on the vessel—the result is usually substantially more accurate than it would be if the motion were ignored.

For example, at 15 knots, a vessel will move 500 yards in one minute; if errors in speed or course made good amount to 10 percent of this distance, the expected error in the final position of the running fix will be 50 yards. On the other hand, if the motion of this vessel between bearings is ignored, with the first bearing abeam and a bearing difference between objects of 40 degrees, an error of 765 yards will result.

2.3 Coastwise Navigation Using Distances and Bearings

The calculator instructions in the following sections have been arranged as a series of specific cases; each case includes the appropriate routines for the several calculators and an illustration of an application which can be worked out on any one of the calculators. The HP-67 and HP-97 are suitable for all of the cases, while the SR-52, has slightly more limited capabilities.*

In the routines which follow in this section, the only co-ordinates are distances and bearings; latitude and longitude are not introduced, and the calculations are based upon the plane-earth assumption. Therefore, as indicated earlier, these routines should be utilized only when the distances involved are relatively short; if they are under 50 nautical miles, the errors arising from the plane-earth assumption will probably not cause difficulty in ordinary navigation.

2.3.1 Fixing, Planning, and Estimated Position on the HP-67 and

HP-97   It has been possible to write for the HP-67 and HP-97 a single routine —routine 2.1—which makes these calculators simple to utilize in solving virtually all of the problems in coastwise navigation. Figures 2.7–2.16 illustrate the use of this routine.

*Some of the equations and programs for the SR-52 developed by the author and presented in this chapter are utilized in two publications issued by Texas Instruments: the Navigation Library (Program Manual NG1) for the SR-52 and the manual on Marine Navigation for the TI-58 and TI-59.

Routine 2.1 (HP-67/97)

Btobj Dobj	De Var	PLAN C SMG ΔT	Clear Initialize	EP D Bt R/S Dr
Cc S St Dr	Tstart Tend	Bc1	Bc2	D2

**FIXING, PLANNING, ESTIMATED POSITION, SET AND DRIFT
(DISTANCE AND BEARING)**

Step	Procedure	Input Data/Units	Keys	Output Data/Units
1	Load program—both sides			
	Fixing—Fix on Two Objects			
2	After completion of step 1, clear		f d	
3	Initialize		f d	
4	Enter true bearing between objects, in either direction	DDD.d	f a	
5	Enter distance between objects	naut. mi.	f a	
6	Enter deviation (+E, −W), even if 0	DD.d	f b	
7	Enter variation (+E, −W), even if 0	DD.d	f b	
8	Enter compass bearing to first object	DDD.d	C	
9	Enter compass bearing to second object	DDD.d	D	
10	Calculate and display distance off second object		E	naut. mi.
	Fixing—Running Fix on One Object			
11	After completion of step 1, clear		f d	
12	Initialize		f d	
13	Enter deviation at time of first bearing (+E, −W), even if 0	DD.d	f b	
14	Enter variation (+E, −W), even if 0	DD.d	f b	
15	Enter compass course during run or leg*	DDD.d	A	
16	Enter vessel speed during run or leg	knots	A	
17	Enter set of current, even if 0	DDD.d	A	
18	Enter drift of current, even if 0	knots	A	
19	Enter time of start of run or leg	H.MS	B	
20	Enter time of end of run or leg	H.MS	B	
21	Enter compass bearing to object at start of run	DDD.d	C	

*Correct for leeway; see table 2.2.

(CONTINUED)

Step	Procedure	Input Data/Units	Keys	Output Data/Units

For multiple courses or speeds, or changes in set or drift between bearings, repeat as necessary steps 13–14 and 15–18; deviation and variation are handled as a pair—if even one of them changes, *both* must be re-entered; similarly, if course, speed, set, or drift changes, *all four* must be re-entered. Steps 19–20 are then repeated for each new leg.

Step	Procedure	Input Data/Units	Keys	Output Data/Units
22	Enter compass bearing to object at end of run, or end of last leg	DDD.d	D	
23	Calculate and display distance off object		E	naut. mi.

Fixing—Running Fix on Two Objects

Step	Procedure	Input Data/Units	Keys	Output Data/Units
24	After completion of step 1, clear		f d	
25	Initialize		f d	
26	Enter true bearing from first object to second object	DDD.d	f a	
27	Enter distance between objects	naut. mi.	f a	
28	Enter deviation at time of first bearing (+E, −W), even if 0	DD.d	f b	
29	Enter variation (+E, −W), even if 0	DD.d	f b	
30	Enter compass course during run or leg*	DDD.d	A	
31	Enter vessel speed during run or leg	knots	A	
32	Enter set of current, even if 0	DDD.d	A	
33	Enter drift of current, even if 0	knots	A	
34	Enter time of start of run or leg	H.MS	B	
35	Enter time of end of run or leg	H.MS	B	
36	Enter compass bearing to first object at start of run	DDD.d	C	

For multiple courses or speeds, or changes in set or drift between bearings, repeat as necessary steps 28–29 and 30–33; deviation and variation are handled as a pair—if even one of them changes, *both* must be re-entered; similarly, if course, speed, set, or drift changes, *all four* must be re-entered. Steps 34–35 are then repeated for each leg.

Step	Procedure	Input Data/Units	Keys	Output Data/Units
37	Enter compass bearing to second object at end of run, or end of last leg	DDD.d	D	
38	Calculate and display distance off second object		E	naut. mi.

Planning

Step	Procedure	Input Data/Units	Keys	Output Data/Units
39	After completion of step 1, enter true bearing from start to destination	DDD.d	f a	
40	Enter distance between start and destination	naut. mi.	f a	

The preceding two steps can be omitted if a fix to the destination has just previously been calculated (as at step 10, 23, or 38).

*Correct for leeway; see table 2.2.

Step	Procedure	Input Data/Units	Keys	Output Data/Units
41	Enter deviation as 0[1]	0	f b	
42	Enter variation ($+$E, $-$W), even if 0	DD.d	f b	
43	Enter *any* value of compass course	DDD.d	A	
44	Enter expected vessel speed	knots	A	
45	Enter expected set of current, even if 0	DDD.d	A	
46	Enter expected drift of current, even if 0	knots	A	
47	Calculate and display magnetic course to steer (ignore display of *SMG* and elapsed time)		f c	DDD.d
48	Enter deviation for course displayed, even if 0, and repeat step 42	DD.d	f b	
49	Calculate and display compass course to steer,**		f c	DDD.d
·	Speed made good,			knots
·	Time required to reach destination			H.MS

Estimated Position

Step	Procedure	Input Data/Units	Keys	Output Data/Units
50	After completion of step 1, clear		f d	
51	Enter true bearing from start to destination	DDD.d	f a	
52	Enter distance from start to destination	naut. mi.	f a	

The preceding two steps can be omitted if the position is to be obtained relative to an object for which a fix has just previously been calculated (as at step 10, 23, or 38). For an estimated position relative to the *starting position,* enter bearing and distance as 0 in the preceding two steps.

Step	Procedure	Input Data/Units	Keys	Output Data/Units
53	Enter deviation ($+$E, $-$W), even if 0	DD.d	f b	
54	Enter variation ($+$E, $-$W), even if 0	DD.d	f b	
55	Enter compass course*	DDD.d	A	
56	Enter vessel speed	knots	A	
57	Enter set of current, even if 0	DDD.d	A	
58	Enter drift of current, even if 0	knots	A	

Steps 51–58 can be omitted if the planning part of this routine has just been completed.

Step	Procedure	Input Data/Units	Keys	Output Data/Units
59	Enter time of start of run	H.MS	B	
60	Enter time at end of leg, or at which estimated position is required	H.MS	B	
61	Calculate and display distance to destination,		f e	naut. mi.
·	True bearing to destination			DDD.d

[1]For an alternative method of estimating deviation in planning, see p. 38.
***Un*correct for leeway; see table 2.2.
*Correct for leeway; see table 2.2.

(CONTINUED)

Step	Procedure	Input Data/Units	Keys	Output Data/Units
	For multiple courses or speeds, or changes in set or drift, repeat as necessary steps 53–54 and 55–58; deviation and variation are handled as a pair—if even one of them changes, *both* must be re-entered; similarly, if course, speed, set, or drift changes, *all four* must be re-entered (a method of recalling course, speed, set, and drift from the calculator's memory, to be used if any of these are to be re-entered, is presented on p. 43). Steps 59–61 are then repeated for each leg.			
	Set and Drift			
62	After completion of step 1, clear		f d	
63	Enter true course made good (available from routine 2.12)	DDD.d	f a	
64	Enter distance made good (available from routine 2.12)	naut. mi.	f a	
65	Enter deviation (+E,−W), even if 0	DD.d	f b	
66	Enter variation (+E,−W), even if 0	DD.d	f b	
67	Enter compass course during run*	DDD.d	A	
68	Enter vessel speed during run	knots	A	
69	Enter time of start of run	H.MS	B	
70	Enter time of end of run	H.MS	B	
71	Calculate estimated position, disregard display of first result (distance),		f e	
·	Display set of current			DDD.d
72	Display drift of current		R/S	knots

*Correct for leeway; see table 2.2.

The instructions of routine 2.1 fall into three main categories: fixing, planning, and finding estimated position. A brief additional segment, for calculating current, permits use of the estimated-position procedures for this purpose. A single magnetic card (identical for the HP-67 and the HP-97) stores the program for all of these operations. However, an additional magnetic card is required for routine 2.1A, which is useful under many circumstances for combining fixing and planning.

The *fixing* parts of the routine cover a fix on two objects, a running fix on one object, and a running fix on two objects. Figure 2.7 shows the case in which the bearing observations on two objects are assumed to be simultaneous—having been made from a stationary vessel, for example. Under these circumstances, all of the input values that relate to the motion of the vessel can be either unentered or set at zero. These values are vessel compass course *(Cc)*,

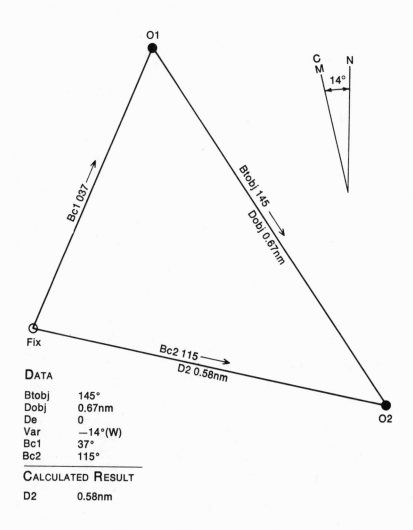

O1

C
M
N
14°

Btobj 145
Dobj 0.67nm

Bc1 037

Fix

Bc2 115
D2 0.58nm

O2

DATA

Btobj	145°
Dobj	0.67nm
De	0
Var	−14°(W)
Bc1	37°
Bc2	115°

CALCULATED RESULT

D2	0.58nm

2.7. Fix on Two Objects (Distance and Bearing)

vessel speed *(S),* set of current *(St),* drift of current *(Dr),* and time of start *(Tstart)* and time of end *(Tend)* of the run. The true bearing between two objects *(Btobj)* can be entered in either sense—from the first object to the second, or from the second to the first. The input bearings *(Bc1* and *Bc2)* can be obtained from single observations taken simultaneously, or nearly so, or they can be calculated from routine 2.6, providing data from regression analysis. The answer is given as distance off the object on which the second observation was made *(D2).*

Figure 2.8 illustrates the running fix on one object. Here, the input data includes values for course, speed, current, and elapsed time, describing the motion of the vessel during the run between observations. As before, the routine accepts compass bearings and converts them to true bearings, since

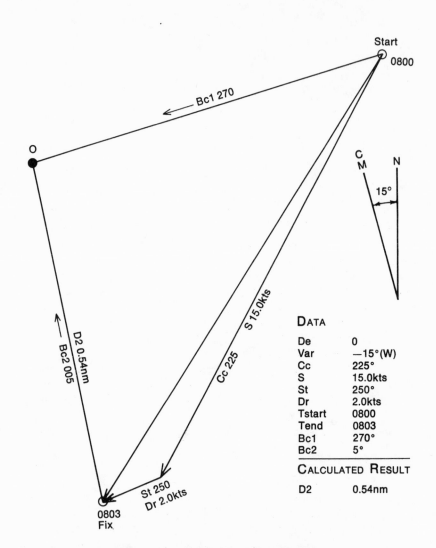

DATA

De	0
Var	−15°(W)
Cc	225°
S	15.0kts
St	250°
Dr	2.0kts
Tstart	0800
Tend	0803
Bc1	270°
Bc2	5°

CALCULATED RESULT

D2	0.54nm

2.8. Running Fix on One Object (Distance and Bearing)

deviation and variation have been entered into the calculator memory. No data entry is made for the bearing or distance between objects, because only one object is involved.

Since the over-all accuracy of the result depends upon correct values for the course and speed *made good* during the run between bearings, it is important to know the set and drift of the current acting on the vessel during the run. The values for set and drift are entered at the appropriate steps even if they are equal to zero.

The vessel speed used in calculating the running fix should be the *average* speed during the run between bearings. This can be ascertained by subtracting a log reading noted at the time of the first bearing from a reading noted at the time of the second bearing (to obtain the distance traveled) and dividing this

figure by the time interval between the readings. Even if many bearings are taken—for use in a regression, for example—only two log readings, one early in the run, and another at the end, are necessary for determining average speed. Also, in this situation the time interval over which the speed is derived need not be precisely the same as the interval over which the bearings are measured. These intervals need only be approximately the same, provided the speed is relatively uniform throughout.

The accuracy of the calculated result will also depend upon the crossing angle of the two lines of position. If possible, the run should be long enough so that the difference between the two bearings is close to 90 degrees.

Figure 2.9 illustrates the case of a vessel that makes a change in its motion

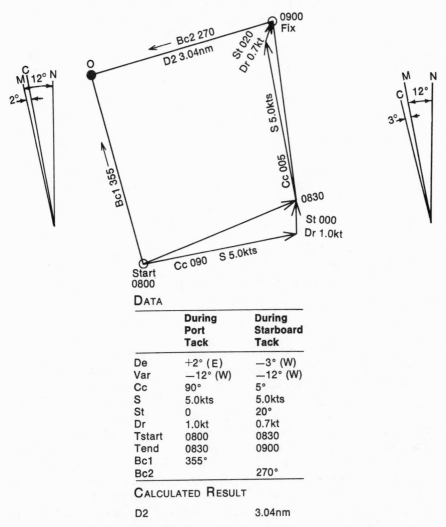

DATA

	During Port Tack	During Starboard Tack
De	+2° (E)	−3° (W)
Var	−12° (W)	−12° (W)
Cc	90°	5°
S	5.0kts	5.0kts
St	0	20°
Dr	1.0kt	0.7kt
Tstart	0800	0830
Tend	0830	0900
Bc1	355°	
Bc2		270°

CALCULATED RESULT

| D2 | | 3.04nm |

2.9. Running Fix on One Object, Multiple Legs (Distance and Bearing)

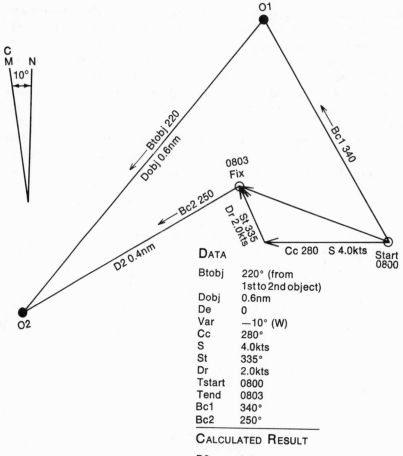

DATA

Btobj	220° (from 1st to 2nd object)
Dobj	0.6nm
De	0
Var	−10° (W)
Cc	280°
S	4.0kts
St	335°
Dr	2.0kts
Tstart	0800
Tend	0803
Bc1	340°
Bc2	250°

CALCULATED RESULT

D2	0.4nm

2.10. Running Fix on Two Objects (Distance and Bearing)

during the period between the first bearing observation and the second. Changes of this sort are accounted for in the calculations as long as the data is properly entered.

A course change may result in alterations in deviation, variation, course, speed, set, drift, time of start, and time of end. In this situation, data is first entered for the initial leg, and the first bearing is included as part of that sequence. Successive legs are treated in turn, with entries being made for all of the changes appropriate for the portion of the run in question. When there is a change in any one of the values entered at ⬛ A —course, speed, set, and drift—all four must be re-entered. Similarly, if there is a change in either variation or deviation, both must be re-entered. For each of the intermediate legs, the last items to be entered are the time of start and time of end of the leg. However, the first bearing to the object is entered when the *first* value of deviation is still present in the calculator; the second bearing to the object is entered when the *last* value of deviation is in the calculator. If this sequence

is maintained, the fixing information—distance off the object at the time of the second observation—is displayed after the second bearing is entered and $\boxed{E}$ is pressed.

Figure 2.10 illustrates the running fix on two objects. This problem is encountered when, for example, there is a significant difference between the time of the bearing on the first object and the time of the bearing on the second. The run made between the two bearings is accounted for in the calculation, to preserve the accuracy of the fix.

The bearing between the two objects *(Btobj)* must be entered in the proper sense: it is measured *from* the first object observed *to* the second object. This is the only case where this order is significant.

The distance between the objects, deviation, variation, course, speed, set, drift, time of start and end of run, and bearings from the vessel to the objects are entered as before. If the vessel's motion changes during the run between bearings, appropriate data entries are made for each new leg. The procedures previously described for entering data changes during a running fix on one object are applicable here as well.

Figure 2.11 illustrates *planning.* In this instance, the input values are the bearing and distance between the start and destination of a planned run, the expected speed of the vessel, and the expected set and drift of the current during the run or leg of the journey.

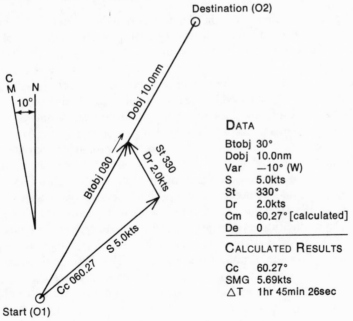

DATA

Btobj	30°
Dobj	10.0nm
Var	−10° (W)
S	5.0kts
St	330°
Dr	2.0kts
Cm	60.27° [calculated]
De	0

CALCULATED RESULTS

Cc	60.27°
SMG	5.69kts
△T	1hr 45min 26sec

2.11. Planning (Distance and Bearing)

In the planning part of the routine, even though the compass course is to be obtained as an answer, an entry for this item is necessary to make possible the acceptance of the values for speed, set, and drift that follow. An arbitrary value for course may be used, or the entry may be made by simply pressing $\boxed{A}$, without first entering a particular value.

Deviation and variation should be entered at some point in the sequence before $\boxed{f}$ $\boxed{c}$ are pressed, since they are required as part of the calculation for a *compass* course to steer. But though variation is independent of the calculated course, deviation is not, since it depends on the compass heading of the vessel. Therefore, the preferred method is to make the calculation first with deviation set at zero; this provides the magnetic course to steer as the answer. Then, any required correction for deviation at this magnetic heading can be obtained from the deviation card, and the planning calculation can be performed a second time—with the appropriate deviation for that magnetic course—to provide the compass course to steer.

A less time-consuming approach is to examine the planned course, estimate the effect of current on the final result, and assume a value for deviation. If —according to the deviation card—the resulting calculated compass course would require a deviation correction of the amount initially assumed, then no further calculation of the compass course to steer is necessary. If the result is a compass course whose accompanying deviation is different by a degree or more from that used to obtain the answer, then the calculation should be repeated, with the proper value for deviation.

The answer obtained from the planning part of the routine should be further modified by the adjustment for leeway (if appropriate, as in the case of a sailing vessel). Reference to table 2.1 shows that for planning, an *uncorrection* will be required. This means that if the wind is on the starboard side of the vessel, the leeway figure is added to the course to obtain the correct vessel heading.

The length of the run used in planning should be limited to the interval over which the expected values for the effects of current are reasonably accurate. When tidal currents with continuously changing set and drift are involved, the values used in this calculation are, at best, approximate. Similarly, if the vessel's passage through a current will itself cause changes in the current, then any single set of values for set and drift will be approximate. The remedy is to break down the planned journey into short sections over which the current can be assumed to be constant. The length of the interval will depend, of course, upon the rate of change of the current *as experienced by the moving vessel.* The more rapid this rate, the shorter the chosen interval. As before, when new values for set and drift are entered, the other items associated with $\boxed{A}$—course (entered as an arbitrary value or simply by pressing $\boxed{A}$) and speed—must be re-entered as well, before $\boxed{f}$ $\boxed{c}$ are pressed to obtain the course to steer.

In addition to compass course, the planning part of the routine supplies speed made good and time required to reach the destination. The latter, given

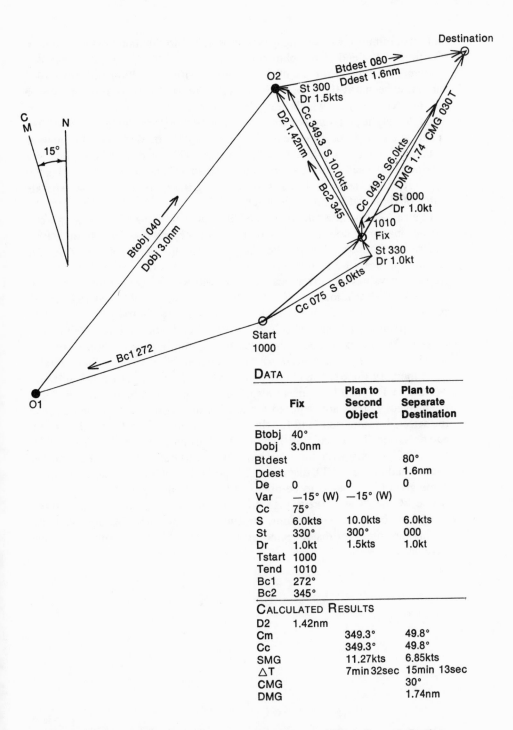

	Fix	Plan to Second Object	Plan to Separate Destination
Btobj	40°		
Dobj	3.0nm		
Btdest			80°
Ddest			1.6nm
De	0	0	0
Var	—15° (W)	—15° (W)	
Cc	75°		
S	6.0kts	10.0kts	6.0kts
St	330°	300°	000
Dr	1.0kt	1.5kts	1.0kt
Tstart	1000		
Tend	1010		
Bc1	272°		
Bc2	345°		

Calculated Results

	Fix	Plan to Second Object	Plan to Separate Destination
D2	1.42nm		
Cm		349.3°	49.8°
Cc		349.3°	49.8°
SMG		11.27kts	6.85kts
△T		7min 32sec	15min 13sec
CMG			30°
DMG			1.74nm

2.12. Running Fix on Two Objects, with Plan to Second Object and Plan to Separate Destination (Distance and Bearing)

in hours, minutes, and seconds, should be added to the time of start to obtain the time at the end of the planning interval.

Figure 2.12 shows the use of the routine to both fix position and plan. After a run that begins at 1000, the position fix is completed at 1010, and the distance off the second object, which bears 345°C, turns out to be 1.42 nautical miles. Next, use of the planning portion of the routine yields the course to steer, speed made good, and the time required to reach *O2*. In this case, the answer obtained from the fix calculation—distance off *O2*—and the bearing *Bc2,* are retained in the calculator's memory as the distance and course to the planned destination, and serve as the basis for obtaining the course to steer. No separate entry of these data items is required.

Figure 2.12 also illustrates a method of combining fixing with planning when the destination is not identical with any of the objects used in obtaining a fix, but rather is a completely different place. In this particular example, the destination bears 80°T from the second object, at a distance of 1.6 nautical miles. New values for current are assumed, with set now equal to 000° and drift to 1.0 knot. Variation (15°W), deviation (0), and vessel speed (6.0 knots) remain the same as during the run between bearing observations.

This planning problem is solved by means of routine 2.1A, which is employed after the fix has been provided by the appropriate portion of routine 2.1. The vessel's position need not be re-entered, since the calculator retains in its memory the bearing and distance to the second object (in this instance 345°C and 1.42 nautical miles); also, variation need not be re-entered if it is unchanged. Entries are required for bearing and distance from the object to the selected destination, and for the expected values of vessel speed, current, and deviation. The calculator then displays the compass course to the destination (49.8°), along with the time required (15 minutes, 13 seconds) and the course made good (30°T), distance made good (1.74 nautical miles), and speed made good (6.85 knots) to be obtained by following the plan.

Use of the "Clear" keys ([f] [d]) permits solving additional planning problems, for other destinations, starting from the same fix; the calculator retains the values for distance and bearing to the object even after these keys have been pressed.

Routine 2.1A (HP-67/97)

			Clear	CMG DMG SMG
Btdest Ddest	Var	S St Dr→Cm	De→Cc	ΔT

PLANNING TO A SEPARATE DESTINATION (DISTANCE AND BEARING)

Step	Procedure	Input Data/Units	Keys	Output Data/Units
1	After obtaining a fix by means of routine 2.1, steps 2–10, 11–23, or 24–38, load program—both sides			
2	Enter true bearing from second object (if two objects were used for the fix) or from object to new destination	DDD.d	A	
3	Enter distance from object to new destination	naut. mi.	A	
4	Enter variation (+E, −W) if it is to be different than for the fix just obtained	DD.d	B	
5	Enter expected vessel speed	knots	C	
6	Enter expected set of current, even if 0	DDD.d	C	
7	Enter expected drift of current, even if 0,	knots	C	
·	Calculate and display magnetic course to steer to new destination			DDD.d
8	Enter deviation for course displayed, even if 0,	DD.d	D	
·	Calculate and display compass course to steer to new destination**			DDD.d
9	Calculate and display time required to reach new destination		E	H.MS
10	Calculate and display true course made good from fix to new destination,		f e	DDD.d
·	Distance from fix to new destination,			naut. mi.
·	Speed made good between fix and new destination			knots
11	Clear before calculating a plan to reach a different destination, starting from the fix obtained by routine 2.1		f d	

**Uncorrect for leeway; see table 2.2.

41

Figures 2.13 and 2.14 illustrate the use of routine 2.1 for calculating *estimated position.* By definition, an estimated position is one which is found by combining data on the vessel's motion through the water with data on the motion of the water itself, to determine the geographic position of the vessel at the end of a specified time interval. Thus, the problem is one of summing two vectors—the vessel's motion (course and speed) and the water's motion (set and drift)—to obtain the vessel's net motion (course and speed made good). Once the speed made good has been calculated, it is multiplied by the elapsed time to obtain the distance traveled.

In the case shown in figure 2.13, the answers are given as distance and bearing to a designated starting point. As in previous calculations, it is impor-

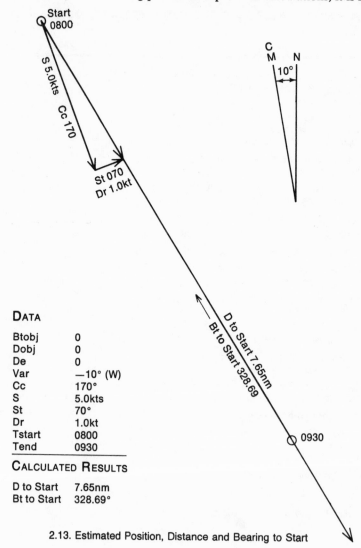

DATA

Btobj	0
Dobj	0
De	0
Var	−10° (W)
Cc	170°
S	5.0kts
St	70°
Dr	1.0kt
Tstart	0800
Tend	0930

CALCULATED RESULTS

D to Start	7.65nm
Bt to Start	328.69°

2.13. Estimated Position, Distance and Bearing to Start

tant to choose a time interval over which speed through the water and set and drift of current are reasonably constant, and this may require breaking a projected journey into a series of shorter legs.

"Clear" ($\boxed{f}$ $\boxed{d}$) must be pressed at the *start* of a series of estimated-position calculations. However, these keys should *not* be pressed after a series of estimated-position calculations has been begun, since doing so would erase the stored figures for distances traveled on earlier legs of the journey.

Whenever a change is necessary in any one of the four values associated with $\boxed{A}$—course, speed, set, and drift—*all four* must be re-entered. It is possible to recall these from the calculator's memory. This should be done in the sequence given on the label for $\boxed{A}$—*Cc, S, St, Dr*—so that the data as it appears in the display can be re-entered by pressing $\boxed{A}$. When course has to be recalled from the memory, it should be done as follows:

$\boxed{f}$ $\boxed{p \leftrightarrow s}$ $\boxed{RCL}$ $\boxed{4}$ $\boxed{f}$ $\boxed{p \leftrightarrow s}$ $\boxed{RCL}$ $\boxed{C}$ $\boxed{-}$ $\boxed{RCL}$ $\boxed{E}$ $\boxed{-}$

The previous compass course will then be displayed. (If the result is negative, or greater than 360°, one simply adds or subtracts 360° to place it in the proper range.) Now, if $\boxed{A}$ is pressed, this quantity is properly converted into a true course. This procedure is necessary because course is stored as "true," and if recalled and re-entered by the method used for the other items, it would be "corrected" twice, and hence be incorrectly stored. The method of recalling speed, set, and drift from memory is as follows:

Item	Press	To Enter, Press
Speed	$\boxed{f}$ $\boxed{p \leftrightarrow s}$ $\boxed{RCL}$ $\boxed{5}$ $\boxed{f}$ $\boxed{p \leftrightarrow s}$	$\boxed{A}$
Set	$\boxed{f}$ $\boxed{p \leftrightarrow s}$ $\boxed{RCL}$ $\boxed{6}$ $\boxed{f}$ $\boxed{p \leftrightarrow s}$	$\boxed{A}$
Drift	$\boxed{f}$ $\boxed{p \leftrightarrow s}$ $\boxed{RCL}$ $\boxed{7}$ $\boxed{f}$ $\boxed{p \leftrightarrow s}$	$\boxed{A}$

If any one of these has changed since its previous entry, the recall sequence is not used when it is to be re-entered; instead, the new value is inserted by means of the number keys, and then $\boxed{A}$ is pressed.

Figure 2.14 illustrates the use of the estimated-position part of the routine when the distance and bearing calculations are made with respect to a selected destination. The data-entry sequence starts at $\boxed{f}$ $\boxed{a}$, with entry of bearing and distance to the object. Answers are displayed as bearing and distance to the selected destination at the time specified.

Once the data has been entered, and the first answers have been calculated and displayed, positions at successive times can be obtained by simply keying in, at $\boxed{B}$, the start and end times of the succeeding legs of the journey. If no changes in vessel speed, course, or current are anticipated during these succeeding legs, no other data need be re-entered.

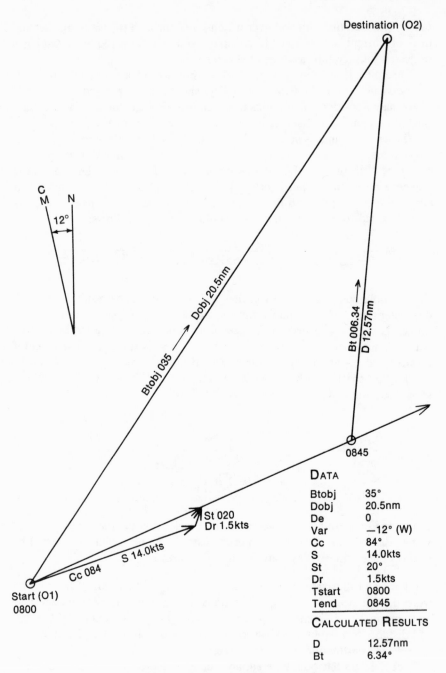

Destination (O2)

C
M N

12°

Dobj 20.5nm

Bt 006.34 →
D 12.57nm

Btobj 035 →

0845

St 020
Dr 1.5kts

S 14.0kts

Cc 084

Start (O1)
0800

DATA	
Btobj	35°
Dobj	20.5nm
De	0
Var	−12° (W)
Cc	84°
S	14.0kts
St	20°
Dr	1.5kts
Tstart	0800
Tend	0845

CALCULATED RESULTS	
D	12.57nm
Bt	6.34°

2.14. Estimated Position (Distance and Bearing)

Figure 2.15 illustrates the use of routine 2.1 in all three of its modes. In this case, a running fix is made on one object; the run starts at 0900, when the object bears 341°C; at 1020, the object bears 267°C. The fix is calculated, placing the

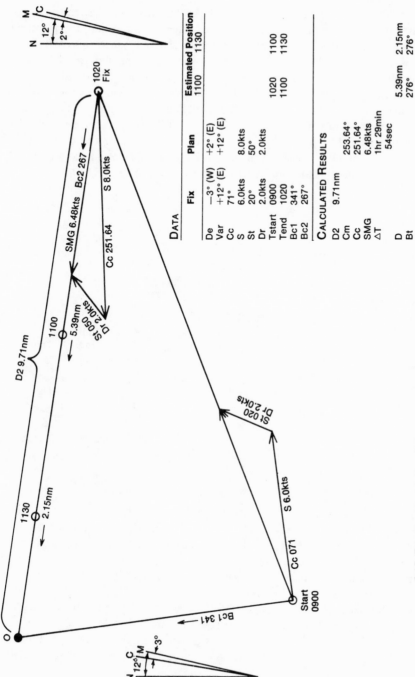

Data

	Fix	Plan	Estimated Position	
			1100	1130
De	−3° (W)	+2° (E)		
Var	+12° (E)	+12° (E)		
Cc	71°			
S	6.0kts	8.0kts		
St	20°	50°		
Dr	2.0kts	2.0kts		
Tstart	0900		1020	1100
Tend	1020		1100	1130
Bc1	341°			
Bc2	267°			

Calculated Results

D2	9.71nm	
Cm	253.64°	
Cc	251.64°	
SMG	6.48kts	
ΔT	1hr 29min	
	54sec	
D	5.39nm	2.15nm
Bt	276°	276°

2.15. Running Fix on One Object, Plan, and Estimated Position (Distance and Bearing)

vessel at 9.71 nautical miles off the object. At that time, it is desired to change course in order to reach the object. Since a current is running, the planning part of the routine is used to obtain a compass course to steer; this calculation yields an answer of 251.64° for an assumed speed of 8 knots on this leg. Speed made good and elapsed time to reach the object are also displayed.

The estimated-position part of the routine is then used to show the anticipated progress along the planned route. The "Clear" keys ([f] [d]) are pressed once, and the first interval of time (1020 to 1100) is then entered. The display, obtained by pressing [f] [e], provides the distance and true bearing to the object at 1100. Entering the interval 1100 to 1130 at [B] and pressing [f] [e] yields the distance and true bearing to the object at 1130.

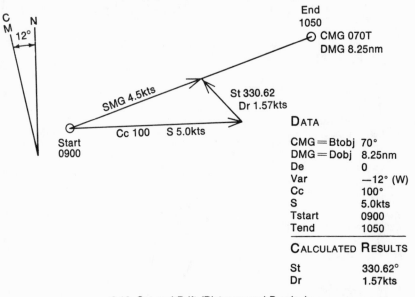

2.16. Set and Drift (Distance and Bearing)

Figure 2.16 illustrates an additional use of routine 2.1. A vector-subtraction operation built into the estimated-position portion of the routine can be employed to calculate the set and drift of a current that has been acting on a vessel.

If the calculator has been in use *and has not since been turned off,* the "Clear" keys should first be pressed.

For this calculation, the course and the distance made good for one leg of a journey, obtainable from two successive fixes on two objects, are entered as *Btobj* and *Dobj,* at [f] [a] ; compass course steered and average speed made good during the run are entered at [A]; but *no* entry is made for set or drift of current.

Next, the times of start and end of the run are entered at [B], and [f] [e] are pressed. The first quantity displayed is ignored; the second is the set of the current. By then pressing [R/S], the drift of the current is obtained.

46

2.3.2 Fixing and Planning on the SR-52 Routine 2.2 provides the keystroke instructions for fixing on the SR-52, and like the preceding routine, includes instructions for all three of the fixing applications. An illustration of the use of this routine to obtain a running fix on two objects when vessel course and speed change between bearings is provided in figure 2.17.

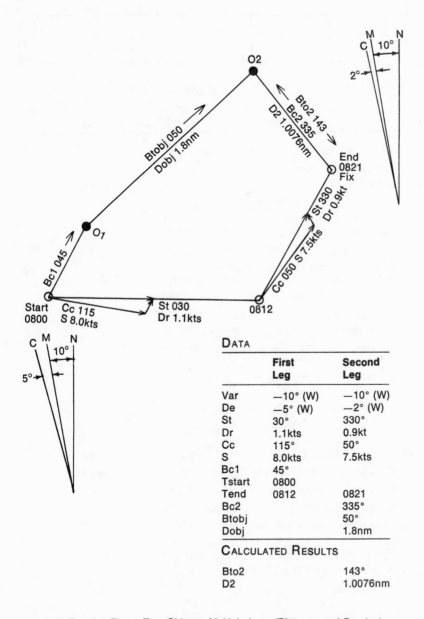

DATA

	First Leg	Second Leg
Var	−10° (W)	−10° (W)
De	−5° (W)	−2° (W)
St	30°	330°
Dr	1.1kts	0.9kt
Cc	115°	50°
S	8.0kts	7.5kts
Bc1	45°	
Tstart	0800	
Tend	0812	0821
Bc2		335°
Btobj		50°
Dobj		1.8nm

CALCULATED RESULTS

Bto2		143°
D2		1.0076nm

2.17. Running Fix on Two Objects, Multiple Legs (Distance and Bearing)

Routine 2.2 (SR-52)

Var De	St Dr	Cc S		Initialize
Time	Bc1 Bc2	Btobj Dobj	Bto2	D2

FIXING (DISTANCE AND BEARING)

Step	Procedure	Input Data/Units	Keys	Output Data/Units
	Before beginning, make sure D/R switch is set to D.			
1	Load program—both sides			
2	Initialize		2nd E'	
	Fix on Two Objects			
3	After completion of steps 1–2, enter variation (+E,−W), even if 0	DD.d	2nd A'	
4	Enter deviation (+E,−W), even if 0	DD.d	2nd A'	
5	Enter true bearing between objects, in either direction	DDD.d	C	
6	Enter distance between objects	naut. mi.	C	
7	Enter compass bearing to first object	DDD.d	B	
8	Enter compass bearing to second object	DDD.d	B	
9	Calculate and display true bearing from second object to vessel		D	DDD.d
10	Calculate and display distance off second object		E	naut. mi.
	Running Fix on One Object			
11	After completion of steps 1–2, enter variation (+E,−W), even if 0	DD.d	2nd A'	
12	Enter deviation (+E,−W), even if 0	DD.d	2nd A'	
13	Enter set of current, even if 0	DDD.d	2nd B'	
14	Enter drift of current, even if 0	knots	2nd B'	
15	Enter compass course during run or leg*	DDD.d	2nd C'	
16	Enter vessel speed during run or leg	knots	2nd C'	
17	Enter compass bearing to object at start of run	DDD.d	B	
18	Enter time of first bearing	H.MS	A	

*Correct for leeway; see table 2.2.

48

Step	Procedure	Input Data/Units	Keys	Output Data/Units
	For multiple courses or speeds, or changes in set or drift between bearings, proceed as follows (steps 19–20):			
19	Enter time of end of preceding leg—i.e., time of change(s)	H.MS	A	
20	Clear display, then repeat steps 11–12, even if variation and deviation are unchanged, and repeat as necessary steps 13–14 and 15–16; set and drift, and course and speed, are to be handled as pairs—if even one member of the pair changes, *both* must be re-entered		CLR	
21	Enter time of end of run	H.MS	A	
22	Enter compass bearing to object at end of run	DDD.d	B	
23	Enter 0 for bearing between objects	0	C	
24	Enter 0 for distance between objects	0	C	
25	Calculate and display true bearing from object to vessel		D	DDD.d
26	Calculate and display distance off object		E	naut. mi.
	Running Fix on Two Objects			
27	After completion of steps 1–2, enter variation (+E, −W), even if 0	DD.d	2nd A′	
28	Enter deviation (+E, −W), even if 0	DD.d	2nd A′	
29	Enter set of current, even if 0	DDD.d	2nd B′	
30	Enter drift of current, even if 0	knots	2nd B′	
31	Enter compass course during run or leg*	DDD.d	2nd C′	
32	Enter vessel speed during run or leg	knots	2nd C′	
33	Enter compass bearing to first object at start of run	DDD.d	B	
34	Enter time of first bearing	H.MS	A	
	For multiple courses or speeds, or changes in set or drift between bearings, proceed as follows (steps 35–36):			
35	Enter time of end of preceding leg—i.e., time of change(s)	H.MS	A	
36	Clear display, then repeat steps 27–28 even if variation and deviation are unchanged, and repeat as necessary steps 29–30 and 31–32; set and drift, and course and speed, are handled as pairs—if even one member of the pair changes, *both* must be re-entered		CLR	
37	Enter time of end of run	H.MS	A	
38	Enter compass bearing to second object at end of run	DDD.d	B	

*Correct for leeway; see table 2.2.

(CONTINUED)

49

Step	Procedure	Input Data/Units	Keys	Output Data/Units
39	Enter true bearing from first object to second object	DDD.d	C	
40	Enter distance between objects	naut. mi.	C	
41	Calculate and display true bearing from second object to vessel		D	DDD.d
42	Calculate and display distance off second object		E	naut. mi.

Although separate routines for fixing and planning are required with the SR-52, some integration between the two is possible. When a position fix has been calculated by means of routine 2.2, the calculated distance off the object and the bearing from the object to the vessel are left in the calculator's memory, so this data can be used in routine 2.3—the Planning routine—without being re-entered. Additional inputs for this part of routine 2.3 include distance and bearing from the object to the destination. The result is given as a course to steer and elapsed time for the run. If the fix has been obtained from two objects, the calculator stores the distance and bearing from the *second* object, and the additional data input required in planning is the distance and bearing from the *second* object to the destination.

Routine 2.3 (SR-52)

CMG	DMG	Cm	De→Cc	ΔT
Var	St Dr	Btdest Ddest		S

PLANNING (DISTANCE AND BEARING)

Step	Procedure	Input Data/Units	Keys	Output Data/Units
	Before beginning, make sure D/R switch is set to D.			
1	Load program—both sides			
2	Enter variation (+E, −W), even if 0	DD.d	A	
3	Enter expected set of current, even if 0	DDD.d	B	
4	Enter expected drift of current, even if 0	knots	B	
5	Enter true bearing from start to destination	DDD.d	C	
6	Enter distance between start and destination	naut. mi.	C	
7	Enter expected vessel speed	knots	E	
8	Calculate and display true course made good		2nd A′	DDD.d
9	Calculate and display distance made good		2nd B′	naut. mi.
10	Calculate and display magnetic course to steer		2nd C′	DDD.d
11	Enter compass deviation (+E, −W), even if 0,	DD.d	2nd D′	
·	Calculate and display compass course to steer**			DDD.d
12	Calculate and display time required to reach destination		2nd E′	H.MS
	Planning Integrated with Fixing			
13	After completion of routine 2.2, which leaves true bearing and distance from object to vessel in calculator memory, load planning program—both sides			
14	Enter variation (+E, −W), even if 0	DD.d	A	

**Uncorrect for leeway; see table 2.2.

(CONTINUED)

Step	Procedure	Input Data/Units	Keys	Output Data/Units
	If expected current is not exactly as last entered in routine 2.2, proceed as follows (steps 15–16):			
15	Enter expected set of current, even if 0	DDD.d	B	
16	Enter expected drift of current, even if 0	knots	B	
17	Enter true bearing from object (if fix was on one object) or from second object (if fix was on two objects) to destination	DDD.d	C	
18	Enter distance from object to destination	naut. mi.	C	
19	Enter expected vessel speed	knots	E	
20	Calculate and display true course made good		2nd A'	DDD.d
21	Calculate and display distance made good		2nd B'	naut. mi.
22	Calculate and display magnetic course to steer		2nd C'	DDD.d
23	Enter compass deviation (+E, −W), even if 0,	DD.d	2nd D'	
·	Calculate and display compass course to steer**			DDD.d
24	Calculate and display time required to reach destination		2nd E'	H.MS
25	Clear, to start a new problem, or		2nd CMs 0 STO 9 8 STO 9 9	

To make certain all registers are cleared, turn off the calculator.

**_Un_correct for leeway; see table 2.2.

The combined use of the two routines on the SR-52 is shown in figure 2.18, which illustrates the commonly encountered situation in which a running fix has been made on one object, and a course to steer to a destination other than that object is required. Routine 2.2 is used for the fix, and routine 2.3 (steps 13–24) is used for the plan. The bearing and the distance from the object to the vessel are stored in the calculator at the end of routine 2.2, and need not be re-entered.

The use of routine 2.3 for planning a journey from start to destination without a position fix is shown in steps 1–12.

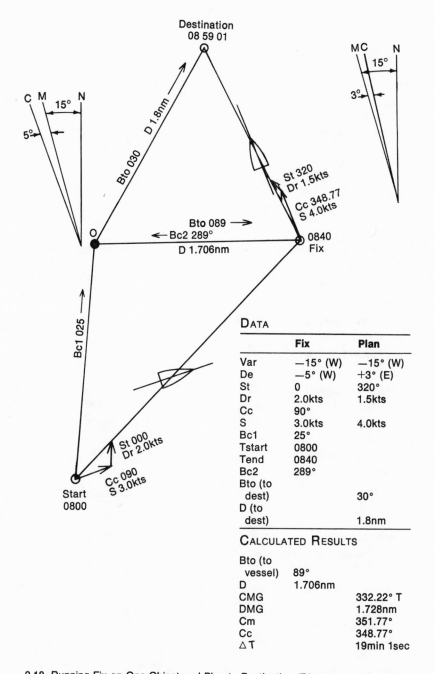

| Destination 08 59 01 | | | |

DATA

	Fix	Plan
Var	−15° (W)	−15° (W)
De	−5° (W)	+3° (E)
St	0	320°
Dr	2.0kts	1.5kts
Cc	90°	
S	3.0kts	4.0kts
Bc1	25°	
Tstart	0800	
Tend	0840	
Bc2	289°	
Bto (to dest)		30°
D (to dest)		1.8nm

CALCULATED RESULTS

Bto (to vessel)	89°	
D	1.706nm	
CMG		332.22° T
DMG		1.728nm
Cm		351.77°
Cc		348.77°
△T		19min 1sec

2.18. Running Fix on One Object and Plan to Destination (Distance and Bearing)

2.3.3 Estimated Position on the SR-52 Routine 2.4 is used for calculating estimated position on the SR-52. This routine yields the same results as the estimated-position portion of routine 2.1 for the HP-67 and HP-97.

Routine 2.4 (SR-52)

Tstart	Tend	Btdest Ddest	D	Bt
Var	De	St Dr	Cc	S

ESTIMATED POSITION (DISTANCE AND BEARING)

Step	Procedure	Input Data/Units	Keys	Output Data/Units
	Before beginning, make sure D/R switch is set to D.			
1	Load program—both sides			
2	Enter variation (+E, −W), even if 0	DD.d	A	
3	Enter deviation (+E, −W), even if 0	DD.d	B	
4	Enter set of current, even if 0	DDD.d	C	
5	Enter drift of current, even if 0	knots	C	
6	Enter compass course*	DDD.d	D	
7	Enter vessel speed	knots	E	
8	Enter time of start of run or leg	H.MS	2nd A'	
9	Enter time of end of run or leg	H.MS	2nd B'	
10	Enter true bearing from start to destination	DDD.d	2nd C'	
11	Enter distance from start to destination	naut. mi.	2nd C'	

For estimated position relative to the *starting position*, enter bearing and distance as 0 in the preceding two steps.

Step	Procedure	Input Data/Units	Keys	Output Data/Units
12	Calculate and display distance to destination at end of leg or run		2nd D'	naut. mi.
13	Calculate and display true bearing to destination at end of leg or run		2nd E'	DDD.d

For multiple courses or speeds, or changes in set or drift, repeat as necessary steps 2–7; set and drift (steps 4–5) are handled as a pair—if even one member of the pair changes, *both* must be re-entered. Steps 8–9 and 12–13 are then repeated for each new leg.

*Correct for leeway; see table 2.2.

Figure 2.19 provides an example of the calculation of estimated positions. In all cases of this sort, an estimate of current is included in the input data, and variation and deviation are automatically taken into account.

54

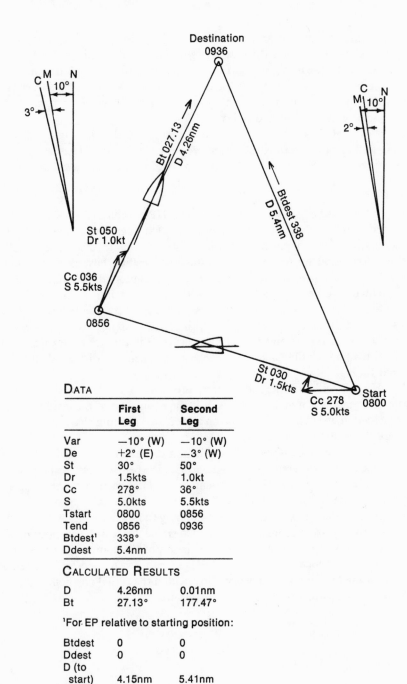

DATA

	First Leg	Second Leg
Var	−10° (W)	−10° (W)
De	+2° (E)	−3° (W)
St	30°	50°
Dr	1.5kts	1.0kt
Cc	278°	36°
S	5.0kts	5.5kts
Tstart	0800	0856
Tend	0856	0936
Btdest[1]	338°	
Ddest	5.4nm	

CALCULATED RESULTS

D	4.26nm	0.01nm
Bt	27.13°	177.47°

[1]For EP relative to starting position:

Btdest	0	0
Ddest	0	0
D (to start)	4.15nm	5.41nm
Bt (to start)	107°	158.03°

2.19. Estimated Position, Multiple Legs (Distance and Bearing)

This routine is able to accommodate multiple changes in such items as course, speed, and set and drift. A series of estimated positions can be calculated, showing the movement of the vessel relative to the initial destination. Thus, the bearing and distance to the destination displayed for the successive legs of the journey constitute a "plot" of the progress of the vessel toward, or in the vicinity of, the selected point.

If the estimated position is to be found relative to the starting point, the bearing and distance to the destination are set equal to zero. The destination then coincides with the starting point, and the results are calculated with reference to that point.

2.3.4 Estimated Position—Tracking

The HP-67 and HP-97 can be programmed to repeat a calculation endlessly, and can therefore be used not just to calculate estimated position at selected times, but to display a vessel's position continuously. As soon as an estimated position has been calculated and displayed, the calculation is repeated, with an automatic change in input equivalent to the vessel's motion during the time required to complete the calculation. The calculating cycle pauses periodically for the few seconds it takes to read from the display the bearing and distance to a preselected destination. The HP-67 and HP-97 also display the time of each calculated position, making possible a simple check on the accuracy of the calculator's internal timing.

The HP-97, with its integral printer, produces a written version of the continuing readout. In many respects, it is the equivalent of the dead-reckoning tracers that are used to plot a line on a Mercator plotting chart, portraying the vessel's position as it moves.

The routine for tracking estimated position on the HP-67 and HP-97 has been prepared in two versions: one—described just below—uses distance and bearing as input data; the other—presented in a later section of this chapter—is based upon latitude and longitude.

The program includes a provision for stopping the tracking action to permit a change in any of the quantities that determine the displayed position—vessel course and speed, variation and deviation of the compass, and set and drift of current. Since the HP-67 and HP-97 can be stopped and restarted without losing tracking accuracy or falling behind the actual position, changes in these input quantities can be made at leisure.

56

Routine 2.5 (HP-67/97)

St Dr	Btdest Ddest	Tstart	Tstop	Clear
Cc Var De	S	Start	Stop	Position

ESTIMATED POSITION—TRACKING (DISTANCE AND BEARING)

Step	Procedure	Input Data/Units	Keys	Output Data/Units
1	Load program—both sides			
2	Enter compass course*	DDD.d	A	
3	Enter variation (+E, −W), even if 0	DD.d	A	
4	Enter deviation (+E, −W), even if 0	DD.d	A	
5	Enter set of current, even if 0	DDD.d	f a	
6	Enter drift of current, even if 0	knots	f a	
7	Enter true bearing from start to destination	DDD.d	f b	
8	Enter distance from start to destination	naut. mi.	f b	

For estimated position relative to the *starting position,* enter bearing and distance as 0 in the preceding two steps.

Step	Procedure	Input Data/Units	Keys	Output Data/Units
9	Enter vessel speed	knots	B	
10	Enter time of start (at least 30 seconds later than present time)	H.MS	f c	
11	When selected time is reached, start calculation, and repeatedly display		C	
·	Distance to destination,			naut. mi.
·	True bearing to destination,			DDD.d
·	Time of displayed position			H.MS

To eliminate timing errors, proceed as follows (steps 12–16):

Step	Procedure	Input Data/Units	Keys	Output Data/Units
12	Allow tracking to proceed for 3–5 minutes; then, if time displayed is in error by more than a few seconds, stop calculator, during a pause for display of time on the HP-67, or while time is being printed on the HP-97		D	
13	Enter watch time at which calculator was stopped; this entry automatically corrects timing error	H.MS	f d	

*Correct for leeway; see table 2.2.

(CONTINUED)

Step	Procedure	Input Data/Units	Keys	Output Data/Units
14	If required, calculate and display distance to destination,		E	naut. mi.
·	True bearing to destination,			DDD.d
·	Time of stop			H.MS
15	Select time of restart (at least 30 seconds later)	H.MS	f c	
16	When selected time is reached, restart calculation		C	

For multiple courses or speeds, or changes in set or drift, stop calculator, as described in steps 12–13. To enter changes, repeat steps 2–6 and 9. Then restart calculation, as described in steps 15–16.

17	Clear, either to eliminate errors in data entry (and to restart the procedure) or to start a new problem		f e	

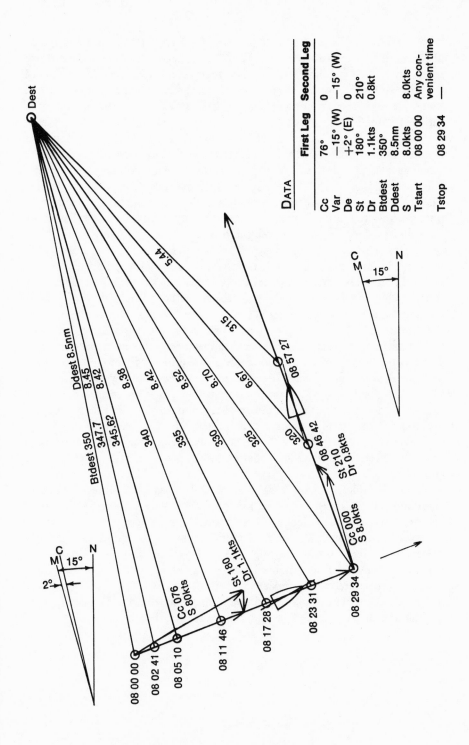

DATA	First Leg	Second Leg
Cc	76°	0
Var	−15° (W)	−15° (W)
De	+2° (E)	0
St	180°	210°
Dr	1.1kts	0.8kt
Btdest	350°	
Ddest	8.5nm	
S	8.0kts	8.0kts
Tstart	08 00 00	Any con-
		venient time
Tstop	08 29 34	—

2.20. Estimated Position—Tracking (Distance and Bearing)

59

Routine 2.5 has been prepared for the HP-67 and HP-97, and figure 2.20 illustrates it. The instructions in steps 12–16 of this routine list the procedures necessary to obtain timing accuracy and then resume tracking. The timing of the programming "loop" is adjusted (by the program) to conform to the actual time intervals of the repeating display, once the necessary information has been supplied. This is accomplished by setting and starting the calculator at a particular watch time. After about five minutes have elapsed, the watch time is noted and compared with the displayed time. In the HP-67, the latter is shown just before the display blanks out. If there is a discrepancy of more than a few seconds, the calculator is stopped during a subsequent display of time. The actual watch time is then entered, and the calculator measures its own timing error, resets its timing, and corrects any component of error in its calculated position due to the timing error. Next, a starting time at least thirty or more seconds in the future is keyed into the calculator (a procedure which resets the estimated position to that of the new starting time), and the "Start" key (C) is pressed when the designated time has been reached. Thus, the stopping and starting can be done at leisure, without fear of losing track of position during the halt in calculation.

It is also possible to make a permanent change in the recorded value of loop time. This procedure is desirable because the exact value of calculation time varies with the particular calculator (even within a single model). Once the user has determined the loop time for his own calculator, by means of steps 12–13, he can insert the appropriate constants into his program for this routine, as described in the discussion of customized programs in the Appendix. Making this change assures that the loop time will henceforth be very nearly correct. Nevertheless, it should be checked each time the routine is used, since it is affected somewhat by variations in temperature, battery voltage, and even the data itself.

In the example of figure 2.20, the calculator has been stopped once, at approximately 08 05 00, to be reset for accurate timing. At 08 29 34, when the course is changed, the calculator is stopped, the time of stopping is entered, and then the new values for compass course, variation, deviation, set, and drift are entered. Next, a new starting time is keyed in, and the calculator is restarted when that time has been reached. For any subsequent changes in data, the procedure can be repeated as necessary.

The calculator will display bearing and distance from the starting point if bearing and distance to the destination are set equal to zero.

2.3.5 Bearing Regression

In section 2.2.2, we discussed the method of linear regression in terms of the increased accuracy it offers in the calculation of position fixes. In this section, and the sections that follow, a number of examples of the use of regression are presented.

Two different forms of regression analysis are useful in coastwise navigation. The first, illustrated by figures 2.21 and 2.22, establishes a smooth regression line among the bearing numbers. This form of regression can be used for fixes on two objects, running fixes on one object, and course made good from three bearings. Examples of all three are given. The second form, which can be used only for a running fix on one object, is discussed in a later section.

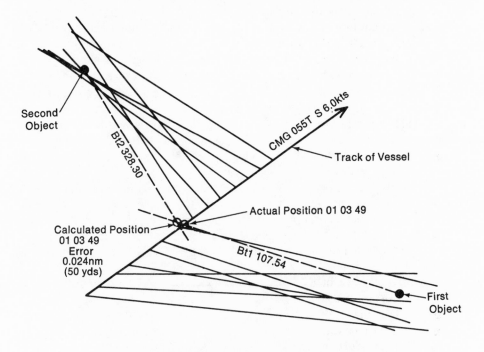

2.21. Observations on Two Objects from a Moving Vessel

In figure 2.21, a vessel is shown on a course made good of 55°, with a speed made good of 6.0 knots. Observations are made successively on two objects, the first with a true bearing of approximately 100°, and the second with a true bearing of approximately 320°. The bearings are taken in succession; in this case, seven observations are made on each of the objects. Figure 2.21 illustrates the effect of fluctuating bearings; the bearing lines of position are shown as radiating from the vessel's successive actual positions. Because of the swinging compass, not a single one of the observed bearing lines passes through the first object. The data is tabulated in figure 2.22; in some instances the bearing error (the difference between the observed value and the actual bearing at the time specified) is quite large, reaching as much as 8 degrees.

61

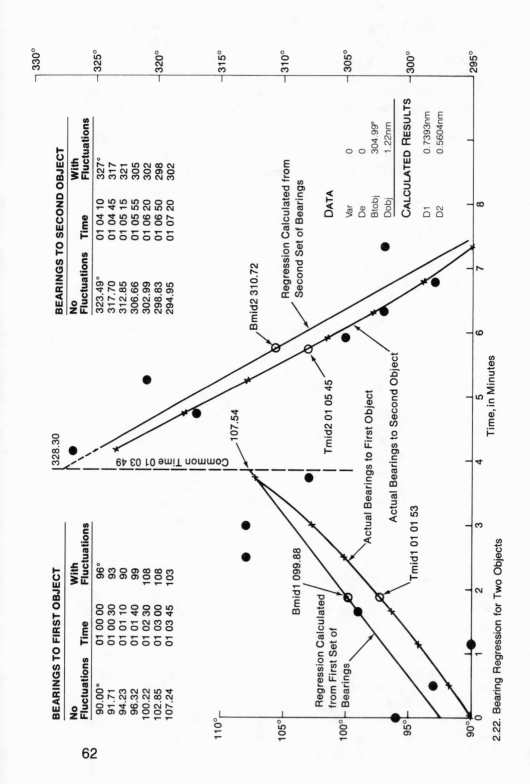

BEARINGS TO FIRST OBJECT

No Fluctuations	Time	With Fluctuations
90.00°	01 00 00	96°
91.71	01 00 30	93
94.23	01 01 10	90
96.32	01 01 40	99
100.22	01 02 30	108
102.85	01 03 00	108
107.24	01 03 45	103

BEARINGS TO SECOND OBJECT

No Fluctuations	Time	With Fluctuations
323.49°	01 04 10	327°
317.70	01 04 45	317
312.85	01 05 15	321
306.66	01 05 55	305
302.99	01 06 20	302
298.83	01 06 50	298
294.95	01 07 20	302

DATA

Var	0
De	0
Btobj	304.99nm
Dobj	1.22nm

CALCULATED RESULTS

D1	0.7393nm
D2	0.5604nm

Regression Calculated from Second Set of Bearings

Bmid2 310.72

Tmid2 01 05 45

Actual Bearings to First Object

Actual Bearings to Second Object

Tmid1 01 01 53

328.30

Common Time 01 03 49

107.54

Bmid1 099.88

Regression Calculated from First Set of Bearings

Time, in Minutes

2.22. Bearing Regression for Two Objects

62

The first step in establishing a fix with the aid of regression methods is to utilize a specially prepared regression routine, with the sequence of bearing–time pairs for each of the objects as the input data. No concern is given to variation or deviation at this point, since the regression process is used only to smooth the data, and to obtain the single values for bearing and time which will serve as input quantities in a fixing routine. Variation and deviation are accommodated when the actual fixing is performed.

In figure 2.22, the observed bearings entered in the regression routine are shown graphically; each is represented by a solid black dot. The actual bearings for the time intervals in question fall on the slightly curved lines; the calculated regressions are represented by the straight lines, on the left for the series of bearings observed at successive times on the first object and on the right for the series of bearing observations on the second object. In each case the fluctuations are smoothed so that the regression line makes a "best fit" approximation to the observed data. Any value of bearing and time picked off the regression line is valid for the observed set of data.

At this point, a choice can be made between two possible approaches: the first is to ascertain for each sequence the bearing value for a time close to the center of the interval, and to use the two bearings as input for a running fix on two objects; the second is to extend the trend lines respectively forward and backward to a common time and use as inputs the indicated values of the bearings to the two objects at that single time. This data can then be used for a fix on two objects.

The latter method is probably more convenient, since it does not require values for vessel speed, course, and set and drift of current, all necessary in a running fix. Moreover, when the regression lines are extended to a common time, they include the effects of the vessel's motion, and the bearings take on very nearly the values that would have been obtained if they had indeed been simultaneously observed. To be sure, as the gaps between the regression lines and the curves of the actual bearings indicate, the presence of substantial fluctuations in the bearings will shift the regression lines; therefore, the values read on their extensions to a common time will not exactly coincide with those obtained through accurate simultaneous observation of the two objects. However, when the data is fluctuating, the results yielded by the method of smoothing and extrapolation are much better than those obtained from a single set of observations on each object. The additional convenience of not having to calculate a running fix makes the method even more attractive.

It should also be noted that the accuracy of this application of linear regression is limited by the fact that it results in a straight-line approximation of a bearing–time relationship more precisely represented as a curve (exemplified in the curve of the actual bearings to the first object in the left-hand section of figure 2.22). The departure from the straight line is greatest for observations of an object close at hand; however, this tendency is offset by the fact that when the object is nearby, the inaccuracy in position fixing due to bearing errors is actually reduced. A bearing error of 2 degrees to one of two objects which are

63

0.35 of a nautical mile away and 0.5 of a mile apart can result in a position error of 0.012 of a mile. If the objects are 1.4 miles away and 2.0 miles apart, a 2-degree bearing error to one of them will result in a position error of 0.05 of a mile—four times as much. Thus, the nearer the objects being observed, the less damaging are the bearing errors.

When values obtained by extending regression lines to a common time are to be used, the time interval between the last observation on the first object and the first observation on the second should be kept to a minimum. As examination of the left-hand section of figure 2.22 makes evident, if the calculated regression line is extended much beyond the common time used here, it will diverge considerably from the curve of the actual bearings. If the common time in this example were to be placed another minute beyond the time of the last observation in the sequence, the error in calculated bearing to the first object would be as great as 3 degrees.

Routine 2.6 provides the keystroke instructions for the Bearing Regression routine on the HP-67 and HP-97. Two sequences of bearing and time can be accommodated. After the first has been entered, pressing $\boxed{C}$ results in display of the time of the middle of the bearing sequence, and then of the value of bearing corresponding to that time. These results are useful as smoothed input for any fixing routine, and for the routine for course made good from three bearings (to be discussed shortly).

After the second sequence has been entered, pressing $\boxed{D}$ results in display of the mid-time and mid-bearing of the second set of bearing–time pairs. Pressing $\boxed{E}$ then extends the two lines of regression to a common time; this common time is displayed first, followed by the bearing to the first object at the common time, and then by the bearing to the second object at that time. Utilizing this data, a fix on two objects can be calculated, as shown in the final steps of the routine.

When the mid-bearings for the data shown in figure 2.22 are calculated by means of this routine, *Bmid1* turns out to be 99.88° at 01 01 53, and *Bmid2* is 310.72° at 01 05 45. At the common time of 01 03 49, the bearings are 107.54° and 328.30°.

A fix has been calculated using the latter two values, and the resulting position—0.56 nautical miles off the second object, on a bearing of 328.30° —is approximately 50 yards in error, as shown in figure 2.21, primarily because of the fluctuations in the original bearing observations.

Routine 2.6 (HP-67/97)

Clear	Var De	Btobj Dobj	D1 Bt1	D2 Bt2
Bearings	Times	Tmid1 Bmid1	Tmid2 Bmid2	Tcom Bcom1 Bcom2

BEARING REGRESSION AND REGRESSION FIX ON TWO OBJECTS

Step	Procedure	Input Data/Units	Keys	Output Data/Units
1	Load program—both sides			
2	Enter sequence of bearing-time pairs obtained with respect to first object; for each pair, enter bearing, followed by	DDD.d	A	
3	Time of bearing	H.MS	B	

If an error is noted in the entry of bearing or time data before the corresponding letter key (A or B) is pressed, eliminate the incorrect data by pressing CLx ; if the error is noted after the letter key has been pressed, clear the calculator by pressing f a , and re-enter all data, starting at step 2.

Step	Procedure	Input Data/Units	Keys	Output Data/Units
4	Calculate and display mid-time of first bearing sequence,		C	H.MS
·	Bearing corresponding to this mid-time			DDD.d
5	Enter sequence of bearing-time pairs obtained with respect to second object; for each pair, enter bearing, followed by	DDD.d	A	
6	Time of bearing	H.MS	B	
7	Calculate and display mid-time of second bearing sequence,		D	H.MS
·	Bearing corresponding to this mid-time			DDD.d
8	Calculate and display the common time (mid-point of time interval between end of first sequence and start of second sequence),		E	H.MS
·	Bearing to first object corresponding to the common time,			DDD.d
·	Bearing to second object corresponding to the common time			DDD.d
9	Unless a regression fix on two objects is to be calculated, clear, to start a new problem		f a	

(CONTINUED)

Step	Procedure	Input Data/Units	Keys	Output Data/Units
	Regression Fix on Two Objects			
10	After completion of step 8, enter variation (+E, −W), even if 0	DD.d	f b	
11	Enter deviation (+E, −W), even if 0	DD.d	f b	
12	Enter true bearing between objects, in either direction	DDD.d	f c	
13	Enter distance between objects	naut. mi.	f c	
14	Calculate and display distance off first object at the common time,		f d	naut. mi.
·	True bearing from vessel to first object at the common time			DDD.d
15	Calculate and display distance off second object at the common time,		f e	naut. mi.
·	True bearing from vessel to second object at the common time			DDD.d

If only one object can be viewed, a running fix on that object can be calculated from the sequences of bearing–time pairs. This process is illustrated in figure 2.23. When the first set of bearings, taken between 01 04 10 and 01 07 20, is used in a regression calculation, a mid-bearing of 125.52° at 01 05 45 results. The second set, beginning at 01 11 00 and ending at 01 14 25, yields a mid-bearing of 179.09°. These two bearings can then be used as input for the running-fix portion of routine 2.1, which establishes the vessel's position at 01 12 43 as 0.82 nautical miles from the object, on a bearing of 179.09°. This answer is in error by 0.10 miles, or 200 yards, with respect to the vessel's actual position at that time.

The value of the regression method is apparent if we compare with this result a position calculated from one pair of the originally observed bearings. A particularly bad pair yields a position that is 0.32 miles in error, as shown in figure 2.23. Other pairs will yield other positions and errors, and it is evident that if just two bearings are taken for a running fix, the probable error will be greater than it is when, for the regression method, many observations are taken.

BEARINGS TO OBJECT

No Fluctuations	Time	With Fluctuations
109.94°	01 04 10	110°
114.03	01 04 45	115
117.85	01 05 15	118
123.36	01 05 55	129
127.05	01 06 20	135
131.68	01 06 50	133
136.49	01 07 20	142
121.94° Tmid 01 05 45	Bmid 125.52°	Error 3.58°
171.09	01 11 00	169
174.98	01 11 30	174
180.29	01 12 15	171
184.49	01 12 55	176
186.88	01 13 20	191
189.96	01 13 55	186
192.35	01 14 25	189
183.27° Tmid 01 12 43	Bmid 179.09°	Error 4.18°

CMG 055.00°T
SMG 6.0kts

Position Calculated from
Bearings at 01 06 20 and 01 12 15
D to obj 0.99nm Error 0.32nm

Actual Position 01 12 43
D to obj 0.73nm

Actual Position 01 12 15
D to obj 0.70nm

Position Calculated from
Mid-bearings for 01 05 45 and 01 12 43
D to obj 0.82nm Error 0.10nm

Actual Position 01 05 45

Object

2.23. Running Fix on One Object Using Bearing Regression

67

Routine 2.7 (SR-52)

			REGRESSION	
Time	First Bearing	Other Bearings	Time	Bearing

BEARING REGRESSION

Step	Procedure	Input Data/Units	Keys	Output Data/Units
	Before beginning, make sure D/R switch is set to D.			
1	Load program—first side			
2	Load program—second side			
3	Enter time of first bearing of sequence	H.MS	A	
4	Enter first bearing of sequence	DDD.d	B	
5	For each subsequent time-bearing pair, enter time, followed by	H.MS	A	
6	Corresponding bearing	DDD.d	C	

If an error is noted in the entry of bearing or time data before the corresponding letter key ([A], [B], or [C]) is pressed, eliminate the incorrect data by pressing [CLR]; if the error is noted after the letter key has been pressed, clear the calculator by pressing [2nd] [CMs] [CLR], and re-enter all data, starting at step 3.

Step	Procedure	Input Data/Units	Keys	Output Data/Units
7	Enter time for which regression bearing is required	H.MS	D	
8	Calculate and display bearing corresponding to time entered in preceding step		E	DDD.d
9	If bearing displayed is greater than 360°, but less than 720°, reduce answer		− 3 6 0	
			=	DDD.d
10	If bearing displayed is 720° or greater, reduce answer		− 7 2 0	
			=	DDD.d
11	If required, calculate *Tmean*		RCL 0 7 ÷ RCL 0 6 = INV 2nd D.MS 2nd fix 4	H.MS
12	Enter *Tmean*		D	
13	Calculate and display bearing corresponding to *Tmean*		E	DDD.d

Routine 2.7 is the Bearing Regression routine for the SR-52. Because of the memory and program limitations in this calculator, the routine can handle only one sequence of bearing–time pairs, rather than the two included in the routine for the HP-67 and HP-97.

When the SR-52 is employed for a fix on two objects, a common time lying in the interval between the two sets of observations is selected, and the regression routine is carried out twice—once to calculate the regression bearing for the first set of observations at the common time, and a second time to obtain the second bearing. In the example shown in figure 2.22, the time is 01 03 49.

If a running fix on one object is to be obtained, the first sequence of bearing –time pairs is entered, and then a quantity *Tmean* is calculated manually, as shown in step 11 of routine 2.7. *Tmean,* which is not to be confused with the common time, is the average of the times of the successive bearing observations. It is essentially equivalent to the mid-time calculated on the HP-67 and HP-97. The two may not be exactly equal, but both represent values of time approximately centered within the overall interval, for use in calculating the bearing required in a running fix. With *Tmean* still in the display, pressing ⬛D followed by ⬛E results in calculation and display of the regression bearing corresponding to *Tmean.* For the sequence in figure 2.23 starting at 01 04 10 and ending at 01 07 20, a regression bearing of 126.02° for a *Tmean* of 01 05 48 is obtained. Since the *Tmean* calculated on the SR-52 differs somewhat from the mid-time of 01 05 45 calculated on the HP-67 and HP-97, there is a shift (of 0.5 of a degree) in the regression bearing, corresponding to the vessel's motion during the interval between the two times specified. Both values are valid, since both are obtained from the same regression equation; they just represent bearings at slightly differing times.

The process of obtaining a regression bearing–time pair is repeated for the second sequence of observed bearings, and the running fix is calculated in the usual way.

Answers obtained with the SR-52 may exceed 360 degrees, so instructions for manually reducing them are included in routine 2.7.

2.3.6 Regression Running Fix   The second method of regression calculation can be used only for a running fix on one object. Its particular virtue is that no limitations need to be observed concerning closeness to the object, the time between bearings, or the speed of the vessel. In the method previously described, regression was used to determine the trend of bearing variation —the manner in which a sequence of bearings changed—with time. In the present method, the regression calculation establishes the trend of the vessel's position as it passes an object. It supplies not only bearing (as did the method previously described), but also distance to the object.

Since this regression method is used for a running fix, it is necessary to know the vessel's course and speed, and the set and drift of any currents. In the routine for the HP-67 and HP-97, these values are included in the input data. The corresponding routine for the SR-52 calls for inputs of course and speed

Data

No Fluctuations	Time	With Fluctuations
109.94°	01 04 10	110°
114.03	01 04 45	115
117.85	01 05 15	118
123.36	01 05 55	129
127.05	01 06 20	135
131.68	01 06 50	133
136.49	01 07 20	142
171.09	01 11 00	169
174.98	01 11 30	174
180.29	01 12 15	171
184.49	01 12 55	176
186.88	01 13 20	191
189.96	01 13 55	186
192.35	01 14 25	189

De 0
Var 0
Cc(CMG) 55.008°
S(SMG) 6.0kts
St 0
Dr 0

Calculated Results

Time	Distance	Bearing
01 04 10	0.76nm	113.1°
01 05 55	0.68	125.7
01 06 50	0.65	133.3
01 11 00	0.70	168.9
01 12 55	0.80	181.6

Tn 01 08 10
Dn 0.64nm

Error 0.07nm (148yds)

2.24. Regression Running Fix on One Object

made good, to be found by a routine requiring the values for the motion of the vessel and the current. Any inaccuracy in these values results in an error in the calculation for the vessel's track, which is in addition to the error resulting from fluctuations in the bearings being observed.

The calculated regression track is always parallel to the vessel's course made good. Therefore, when error in the data concerning the vessel's path over the bottom causes a shift in the course made good, the calculated track shifts in the same direction by an equal amount. If the calculated speed made good is less than the actual speed made good, the calculated regression track will be *closer* to the object than it otherwise would have been; a faster speed made good will shift the calculated track *away* from the object.

An example of a regression running fix is shown in figure 2.24. The bearing –time pairs used here are the same as those in the preceding figure, for the running fix using bearing regression. The scattering of the bearing lines of position, few of which pass through the object, indicates the extent of the fluctuation in the individual observations. Yet the final result is a track that is displaced by only 148 yards, demonstrating the value of the method.

The plots of bearing against time that correspond to the input observations (black dots), the actual bearings, and the calculated values for this example are shown in figure 2.25. Here, in contrast to figure 2.22, the calculated regression line is a curve, rather than a straight line. This difference arises because the regression running fix provides an exact statement of the vessel's position (if the data for bearing and course and speed made good is correct), while the bearing regression gives a close, straight-line approximation.

The data tabulated in figure 2.24 can be used by the reader who wishes to try out routine 2.8 or 2.9, checking his calculations against the results shown.

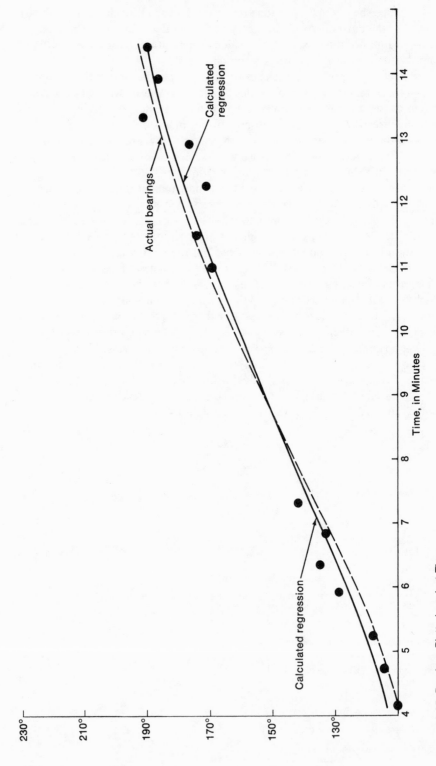

2.25. Bearings Plotted against Time

72

Routine 2.8 (HP-67/97)

Clear	De Var		Tn Dn	Tp
Cc S	St Dr	Bc	Time	Dp Btp

REGRESSION RUNNING FIX

Step	Procedure	Input Data/Units	Keys	Output Data/Units
	This routine cannot be used when the vessel is proceeding directly toward or away from the object being observed. Also, it should not be used when the relative bearing to the object is much less than ±45 degrees off the bow or stern, especially when there are bearing fluctuations of 2 degrees or more.			
1	Load program—both sides			
2	Enter deviation ($+$E, $-$W), even if 0	DD.d	f b	
3	Enter variation ($+$E, $-$W), even if 0	DD.d	f b	
4	Enter compass course*	DDD.d	A	
5	Enter vessel speed	knots	A	
6	Enter set of current, even if 0	DDD.d	B	
7	Enter drift of current, even if 0	knots	B	
8	Enter bearing-time pairs; for each pair, enter compass bearing, followed by	DDD.d	C	
9	Time of bearing	H.MS	D	
	If an error is noted in the entry of bearing or time data before the corresponding letter key ($\boxed{C}$ or $\boxed{D}$) is pressed, eliminate the incorrect data by pressing $\boxed{CLx}$; if the error is noted after the letter key has been pressed, clear the calculator by pressing $\boxed{f}$ $\boxed{a}$, and re-enter all data, starting at step 2.			
10	Enter watch time for which running fix is required	H.MS	f e	
11	Calculate and display distance off object at time selected,		E	naut. mi.
·	True bearing to object at time selected			DDD.d
	The preceding step is an absolute prerequisite to the calculation of time and distance of nearest approach in steps 12–13, following.			
	Display of ERROR after execution of the preceding step indicates that the routine will not function because the vessel is on a constant course made good to or from the object.			
12	Calculate and display watch time of nearest approach to object		f d	H.MS
13	Calculate and display distance off object at time of nearest approach		f d	naut. mi.
14	Clear, to start a new problem		f a	

*Correct for leeway; see table 2.2.

Routine 2.9 (SR-52)

Tp→Dp	Btp	Tn	ΔTn	Initialize
Var De	CMG SMG	Bc	Time	

REGRESSION RUNNING FIX

Step	Procedure	Input Data/Units	Keys	Output Data/Units
	This routine cannot be used when the vessel is proceeding directly toward or away from the object being observed. Also, it should not be used when the relative bearing to the object is much less than ± 45 degrees off the bow or stern, especially when there are bearing fluctuations of 2 degrees or more.			
	Before beginning, make sure D/R switch is set to D.			
1	Load program—first side			
2	Load program—second side			
3	Initialize		2nd E′	
4	Enter variation ($+$E, $-$W), even if 0	DD.d	A	
5	Enter deviation ($+$E, $-$W), even if 0	DD.d	A	
6	Enter true course made good	DDD.d	B	
7	Enter speed made good	knots	B	
8	Enter bearing-time pairs; for each pair, enter compass bearing, followed by	DDD.d	C	
9	Time of bearing	H.MS	D	
	If an error is noted in the entry of bearing or time data before the corresponding letter key ([C] or [D]) is pressed, eliminate the incorrect data by pressing [CLR]; if the error is noted after the letter key has been pressed, clear the calculator by pressing [2nd] [CMs] [CLR], and re-enter all data, starting at step 4.			
10	Enter watch time for which running fix is required,	H.MS	2nd A′	
·	Calculate and display distance off object at time selected			naut. mi.
	The preceding step is an absolute prerequisite to the calculation of time and distance of nearest approach in steps 12–13, following.			
11	Calculate and display true bearing to object at time selected		2nd B′	DDD.d
12	Calculate and display time of nearest approach to object		2nd C′	H.MS

74

Step	Procedure	Input Data/Units	Keys	Output Data/Units
13	Calculate and display distance of nearest approach to object (the time of nearest approach obtained in step 12 is left in the display)		2nd A'	naut. mi.
14	Calculate and display time interval between time selected in step 10 and time of nearest approach		2nd D'	H.MS
15	Initialize, either to restart the procedure or to start a new problem		2nd E'	

In these procedures, variation and deviation need to be entered, since the input quantities include compass course (in routine 2.8) and compass bearings (in both routines), while the results are given in terms of distance and *true* bearing to the object.

Two reservations accompany the instructions. The first specifies that these routines cannot be used when the vessel is proceeding directly toward or away from the object being observed. The reason is that there is no way to calculate distance toward or away from the object when the bearings are aligned with the vessel's track. Headings resulting in a course made good that is within less than a degree of the bearings to the object are not acceptable. Since currents may cause a net motion in line with an object even though the vessel is not headed directly toward or away from it, the vessel's course made good rather than its heading is relevant here.

The second reservation involves the fact that these routines tend to exaggerate the effect of bearing fluctuations when the relative bearing to the object is much less than 45 degrees off the bow or stern on either side of the vessel. Consequently, bearings within these ranges should not be used as input data at times when bearing fluctuations are substantial—swings of 2 degrees or more.

Since the regression running fix establishes the vessel's track, it can be employed to calculate the time and distance of the nearest approach to the object. In routine 2.8, this is done after the data has been entered in steps 1–9, and steps 10–11 have been executed at least once. Pressing $\boxed{f}$ $\boxed{d}$ once for time of nearest approach and once for distance of nearest approach will provide the desired results.

In routine 2.9, for the SR-52, the time of nearest approach is calculated by pressing $\boxed{2nd}$ $\boxed{C'}$ after the sequence of bearing–time pairs has been entered (steps 8–9) and the bearing and distance for a selected time have been calculated (steps 10–11). The distance of nearest approach is then obtained by pressing $\boxed{2nd}$ $\boxed{A'}$.

On the HP-67 and HP-97, pressing $\boxed{f}$ $\boxed{a}$ enables one to clear and initialize the calculator for a new problem, or to restart the calculation. The same result is obtained on the SR-52 by pressing $\boxed{2nd}$ $\boxed{E'}$.

75

2.3.7 Course Made Good from Three Bearings Another example of the use of regression in coastwise navigation is its role in the preparation of data for routines 2.10 and 2.11, for finding course made good from three bearings. This procedure is valuable because the determination of course made good can be made without any knowledge of current. However, it must be used properly: unless widely spaced bearings are selected, very large errors may result, as figure 2.26 shows. In this case, the vessel is proceeding due west, and a number of observations are made on a single object. When the successive bearing observations supplying the basis for calculating the course made good are spaced at intervals of only 10 degrees, an error in the first and third bearings of 1 degree (too low) causes an error of almost 30 degrees in the calculated course. However, when the intervals between the observations are 40 degrees and 25 degrees, 1-degree errors in the first and third bearings result in an error in the calculated course of just over 3 degrees. (In each of these cases, the calculated answer is actually the reciprocal of the *CMG*, because of a 180-degree ambiguity.)

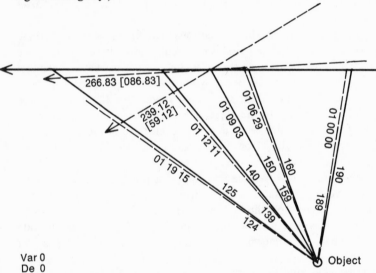

Var 0
De 0

	WITHOUT BEARING ERROR		WITH BEARING ERROR	
	True Bearing	**Time**	**True Bearing**	**Time**
Narrowly	160°	01 06 29	159°	01 06 29
Spaced	150	01 09 03	150	01 09 03
Bearings	140	01 12 11	139	01 12 11
	CMG[1] 89.42° + 180°, or 269.42° T		CMG[1] 59.12° + 180°, or 239.12° T	
Widely	190°	01 00 00	189°	01 00 00
Spaced	150	01 09 03	150	01 09 03
Bearings	125	01 19 15	124	01 19 15
	CMG[1] 89.94° + 180°, or 269.94° T		CMG[1] 86.83° + 180°, or 266.83° T	

[1]Since the calculated result is the reciprocal of the actual value, 180° is added.

2.26. Course Made Good from Three Bearings (Sensitivity to Error)

Routine 2.10 (HP-67/97)

T1	T2	T3		Var De
Bc1	Bc2	Bc3	CMG	

COURSE MADE GOOD FROM THREE BEARINGS

Step	Procedure	Input Data/Units	Keys	Output Data/Units
1	Load program			
2	Enter variation (+E,−W), even if 0	DD.d	f e	
3	Enter deviation (+E,−W), even if 0	DD.d	f e	
4	Enter first compass bearing to object	DDD.d	A	
5	Enter time of first bearing	H.MS	f a	
6	Enter second compass bearing to object	DDD.d	B	
7	Enter time of second bearing	H.MS	f b	
8	Enter third compass bearing to object	DDD.d	C	
9	Enter time of third bearing	H.MS	f c	
10	Calculate and display true course made good (the result contains a 180-degree ambiguity that must be resolved by the user)		D	DDD.d

Errors in the calculated result can also be minimized by the use of bearing regression. Three different sequences of bearing observations are taken, separated by enough time to allow substantial movement of the vessel between sequences. Next, a regression value of bearing is obtained for the mid-time of each sequence (from routine 2.6, for the HP-67 and HP-97) or the *Tmean* of each sequence (from routine 2.7, for the SR-52). These routines are discussed in section 2.3.5. When routine 2.6 is used, step 8 can be omitted, since no bearing extension to a common time is needed. The resulting values of time and bearing for each of the three groups of observations then serve as input for routines 2.10 and 2.11.

Routine 2.10 has been prepared for the HP-67 and HP-97. The calculated result contains a 180-degree ambiguity, inherent in the equations used to solve the problem, but the navigator should be able to resolve this without any difficulty. The data presented in figure 2.27, which shows both the original

77

observations and the answers obtained from the HP-67 and HP-97, can be used to test the program.

As this data indicates, when regression methods are used and widely spaced bearings are chosen, even fluctuating observations can yield quite acceptable results. In this instance, though some of the original bearings are many degrees away from the correct values, they yield a course made good which is in error by only 0.7 of a degree. Since, in addition, course made good is determined without any knowledge of current, the effort of employing the regression method is probably well worth while.

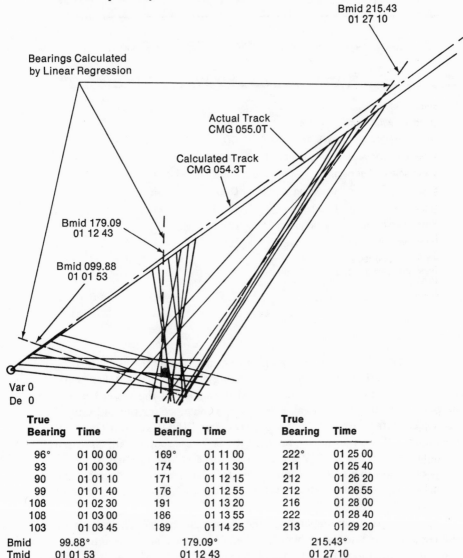

True Bearing	Time	True Bearing	Time	True Bearing	Time
96°	01 00 00	169°	01 11 00	222°	01 25 00
93	01 00 30	174	01 11 30	211	01 25 40
90	01 01 10	171	01 12 15	212	01 26 20
99	01 01 40	176	01 12 55	212	01 26 55
108	01 02 30	191	01 13 20	216	01 28 00
108	01 03 00	186	01 13 55	222	01 28 40
103	01 03 45	189	01 14 25	213	01 29 20

Bmid   99.88°   179.09°   215.43°
Tmid   01 01 53   01 12 43   01 27 10
Calculated CMG 54.3° T

2.27. Course Made Good from Three Bearings Using Bearing Regression

Routine 2.11 (SR-52)

No. of Bearings	Var De	Bc	Time	CMG

COURSE MADE GOOD FROM THREE, SIX, OR NINE BEARINGS

Step	Procedure	Input Data/Units	Keys	Output Data/Units
	Before beginning, make sure D/R switch is set to D.			
1	Load program—first side			
2	Load program—second side			
3	Enter number of bearings	3, 6, or 9	A	
4	Enter variation (+E, −W), even if 0	DD.d	B	
5	Enter deviation (+E, −W), even if 0	DD.d	B	
6	Enter bearing-time pairs; for each pair, enter compass bearing, followed by	DDD.d	C	
7	Time of bearing	H.MS	D	
8	Calculate and display true course made good (the result contains a 180-degree ambiguity that must be resolved by the user)		E	DDD.d

A similar procedure—routine 2.11—has been prepared for the SR-52. This routine can accept as input three, six, or nine bearings. When regression is used as a preliminary step, three bearing–time pairs are obtained, so the entry of the number of bearings, in step 3, should be made accordingly.

Figure 2.28 presents a set of data and the calculated answers obtained through routine 2.11 without any preliminary calculation of *Tmean*. The routine was used three times—once with three bearings (widely spaced, for best results), once with three pairs of bearings, and once with all nine bearings. The most accurate answer is the last: the error of 0.83 of a degree compares quite favorably with the result, shown in figure 2.27, obtained from the same data when bearing regression is used.

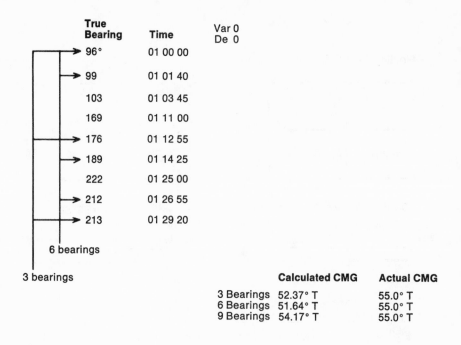

True Bearing	Time	Var 0 De 0
96°	01 00 00	
99	01 01 40	
103	01 03 45	
169	01 11 00	
176	01 12 55	
189	01 14 25	
222	01 25 00	
212	01 26 55	
213	01 29 20	

6 bearings

3 bearings

	Calculated CMG	Actual CMG
3 Bearings	52.37° T	55.0° T
6 Bearings	51.64° T	55.0° T
9 Bearings	54.17° T	55.0° T

2.28. Course Made Good from Three, Six, or Nine Bearings

2.3.8   Course and Speed Made Good from Two Fixes   A set of routines has been prepared which will be useful in coastal and tidal waters, where currents may set a vessel to one side or the other, or ahead of or behind an expected track. These are based on the fact that if two successive fixes can be obtained, the course and speed made good over the bottom *during the time interval between the two fixes* can be determined. Since the course being steered and the vessel's speed during the interval are known, a further calculation will yield the set and drift of the current acting on the vessel during this time.

The position fixes in this instance should be calculated from successive bearings on two charted objects, since pairs of observations made in this manner will accommodate the vessel's motion without requiring a knowledge of the current. Running fixes, which do require knowledge of the current, are not acceptable. When—on either the first or the second round of bearings —considerable time intervenes between the observation of the first and of the second object, the technique of bearing regression (employing a common time) should be used.

If, as is often the case, at the time of either the first or the second set of observations the vessel is at a known location (such as a buoy, pier, or mooring) which serves as one of the objects, the calculator routines will still provide correct answers; the calculated distance off this object will be zero, and course and speed made good will be properly shown.

80

Routine 2.12 (HP-67/97)

Var De	Cc S	D1o1 D1o2 T1	D2o1 D2o2 T2	Clear
Btobj Dobj	Bc1o1 Bc1o2 T1	Bc2o1 Bc2o2 T2	SMG CMG	Dr St

COURSE MADE GOOD AND SPEED MADE GOOD FROM TWO FIXES, SET AND DRIFT (DISTANCE AND BEARING)

Step	Procedure	Input Data/Units	Keys	Output Data/Units
1	Load program—both sides			
2	Enter variation (+E,−W), even if 0	DD.d	f a	
3	Enter deviation (+E,−W), even if 0	DD.d	f a	
4	Enter true bearing between objects, in either direction	DDD.d	A	
5	Enter distance between objects	naut. mi.	A	
6	Enter first compass bearing to first object	DDD.d	B	
7	Enter first compass bearing to second object	DDD.d	B	
8	Enter time of first set of bearings	H.MS	B	
9	Enter second compass bearing to first object	DDD.d	C	
10	Enter second compass bearing to second object	DDD.d	C	
11	Enter time of second set of bearings	H.MS	C	

If the vessel is alongside either object at time of first or second set of bearings, enter an arbitrary bearing (*not* 0) at the appropriate step (6, 7, 9, or 10). The result will be a display of 0 for distance off that object (in step 12 or 13), and all other distances will be correct.

Step	Procedure	Input Data/Units	Keys	Output Data/Units
12	Calculate and display distance off first object at time of first set of bearings,		f c	naut. mi.
·	Distance off second object at time of first set of bearings,			naut. mi.
·	Display time of first set of bearings			H.MS
13	Calculate and display distance off first object at time of second set of bearings,		f d	naut. mi.
·	Distance off second object at time of second set of bearings,			naut. mi.
·	Display time of second set of bearings			H.MS

(CONTINUED)

81

Step	Procedure	Input Data/Units	Keys	Output Data/Units
14	Calculate and display speed made good between two sets of bearings,		D	knots
·	True course made good between two sets of bearings			DDD.d
15	Enter compass course of vessel between two sets of bearings*	DDD.d	f b	
16	Enter speed of vessel between two sets of bearings	knots	f b	
17	Calculate and display drift of current,		E	knots
·	Set of current			DDD.d
18	Clear, either to eliminate errors in data entry (and to restart the procedure) or to start a new problem		f e	

*Correct for leeway; see table 2.2.

Routine 2.13 (SR-52)

Bc2o1 Bc2o2	T2	D2o1 D2o2	CMG	SMG
Var De	Btobj Dobj	Bc1o1 Bc1o2	T1	D1o1 D1o2

COURSE MADE GOOD AND SPEED MADE GOOD FROM TWO FIXES (DISTANCE AND BEARING)

Step	Procedure	Input Data/Units	Keys	Output Data/Units
	Before beginning, make sure D/R switch is set to D.			
1	Load program—first side			
2	Load program—second side			
3	Initialize		2nd CMs 2nd rset CLR	
4	Enter variation (+E, −W), even if 0	DD.d	A	
5	Enter deviation (+E, −W), even if 0	DD.d	A	
6	Enter true bearing between objects, in either direction	DDD.d	B	
7	Enter distance between objects	naut. mi.	B	
8	Enter first compass bearing to first object	DDD.d	C	
9	Enter first compass bearing to second object	DDD.d	C	

If the vessel is alongside either object at time of first set of bearings, enter an arbitrary bearing (*not* 0) at the appropriate step (8 or 9). The result will be a display of 0 for distance off that object in step 11 or 12, and the other distance will be correct.

Step	Procedure	Input Data/Units	Keys	Output Data/Units
10	Enter time of first set of bearings	H.MS	D	
11	Calculate and display distance off first object at time of first set of bearings		E	naut. mi.
12	Calculate and display distance off second object at time of first set of bearings		E	naut. mi.
13	Enter second compass bearing to first object	DDD.d	2nd A′	
14	Enter second compass bearing to second object	DDD.d	2nd A′	

(CONTINUED)

Step	Procedure	Input Data/Units	Keys	Output Data/Units
	If the vessel is alongside either object at time of second set of bearings, enter an arbitrary bearing (*not* 0) at the appropriate step (13 or 14). The result will be a display of 0 for distance off that object in step 16 or 17, and the other distance will be correct.			
15	Enter time of second set of bearings	H.MS	2nd B′	
16	Calculate and display distance off first object at time of second set of bearings		2nd C′	naut. mi.
17	Calculate and display distance off second object at time of second set of bearings		2nd C′	naut. mi.
18	Calculate and display true course made good between two sets of bearings		2nd D′	DDD.d
19	Calculate and display speed made good between two sets of bearings		2nd E′	knots
20	Clear, either to eliminate errors in data entry (and to restart the procedure) or to start a new problem		2nd CMs 2nd rset[1] CLR	

[1]This step is essential in order to clear flags set by the running program.

Routine 2.14 (SR-52)

	S	Dr or SMG	SMG	Dr
Var De	Cc	St or CMG	CMG	St

COURSE MADE GOOD AND SPEED MADE GOOD, SET AND DRIFT

Step	Procedure	Input Data/Units	Keys	Output Data/Units
	Before beginning, make sure D/R switch is set to D.			
1	Load program			
2	Enter variation ($+$E,$-$W), even if 0	DD.d	A	
3	Enter deviation ($+$E,$-$W), even if 0	DD.d	A	
4	Enter compass course*	DDD.d	B	
5	Enter vessel speed	knots	2nd B'	
	Course Made Good and Speed Made Good			
6	After completion of steps 1–5, enter set of current, even if 0	DDD.d	C	
7	Enter drift of current, even if 0	knots	2nd C'	
8	Calculate and display true course made good		D	DDD.d
9	Calculate and display speed made good		2nd D'	knots
	Set and Drift			
10	After completion of steps 1–5, enter true course made good (available from routine 2.13 or routine 2.28)	DDD.d	C	
11	Enter speed made good (available from routine 2.13 or routine 2.28)	knots	2nd C'	
12	Calculate and display set of current		E	DDD.d
13	Calculate and display drift of current		2nd E'	knots

*Correct for leeway; see table 2.2.

85

On the HP-67 and HP-97 a single routine—routine 2.12—can be used both for finding course and speed and for calculating set and drift of current. On the SR-52, two separate routines are required for these operations. These are presented as routines 2.13 and 2.14.

Figure 2.29 illustrates the situation in which these calculator routines are employed. The accompanying data can be used to verify the accuracy of the procedures described.

DATA

	SMG, CMG	Set and Drift
Var	−15° (W)	
De	+3° (E)	
Btobj	143°	
Dobj	5.0nm	
Bc1o1	122°	
Bc1o2	12°	
T1	0800	
Bc2o1	209°	
Bc2o2	282°	
T2	0905	
Cc		77°
S		6.0kts

CALCULATED RESULTS

D1o1	3.2nm	
D1o2	2.9nm	
D2o1	4.18nm	
D2o2	4.23nm	
SMG	4.73kts	
CMG	55.58° T	
Dr		1.5kts
St		275.19°

2.29. Course Made Good and Speed Made Good from Two Fixes (Distance and Bearing)

86

2.4 Coastwise Navigation Using Latitude and Longitude Co-ordinates

In the calculator routines discussed so far, positions have been defined in terms of distances and bearings to and from vessels and objects. The remainder of this chapter covers the cases in which objects, obstacles, and vessel positions are located in terms of latitude and longitude.

As was pointed out in section 2.2.1, the use of latitude and longitude is accompanied by the assumption of a non-planar earth; this must be taken into account in the calculations, and either the Mercator chart-factor method of calculation or the mid-latitude method may therefore be employed. The chart factor *(lm)* is the ratio of the actual length in nautical miles of a given interval of longitude (in minutes and seconds) to the same interval of latitude, at the latitude in question, and reflects the actual shape of the aspheric earth. The mid-latitude method, which assumes a perfectly spherical earth, involves computing the average latitude (the mid-latitude) of the area in question, and determining the equivalent of the chart factor by taking the cosine of the mid-latitude.

In most cases, the difference in position as calculated by the two methods is small enough to be ignored. However, in some situations, especially those in which position is calculated from a running fix on two objects, errors can reach as much as a quarter of a nautical mile, depending on the orientation of objects and course made good during the run. Hence, in the fixing routines, the chart-factor method is preferable when maximum accuracy is required. This method is particularly suitable for position fixing because the distances involved are relatively short, especially if bearings are being taken on visual objects. Hence, a single chart factor applies to the whole area involved. This can be obtained by taking from the chart the length of the interval of longitude and dividing it by the length of the corresponding interval of latitude, or the task of making the measurements may be avoided by using table 2.3, which provides the same information in convenient form. The distances are specified for the nearest degree of latitude, which is probably quite adequate for computational purposes. Fixing routines based on mid-latitude calculations are also provided, for those cases where they are more convenient, or where the chart factor is not readily available.

For planning, estimating position, and tracking, it is often easier and equally accurate to use the mid-latitude method. This is true for a journey in excess of 10 nautical miles, especially if considerable north–south movement is involved, since it is difficult to define chart factor accurately for a wide latitude interval.

Operations involving latitude and longitude are facilitated in the HP-67, HP-97, and SR-52, by the external magnetic memories, which make possible the prerecording of the latitude and longitude of places and objects. Each location, defined by a co-ordinate system of many numerical units (say, a

87

Lat.	Degree of latitude				Degree of longitude				Lat.
	Nautical miles·	Statute miles	Feet	Meters	Nautical miles	Statute miles	Feet	Meters	
°									°
0	59. 701	68. 703	362 753	110 567	60. 109	69. 172	365 226	111 321	0
1	. 702	. 704	756	568	60. 099	69. 161	365 171	111 304	1
2	. 702	. 704	759	569	60. 072	69. 129	365 003	111 253	2
3	. 703	. 705	762	570	60. 026	69. 077	364 728	111 169	3
4	. 705	. 707	772	573	59. 963	69. 004	364 341	111 051	4
5	59. 706	68. 709	362 782	110 576	59. 881	68. 910	363 845	110 900	5
6	. 708	. 711	795	580	59. 781	68. 795	363 238	110 715	6
7	. 711	. 714	808	584	59. 664	68. 660	362 523	110 497	7
8	. 713	. 717	825	589	59. 528	68. 503	361 696	110 245	8
9	. 717	. 721	844	595	59. 373	68. 325	360 758	109 959	9
10	59. 720	68. 724	362 864	110 601	59. 201	68. 128	359 715	109 641	10
11	. 724	. 729	887	608	59. 011	67. 909	358 560	109 289	11
12	. 728	. 734	913	616	58. 803	67. 670	357 297	108 904	12
13	. 732	. 739	940	624	58. 578	67. 410	355 925	108 486	13
14	. 737	. 744	969	633	58. 335	67. 130	354 449	108 036	14
15	59. 742	68. 750	363 002	110 643	58. 074	66. 830	352 864	107 553	15
16	. 748	. 757	035	653	57. 795	66. 509	351 168	107 036	16
17	. 753	. 763	068	663	57. 498	66. 168	349 367	106 487	17
18	. 760	. 770	107	675	57. 185	65. 807	347 461	105 906	18
19	. 766	. 777	143	686	56. 854	65. 427	345 453	105 294	19
20	59. 773	68. 785	363 186	110 699	56. 506	65. 026	343 337	104 649	20
21	. 780	. 793	228	712	56. 140	64. 605	341 115	103 972	21
22	. 787	. 801	271	725	55. 758	64. 165	338 793	103 264	22
23	. 794	. 810	317	739	55. 359	63. 705	336 365	102 524	23
24	. 802	. 819	363	753	54. 943	63. 227	333 839	101 754	24
25	59. 810	68. 828	363 412	110 768	54. 510	62. 729	331 207	100 952	25
26	. 818	. 837	461	783	54. 060	62. 211	328 474	100 119	26
27	. 827	. 847	514	799	53. 594	61. 675	325 646	99 257	27
28	. 835	. 857	566	815	53. 112	61. 121	322 717	98 364	28
29	. 844	. 868	622	832	52. 614	60. 547	319 688	97 441	29
30	59. 853	68. 878	363 675	110 848	52. 099	59. 955	316 562	96 488	30
31	. 863	. 889	734	866	51. 569	59. 345	313 340	95 506	31
32	. 872	. 900	789	883	51. 023	58. 716	310 023	94 495	32
33	. 882	. 911	848	901	50. 462	58. 070	306 611	93 455	33
34	. 891	. 922	907	919	49. 885	57. 407	303 107	92 387	34
35	59. 902	68. 934	363 970	110 938	49. 293	56. 725	299 508	91 290	35
36	. 911	. 945	364 029	956	48. 686	56. 027	295 820	90 166	36
37	. 922	. 957	091	975	48. 064	55. 311	292 041	89 014	37
38	. 932	. 968	154	994	47. 427	54. 578	288 173	87 835	38
39	. 942	. 980	216	111 013	46. 776	53. 829	284 216	86 629	39
40	59. 953	68. 993	364 281	111 033	46. 110	53. 063	280 171	85 396	40
41	. 963	69. 005	344	052	45. 430	52. 280	276 040	84 137	41
42	. 974	. 017	409	072	44. 737	51. 482	271 827	82 853	42
43	. 984	. 029	472	091	44. 030	50. 668	267 530	81 543	43
44	. 995	. 041	537	111	43. 309	49. 839	263 150	80 208	44
45	60. 006	69. 054	364 603	111 131	42. 575	48. 994	258 691	78 849	45

Table 2.3   Length of a Degree of Latitude and Longitude[1]

[1]Table 6 in *American Practical Navigator,* vol. 2 (Defense Mapping Agency Hydrographic Center, 1975), pp. 124–25.

Lat.	Degree of latitude				Degree of longitude				Lat.
	Nautical miles	Statute miles	Feet	Meters	Nautical miles	Statute miles	Feet	Meters	
°									°
45	60. 006	69. 054	364 603	111 131	42. 575	48. 994	258 691	78 849	45
46	. 017	. 066	669	151	41. 828	48. 135	254 154	77 466	46
47	. 027	. 078	731	170	41. 068	47. 260	249 534	76 058	47
48	. 038	. 090	797	190	40. 296	46. 372	244 843	74 628	48
49	. 049	. 103	862	210	39. 511	45. 468	240 072	73 174	49
50	60. 059	69. 114	364 925	111 229	38. 714	44. 551	235 230	71 698	50
51	. 070	. 127	990	249	37. 905	43. 620	230 315	70 200	51
52	. 080	. 139	365 052	268	37. 084	42. 676	225 328	68 680	52
53	. 090	. 151	115	287	36. 253	41. 719	220 276	67 140	53
54	. 100	. 162	177	306	35. 409	40. 748	215 151	65 578	54
55	60. 111	69. 174	365 240	111 325	34. 555	39. 765	209 961	63 996	55
56	. 120	. 185	299	343	33. 691	38. 770	204 708	62 395	56
57	. 130	. 197	358	361	32. 815	37. 763	199 390	60 774	57
58	. 140	. 208	417	379	31. 930	36. 745	194 012	59 135	58
59	. 150	. 219	476	397	31. 036	35. 715	188 576	57 478	59
60	60. 159	69. 229	365 531	111 414	30. 131	34. 674	183 077	55 802	60
61	. 168	. 241	591	432	29. 217	33. 622	177 526	54 110	61
62	. 177	. 251	643	448	28. 294	32. 560	171 916	52 400	62
63	. 186	. 261	696	464	27. 362	31. 488	166 257	50 675	63
64	. 194	. 270	748	480	26. 422	30. 406	160 545	48 934	64
65	60. 203	69. 280	365 801	111 496	25. 474	29. 314	154 780	47 177	65
66	. 211	. 290	850	511	24. 518	28. 215	148 973	45 407	66
67	. 219	. 298	896	525	23. 554	27. 105	143 117	43 622	67
68	. 226	. 307	942	539	22. 583	25. 988	137 215	41 823	68
69	. 234	. 316	988	553	21. 605	24. 862	131 273	40 012	69
70	60. 241	69. 324	366 030	111 566	20. 620	23. 729	125 289	38 188	70
71	. 247	. 331	070	578	19. 629	22. 589	119 268	36 353	71
72	. 254	. 339	109	590	18. 632	21. 441	113 209	34 506	72
73	. 260	. 346	148	602	17. 629	20. 287	107 113	32 648	73
74	. 266	. 353	184	613	16. 620	19. 126	100 988	30 781	74
75	60. 272	69. 359	366 217	111 623	15. 606	17. 959	94 826	28 903	75
76	. 276	. 365	247	632	14. 588	16. 788	88 638	27 017	76
77	. 282	. 371	280	642	13. 565	15. 611	82 425	25 123	77
78	. 286	. 376	306	650	12. 538	14. 428	76 181	23 220	78
79	. 290	. 381	332	658	11. 507	13. 242	69 918	21 311	79
80	60. 294	69. 385	366 355	111 665	10. 472	12. 051	63 629	19 394	80
81	. 298	. 389	375	671	9. 434	10. 857	57 323	17 472	81
82	. 301	. 393	394	677	8. 394	9. 659	51 001	15 545	82
83	. 303	. 396	411	682	7. 350	8. 458	44 659	13 612	83
84	. 306	. 399	427	687	6. 304	7. 255	38 304	11 675	84
85	60. 308	69. 402	366 440	111 691	5. 256	6. 049	31 939	9 735	85
86	. 310	. 403	450	694	4. 207	4. 842	25 564	7 792	86
87	. 311	. 405	457	696	3. 157	3. 633	19 180	5 846	87
88	. 312	. 406	463	698	2. 105	2. 422	12 789	3 898	88
89	. 313	. 407	467	699	1. 052	1. 211	6 394	1 949	89
90	60. 313	69. 407	366 467	111 699	0. 000	0. 000	0	0	90

latitude of 41°17′23″N and a longitude of 68°14′32″W) is assigned an identification number in the HP-67 and HP-97, and an identification letter in the SR-52.

In addition, in the HP-67 and HP-97, the magnetic compass variation and the Mercator chart factor for the section of the chart being used can be stored on the card, and are then automatically extracted by the routine that uses the prerecorded data. In the SR-52, the chart factor can be stored, but the variation must be keyed in manually, where needed. Once prerecording has been completed, utilization of the data as part of the input for a routine requires just keying in the identification number or letter, and then (in the HP-67 and HP-97) pressing the appropriate keys to load the data. These simple procedures may replace as many as seventeen individual keystrokes. The co-ordinates are entered quickly and accurately.

Simplicity in performing calculations is gained in another way as well. In the preceding routines for coastwise fixing and planning, when the distance and bearing between charted objects were required as input data, the information had to be obtained by measurement on the chart. However, if the latitude and longitude have been prerecorded, once the numbers or letters designating the two positions have been keyed in, the calculator will automatically determine the values of distance and bearing between the objects, for use in the remainder of the calculation.

The answers yielded by calculations made with latitude and longitude are convenient and flexible. The planning routines provide course to steer, time of arrival (on the HP-67 and HP-97 or elapsed time (on the SR-52), and course and distance made good. The position fix is displayed in the form of latitude and longitude, but on the HP-67 and HP-97, the distance off one of the objects observed is also provided; the user can choose the terms most convenient for his purposes.

2.4.1 Prerecorded Lists of Objects

All of the routines developed for latitude and longitude can accept prerecorded data from one or more cards, and also data inserted manually, at the keyboard, so they can be used even when there has been no opportunity to prerecord the co-ordinates of a particular place. However, it is most convenient to employ prerecorded data.

The best sources of co-ordinates for prerecording are nautical charts with a scale of 1 to 20,000 or 1 to 40,000; these can be read with sufficient accuracy to provide degrees, minutes, and seconds of latitude and longitude. Taking data from light lists, such as those published by the U.S. Coast Guard, appears to be somewhat risky, since positions shown in those publications are occasionally different—and less accurate—than the ones on a nautical chart.

A further caution should also be observed. The position of floating aids to navigation, such as buoys, is constantly subject to change as a result of heavy weather, collisions, and the like. The U.S. government publishes notices to

mariners describing shifts, removals, and new locations of buoys and other floating aids. Hence, the data on the prerecorded cards must be updated from time to time in exactly the same manner as the data on nautical charts.

In the prerecording of latitude and longitude, it is customary to employ degrees, minutes, and seconds *(DD.MMSS)*, rather than degrees, minutes, and tenths of minutes, since conversion to decimal degrees can be accomplished by the calculator automatically. (Tenths of minutes are employed for celestial navigation, because sextant scales are normally calibrated in tenths of minutes of arc.)

Once the co-ordinates have been recorded and checked for accuracy, care should be taken to protect the data cards from inadvertent erasure in the calculator. On the HP-67 and HP-97, this is done by clipping the corners of the cards; on the SR-52, the cards are protected against inadvertent erasure by the fact that they cannot be re-used unless small, black adhesive tabs are properly attached. When any positions need to be changed completely, new cards should be prepared; attempting to alter the old ones is likely to result in the accidental deletion of data that is supposed to be retained. Also, since the small data cards—and program cards—can easily become lost or wedged into inaccessible places, duplicates should be made. Otherwise, the labor of remeasuring positions may become necessary.

Data cards should be prepared, as convenient, for all the areas the navigator expects to enter. In this way, a library of positions can be accumulated.

2.4.2 Prerecorded Magnetic Cards for the HP-67 and HP-97   Routine 2.15 is the set of instructions for preparing a prerecorded latitude and longitude data card for the HP-67 and HP-97. A single card can store latitude and longitude for eleven different objects, along with the magnetic compass variation and the Mercator chart factor *(lm)* for the section of the chart being used. When constructing this card, it is important to note step 11 of the routine, in which storage is shifted from the primary to the secondary register. If this is not done, beginning with the sixth object, the recording of additional co-ordinates will result in the successive erasure of the positions of the first five objects.

Routine 2.15 (HP-67/97)

```
┌─────────────────────────────────────────────────────────────┐
│                                                               │
│            Latitude and Longitude Data Card, No. N            │
│                                                               │
└─────────────────────────────────────────────────────────────┘
```

LATITUDE AND LONGITUDE DATA CARD

Step	Procedure	Input Data/Units	Keys	Output Data/Units
1	Enter 1st latitude (+N,−S)	DD.MMSS	STO 0	
2	Enter 1st longitude (+W,−E)	DD.MMSS	STO 1	

In entering latitude and longitude, signs should be employed throughout as indicated in steps 1 and 2.

Step	Procedure	Input Data/Units	Keys	Output Data/Units
3	Enter 2nd latitude	DD.MMSS	STO 2	
4	Enter 2nd longitude	DD.MMSS	STO 3	
5	Enter 3rd latitude	DD.MMSS	STO 4	
6	Enter 3rd longitude	DD.MMSS	STO 5	
7	Enter 4th latitude	DD.MMSS	STO 6	
8	Enter 4th longitude	DD.MMSS	STO 7	
9	Enter 5th latitude	DD.MMSS	STO 8	
10	Enter 5th longitude	DD.MMSS	STO 9	
11	Shift to secondary storage		f p↔s	
12	Enter 6th latitude	DD.MMSS	STO 0	
13	Enter 6th longitude	DD.MMSS	STO 1	
14	Enter 7th latitude	DD.MMSS	STO 2	
15	Enter 7th longitude	DD.MMSS	STO 3	
16	Enter 8th latitude	DD.MMSS	STO 4	
17	Enter 8th longitude	DD.MMSS	STO 5	
18	Enter 9th latitude	DD.MMSS	STO 6	
19	Enter 9th longitude	DD.MMSS	STO 7	
20	Enter 10th latitude	DD.MMSS	STO 8	
21	Enter 10th longitude	DD.MMSS	STO 9	
22	Enter 11th latitude	DD.MMSS	STO A	
23	Enter 11th longitude	DD.MMSS	STO B	
24	Enter chart factor[1]	0.nnnn	STO D	

[1]Chart factor is calculated by dividing the length in nautical miles of an interval of longitude (say five minutes) at the location in question by the length in nautical miles of an *equal* interval of latitude at that location. The quotient—the chart factor—should be brought to four decimal places. The necessary figures can be obtained either from direct measurement on a chart or from table 2.3.

Step	Procedure	Input Data/Units	Keys	Output Data/Units
25	Enter variation of compass (+E,−W), even if 0	DD.d	STO E	
26	Prepare to record data card		f W/DATA	CRD
27	Record data card—both sides			CRD

When the co-ordinates of two objects are used in a problem, it is not necessary that the data for both objects be contained on one card. However, if two cards are required, it should be remembered that the calculator will retain the values for variation and chart factor supplied by the *second* card inserted. If this presents a problem, the user can override these manually, at the keyboard, and substitute any desired values.

2.4.3 Prerecorded Magnetic Cards for the SR-52

Routine 2.16 is the set of instructions for preparing a prerecorded data card for the SR-52. When both sides of the card are used, a chart factor and nine latitude and longitude pairs can be stored; because of space limitations, variation is not included, and must be entered manually, as needed. The program memory is employed for recording the co-ordinates, so steps to transfer information from the program memory to the data memory are built into the routine.

Where a routine includes an instruction to "Clear" or "Initialize," this should be carried out with the calculation program in place, and *before* any prerecorded data is entered, since co-ordinates which have been loaded previously will be erased by this operation. After initialization, the data can be entered, and the program is then reinserted for completion of the routine.

2.4.4 The Application of Leeway

In all of the planning routines, care should be taken to correct for leeway whenever necessary (most often, that is, in the case of sailing vessels). The specific instructions concerning leeway are in section 2.2.5.

Routine 2.16 (SR-52)

A′	B′	C′	D′	
A	B	C	D	E

LATITUDE AND LONGITUDE DATA CARD

Step	Procedure	Input Data/Units	Keys	Output Data/Units
1	Latitudes, longitudes, and chart factor are recorded in the program memory. Hence, entries are made by shifting the calculator into LRN mode.		2nd rset LRN	000 00
2	Enter subroutine		2nd LBL 2nd E′ 2nd D.MS 2nd EXC 0 5 2nd EXC 0 6 2nd EXC 0 7 2nd EXC 0 8 . n n n n[1] STO 1 1 2nd rtn	025 00

Nine latitude and longitude pairs can be entered on the two sides of one card. They should be close enough to each other to require the same chart factor, as entered in step 2. Recording of co-ordinates starts at program step 25. Each pair of co-ordinates is separated by a lettered label—A–E and (2nd) A′–D′. The symbols *DD.MMSS* represent the individual digits of degrees, minutes, and seconds, and the decimal-point key is pressed to separate degrees from minutes. The sample entry steps shown are for co-ordinates of up to 99°59′59″, but the memory can accommodate nine sets of co-ordinates all 100° or larger.

[1]Each n stands for one digit of the chart factor. For the method of calculating this four-place decimal, see footnote 1 to routine 2.15.

Step	Procedure	Input Data/Units	Keys	Output Data/Units
3	Enter 1st latitude (+N,−S)		2nd LBL A *D D* . *M M S* *S* 2nd E'	
4	Enter 1st longitude (+W,−E)		*D D* . *M M S* *S* 2nd E' HLT	
5	Enter 2nd latitude (+N,−S)		2nd LBL B *D D* . *M M S* *S* 2nd E'	
6	Enter 2nd longitude (+W,−E)		*D D* . *M M S* *S* 2nd E' HLT	
	. . .			
19	Enter 9th latitude (+N,−S)		2nd LBL 2nd D' *D D* . *M M S* *S* 2nd E'	
20	Enter 9th longitude (+W,−E)		*D D* . *M M S* *S* 2nd E' HLT	
21	Record data card—first side		LRN CLR INV 2nd read	
22	Record data card—second side		INV 2nd read	

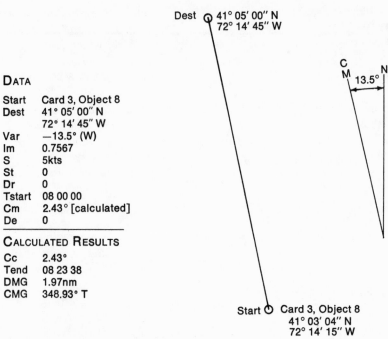

DATA

Start	Card 3, Object 8
Dest	41° 05′ 00″ N
	72° 14′ 45″ W
Var	−13.5° (W)
Im	0.7567
S	5kts
St	0
Dr	0
Tstart	08 00 00
Cm	2.43° [calculated]
De	0

CALCULATED **R**ESULTS

Cc	2.43°
Tend	08 23 38
DMG	1.97nm
CMG	348.93° T

2.30. Planning (Chart Factor)

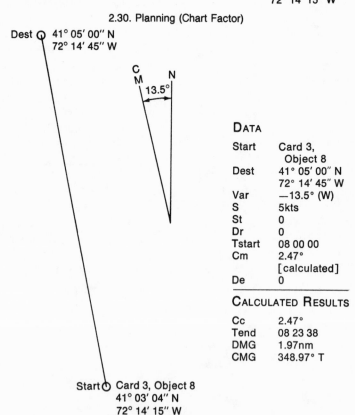

DATA

Start	Card 3, Object 8
Dest	41° 05′ 00″ N
	72° 14′ 45″ W
Var	−13.5° (W)
S	5kts
St	0
Dr	0
Tstart	08 00 00
Cm	2.47° [calculated]
De	0

CALCULATED **R**ESULTS

Cc	2.47°
Tend	08 23 38
DMG	1.97nm
CMG	348.97° T

96

2.31. Planning (Mid-latitude)

2.4.5   Planning on the HP-67 and HP-97   The Planning routines for the HP-67 and HP-97—routine 2.17, using chart factor, and routine 2.18, using mid-latitude calculations—are part of an integrated set which also includes calculating and tracking estimated position (routines 2.20 and 2.21) and fixing (routines 2.24 and 2.25). Once the co-ordinates have been entered for the first and second object (in fixing) or the necessary data has been obtained (in planning), the information can be used as well for the later calculation or tracking of estimated position. Re-entry of this data is then unnecessary. This design was adopted in part because of certain memory limitations in the calculator, but is also convenient because it is often necessary to move from planning to tracking. The fact that the Planning routines also provide data-input steps for the routines involving estimated position is another reason for their being given in both chart-factor and mid-latitude versions; the latter routines exist in both forms.

Figure 2.30 (for chart factor) and figure 2.31 (for mid-latitude) illustrate the use of routine 2.17 and routine 2.18, respectively, in planning. In this instance, the starting position is object 8 on data card 3. Pressing ⑧ Ⓕ Ⓐ results in entry of the object's co-ordinates (latitude of 41°03′04″N and longitude of 72°14′15″W) and also, automatically, of the variation (13.5 degrees W) and the chart factor (0.7567). If the necessary data has not been stored on a magnetic card, it is entered manually, as specified in steps 8–23 (for chart factor) or steps 8–22 (for mid-latitude).

Since a vessel's deviation depends on the heading, it cannot be determined until the planned course has been calculated. Therefore, it is added when the magnetic course to steer has been displayed and the vessel's expected heading is known (i.e., after step 29 of routine 2.17 or step 28 of routine 2.18). Even if the value for deviation at this heading is zero, it should be keyed into the calculator. The resulting display is the compass course to steer.

The complete answer to this problem includes the course to steer, the expected time of arrival, the distance made good, and the course made good (this may be different from the course steered if current data has been inserted).

2.4.6   Planning (Mid-latitude) on the SR-52   Routine 2.19 is the Planning routine for the SR-52, employing the mid-latitude method of calculation. Any combination of prerecorded and manually entered data may be used. As in the routines previously described, deviation is added after a magnetic course has been displayed (i.e., after step 35); the result is conversion of any negative magnetic course to a compass course within the range of 0–360° degrees.

The data supplied in figure 2.31 can be used to test the method on the SR-52.

Routine 2.17 (HP-67/97)

Select Start	Select Dest	Load		Var lm
S St Dr	Tstart	Cm De→Cc	Tend	DMG CMG

PLANNING (CHART FACTOR)

Step	Procedure	Input Data/Units	Keys	Output Data/Units
1	Load program—both sides			
	If both start and destination co-ordinates are on data cards, proceed as follows (steps 2–7):			
2	Load data card containing start co-ordinates			
3	Enter identification number corresponding to start co-ordinates (an even number from 0 to 20)	0–20	f a	
	If destination co-ordinates are on same data card,			
4	Enter identification number corresponding to destination co-ordinates (an even number from 0 to 20), and continue at step 7	0–20	f b	
	If destination co-ordinates are on a different data card,			
5	Load second data card			
6	Enter identification number corresponding to destination co-ordinates (an even number from 0 to 20)	0–20	f b	
7	Load start and destination co-ordinates into memory, and continue at step 23		f c	
	If only start co-ordinates are on a data card, proceed as follows (steps 8–12):			
8	Load data card			
9	Enter identification number corresponding to start co-ordinates (an even number from 0 to 20)	0–20	f a	
10	Enter destination latitude (+N, −S)	DD.MMSS	ENTER	
11	Enter destination longitude (+W, −E), but *do not press* $\boxed{\text{ENTER}}$	DD.MMSS		
12	Load start and destination co-ordinates into memory, and continue at step 23		f c	

98

Step	Procedure	Input Data/Units	Keys	Output Data/Units
	If only destination co-ordinates are on a data card, proceed as follows (steps 13–17):			
13	Enter start latitude (+N,−S)	DD.MMSS	ENTER	
14	Enter start longitude (+W,−E)	DD.MMSS	ENTER	
15	Load data card			
16	Enter identification number corresponding to destination co-ordinates (an even number from 0 to 20	0–20	f b	
17	Load start and destination co-ordinates into memory, and continue at step 23		f c	
	If neither start nor destination co-ordinates are on data cards, proceed as follows (steps 18–33):			
18	Enter start latitude (+N,−S)	DD.MMSS	ENTER	
19	Enter start longitude (+W,−E)	DD.MMSS	ENTER	
20	Enter destination latitude (+N,−S)	DD.MMSS	ENTER	
21	Enter destination longitude (+W,−E), but *do not press* ENTER	DD.MMSS		
22	Load start and destination co-ordinates into memory		f c	
23	Enter variation (+E,−W), even if 0, if no data card has been used, if variation is to be different from value on last data card used, or if chart factor is to be entered in the following step	DD.d	f e	
24	Enter chart factor if no data card has been used, or if chart factor is to be different from value on last data card used	0.nnnn	f e	
25	Enter expected vessel speed	knots	A	
26	Enter expected set of current, even if 0	DDD.d	A	
27	Enter expected drift of current, even if 0	knots	A	
28	Enter time of start of run	H.MS	B	
29	Calculate and display magnetic course to steer		C	DDD.d
30	Enter deviation for planned magnetic course (+E,−W), even if 0,	DD.d	C	
·	Calculate and display compass course to steer**			DDD.d
31	Calculate and display time destination will be reached		D	H.MS
32	Calculate and display distance made good		E	naut. mi.
33	Calculate and display true course made good		E	DDD.d

**Uncorrect for leeway; see table 2.2.

Routine 2.18 (HP-67/97)

Select Start	Select Dest	Load		Var
S St Dr	Tstart	Cm De→Cc	Tend	DMG CMG

PLANNING (MID-LATITUDE)

Step	Procedure	Input Data/Units	Keys	Output Data/Units
1	Load program—both sides			
	If both start and destination co-ordinates are on data cards, proceed as follows (steps 2–7):			
2	Load data card containing start co-ordinates			
3	Enter identification number corresponding to start co-ordinates (an even number from 0 to 20)	0–20	f a	
	If destination co-ordinates are on same data card,			
4	Enter identification number corresponding to destination co-ordinates (an even number from 0 to 20), and continue at step 7	0–20	f b	
	If destination co-ordinates are on a different data card,			
5	Load second data card			
6	Enter identification number corresponding to destination co-ordinates (an even number from 0 to 20)	0–20	f b	
7	Load start and destination co-ordinates into memory, and continue at step 23		f c	
	If only start co-ordinates are on a data card, proceed as follows (steps 8–12):			
8	Load data card			
9	Enter identification number corresponding to start co-ordinates (an even number from 0 to 20)	0–20	f a	
10	Enter destination latitude ($+N, -S$)	DD.MMSS	ENTER	
11	Enter destination longitude ($+W, -E$), *but do not press* ENTER	DD.MMSS		
12	Load start and destination co-ordinates into memory, and continue at step 23		f c	

100

Step	Procedure	Input Data/Units	Keys	Output Data/Units
	If only destination co-ordinates are on a data card, proceed as follows (steps 13–17):			
13	Enter start latitude (+N,−S)	DD.MMSS	ENTER	
14	Enter start longitude (+W,−E)	DD.MMSS	ENTER	
15	Load data card			
16	Enter identification number corresponding to destination co-ordinates (an even number from 0 to 20)	0–20	f b	
17	Load start and destination co-ordinates into memory, and continue at step 23		f c	
	If neither start nor destination co-ordinates are on data cards, proceed as follows (steps 18–32):			
18	Enter start latitude (+N,−S)	DD.MMSS	ENTER	
19	Enter start longitude (+W,−E)	DD.MMSS	ENTER	
20	Enter destination latitude (+N,−S)	DD.MMSS	ENTER	
21	Enter destination longitude (+W,−E), *but do not press* ENTER	DD.MMSS		
22	Load start and destination co-ordinates into memory		f c	
23	Enter variation (+E,−W), even if 0, if no data card has been used, or if variation is to be different from value on last data card used	DD.d	f e	
24	Enter expected vessel speed	knots	A	
25	Enter expected set of current, even if 0	DDD.d	A	
26	Enter expected drift of current, even if 0	knots	A	
27	Enter time of start of run	H.MS	B	
28	Calculate and display magnetic course to steer		C	DDD.d
29	Enter deviation for planned magnetic course (+E,−W), even if 0,	DD.d	C	
·	Calculate and display compass course to steer**			DDD.d
30	Calculate and display time destination will be reached		D	H.MS
31	Calculate and display distance made good		E	naut. mi.
32	Calculate and display true course made good		E	DDD.d

**Uncorrect for leeway; see table 2.2.

Routine 2.19 (SR-52)

Ct	Var→Cm De→Cc	ΔT	CMG	DMG
St Dr	S	Lstart Lostart	Ldest Lodest	

PLANNING (MID-LATITUDE)

Step	Procedure	Input Data/Units	Keys	Output Data/Units
	Before beginning, make sure D/R switch is set to D.			
	If both start and destination co-ordinates are on data cards, proceed as follows (steps 1–9):			
1	Load data card containing start co-ordinates			
2	Enter identification letter corresponding to start co-ordinates		A–2nd D'	
	If destination co-ordinates are on same data card,			
3	Enter identification letter corresponding to destination co-ordinates, and continue at step 6		A–2nd D'	
	If destination co-ordinates are on a different data card,			
4	Load second data card			
5	Enter identification letter corresponding to destination co-ordinates		A–2nd D'	
6	Load program—both sides			
7	Enter expected set of current, even if 0	DDD.d	A	
8	Enter expected drift of current, even if 0	knots	A	
9	Enter expected vessel speed, and continue at step 34	knots	B	
	If only start co-ordinates are on a data card, proceed as follows (steps 10–17):			
10	Load data card			
11	Enter identification letter corresponding to start co-ordinates		A–2nd D'	
12	Load program—both sides			
13	Enter expected set of current, even if 0	DDD.d	A	

Step	Procedure	Input Data/Units	Keys	Output Data/Units
14	Enter expected drift of current, even if 0	knots	A	
15	Enter expected vessel speed	knots	B	
16	Enter destination latitude (+N,−S)	DD.MMSS	D	
17	Enter destination longitude (+W,−E), and continue at step 34	DD.MMSS	D	

If only destination co-ordinates are on a data card, proceed as follows (steps 18–26):

Step	Procedure	Input Data/Units	Keys	Output Data/Units
18	Load program—both sides			
19	Enter expected set of current, even if 0	DDD.d	A	
20	Enter expected drift of current, even if 0	knots	A	
21	Enter expected vessel speed	knots	B	
22	Enter start latitude (+N,−S)	DD.MMSS	C	
23	Enter start longitude (+W,−E)	DD.MMSS	C	
24	Load data card			
25	Enter identification letter corresponding to destination co-ordinates		A–2nd D'	
26	Load program—both sides—and continue at step 34			

If neither start nor destination co-ordinates are on data cards, proceed as follows (steps 27–39):

Step	Procedure	Input Data/Units	Keys	Output Data/Units
27	Enter expected set of current, even if 0	DDD.d	A	
28	Enter expected drift of current, even if 0	knots	A	
29	Enter expected vessel speed	knots	B	
30	Enter start latitude (+N,−S)	DD.MMSS	C	
31	Enter start longitude (+W,−E)	DD.MMSS	C	
32	Enter destination latitude (+N,−S)	DD.MMSS	D	
33	Enter destination longitude (+W,−E)	DD.MMSS	D	
34	Calculate and display true course to steer		2nd A'	DDD.d
35	Enter variation (+E,−W), even if 0,	DD.d	2nd B'	
·	Display magnetic course to steer			DDD.d
36	Enter deviation (+E,−W), even if 0,	DD.d	2nd B'	
·	Display compass course to steer**			DDD.d
37	Calculate and display time required to reach destination		2nd C'	H.MS
38	Calculate and display true course made good		2nd D'	DDD.d
39	Calculate and display distance made good		2nd E'	naut. mi.

**Uncorrect for leeway; see table 2.2.

2.4.7 Estimated Position and Tracking Routine 2.20 (for chart factor) and routine 2.21 (for mid-latitude) can be used to calculate a single estimated position for a preselected time, and also to provide continuous real-time tracking of estimated position. On the HP-67, an updated display of position, in the form of distance and bearing to the destination, appears at intervals of about twenty-four seconds. On the HP-97, a printout at approximately thirteen-second intervals provides the same information. This real-time position display is not available in the SR-52; however, a series of estimated positions can be calculated by means of routine 2.23.

2.4.8. Calculating a Single Estimated Position on the HP-67 and HP-97 When routine 2.20 is to be used, the necessary data may be retained after the completion of routine 2.17, or the co-ordinates may be entered by means of the Fixing routine (2.24), with the "first object" serving as the equivalent of the starting position and the "second object" as the equivalent of the destination. If the co-ordinates are entered manually, variation and chart factor must also be entered, as shown in this routine. When routine 2.21 (mid-latitude) is to be used for calculating an estimated position, the necessary data may be retained after the completion of routine 2.18, or the co-ordinates may be entered by means of routine 2.25. Destination co-ordinates are required because the estimated position may be expressed not only in terms of the latitude and longitude which will be reached at the time selected, but also in terms of the distance and bearing to the destination at that time. The more conventional way of describing the result of an estimated-position calculation is in the form of latitude and longitude, but in some instances, the result in the form of distance and bearing may be more convenient, so both are provided. It is also possible to calculate estimated distance and bearing to the starting position. To obtain this result, one need only re-enter the start co-ordinates in the steps calling for the destination co-ordinates.

The "EP" key (B in these routines) disables the continuous real-time tracking mechanism when a single estimated position is desired. Thus, step 7 in routine 2.20 or routine 2.21 is performed when no tracking is needed, and steps 8–12 then provide the desired result.

Routine 2.20 (HP-67/97)

		Tstart	Tend or Tstop	
Cc S St Dr	EP	Start	Stop	D Bt L Lo

TRACKING AND ESTIMATED POSITION (CHART FACTOR)

Step	Procedure	Input Data/Units	Keys	Output Data/Units
	If this routine is to be used directly following completion of routine 2.17, steps 1–31 or 1–33, load program (step 2, below) and continue at step 7 or step 13. If data has not been retained from routine 2.17, proceed as follows:			
1	Enter co-ordinates, deviation, variation, and chart factor by means of routine 2.24, steps 1–25; for calculation of distance and bearing to starting position (first object), re-enter co-ordinates of start in the steps calling for co-ordinates of destination (second object)			
2	Load program—both sides			
3	Enter compass course*	DDD.d	A	
4	Enter vessel speed	knots	A	
5	Enter set of current, even if 0	DDD.d	A	
6	Enter drift of current, even if 0	knots	A	
	Estimated Position			
7	After completion of steps 1–6, as appropriate, set EP		B	
8	Enter time of start of run	H.MS	f c	
9	Enter time of end of run	H.MS	f d	
10	Calculate and display distance to destination at end of run,		E	naut. mi.
·	True bearing to destination at end of run			DDD.d
11	If required, calculate and display latitude at end of run		E	$\pm$DD.MMSS
12	Calculate and display longitude at end of run		E	$\pm$DD.MMSS
	Tracking			
13	After completion of steps 1–6, as appropriate, enter time of start (at least 30 seconds later than present time)	H.MS	f c	

*Correct for leeway; see table 2.2.

(CONTINUED)

105

Step	Procedure	Input Data/Units	Keys	Output Data/Units
14	When selected time is reached, start calculation, and repeatedly display distance to destination,		C	naut. mi.
·	True bearing to destination,			DDD.d
·	Time of displayed position			H.MS
	To eliminate timing errors, proceed as follows (steps 15–18):			
15	Allow tracking to continue for 3–5 minutes; then, if time displayed is in error by more than a few seconds, stop calculator, during a pause for display of time on the HP-67, or while time is being printed on the HP-97		D	
16	Enter watch time at which calculator was stopped; this entry automatically corrects timing error	H.MS	f d	
17	Select time of restart (at least 30 seconds later)	H.MS	f c	
18	When selected time is reached, restart calculation		C	
	For multiple courses or speeds, or changes in set or drift, stop calculator, as described in steps 15–16, and proceed as follows (steps 19–26):			
19	If variation has changed, enter variation (+E, −W)	DD.d	STO E	
20	If deviation has changed, enter deviation (+E, −W)	DD.d	STO C	
21	Enter compass course*	DDD.d	A	
22	Enter speed	knots	A	
23	Enter set of current, even if 0	DDD.d	A	
24	Enter drift of current, even if 0	knots	A	
	When any one of the values listed in the preceding four steps has changed, *all four* must be re-entered.			
25	Select time of restart (at least 30 seconds later)	H.MS	f c	
26	When selected time is reached, restart calculation		C	

For use of the tracking program in the calculation of set and drift, see routine 2.24, steps 64–81.

If destination is to be changed, stop calculator, as described in steps 15–16, and proceed as follows (steps 27–31):

*Correct for leeway; see table 2.2.

106

Step	Procedure	Input Data/Units	Keys	Output Data/Units
27	Calculate and display distance to original destination,		E	naut. mi.
·	True bearing to original destination			DDD.d
28	Calculate and display latitude of present position		E	$\pm$DD.MMSS
29	Calculate and display longitude of present position		E	$\pm$DD.MMSS
	These co-ordinates are automatically stored, for use in planning.			
30	Load planning program, as used in routine 2.17, and perform steps 1–31 of routine 2.17, as necessary, to enter new destination and complete new plan			
31	Reload tracking program, and resume tracking at step 13			

Routine 2.21 (HP-67/97)

		Tstart	Tend or Tstop	
Cc S St Dr	EP	Start	Stop	D Bt L Lo

TRACKING AND ESTIMATED POSITION (MID-LATITUDE)

Step	Procedure	Input Data/Units	Keys	Output Data/Units
	If this routine is to be used directly following completion of routine 2.18, steps 1–30 or 1–32, load program (step 2, below) and continue at step 7 or step 13. If data has not been retained from routine 2.18, proceed as follows:			
1	Enter co-ordinates, deviation, and variation by means of routine 2.25, steps 1–24; for calculation of distance and bearing to starting position (first object), re-enter co-ordinates of start in the steps calling for destination (second object)			
2	Load program—both sides			
3	Enter compass course*	DDD.d	A	
4	Enter vessel speed	knots	A	
5	Enter set of current, even if 0	DDD.d	A	
6	Enter drift of current, even if 0	knots	A	
	Estimated Position			
7	After completion of steps 1–6, as appropriate, set EP		B	
8	Enter time of start of run	H.MS	f c	
9	Enter time of end of run	H.MS	f d	
10	Calculate and display distance to destination at end of run,		E	naut. mi.
·	True bearing to destination at end of run			DDD.d
11	If required, calculate and display latitude at end of run		E	$\pm$DD.MMSS
12	Calculate and display longitude at end of run		E	$\pm$DD.MMSS
	Tracking			
13	After completion of steps 1–6, as appropriate, enter time of start (at least 30 seconds later than present time)	H.MS	f c	

*Correct for leeway; see table 2.2.

108

Step	Procedure	Input Data/Units	Keys	Output Data/Units
14	When selected time is reached, start calculation, and repeatedly display distance to destination,		C	naut. mi.
·	True bearing to destination,			DDD.d
·	Time of displayed position			H.MS

To eliminate timing errors, proceed as follows (steps 15–18):

15	Allow tracking to continue for 3–5 minutes; then, if time displayed is in error by more than a few seconds, stop calculator, during a pause for display of time on the HP-67, or while time is being printed on the HP-97		D	
16	Enter watch time at which calculator was stopped; this entry automatically corrects timing error	H.MS	f d	
17	Select time of restart (at least 30 seconds later)	H.MS	f c	
18	When selected time is reached, restart calculation		C	

For multiple courses or speeds, or changes in set or drift, stop calculator, as described in steps 15–16, and proceed as follows (steps 19–26):

19	If variation has changed, enter variation (+E, −W)	DD.d	STO E	
20	If deviation has changed, enter deviation (+E, −W)	DD.d	STO C	
21	Enter compass course*	DDD.d	A	
22	Enter speed	knots	A	
23	Enter set of current, even if 0	DDD.d	A	
24	Enter drift of current, even if 0	knots	A	

When any one of the values listed in the preceding four steps has changed, *all four* must be re-entered.

25	Select time of restart (at least 30 seconds later)	H.MS	f c	
26	When selected time is reached, restart calculation		C	

For the use of the tracking program in the calculation of set and drift, see routine 2.25, steps 62–81.

If destination is to be changed, stop calculator, as described in steps 15–16, and proceed as follows (steps 27–31):

27	Calculate and display distance to original destination,		E	naut. mi.
·	True bearing to original destination			DDD.d

*Correct for leeway; see table 2.2.

(CONTINUED)

109

Step	Procedure	Input Data/Units	Keys	Output Data/Units
28	Calculate and display latitude of present position		E	±DD.MMSS
29	Calculate and display longitude of present position		E	±DD.MMSS

These co-ordinates are automatically stored for use in planning.

30	Load planning program, as used in routine 2.18, and perform steps 1–30, as necessary, to enter new destination and complete new plan			
31	Reload tracking program, and resume tracking at step 13			

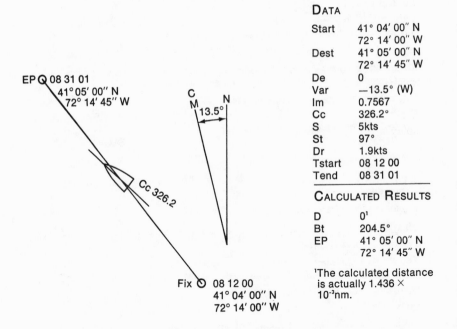

DATA

Start	41° 04′ 00″ N
	72° 14′ 00″ W
Dest	41° 05′ 00″ N
	72° 14′ 45″ W
De	0
Var	−13.5° (W)
Im	0.7567
Cc	326.2°
S	5kts
St	97°
Dr	1.9kts
Tstart	08 12 00
Tend	08 31 01

CALCULATED RESULTS

D	0¹
Bt	204.5°
EP	41° 05′ 00″ N
	72° 14′ 45″ W

¹The calculated distance is actually 1.436 × 10⁻³nm.

EP ◐ 08 31 01
41° 05′ 00″ N
72° 14′ 45″ W

Cc 326.2

C M N
13.5°

Fix ◐ 08 12 00
41° 04′ 00″ N
72° 14′ 00″ W

2.32. Estimated Position (Latitude and Longitude)

Figure 2.32 illustrates the use of the HP-67 and HP-97 for the calculation of estimated position. This example should be worked out by the reader to test whether he has properly recorded the program for this operation.

A routine for the convenient calculation of a series of estimated positions on a longer journey with several legs is discussed in section 2.4.13.

2.4.9 Calculating Current on the HP-67 and HP-97 When the starting position of a run is known, and a position fix is obtained at some time after the start, it is possible to calculate current by comparing the actual course made good and speed made good with the vessel's heading and speed through the water. The necessary vector subtraction is done by the calculator, and the answer is displayed as set and drift.

The procedure followed is another example of the integration among programs that is possible with the HP-67 and HP-97. For chart-factor calculations, the sequence begins with the use of routine 2.24 to obtain a fix on two objects. The resulting position is left in the calculator, and after the entry of start co-ordinates, the tracking and estimated-position program of routine 2.20 is loaded, and steps 72–77 of routine 2.24 are performed, with set and drift automatically set to zero, and with *Tstart* and *Tstop* representing the start of the run and the time of the fix. Completion of steps 78–80 then results in display of the set and drift of the current acting on the vessel during the run. The illustration of current calculation given in figure 2.38 (in connection with routine 2.24) can be used for testing these operations.

An almost identical procedure is possible when the mid-latitude method of calculation is employed. The fix on two objects is obtained by means of routine 2.25, and after the entry of start co-ordinates, the program of routine 2.21 is loaded. The procedure does differ in one respect from the chart-factor version previously described. Set and drift are not automatically set to zero when vessel speed is entered; instead, this is done in steps 72–73 of routine 2.25. Steps 74–77 are then performed, and completion of steps 78–80 once again results in display of the set and drift of the current.

2.4.10 Tracking (Chart Factor) on the HP-67 and HP-97 Routine 2.20 can be used to calculate and display estimated position repeatedly, taking into account the influence of any known current, and thereby tracking the position of the vessel as it moves through the water.

Each time the calculation of estimated position is performed, the result is displayed or printed, and the calculation is then repeated from the updated position. The time interval required to complete one cycle of calculation is approximately twenty-four seconds in the HP-67, and thirteen seconds in the HP-97.

Clearly, correct timing is needed for position tracking. Unfortunately, however, timing precision of a high order is not a prerequisite for accurate performance in a calculator, so adjustments may be required when tracking is begun.

The method for making these adjustments, shown in routine 2.20, is the equivalent of the method previously described in routine 2.5. At step 13, the time of start—perhaps thirty seconds ahead of the present time—is entered, and $\boxed{f}$ $\boxed{c}$ are pressed. Once the display has stopped fluctuating, *Tstart* is visible. When watch time is the same as *Tstart,* $\boxed{C}$ is pressed (step 14), and the tracking calculation begins. After about eight to twelve cycles of calculation, the displayed time is compared to watch time. If—as is likely—these are

111

substantially different, calculation is stopped by pressing D *while time is being displayed;* next, the watch time at which that key was pressed is entered, as *Tstop,* and f d are pressed.

With completion of this sequence, the timing of the calculator is changed, so that it will be more nearly correct when the routine is resumed, and the position error due to incorrect timing is eliminated.

Restarting the tracking routine essentially requires repetition of steps 13 and 14, with a time in the near future entered, and C pressed when that time has been reached to restart calculation. After a few cycles, displayed time and watch time should be compared; they should now correspond closely. It should be understood that if the calculator's timing is still not absolutely precise, the position displayed will be correct for the time displayed, rather than for the actual time at that moment.

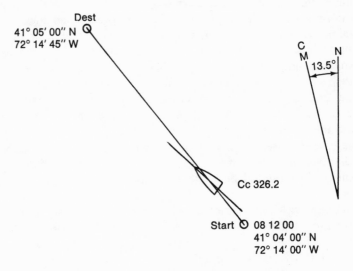

DATA

Start	41° 04′ 00″ N
	72° 14′ 00″ W
Dest	41° 05′ 00″ N
	72° 14′ 45″ W
De	0
Var	—13.5° (W)
Im	0.7567
Cc	326.2°
S	5.0kts
St	97°
Dr	1.9kts
Tstart	08 12 00

DISPLAY

Distance	True Bearing	Time	
1.1nm	330.4°	08 13 16	12 seconds
1.1	330.4	08 13 28	
1.0	330.4	08 15 09	
0.9	330.4	08 16 12	
Timing reset			
0.8	330.4	08 17 13	13 seconds
0.8	330.4	08 17 26	
0.7	330.4	08 19 35	
0.4	330.3	08 25 10	
0.2	330.1	08 27 45	
0.1	329.8	08 29 28	
0	326.0	08 30 46	
0.1	151.4	08 32 16	

2.33. Tracking (Latitude and Longitude)

112

The accuracy of the displayed position also depends, of course, on the correctness of the input data concerning course, speed, and set and drift of current. What is calculated is the best estimate of position, based upon the navigator's knowledge of these factors.

As in routine 2.5, a permanent change in the recorded value of loop time can be made, by the method shown in the section on customized programs in the Appendix. Even when this has been done, however, the correctness of the loop time should be checked whenever the routine is used.

Figure 2.33 illustrates the operation of the tracking routine. After the calculator had run for several minutes, it was stopped and reset for proper timing, and the assumed length of the interval between successive displays changed from twelve seconds to thirteen seconds. The latter figure was nearly correct for that particular calculator; after it had run for the next fifteen minutes, the apparent timing error was only six seconds.

In this illustration, the value for distance appears to remain constant for several successive displays; this is the result of setting the decimal point to only one place, for tenth-of-a-mile increments. Since at the speed made good involved in the example (less than 4 knots), it takes approximately one minute and thirty seconds to move one-tenth of a mile, the display necessarily shows no change during some of the shorter intervals listed. This effect could be eliminated by programming the display to show distance to two decimal places.

The bearing shows virtually no change because the course being steered (326.2°) has been correctly chosen for reaching the destination in the existing current. A small error in heading becomes apparent when the destination has nearly been reached; there the bearing begins to shift. When the track is continued beyond the destination, the bearings in the display shift by 180 degrees, and the distance begins to increase, as shown in the final row of data in figure 2.33.

Routine 2.20 includes the means to change the values for any of the factors that affect estimated position. It is only necessary that tracking be stopped (by pressing $\boxed{D}$) while time is being displayed, and that the watch time at that moment be inserted at once as *Tstop*—that is, the time is entered, and $\boxed{f}$ $\boxed{d}$ are pressed. New values for variation and deviation, and for vessel course, vessel speed, and set and drift of current can then be entered as necessary. (If any one of these last four is changed, all of them must be re-entered.) The calculator is then restarted exactly as previously described, and the display incorporates the effects of the new motion.

If the destination is to be changed, the calculator is stopped, as previously described, and after the entry of *Tstop*, $\boxed{E}$ is pressed three times. Pressing this key the first time results in display of the distance and bearing to the original destination; pressing it a second time displays the latitude of the present position; and pressing it a third time, the longitude. This operation also positions these co-ordinates in the calculator's storage, for use in calculating a plan to reach the new destination. Next, the planning program card is inserted, and

113

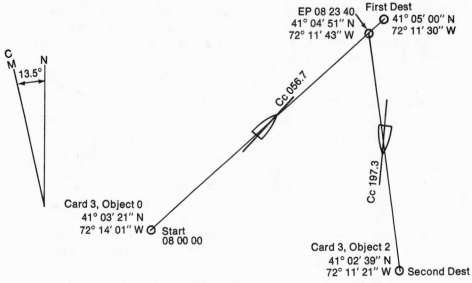

PLANNING

DATA

Start   Card 3, Object 0
First Dest   41° 05' 00" N
             72° 11' 30" W
Var   —13.5° (W)
Im   0.7567
S   5.0kts
St   80°
Dr   1.0kt
Tstart   08 00 00
Cm   56.7° [calculated]
De   0

CALCULATED RESULTS

Cc   56.7°
Tend 08 25 55
DMG   2.52nm
CMG   49.09° T

TRACKING AND ESTIMATED POSITION

Distance	True Bearing	Time	Latitude	Longitude
2.3nm	49.1°	08 02 02		
1.3	49.1	08 12 39		
0.3	49.1	08 22 26		
0.2	49.0	08 23 40	41° 04' 51" N	72° 11' 43" W

PLANNING

DATA

Second Dest Card 3, Object 2
S   5.0kts
St   100°
Dr   1.0kt
Tstart   08 23 40
Cm   197.3°
De   0

CALCULATED RESULTS

Cc   197.3°
Tend 08 49 18
DMG   2.22nm
CMG   172.8° T

2.34. Tracking Combined with Planning (Latitude and Longitude)

in accordance with steps 1–31 (as necessary) of routine 2.17, the new destination co-ordinates and other required data are entered, and a plan for reaching the new destination is obtained. Then the tracking program card is inserted once again, and tracking is resumed, as specified in the instructions of routine 2.20.

The combination of planning and tracking is illustrated in Figure 2.34. In this case, the vessel's starting point is at a latitude of 41°03'21"N and a longitude of 72°14'01"W; these co-ordinates have been prerecorded as object 0 on card 3. Once the planning program card and data card 3 have been inserted, simply pressing $\boxed{0}$ enters the starting co-ordinates. The destination co-ordinates and other necessary data are entered manually, according to the instructions in routine 2.17. Next, with the planning program still in place, entry of vessel speed, set and drift of current, and starting time (08 00 00) results in the display of a compass course of 56.7° and a time of arrival of 08 25 55.

Now the tracking program is entered; the values for compass course, speed, and set and drift are retained from the preceding operations, and need not be re-entered. The starting time is entered at $\boxed{f}\boxed{c}$, and when that time is reached, $\boxed{C}$ is pressed, and tracking commences. A few representative values of distance, bearing, and time are shown in the figure, typical of the displays on the calculator during the tracking of estimated position.

When 08 23 40 is reached, the tracking is stopped, and by means of steps 27–29, the vessel's location at that time (41°04'51"N, 72°11'43"W) is displayed and positioned in the calculator for use in the planning for the new destination (41°02'39"N, 72°11'21"W, which in this instance is object 2 on card 3). The new compass course turns out to be 197.3°, and the expected time of arrival is 08 49 18.

Some time will of course be lost during the calculation of the new plan and the maneuvering onto the new course, and this lost time can be taken into account in routine 2.20. For this purpose, the estimated-position portion of the routine (steps 7–12) is used to determine the position of the vessel on the old heading at a time a few minutes in the future. The plan is then calculated from that future position.

If the example in figure 2.34 is altered by assuming that because of the time required to calculate the new plan, the actual change to the new course will occur at 08 25 00, the estimated position at that time turns out to be 41°04'56"N, 72°11'35"W. This is obtained by pressing $\boxed{B}$ (step 7) and setting *Tstart* at 08 23 40 and *Tstop* at 08 25 00. Then, pressing $\boxed{E}$ three times results in calculation of the anticipated position and placement of its latitude and longitude in the calculator's memory, for use in planning, in routine 2.17. The new course to steer, starting from the vessel's position at 08 25 00, turns out to be 200.1°, and the predicted arrival time is 08 51 45.

2.4.11 Tracking (Mid-latitude) on the HP-67 and HP-97   Routine 2.21, for mid-latitude tracking and estimated position, has been written for use on long-distance journeys, when chart-factor calculations are not appropriate. The starting and destination co-ordinates may be obtained from the mid-latitude Fixing routine (2.25), or all of the initial data, including course, speed, set, and drift, may be retained from steps 1–30 of the Planning routine (2.18).

The instructions for using this routine for tracking are virtually identical with those for routine 2.20. The method of making a permanent change in the recorded loop time is shown in the Appendix.

Use of the mid-latitude routines with the data supplied in figure 2.33 will yield answers slightly different from those listed in the figure. However, these discrepancies have no practical significance.

2.4.12 Nonprint Tracking on the HP-97   To conserve paper and extend battery life on a long journey, the programs for chart-factor and mid-latitude tracking on the HP-97 can be modified to eliminate the printing of every calculated distance, bearing, and time. This is accomplished, once the programs have been loaded, by replacing the "Print" instructions with "Pause" instructions, and changing the "Stop" key, as shown in the section on nonprint operation in the Appendix.

2.4.13 Estimated Position (Mid-latitude) on the HP-67 and HP-97   An additional estimated-position program for the HP-67 and HP-97 permits easy and rapid calculation of successive estimated positions for a run or journey that has a number of changes in course, speed, set, or drift. Values for course made good and speed made good, which are required in the Sight Reduction routines in chapter 4, can also be displayed. Routine 2.22 (for mid-latitude calculations only) provides the instructions for this program, and figure 2.35 illustrates its use.

If the distances and bearings obtained as answers in this routine are to be displayed relative to the starting position of the vessel, the latitude and longitude of the destination should be set equal to those of the start.

2.35. Estimated Position, Multiple Legs (Latitude and Longitude)

START OF LEG

Latitude	Longitude	De	Var	Cc	S	St	Dr	T
41° 05' 00" N	71° 52' 00" W	+2° (E)	—13.75° (W)	61°	6.0kts	250°	1.0kt	08
(41° 06' 29" N	71° 50' 00" W)[1]	—3° (W)	—13.75° (W)	26°	6.0	250°	1.1	08
(41° 07' 58" N	71° 50 02" W)[1]	—2° (W)	—13.75° (W)	285°	6.0	(250°	1.1)[1]	08

[1] Because they are unchanged, these values need not be re-entered.

116

Routine 2.22 provides no continuous tracking and display of estimated position.

2.4.14 Estimated Position on the SR-52 Routine 2.23 is used for the calculation of estimated position on the SR-52. The calculated true bearing and distance from the starting position to the estimated position of the vessel are also displayed.

A prerecorded data card, prepared in accordance with the instructions of routine 2.16, may supply the starting latitude and longitude. And in this routine, as in those for the HP-67 and HP-97, the calculated estimated position at the end of one leg can serve without re-entry as the starting point of the next.

The example given in figure 2.35 can be used to test the program; calculated answers should fall within one second of arc of latitude and longitude.

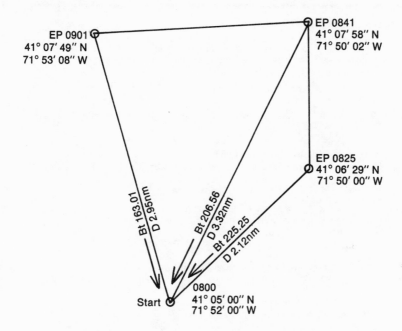

END OF LEG

T2	Latitude	Longitude	Bt (EP to Start)	D (to EP)	Bt (Start to EP)
825	41° 06' 29" N	71° 50' 00" W	225.25°	2.12nm	45.25°
·841	41° 07' 58" N	71° 50' 02" W	206.56°	3.32	26.56°
901	41° 07' 49" N	71° 53' 08" W	163.01°	2.95	343.01°

117

Routine 2.22 (HP-67/97)

Select Start	Select Dest	Load	LEP LoEP	D Bt DMG CMG SMG
De Var	Cc S	St Dr	Tstart	Tend

ESTIMATED POSITION (MID-LATITUDE)

Step	Procedure	Input Data/Units	Keys	Output Data/Units
1	Load program—both sides			
	For calculation of distance and bearing to starting position, re-enter start co-ordinates in the steps calling for destination co-ordinates.			
	If both start and destination co-ordinates are on data cards, proceed as follows (steps 2–7):			
2	Load data card containing start co-ordinates			
3	Enter identification number corresponding to start co-ordinates (an even number from 0 to 20)	0–20	f a	
	If destination co-ordinates are on same data card,			
4	Enter identification number corresponding to destination co-ordinates (an even number from 0 to 20), and continue at step 7	0–20	f b	
	If destination co-ordinates are on a different data card,			
5	Load second data card			
6	Enter identification number corresponding to destination co-ordinates (an even number from 0 to 20)	0–20	f b	
7	Load start and destination co-ordinates into memory, and continue at step 23		f c	
	If only start co-ordinates are on a data card, proceed as follows (steps 8–12):			
8	Load data card			
9	Enter identification number corresponding to start co-ordinates (an even number from 0 to 20)	0–20	f a	
10	Enter destination latitude (+N,−S)	DD.MMSS	ENTER	
11	Enter destination longitude (+W,−E), *but do not press* [ENTER]	DD.MMSS		

118

Step	Procedure	Input Data/Units	Keys	Output Data/Units
12	Load start and destination co-ordinates into memory, and continue at step 23		f c	

If only destination co-ordinates are on a data card, proceed as follows (steps 13–17):

Step	Procedure	Input Data/Units	Keys	Output Data/Units
13	Enter start latitude (+N, −S)	DD.MMSS	ENTER	
14	Enter start longitude (+W, −E)	DD.MMSS	ENTER	
15	Load data card			
16	Enter identification number corresponding to destination co-ordinates (an even number from 0 to 20)	0–20	f b	
17	Load start and destination co-ordinates into memory, and continue at step 23		f c	

If neither start nor destination co-ordinates are on data cards, proceed as follows (steps 18–34):

Step	Procedure	Input Data/Units	Keys	Output Data/Units
18	Enter start latitude (+N, −S)	DD.MMSS	ENTER	
19	Enter start longitude (+W, −E)	DD.MMSS	ENTER	
20	Enter destination latitude (+N, −S)	DDMMSS	ENTER	
21	Enter destination longitude (+W, −E), but *do not press* ENTER	DD.MMSS		
22	Load start and destination co-ordinates into memory		f c	
23	Enter deviation (+E, −W), even if 0	DD.d	A	
24	Enter variation (+E, −W), even if 0, if no data card has been used, or if variation is to be different from value on last data card used	DD.d	A	
25	Enter compass course during run or leg*	DDD.d	B	
26	Enter vessel speed during run or leg	knots	B	
27	Enter set of current during run or leg, even if 0	DDD.d	C	
28	Enter drift of current during run or leg, even if 0	knots	C	
29	Enter time of start of run or leg	H.MS	D	
30	Enter time of end of run or leg	H.MS	E	
31	Calculate and display latitude of estimated position at end of run or leg		f d	±DD.MMSS
32	Calculate and display longitude of estimated position at end of run or leg		f d	±DD.MMSS
33	Calculate and display distance to destination at end of run or leg		f e	naut. mi.
34	Calculate and display true bearing to destination at end of run or leg		f e	DDD.d

*Correct for leeway; see table 2.2.

(CONTINUED)

119

Step	Procedure	Input Data/Units	Keys	Output Data/Units
35	Calculate and display distance made good at end of run or leg,		f e	naut. mi.
·	Course made good at end of run or leg,			DDD.d
·	Speed made good at end of run or leg			knots

For multiple courses or speeds, or changes in set or drift between estimated positions, steps 23–24, 25–26, and 27–28 are repeated as necessary; deviation and variation, course and speed, and set and drift are handled as pairs—if even one member of the pair changes, *both* must be re-entered. Steps 29–34 are then repeated for each leg.

Routine 2.23 (SR-52)

BtEP	Distance	LEP	LoEP	Initialize
Time	Var De	St Dr	Cc S	Lstart Lostart

ESTIMATED POSITION (MID-LATITUDE)

Step	Procedure	Input Data/Units	Keys	Output Data/Units
	Before beginning, make sure D/R switch is set to D.			
	If start co-ordinates are on a data card, proceed as follows (steps 1–2):			
1	Load data card			
2	Enter identification letter corresponding to start co-ordinates, and continue at step 3, omitting steps 11–12		A–2nd D′	
	If start co-ordinates are not on a data card, begin at step 3.			
3	Load program—both sides			
4	Enter time of start of run or leg	H.MS	A	
5	Enter variation (+E,−W), even if 0	DD.d	B	
6	Enter deviation (+E,−W), even if 0	DD.d	B	
7	Enter set of current, even if 0	DDD.d	C	
8	Enter drift of current, even if 0	knots	C	
9	Enter compass course*	DDD.d	D	
10	Enter vessel speed during run or leg	knots	D	
11	Enter latitude of start (+N,−S), if not on a data card	DD.MMSS	E	
12	Enter longitude of start (+W,−E), if not on a data card	DD.MMSS	E	
13	Enter time of end of run or leg	H.MS	A	
14	Calculate and display true bearing from start to estimated position		2nd A′	DDD.d
15	Calculate and display distance from start to estimated position		2nd B′	naut. mi.
16	Calculate and display latitude of estimated position		2nd C′	+DD.MMSS

*Correct for leeway; see table 2.2.

(CONTINUED)

Step	Procedure	*Input* Data/Units	Keys	*Output* Data/Units
17	Calculate and display longitude of estimated position		2nd D'	±DD.MMSS

For multiple courses or speeds, or changes in set or drift between estimated positions, *do not initialize* between successive legs. Steps 1–4 and 11–12 need not be repeated; the time of end of the preceding leg, already entered at step 13, automatically becomes the time of start of the new leg. Steps 5–6, 7–8, and 9–10 are repeated as necessary; variation and deviation, set and drift, and course and speed are handled as pairs—if even one member of the pair changes, *both* must be re-entered. Steps 13–17 are then repeated for each leg.

Step	Procedure	Input Data/Units	Keys	Output Data/Units
18	Initialize *only for an entirely new calculation*		2nd E'	

2.4.15 Fixing on the HP-67 and HP-97 Routine 2.24 (for chart factor) provides instructions for obtaining three different forms of position fix with the HP-67 and HP-97: the fix on two objects, the running fix on one object, and the running fix on two objects. Routine 2.25 provides an almost identical set of instructions for calculating positions fixes by the mid-latitude method.

Where possible, prerecorded data cards should be used for entering the positions of the observed objects. The elimination of the need to enter all the digits of latitude and longitude for two positions reduces the chances for inaccuracy and increases convenience. Instructions for preparation of the cards are given in routine 2.15.

As was noted earlier, the Fixing routine for the HP-67 and HP-97 is integrated with both the Planning and the Tracking routines (2.17 and 2.20 for chart factor, 2.18 and 2.21 for mid-latitude). Positions calculated by means of the Fixing routine may become input data for the other two, with re-entry of calculated results kept to a minimum. Thus, a calculated fix can be the starting point for a new plan—obtained by means of routine 2.17 or 2.18, as appropriate—either to complete a journey, or to determine the course to a changed destination. Or the fix can be the basis for calculating the current (or current plus leeway) acting on the vessel, by means of the program for the tracking routine.

122

Routine 2.24 (HP-67/97)

Select O1	Select O2	Load O1 & O2	Select Start	De Var Im
Cc S St Dr	Tstart Tend	Bc1	Bc2	Lfix Lofix D2

FIXING, SET AND DRIFT (CHART FACTOR)

Step	Procedure	Input Data/Units	Keys	Output Data/Units
1	Load program—both sides			
	Fix on Two Objects			
	After completion of step 1, enter co-ordinates—			
	If co-ordinates of both objects are on data cards, proceed as follows (steps 2–7):			
2	Load data card containing co-ordinates of first object			
3	Enter identification number corresponding to co-ordinates of first object (an even number from 0 to 20)	0–20	f a	
	If co-ordinates of second object are on same data card,			
4	Enter identification number corresponding to co-ordinates of second object (an even number from 0 to 20), and continue at step 7	0–20	f b	
	If co-ordinates of second object are on a different card,			
5	Load second data card			
6	Enter identification number corresponding to co-ordinates of second object (an even number from 0 to 20)	0–20	f b	
7	Load co-ordinates of first and second objects into memory, and continue at step 23		f c	
	If only co-ordinates of first object are on a data card, proceed as follows (steps 8–12):			
8	Load data card			
9	Enter identification number corresponding to co-ordinates of first object (an even number from 0 to 20)	0–20	f a	
10	Enter latitude of second object ($+N, -S$)	DD.MMSS	ENTER	

(CONTINUED)

123

Step	Procedure	Input Data/Units	Keys	Output Data/Units
11	Enter longitude of second object (+W, −E), but *do not press* ENTER	DD.MMSS		
12	Load co-ordinates of first and second objects into memory, and continue at step 23		f c	

If only co-ordinates of second object are on a data card, proceed as follows (steps 13–17):

Step	Procedure	Input Data/Units	Keys	Output Data/Units
13	Enter latitude of first object (+N,−S)	DD.MMSS	ENTER	
14	Enter longitude of first object (+W,−E)	DD.MMSS	ENTER	
15	Load data card			
16	Enter identification number corresponding to second object (an even number from 0 to 20)	0–20	f b	
17	Load co-ordinates of first and second objects into memory, and continue at step 23		f c	

If co-ordinates of neither first nor second object are on data cards, proceed as follows (steps 18–30):

Step	Procedure	Input Data/Units	Keys	Output Data/Units
18	Enter latitude of first object (+N,−S)	DD.MMSS	ENTER	
19	Enter longitude of first object (+W,−E)	DD.MMSS	ENTER	
20	Enter latitude of second object (+N,−S)	DD.MMSS	ENTER	
21	Enter longitude of second object (+W, −E), but *do not* press ENTER	DD.MMSS		
22	Load co-ordinates of first and second objects into memory		f c	
23	Enter deviation (+E,−W), even if 0	DD.d	f e	
24	Enter variation (+E,−W), even if 0, if no data card has been used, if variation is to be different from value on last data card used, or if chart factor is to be entered in the following step	DD.d	f e	
25	Enter chart factor if no data card has been used or if chart factor is to be different from value on last data card used	0.nnnn	f e	
26	Enter compass bearing to first object	DDD.d	C	
27	Enter compass bearing to second object	DDD.d	D	
28	Calculate and display latitude of fix		E	±DD.MMSS
29	Calculate and display longitude of fix		E	±DD.MMSS
30	Unless fix is to be used in calculation of current in steps 64–80, or in planning (routine 2.17), calculate and display distance from fix to second object		E	naut. mi.

124

Step	Procedure	Input Data/Units	Keys	Output Data/Units
	Running Fix on One Object			
	After completion of step 1, enter co-ordinates—			
	If co-ordinates of object are on a data card, proceed as follows (steps 31–33):			
31	Load data card			
32	Enter identification number corresponding to object (an even number from 0 to 20)	0–20	f a	
33	Re-enter identification number corresponding to object, and continue at step 38	0–20	f b	
	If co-ordinates of object are not on a data card, proceed as follows (steps 34–52):			
34	Enter latitude of object ($+$N,$-$S)	DD.MMSS	ENTER	
35	Enter longitude of object ($+$W,$-$E)	DD.MMSS	ENTER	
36	Re-enter latitude of object ($+$N,$-$S)	DD.MMSS	ENTER	
37	Re-enter longitude of object ($+$W,$-$E), but *do not press* ENTER	DD.MMSS		
38	Load co-ordinates of object into memory		f c	
39	Enter deviation ($+$E,$-$W), even if 0	DD.d	f e	
40	Enter variation ($+$E,$-$W), even if 0, if no data card has been used, if variation is to be different from value on data card, or if chart factor is to be entered in the following step	DD.d	f e	
41	Enter chart factor if no data card has been used or if chart factor is to be different from value on data card	0.nnnn	f e	
42	Enter compass course during run or leg*	DDD.d	A	
43	Enter vessel speed during run or leg	knots	A	
44	Enter set of current, even if 0	DDD.d	A	
45	Enter drift of current, even if 0	knots	A	
46	Enter time of start of run or leg	H.MS	B	
47	Enter time of end of run or leg	H.MS	B	
48	Enter compass bearing to object at start of run	DDD.d	C	
	For multiple courses or speeds, or changes in set or drift between bearings, repeat steps 39–47.			
49	Enter compass bearing to object at time of end of run, or at end of last leg	DDD.d	D	
50	Calculate and display latitude of fix		E	$\pm$DD.MMSS

*Correct for leeway; see table 2.2.

(CONTINUED)

Step	Procedure	Input Data/Units	Keys	Output Data/Units
51	Calculate and display longitude of fix		E	±DD.MMSS
52	Calculate and display distance from fix to object		E	naut. mi.

Running Fix on Two Objects

Step	Procedure	Input Data/Units	Keys	Output Data/Units
53	After completion of steps 1–25, as appropriate, enter compass course during run or leg*	DDD.d	A	
54	Enter vessel speed during run or leg	knots	A	
55	Enter set of current, even if 0	DDD.d	A	
56	Enter drift of current, even if 0	knots	A	
57	Enter time of start of run or leg	H.MS	B	
58	Enter time of end of run or leg	H.MS	B	
59	Enter compass bearing to first object at start of run	DDD.d	C	

For multiple courses or speeds, or changes in set or drift between bearings, repeat steps 23–24, and 53–58.

Step	Procedure	Input Data/Units	Keys	Output Data/Units
60	Enter compass bearing to second object at end of run, or at end of last leg	DDD.d	D	
61	Calculate and display latitude of fix		E	±DD.MMSS
62	Calculate and display longitude of fix		E	±DD.MMSS
63	Calculate and display distance from fix to second object		E	naut. mi.

Set and Drift

This procedure can be used *only* after completion of a fix on two objects, by means of steps 1–29.

If start co-ordinates are on a data card, proceed as follows (steps 64–66):

Step	Procedure	Input Data/Units	Keys	Output Data/Units
64	Load data card			
65	Enter identification number corresponding to start co-ordinates (an even number from 0 to 20)	0–20	f d	
66	Load start co-ordinates into memory, and continue at step 71		f c	

If start co-ordinates are not on a data card, proceed as follows (steps 67–81):

Step	Procedure	Input Data/Units	Keys	Output Data/Units
67	Enter latitude of start (+N, −S)	DD.MMSS	ENTER	
68	Enter longitude of start (+W, −E)	DD.MMSS	R↓ R↓	
69	Load start co-ordinates into memory		f c	
70	Initialize		0 f	
			p ↔ s	
			STO	
			9 f	
			p ↔ s	

*Correct for leeway; see table 2.2.

Step	Procedure	Input Data/Units	Keys	Output Data/Units
71	Load tracking program (as used in routine 2.20)			
72	Enter compass course during run*	DDD.d	A	
73	Enter vessel speed during run (this step results in set and drift being automatically set to zero)	knots	A	
74	Set EP		B	
75	Enter time of start of run	H.MS	f c	
76	Enter time of fix	H.MS	f d	
77	Calculate and display drift distance,		E	naut. mi.
·	Set of current			DDD.d
78	Display drift distance		RCL 7	naut. mi.
79	Display time interval		RCL I	H.hh
80	Calculate and display drift		÷	knots
81	If desired, relocate present position in the memory, for use in the Planning routine (2.17)		RCL 2 RCL 3	

*Correct for leeway; see table 2.2.

Routine 2.25 (HP-67/97)

Select O1	Select O2	Load O1 & O2	Select Start	De Var
Cc S St Dr	T start Tend	Bc1	Bc2	Lfix Lofix D2

FIXING, SET AND DRIFT (MID-LATITUDE)

Step	Procedure	Input Data/Units	Keys	Output Data/Units
1	Load program—both sides			
	Fix on Two Objects			
	After completion of step 1, enter co-ordinates—			
	If co-ordinates of both objects are on data cards, proceed as follows (steps 2–7):			
2	Load data card containing co-ordinates of first object			
3	Enter identification number corresponding to co-ordinates of first object (an even number from 0 to 20)	0–20	f a	
	If co-ordinates of second object are on same data card,			
4	Enter identification number corresponding to co-ordinates of second object (an even number from 0 to 20), and continue at step 7	0–20	f b	
	If co-ordinates of second object are on a different card,			
5	Load second data card			
6	Enter identification number corresponding to co-ordinates of second object (an even number from 0 to 20)	0–20	f b	
7	Load co-ordinates of first and second objects into memory, and continue at step 23		f c	
	If only co-ordinates of first object are on a data card, proceed as follows (steps 8–12):			
8	Load data card			
9	Enter identification number corresponding to co-ordinates of first object (an even number from 0 to 20)	0–20	f a	
10	Enter latitude of second object (+N,−S)	DD.MMSS	ENTER	

128

Step	Procedure	Input Data/Units	Keys	Output Data/Units
11	Enter longitude of second object (+W, −E), but *do not press* ENTER	DD.MMSS		
12	Load co-ordinates of first and second objects into memory, and continue at step 23		f c	

If only co-ordinates of second object are on a data card, proceed as follows (steps 13–17):

Step	Procedure	Input Data/Units	Keys	Output Data/Units
13	Enter latitude of first object (+N, −S)	DD.MMSS	ENTER	
14	Enter longitude of first object (+W, −E)	DD.MMSS	ENTER	
15	Load data card			
16	Enter identification number corresponding to second object (an even number from 0 to 20)	0–20	f b	
17	Load co-ordinates of first and second objects into memory, and continue at step 23		f c	

If co-ordinates of neither first nor second object are on data cards, proceed as follows (steps 18–29):

Step	Procedure	Input Data/Units	Keys	Output Data/Units
18	Enter latitude of first object (+N, −S)	DD.MMSS	ENTER	
19	Enter longitude of first object (+W, −E)	DD.MMSS	ENTER	
20	Enter latitude of second object (+N, −S)	DD.MMSS	ENTER	
21	Enter longitude of second object (+W, −E), but *do not press* ENTER	DD.MMSS		
22	Load co-ordinates of first and second objects into memory		f c	
23	Enter deviation (+E, −W), even if 0	DD.d	f e	
24	Enter variation (+E, −W), even if 0, if no data card has been used, or if variation is to be different from value on last data card used	DD.d	f e	
25	Enter compass bearing to first object	DDD.d	C	
26	Enter compass bearing to second object	DDD.d	D	
27	Calculate and display latitude of fix		E	±DD.MMSS
28	Calculate and display longitude of fix		E	±DD.MMSS
29	Unless fix is to be used in calculation of current in steps 62–80, or in planning (routine 2.18), calculate and display distance from fix to second object		E	naut. mi.

Running Fix on One Object

After completion of step 1, enter co-ordinates—

If co-ordinates of object are on a data card, proceed as follows (steps 30–32):

Step	Procedure	Input Data/Units	Keys	Output Data/Units
30	Load data card			

(CONTINUED)

Step	Procedure	Input Data/Units	Keys	Output Data/Units
31	Enter identification number corresponding to object (an even number from 0 to 20)	0–20	f a	
32	Re-enter identification number corresponding to object, and continue at step 37	0–20	f b	

If co-ordinates of object are not on a data card, proceed as follows (steps 33–50):

Step	Procedure	Input Data/Units	Keys	Output Data/Units
33	Enter latitude of object (+N,−S)	DD.MMSS	ENTER	
34	Enter longitude of object (+W,−E)	DD.MMSS	ENTER	
35	Re-enter latitude of object (+N,−S)	DD.MMSS	ENTER	
36	Re-enter longitude of object (+W,−E), but *do not press* ENTER	DD.MMSS		
37	Load co-ordinates of object into memory		f c	
38	Enter deviation (+E,−W), even if 0	DD.d	f e	
39	Enter variation (+E,−W), even if 0, if no data card has been been used, or if variation is to be different from value on data card	DD.d	f e	
40	Enter compass course during run or leg*	DDD.d	A	
41	Enter vessel speed during run or leg	knots	A	
42	Enter set of current, even if 0	DDD.d	A	
43	Enter drift of current, even if 0	knots	A	
44	Enter time of start of run or leg	H.MS	B	
45	Enter time of end of run or leg	H.MS	B	
46	Enter compass bearing to object at start of run	DDD.d	C	

For multiple courses or speeds, or changes in set or drift between bearings, repeat steps 38–45.

Step	Procedure	Input Data/Units	Keys	Output Data/Units
47	Enter compass bearing to object at time of end of run, or at end of last leg	DDD.d	D	
48	Calculate and display latitude of fix		E	±DD.MMSS
49	Calculate and display longitude of fix		E	±DD.MMSS
50	Calculate and display distance from fix to object		E	naut. mi.

Running Fix on Two Objects

Step	Procedure	Input Data/Units	Keys	Output Data/Units
51	After completion of steps 1–24, as appropriate, enter compass course during run or leg*	DDD.d	A	

*Correct for leeway; see table 2.2.

130

Step	Procedure	Input Data/Units	Keys	Output Data/Units
52	Enter vessel speed during run or leg	knots	A	
53	Enter set of current, even if 0	DDD.d	A	
54	Enter drift of current, even if 0	knots	A	
55	Enter time of start of run or leg	H.MS	B	
56	Enter time of end of run or leg	H.MS	B	
57	Enter compass bearing to first object at start of run	DDD.d	C	

For multiple courses or speeds, or change in set or drift between bearings, repeat steps 23–24 and 51–56.

Step	Procedure	Input Data/Units	Keys	Output Data/Units
58	Enter compass bearing to second object at end of run, or at end of last leg	DDD.d	D	
59	Calculate and display latitude of fix		E	±DD.MMSS
60	Calculate and display longitude of fix		E	±DD.MMSS
61	Calculate and display distance from fix to second object		E	naut. mi.

Set and Drift

This procedure can be used *only* after completion of a fix on two objects, by means of steps 1–28.

If start co-ordinates are on a data card, proceed as follows (steps 62–64):

Step	Procedure	Input Data/Units	Keys	Output Data/Units
62	Load data card			
63	Enter identification number corresponding to start co-ordinates (an even number from 0 to 20)	0–20	f d	
64	Load start co-ordinates into memory, and continue at step 69		f c	

If start co-ordinates are not on a data card, proceed as follows (steps 65–81):

Step	Procedure	Input Data/Units	Keys	Output Data/Units
65	Enter latitude of start (+N, −S)	DD.MMSS	ENTER	
66	Enter longitude of start (+W, −E)	DD.MMSS	R↓ R↓	
67	Load start co-ordinates into memory		f c	
68	Initialize		0 f p ⟷ s STO 9 f p ⟷ s	
69	Load tracking program (as used in routine 2.21)			
70	Enter compass course during run*	DDD.d	A	

*Correct for leeway; see table 2.2.

(CONTINUED)

131

Step	Procedure	Input Data/Units	Keys	Output Data/Units
71	Enter vessel speed during run	knots	A	
72	Enter set of current as 0	0	A	
73	Enter drift of current as 0	0	A	
74	Set EP		B	
75	Enter time of start of run	H.MS	f c	
76	Enter time of fix	H.MS	f d	
77	Calculate and display drift distance,		E	naut. mi.
·	Set of current			DDD.d
78	Display drift distance		RCL 7	naut. mi.
79	Display time interval		RCL I	H.hh
80	Calculate and display drift		÷	knots
81	If desired, relocate present position in the memory, for use in the Planning routine (2.18)		RCL 2 RCL 3	

Figure 2.36 shows the use of the Fixing routine when two objects can be observed simultaneously, or nearly so. If desired, the simultaneous values for two observed bearings can be obtained by means of routine 2.6, for the bearing regression.

In the situation illustrated in the figure, the bearings on two objects of known position are taken at 0812, and the vessel's position is determined by the calculator routine to be 41°04'00"N, 72°14'00"W.

Once a fix has been obtained, the result can be used in planning the course to a new destination.

The co-ordinates of the fix remain in the calculator while the planning program (for routine 2.17 or 2.18) is loaded—but only if one has *not* pressed $\boxed{E}$ for a third time (step 30 of routine 2.24, or step 29 of routine 2.25) to obtain distance off the second object at the fix. Doing so would remove the fix co-ordinates from the memory, making subsequent integration with the Planning routine impossible.

Under the conditions specified, the co-ordinates of the fix become the start co-ordinates for the Planning routine. The destination co-ordinates are then entered either by use of a prerecorded data card or manually, as in steps 16–17 or 20–22 of routines 2.17 and 2.18. Variation, if not changed, does not have to be re-entered. Vessel speed and set and drift are entered, along with the time of the fix (now serving as *Tstart*). The remaining steps of the Planning routine are then followed.

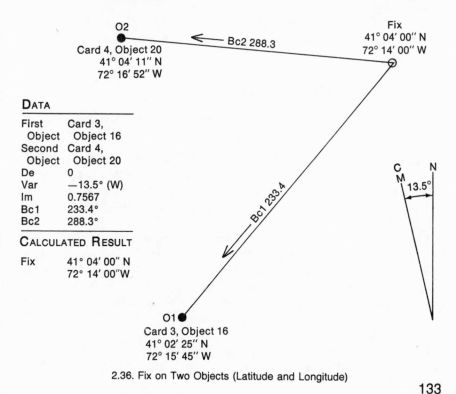

O2
Card 4, Object 20
41° 04' 11" N
72° 16' 52" W

Bc2 288.3

Fix
41° 04' 00" N
72° 14' 00" W

DATA

First Object	Card 3, Object 16
Second Object	Card 4, Object 20
De	0
Var	−13.5° (W)
Im	0.7567
Bc1	233.4°
Bc2	288.3°

CALCULATED RESULT

Fix	41° 04' 00" N
	72° 14' 00"W

Bc1 233.4

O1
Card 3, Object 16
41° 02' 25" N
72° 15' 45" W

2.36. Fix on Two Objects (Latitude and Longitude)

133

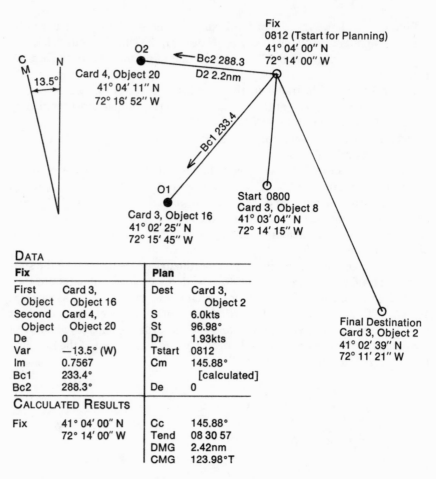

2.37. Fix on Two Objects and Plan to New Destination (Latitude and Longitude)

Figure 2.37 illustrates the combined use of the Fixing and Planning routines. The fix on two objects is as shown in the preceding figure. The fix point becomes the new starting position when it is reached by the vessel at 0812. The new destination is object 2 on data card 3, a buoy at latitude 41°02′39″N, longitude 72°11′21″W.

The employment of the Fixing routines in conjunction with other routines for the calculation of current (also discussed in section 2.4.9) is illustrated by figure 2.38. Since the vessel started northward at 0800 from a known position —object 8 on data card 3 (41°03′04″N, 72°14′15″W)—and its 0812 position is now known, course and speed made good can be calculated, and therefore the current that must have been acting on the vessel between 0800 and 0812 can be ascertained.

The instructions for routines 2.24 and 2.25 include the steps to be followed in this calculation of current. For chart-factor calculations, the vessel's starting

134

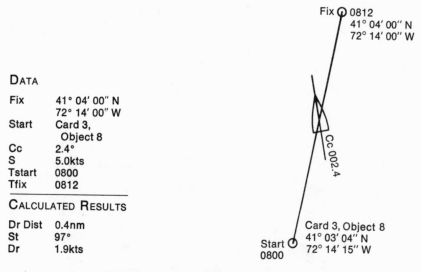

DATA

Fix	41° 04' 00" N
	72° 14' 00" W
Start	Card 3,
	Object 8
Cc	2.4°
S	5.0kts
Tstart	0800
Tfix	0812

CALCULATED RESULTS

Dr Dist	0.4nm
St	97°
Dr	1.9kts

2.38. Set and Drift (Latitude and Longitude)

position is entered by means of steps 64–70 (as appropriate) of routine 2.24; the calculator's memory already contains the co-ordinates of the fix. Next, as described in section 2.4.9, the tracking program of routine 2.20 is loaded (step 71), and steps 72–80 of routine 2.24 are performed, yielding the values of set and drift. For mid-latitude calculations, the corresponding operations in routine 2.25 are listed in steps 62–80.

Once the set and drift of current have been calculated, they can be used as input to the Planning routine (2.17 or 2.18, as appropriate) if a revised course to the destination is to be calculated, perhaps because it is evident that the current has shifted the vessel off the desired track. Among the items of input required are the vessel's present position and its destination. The present position is still in the calculator's memory, but not exactly in the right location for the Planning routine. This can be corrected by pressing $\boxed{\text{RCL}}$ $\boxed{2}$ and $\boxed{\text{RCL}}$ $\boxed{3}$. Then the planning program is re-inserted and the destination is entered, either from a prerecorded data card or manually, as indicated in steps 15–17 and 20–22 of routine 2.17 or 2.18. Speed, set, and drift must be entered at $\boxed{\text{A}}$ (steps 25–27 of routine 2.17 or steps 24–26 of routine 2.18); set and drift are *not* in the memory following the current calculations described above.

If it is inconvenient to integrate these programs, the Planning routine can be used by itself, but it will then be necessary to re-enter the co-ordinates of the vessel's position fix as the start of the new leg.

135

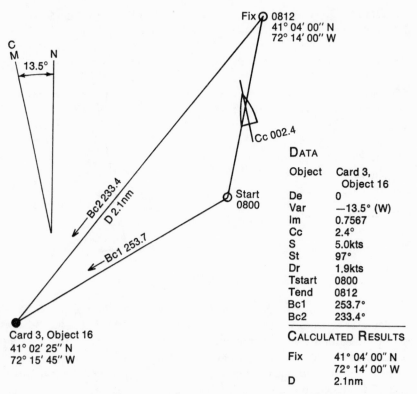

Fix 0812
41° 04′ 00″ N
72° 14′ 00″ W

C
M   N
13.5°

Cc 002.4

Bc2 233.4
D 2.1nm

Bc1 253.7

Start
0800

Card 3, Object 16
41° 02′ 25″ N
72° 15′ 45″ W

DATA

Object	Card 3, Object 16
De	0
Var	−13.5° (W)
Im	0.7567
Cc	2.4°
S	5.0kts
St	97°
Dr	1.9kts
Tstart	0800
Tend	0812
Bc1	253.7°
Bc2	233.4°

CALCULATED RESULTS

Fix	41° 04′ 00″ N
	72° 14′ 00″ W
D	2.1nm

2.39. Running Fix on One Object (Latitude and Longitude)

Figure 2.39 illustrates the running fix on one object. In this instance, only one object is observed, and the vessel is in motion between two successive bearings.

Since there is just one object, its co-ordinates are entered twice, either manually, as shown in the instructions of steps 34–37 of routine 2.24, or from a prerecorded data card, as shown in the instructions of steps 31–33 (that is, [f][a] will be pressed for the first entry and [f][b] for the second). For routine 2.25, the corresponding steps are 33–36 and 30–32. If no data card is employed, the variation and chart factor must be entered manually, at step 40 and step 41 of routine 2.24; variation must be entered at step 39 of routine 2.25.

Because the vessel is not stationary this time, the input data includes not only deviation and variation (both entered at [f][e]), but also course and speed, the set and drift of the current, if any (all entered at [A]), and the time of start and time of end of the leg or run (entered at [B]). All of these can be re-entered whenever necessary. As always, if any one of the values entered at [A] is changed, the other three must be re-entered as well, along with the time of start and time of end for the particular leg of the run.

Figure 2.40 illustrates the situation in which bearings on two different objects are obtained, with the vessel having moved during the time between the two observations. As was shown in section 2.2.6, when this time interval

136

is substantial—say, a few minutes—an error in the calculated fix can result unless the vessel's movement is taken into account.

The co-ordinates for the sighted objects may be entered manually, or taken from prerecorded data cards, or both. Manual entry of variation and chart factor are required if prerecorded cards are not used. As in the running fix on one object, changes in course, speed, set and drift of current, and deviation and variation, can be accommodated, and the same cautions with respect to the re-entry of altered values apply: if any one of the values entered at $\boxed{A}$ changes, the other three must also be re-entered, along with the time of start and time of end for the particular leg of the run.

If the regression method of routine 2.6 is employed, two bearing–time pairs are obtained from two separate regression calculations. The bearing angles, with their associated times (which serve as *Tstart* and *Tend*), are entered at steps 57–60 of routine 2.24 or steps 55–58 of routine 2.25.

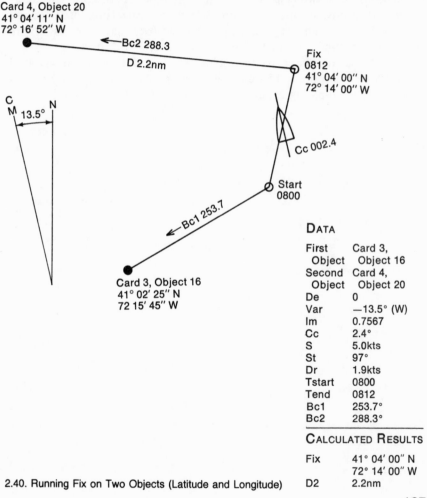

Card 4, Object 20
41° 04′ 11″ N
72° 16′ 52″ W

Bc2 288.3
D 2.2nm

Fix
0812
41° 04′ 00″ N
72° 14′ 00″ W

C M 13.5° N

Cc 002.4

Start
0800

Bc1 253.7

Card 3, Object 16
41° 02′ 25″ N
72 15′ 45″ W

DATA

First Object	Card 3, Object 16
Second Object	Card 4, Object 20
De	0
Var	−13.5° (W)
Im	0.7567
Cc	2.4°
S	5.0kts
St	97°
Dr	1.9kts
Tstart	0800
Tend	0812
Bc1	253.7°
Bc2	288.3°

CALCULATED RESULTS

Fix	41° 04′ 00″ N 72° 14′ 00″ W
D2	2.2nm

2.40. Running Fix on Two Objects (Latitude and Longitude)

137

2.4.16 Fixing on the SR-52 Routine 2.26 (for chart factor) and routine 2.27 (for mid-latitude) provide instructions for using the SR-52 to obtain position fixes by taking bearings on one or two objects whose latitude and longitude co-ordinates are known. Prerecorded data, stored on magnetic cards in accordance with the instructions of routine 2.16, can be employed. Since the cards for the SR-52, unlike those for the HP-67 and HP-97, do not store compass variation, this value must in every case be added manually.

The routines can accommodate changes in variation, deviation, course, speed, and set and drift.

If smoothed values for the bearing angles are obtained by means of routine 2.7, for the bearing regression, they can be entered, along with the corresponding values of time, at steps 46–47 and 50–51 or 75–76 and 79–80 in routine 2.26, or at the equivalent steps in routine 2.27.

For the calculation of current, the most recent position is obtained from a simultaneous fix on two objects, by means of routine 2.26 or 2.27. This information is then used as input in routine 2.28 for the calculation of the course made good and speed made good between the two fixes, and these answers are then used in routine 2.14 for the calculation of set and drift.

The reader can test the correctness of his recording of the programs involved by employing the routines to solve the problems shown in figures 2.36 and 2.38–2.40 and comparing his answers with those supplied in the figures.

Routine 2.26 (SR-52)

Var De	St Dr	Cc S		Im
Time	Bc1 Bc2	Lobj Lo-obj	Lfix	Lofix

FIXING (CHART FACTOR)

Step	Procedure	Input Data/Units	Keys	Output Data/Units
	Before beginning, make sure D/R switch is set to D.			
	Fix on Two Objects			
	If co-ordinates of both objects are on data cards, proceed as follows (steps 1–13):			
1	Clear memories		2nd CMs CLR	
2	Load data card containing co-ordinates of first object			
3	Enter identification letter corresponding to first object		A–2nd D'	
	If co-ordinates of second object are on same data card,			
4	Enter identification letter corresponding to second object, and continue at step 7		A–2nd D'	
	If co-ordinates of second object are on a different data card,			
5	Load second data card			
6	Enter identification letter corresponding to second object		A–2nd D'	
7	Load program—both sides			
8	Enter variation (+E,−W), even if 0	DD.d	2nd A'	
9	Enter deviation (+E,−W), even if 0	DD.d	2nd A'	
10	Enter compass bearing to first object	DDD.d	B	
11	Enter compass bearing to second object	DDD.d	B	
12	Calculate and display latitude of fix		D	±DD.MMSS
13	Calculate and display longitude of fix		E	±DD.MMSS

(CONTINUED)

139

Step	Procedure	Input Data/Units	Keys	Output Data/Units
	If only co-ordinates of first object are on a data card, proceed as follows (steps 14–18):			
14	Perform steps 1–3 and 7–11			
15	Enter latitude of second object ($+$N,$-$S)	DD.MMSS	C	
16	Enter longitude of second object ($+$W, $-$E)	DD.MMSS	C	
17	Calculate and display latitude of fix		D	$\pm$DD.MMSS
18	Calculate and display longitude of fix		E	$\pm$DD.MMSS
	If only co-ordinates of second object are on a data card, proceed as follows (steps 19–26):			
19	Perform steps 1 and 7–11			
20	Enter latitude of first object ($+$N,$-$S)	DD.MMSS	C	
21	Enter longitude of first object ($+$W,$-$E)	DD.MMSS	C	
22	Load data card containing co-ordinates of second object			
23	Enter identification letter corresponding to second object		A–2nd D'	
24	Reload program—both sides			
25	Calculate and display latitude of fix		D	$\pm$DD.MMSS
26	Calculate and display longitude of fix		E	$\pm$DD.MMSS
	If co-ordinates of neither first nor second object are on data cards, proceed as follows (steps 27–34):			
27	Perform steps 1 and 7–11			
28	Enter chart factor	0.nnnn	2nd E'	
29	Enter latitude of first object ($+$N,$-$S)	DD.MMSS	C	
30	Enter longitude of first object ($+$W,$-$E)	DD.MMSS	C	
31	Enter latitude of second object ($+$N,$-$S)	DD.MMSS	C	
32	Enter longitude of second object ($+$W, $-$E)	DD.MMSS	C	
33	Calculate and display latitude of fix		D	$\pm$DD.MMSS
34	Calculate and display longitude of fix		E	$\pm$DD.MMSS

Running Fix on One Object

If co-ordinates of object are on a data card, proceed as follows (steps 35–53):

Step	Procedure	Input Data/Units	Keys	Output Data/Units
35	Clear memories		2nd CMs CLR	
36	Load data card			

Step	Procedure	Input Data/Units	Keys	Output Data/Units
37	Enter identification letter corresponding to object		A–2nd D'	
38	Re-enter identification letter corresponding to object		A–2nd D'	
39	Load program—both sides			
40	Enter variation (+E,−W), even if 0	DD.d	2nd A'	
41	Enter deviation (+E,−W), even if 0	DD.d	2nd A'	
42	Enter set of current, even if 0	DDD.d	2nd B'	
43	Enter drift of current, even if 0	knots	2nd B'	
44	Enter compass course during run or leg*	DDD.d	2nd C'	
45	Enter vessel speed during run or leg	knots	2nd C'	
46	Enter compass bearing to object at start of run	DDD.d	B	
47	Enter time of first bearing	H.MS	A	

For multiple courses or speeds, or changes in set or drift between bearings, proceed as follows (steps 48–49):

Step	Procedure	Input Data/Units	Keys	Output Data/Units
48	Enter time of end of preceding leg—i.e., time of change(s)	H.MS	A	
49	Clear display, then repeat steps 40–41 even if variation and deviation are unchanged, and repeat as necessary steps 42–43 and 44–45; set and drift, and course and speed, are handled as pairs—if even one member of the pair changes, *both* must be re-entered		CLR	
50	Enter time of end of run	H.MS	A	
51	Enter compass bearing to object at end of run	DDD.d	B	
52	Calculate and display latitude of fix		D	±DD.MMSS
53	Calculate and display longitude of fix		E	±DD.MMSS

If co-ordinates of object are not on a data card, proceed as follows (steps 54–61):

Step	Procedure	Input Data/Units	Keys	Output Data/Units
54	Perform steps 35 and 39–51			
55	Enter chart factor	0.nnnn	2nd E'	
56	Enter latitude of object (+N,−S)	DD.MMSS	C	
57	Enter longitude of object (+W,−E)	DD.MMSS	C	
58	Re-enter latitude of object (+N,−S)	DD.MMSS	C	
59	Re-enter longitude of object (+W,−E)	DD.MMSS	C	
60	Calculate and display latitude of fix		D	±DD.MMSS
61	Calculate and display longitude of fix		E	±DD.MMSS

*Correct for leeway; see table 2.2.

(CONTINUED)

Step	Procedure	Input Data/Units	Keys	Output Data/Units

Running Fix on Two Objects

If co-ordinates of both objects are on data cards, proceed as follows (steps 62–82):

Step	Procedure	Input Data/Units	Keys	Output Data/Units
62	Clear memories		2nd CMs CLR	
63	Load data card containing co-ordinates of first object			
64	Enter identification letter corresponding to first object		A–2nd D′	

If co-ordinates of second object are on same data card,

Step	Procedure	Input Data/Units	Keys	Output Data/Units
65	Enter identification letter corresponding to second object, and continue at step 68		A–2nd D′	

If co-ordinates of second object are on a different data card,

Step	Procedure	Input Data/Units	Keys	Output Data/Units
66	Load second data card			
67	Enter identification letter corresponding to second object		A–2nd D′	
68	Load program—both sides			
69	Enter variation (+E, −W), even if 0	DD.d	2nd A′	
70	Enter deviation (+E, −W), even if 0	DD.d	2nd A′	
71	Enter set of current, even if 0	DDD.d	2nd B′	
72	Enter drift of current, even if 0	knots	2nd B′	
73	Enter compass course during run or leg*	DDD.d	2nd C′	
74	Enter vessel speed during run or leg	knots	2nd C′	
75	Enter compass bearing to first object at start of run	DDD.d	B	
76	Enter time of first bearing	H.MS	A	

For multiple courses or speeds, or changes in set or drift between bearings, proceed as follows (steps 77–78):

Step	Procedure	Input Data/Units	Keys	Output Data/Units
77	Enter time of end of preceding leg—i.e., time of change(s)	H.MS	A	
78	Clear display, then repeat steps 69–70 even if variation and deviation are unchanged, and repeat as necessary steps 71–72 and 73–74; set and drift, and course and speed, are handled as pairs—if even one member of the pair changes, *both* must be re-entered		CLR	

*Correct for leeway; see table 2.2.

142

Step	Procedure	Input Data/Units	Keys	Output Data/Units
79	Enter time of end of run	H.MS	A	
80	Enter compass bearing to second object at end of run	DDD.d	B	
81	Calculate and display latitude of fix		D	±DD.MMSS
82	Calculate and display longitude of fix		E	±DD.MMSS

If only co-ordinates of first object are on a data card, proceed as follows (steps 83–87):

83	Perform steps 62–64 and 68–80			
84	Enter latitude of second object (+N,−S)	DD.MMSS	C	
85	Enter longitude of second object (+W, −E)	DD.MMSS	C	
86	Calculate and display latitude of fix		D	±DD.MMSS
87	Calculate and display longitude of fix		E	±DD.MMSS

If only co-ordinates of second object are on a data card, proceed as follows (steps 88–94):

88	Perform steps 62 and 68			
89	Enter latitude of first object (+N,−S)	DD.MMSS	C	
90	Enter longitude of first object (+W,−E)	DD.MMSS	C	
91	Load data card containing co-ordinates of second object			
92	Enter identification letter corresponding to second object		A–2nd D'	
93	Reload program—both sides			
94	Perform steps 69–82			

If co-ordinates of neither first nor second object are on data cards, proceed as follows (steps 95–102):

95	Perform steps 62 and 68–80			
96	Enter chart factor	0.nnnn	2nd E'	
97	Enter latitude of first object (+N,−S)	DD.MMSS	C	
98	Enter longitude of first object (+W,−E)	DD.MMSS	C	
99	Enter latitude of second object (+N,−S)	DD.MMSS	C	
100	Enter longitude of second object (+W, −E)	DD.MMSS	C	
101	Calculate and display latitude of fix		D	±DD.MMSS
102	Calculate and display longitude of fix		E	±DD.MMSS

Routine 2.27 (SR-52)

Var De	St Dr	Cc S		
Time	Bc1 Bc2	Lobj Lo-obj	Lfix	Lofix

FIXING (MID-LATITUDE)

Step	Procedure	Input Data/Units	Keys	Output Data/Units
	Before beginning, make sure D/R switch is set to D.			
	Fix on Two Objects			
	If co-ordinates of both objects are on data cards, proceed as follows (steps 1–13):			
1	Clear memories		2nd CMs CLR	
2	Load data card containing co-ordinates of first object			
3	Enter identification letter corresponding to first object		A–2nd D'	
	If co-ordinates of second object are on same data card,			
4	Enter identification letter corresponding to second object, and continue at step 7		A–2nd D'	
	If co-ordinates of second object are on a different data card,			
5	Load second data card			
6	Enter identification letter corresponding to second object		A–2nd D'	
7	Load program—both sides			
8	Enter variation (+E, −W), even if 0	DD.d	2nd A'	
9	Enter deviation (+E, −W), even if 0	DD.d	2nd A'	
10	Enter compass bearing to first object	DDD.d	B	
11	Enter compass bearing to second object	DDD.d	B	
12	Calculate and display latitude of fix		D	$\pm$DD.MMSS
13	Calculate and display longitude of fix		E	$\pm$DD.MMSS

144

Step	Procedure	Input Data/Units	Keys	Output Data/Units
	If only co-ordinates of first object are on a data card, proceed as follows (steps 14–18):			
14	Perform steps 1–3 and 7–11			
15	Enter latitude of second object (+N,−S)	DD.MMSS	C	
16	Enter longitude of second object (+W, −E)	DD.MMSS	C	
17	Calculate and display latitude of fix		D	±DD.MMSS
18	Calculate and display longitude of fix		E	±DD.MMSS
	If only co-ordinates of second object are on a data card, proceed as follows (steps 19–26):			
19	Perform steps 1 and 7–11			
20	Enter latitude of first object (+N,−S)	DD.MMSS	C	
21	Enter longitude of first object (+W,−E)	DD.MMSS	C	
22	Load data card containing co-ordinates of second object			
23	Enter identification letter corresponding to second object		A–2nd D′	
24	Reload program—both sides			
25	Calculate and display latitude of fix		D	±DD.MMSS
26	Calculate and display longitude of fix		E	±DD.MMSS
	If co-ordinates of neither first nor second object are on data cards, proceed as follows (steps 27–34):			
27	Perform steps 1 and 7–11			
28	Enter latitude of first object (+N,−S)	DD.MMSS	C	
29	Enter longitude of first object (+W,−E)	DD.MMSS	C	
30	Enter latitude of second object (+N,−S)	DD.MMSS	C	
31	Enter longitude of second object (+W, −E)	DD.MMSS	C	
32	Calculate and display latitude of fix		D	±DD.MMSS
33	Calculate and display longitude of fix		E	±DD.MMSS

Running Fix on One Object

Step	Procedure	Input Data/Units	Keys	Output Data/Units
	If co-ordinates of object are on a data card, proceed as follows (steps 34–52):			
34	Clear memories		2nd CMs CLR	
35	Load data card			
36	Enter identification letter corresponding to object		A–2nd D′	
37	Re-enter identification letter corresponding to object		A–2nd D′	

(CONTINUED)

145

Step	Procedure	Input Data/Units	Keys	Output Data/Units
38	Load program—both sides			
39	Enter variation (+E, −W), even if 0	DD.d	2nd A′	
40	Enter deviation (+E, −W), even if 0	DD.d	2nd A′	
41	Enter set of current, even if 0	DDD.d	2nd B′	
42	Enter drift of current, even if 0	knots	2nd B′	
43	Enter compass course during run or leg*	DDD.d	2nd C′	
44	Enter vessel speed during run or leg	knots	2nd C′	
45	Enter compass bearing to object at start of run	DDD.d	B	
46	Enter time of first bearing	H.MS	A	
	For multiple courses or speeds, or changes in set or drift between bearings, proceed as follows (steps 47–48):			
47	Enter time of end of preceding leg—i.e., time of change(s)	H.MS	A	
48	Clear display, then repeat steps 39–40 even if variation and deviation are unchanged, and repeat as necessary steps 41–42 and 43–44; set and drift, and course and speed, are handled as pairs—if even one member of the pair changes, *both* must be re-entered		CLR	
49	Enter time of end of run	H.MS	A	
50	Enter compass bearing to object at end of run	DDD.d	B	
51	Calculate and display latitude of fix		D	±DD.MMSS
52	Calculate and display longitude of fix		E	±DD.MMSS
	If co-ordinates of object are not on a data card, proceed as follows (steps 53–59):			
53	Perform steps 34 and 38–50			
54	Enter latitude of object (+N, −S)	DD.MMSS	C	
55	Enter longitude of object (+W, −E)	DD.MMSS	C	
56	Re-enter latitude of object (+N, −S)	DD.MMSS	C	
57	Re-enter longitude of object (+W, −E)	DD.MMSS	C	
58	Calculate and display latitude of fix		D	±DD.MMSS
59	Calculate and display longitude of fix		E	±DD.MMSS
	Running Fix on Two Objects			
	If co-ordinates of both objects are on data cards, proceed as follows (steps 60–80):			
60	Clear memories		2nd CMs CLR	

*Correct for leeway; see table 2.2.

146

Step	Procedure	Input Data/Units	Keys	Output Data/Units
61	Load data card containing co-ordinates of first object			
62	Enter identification letter corresponding to first object		A–2nd D'	
	If co-ordinates of second object are on same data card,			
63	Enter identification letter corresponding to second object, and continue at step 66		A–2nd D'	
	If co-ordinates of second object are on a different data card,			
64	Load second data card			
65	Enter identification letter corresponding to second object		A–2nd D'	
66	Load program—both sides			
67	Enter variation (+E, −W), even if 0	DD.d	2nd A'	
68	Enter deviation (+E, −W), even if 0	DD.d	2nd A'	
69	Enter set of current, even if 0	DDD.d	2nd B'	
70	Enter drift of current, even if 0	knots	2nd B'	
71	Enter compass course during run or leg*	DDD.d	2nd C'	
72	Enter vessel speed during run or leg	knots	2nd C'	
73	Enter compass bearing to first object at start of run	DDD.d	B	
74	Enter time of first bearing	H.MS	A	
	For multiple courses or speeds, or changes in set or drift between bearings, proceed as follows (steps 75–76):			
75	Enter time of end of preceding leg—i.e., time of change(s)	H.MS	A	
76	Clear display, then repeat steps 67–68 even if variation and deviation are unchanged, and repeat as necessary steps 69–70 and 71–72; set and drift, and course and speed, are handled as pairs—if even one member of the pair changes, *both* must be re-entered		CLR	
77	Enter time of end of run	H.MS	A	
78	Enter compass bearing to second object at end of run	DDD.d	B	
79	Calculate and display latitude of fix		D	±DD.MMSS

*Correct for leeway; see table 2.2.

(CONTINUED)

Step	Procedure	Input Data/Units	Keys	Output Data/Units
80	Calculate and display longitude of fix		E	$\pm$DD.MMSS
	If only co-ordinates of first object are on a data card, proceed as follows (steps 81–85):			
81	Perform steps 60–62 and 66–78			
82	Enter latitude of second object (+N,−S)	DD.MMSS	C	
83	Enter longitude of second object (+W, −E)	DD.MMSS	C	
84	Calculate and display latitude of fix		D	$\pm$DD.MMSS
85	Calculate and display longitude of fix		E	$\pm$DD.MMSS
	If only co-ordinates of second object are on a data card, proceed as follows (steps 86–92):			
86	Perform steps 60 and 66			
87	Enter latitude of first object (+N,−S)	DD.MMSS	C	
88	Enter longitude of first object (+W,−E)	DD.MMSS	C	
89	Load data card containing co-ordinates of second object			
90	Enter identification letter corresponding to second object		A–2nd D'	
91	Reload program—both sides			
92	Perform steps 67–80			
	If co-ordinates of neither first not second object are on data cards, proceed as follows (steps 93–99):			
93	Perform steps 60 and 66–78			
94	Enter latitude of first object (+N,−S)	DD.MMSS	C	
95	Enter longitude of first object (+W,−E)	DD.MMSS	C	
96	Enter latitude of second object (+N,−S)	DD.MMSS	C	
97	Enter longitude of second object	DD.MMSS	C	
98	Calculate and display latitude of fix		D	$\pm$DD.MMSS
99	Calculate and display longitude of fix		E	$\pm$DD.MMSS

Routine 2.28 (SR-52)

DMG	SMG			
Lstart Lostart	Lend Loend	Tstart	Tend	CMG

COURSE MADE GOOD AND SPEED MADE GOOD FROM TWO POSITIONS
(LATITUDE AND LONGITUDE)

Step	Procedure	Input Data/Units	Keys	Output Data/Units
	Before beginning, make sure D/R switch is set to D.			
	If both start and end co-ordinates are on data cards, proceed as follows (steps 1–6):			
1	Load data card containing start co-ordinates			
2	Enter identification letter corresponding to start co-ordinates		A–2nd D′	
	If end co-ordinates are on same data card,			
3	Enter identification letter corresponding to end co-ordinates, and continue at step 6		A–2nd D′	
	If end co-ordinates are on a different data card,			
4	Load second data card			
5	Enter identification letter corresponding to end co-ordinates		A–2nd D′	
6	Load program, and continue at step 18			
	If only start co-ordinates are on a data card, proceed as follows (steps 7–11):			
7	Load data card			
8	Enter identification letter corresponding to start co-ordinates		A–2nd D′	
9	Load program			
10	Enter end latitude (+N,−S)	DD.MMSS	B	
11	Enter end longitude (+W,−E), and continue at step 18	DD.MMSS	B	
	If only end co-ordinates are on a data card, proceed as follows (steps 12–22):			

(CONTINUED)

149

Step	Procedure	Input Data/Units	Keys	Output Data/Units
12	Load program			
13	Enter start latitude (+N,−S)	DD.MMSS	A	
14	Enter start longitude (+W,−E)	DD.MMSS	A	
15	Load data card containing end co-ordinates			
16	Enter identification letter corresponding to end co-ordinates		A–2nd D'	
17	Reload program			
18	Enter time of start	H.MS	C	
19	Enter time of end	H.MS	D	
20	Calculate and display true course made good		E	DDD.d
21	Calculate and display distance made good		2nd A'	naut. mi.
22	Calculate and display speed made good		2nd B'	knots

3
Sailing

ABBREVIATIONS Used in the Routines of Chapter 3

AW   speed of apparent wind

AWo   optimum speed of apparent wind

Btm   true bearing from start to mark or way point

Btmark   true bearing from vessel to mark or way point

Cc   compass course

Cco   optimum compass course

CMG   true course made good

Cmo   optimum magnetic course

Ct   true course

D1   distance from start of tack to lay line

D2   distance from start of next tack to mark or way point

DD.d, DDD.d   degrees and tenths of a degree

De   deviation

Dm   distance from start to mark or way point

Dmark   distance from vessel to mark or way point

Dr   drift of current

E   east

H   angle of heel

H.MS   hour(s), minute(s), and second(s)

MW   speed of modified true wind

MWnom   nominal value of modified true wind

naut. mi.   nautical miles

S   vessel speed

ΔS   difference between *Sdo* and *Sd*

Sc   corrected vessel speed

Sd   due-downwind speed

Sdo   optimum downwind speed

Set Port   set for port calculations

Set Stbd   set for starboard calculations

SMG   speed made good

So   optimum speed to windward

St   set of current

ΔT   time already elapsed on present tack

ΔT1   time required from start of tack to reach lay line

ΔT2   time required from start of next tack to reach mark or way point

ΔTmark   total time required to reach mark or way point

Var   variation

W   west

ΔW/2   angular shift required to go from *Sd* to *Sdo*

Wa   angle of apparent wind

Wao   optimum angle of apparent wind

Wm   direction of modified true wind

Wt   tacking angle

Wto   optimum tacking angle

↑   following a data-entry item indicates that it is entered by pressing [ENTER] instead of a letter key.

→   following a data-entry item indicates that its entry initiates (without further keyboard activity) the calculation and display of one or more results.

;   preceding an item indicates that [RUN] is used instead of a letter key.

+   indicates that the item (e.g., east variation on the HP-67/97) is entered simply by pressing the appropriate numerical keys, on both the HP-67/97 and the SR-52.

−   indicates that the item is entered on the HP-67/97 by pressing the appropriate numerical keys followed by [CHS], and on the SR-52 by pressing the appropriate numerical keys followed by [+/−].

152

3.1 Introduction

When it comes to sailing—whether cruising or racing—the calculator has uses beyond planning and position finding. To reach a mark or destination that lies to windward, tacking is necessary. When the situation is complicated by the presence of currents, the calculator can sort out the variables involved, and display the courses to steer to reach the destination in the shortest time. Similarly, the calculator can quickly solve the question of whether to tack downwind, again taking into account any currents. This chapter shows in detail how the calculator can be used to provide the information needed to optimize sailing performance.

To employ a calculator in this manner, one must know the direction and speed of the apparent (relative) wind, and the vessel speed through the water —information available from wind vanes, anemometers, and knotmeters. The instructions which follow assume the presence on board of such instruments.

3.2 The Combination of Wind and Current

The effect of current on apparent wind can be easily understood if one visualizes a boat without sails or power, on a windless day, moving only to the motion of a current. An anemometer mounted on deck will show a wind speed equal to that of the current, and a wind vane will indicate a wind direction opposite to that of the current. This current wind—created by the motion of the vessel through the air—in combination with any natural true wind, constitutes the actual, or *modified true wind,* for this particular craft. Thus, if the vessel is drifting in a 2-knot current, a 10-knot wind will become an 8-knot modified true wind when blowing in the same direction as the current, and a 12-knot modified true wind when blowing in the opposite direction.

If the wind is coming *from* true north (000°), and the current is flowing *toward* true west (270°), the speed of the resulting modified true wind will be 10.2 knots and the direction it comes from will be 348.7°. These values are obtained by vector addition, as shown in figure 3.1. Here, the true-wind vector (TW) of magnitude 10 knots is seen coming from the north and therefore pointing due south; the current, with a drift west of 2 knots, creates a 2-knot current wind moving the opposite way, and the direction of the current-wind vector (−Dr) is therefore 90°. The addition of −Dr to TW produces the resultant, which represents the direction *(Wm)* and speed *(MW)* of the modified true wind.

In the routines that follow, values for the modified true wind are employed; calculations based on vessel speed and apparent-wind speed and direction yield the necessary information about this wind. The vessel is affected by no other; it moves under the influence of the modified true wind, not of the true wind isolated from the current.

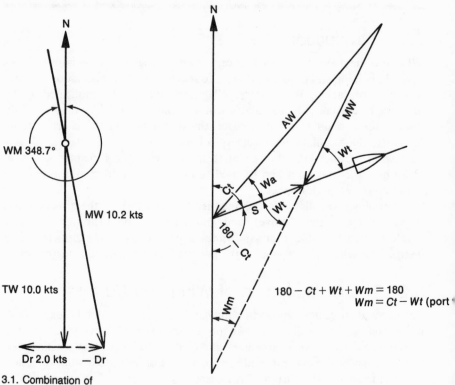

3.1. Combination of Wind and Current

3.2. Calculation of Modified True Wind

3.3 Calculating Modified True Wind

If a vessel is equipped with a compass, and with instruments measuring vessel speed through the water *(S)* and the speed *(AW)* and direction *(Wa)* of the apparent wind, the speed *(MW)* and direction *(Wm)* of the modified true wind can be calculated by standard trigonometrical methods.

The basis for this calculation is shown in figure 3.2. The situation illustrated is a beat to windward, on the port tack. The vector **S**, which represents the vessel's motion through the water, has the direction *Ct,* measured with respect to true north. The tacking angle *(Wt),* between the wind vector and the vessel's motion vector, is a relative angle, measured with respect to the fore-and-aft axis of the vessel. The direction of the modified true wind *(Wm)* is equal to *Ct − Wt,* and is therefore related to a geographic reference—the true course of the vessel. Correspondingly, on the starboard tack, *Wm* is equal to *Ct + Wt.*

154

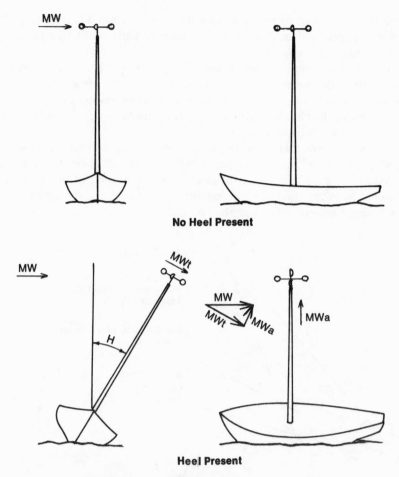

No Heel Present

Heel Present

MWt: tangential component of modified true wind
MWa: axial component of modified true wind

3.3. Effect of Heel Angle on Anemometer

One complication that arises when calculating *MW* from data measured on board is the fact that any heeling of the vessel can affect the accuracy of wind speed measured by the anemometer. The reason for this is made evident in figure 3.3, showing the effect of a wind blowing from the starboard side, with no heel present (upper portion of the figure), and with heel present (lower portion). In the latter case, the effectiveness of the wind in turning the anemometer cups is reduced. The modified wind *(MW)* blowing from the starboard side causes the vessel to heel to port; that portion of the wind that blows across the anemometer cups causes them to rotate, but the portion of the wind that blows up between the cups has no turning effect. When the angle of heel *(H)* is equal to zero, the wind is tangential to the open cup. But with heel present, some of the wind in effect comes from an axial direction (from up or

155

down the mast), and its ability to spin the cups is reduced accordingly. The vector diagram resolves these wind components. Only **MWt** (the tangential portion) turns the cups.

The calculator routines that follow all take this effect into consideration. Heel angle is entered as input, and appropriate corrections are made in the calculated values. Similarly, when apparent-wind speeds are displayed, they have been modified by the calculator to give the results as they would be seen on the vessel's wind-speed meter.

The relationships that underlie the calculator routines in this chapter hold for all points of sailing; no changes in equations or calculator programs are needed as the wind shifts from forward of the beam to aft of the beam. The difference in the method of obtaining *Wm* on the port and on the starboard tack is easily accommodated in the instructions.

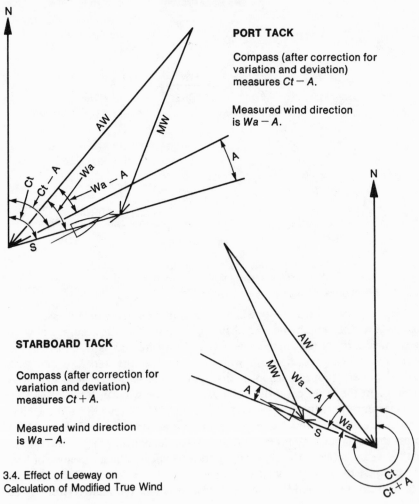

PORT TACK

Compass (after correction for variation and deviation) measures $Ct - A$.

Measured wind direction is $Wa - A$.

STARBOARD TACK

Compass (after correction for variation and deviation) measures $Ct + A$.

Measured wind direction is $Wa - A$.

3.4. Effect of Leeway on Calculation of Modified True Wind

The values for *MW* and *Wm* are not calculated for their own sake. Rather, obtaining these values is part of the procedure for the complete solution of tactical and navigation problems, as in routines 3.1 and 3.3–3.4.

The effect of leeway, explained in section 2.2.5, must be taken into account in calculations involving the wind. As figure 3.4 indicates, this effect is different on the port and on the starboard tack, although the underlying cause is the same. On the port tack, when the vessel moves along **S,** its heading is a few degrees upwind of **S.** The amount of leeway—the difference between the vessel's heading and its course over the bottom, in the absence of current —is shown as angle *A.* The direction exhibited by the vessel's compass will be in error accordingly; on the port tack the course shown by the compass will be less than the vessel's course *(Ct)* by the amount of angle *A.* On the starboard tack (illustrated in the second part of the figure) the course shown by the compass will be correspondingly greater than *Ct.* Hence, as was indicated in table 2.2, the leeway correction involves addition to the compass reading on the port tack, and subtraction from it on the starboard tack. For uncorrection, the opposite is true.

The presence of leeway must also be taken into account when the direction of the apparent wind *(Wa)* is measured. As was shown in figure 3.2, *Wa* represents the angle between the vector for the apparent wind (**AW**) and the vector for the vessel's motion through the water (**S**). This angle is measured in relation to the direction in which the bow is pointing (the fore-and-aft axis of the boat), not the direction of the vessel's track, and since leeway causes some crabbing, so that the bow points a few degrees closer to the wind than the actual course through the water, a correction must be made. In this instance, however, since the angle in question is not a compass direction, but is relative to the vessel, the correction—addition of the amount of angle *A* —will be the same on both tacks. By the same token, when uncorrection of the value for apparent-wind direction is necessary, the amount of the leeway angle is subtracted on both tacks.

A typical vessel beating to windward might encounter the values of leeway* shown in table 3.1.

Table 3.1   Values of Leeway

| Level of Wind | Angle of Apparent Wind, in Degrees | | |
| | 20 | 27 | 35 |
	Leeway Angle, in Degrees		
Light	4	3	2
Moderate	5	4	3
Heavy	6	5	4

*These values are from Alan J. Adler, "The Best Course to Windward," *Sail,* February 1975, p. 26.

In summary, if correction is required, the amount of the leeway angle is *always added* to the value for the apparent wind read on board the vessel, but is *either added or subtracted* to the magnetic compass course (the course after correction for deviation), depending on whether the vessel is on the port or the starboard tack, as shown in table 2.2.

3.4 Beating to Windward—Cruising

The foregoing principles find practical application in the calculation of successive courses to steer and courses and speeds made good while cruising on a beat to windward between two points, as shown in figure 3.5. In this case, the modified-true-wind vector (**MW**) is the reference direction from which port- and starboard-tack vectors (**S**) are drawn. However, the actual direction of the course made good over the bottom is shown not by these tack vectors, but by

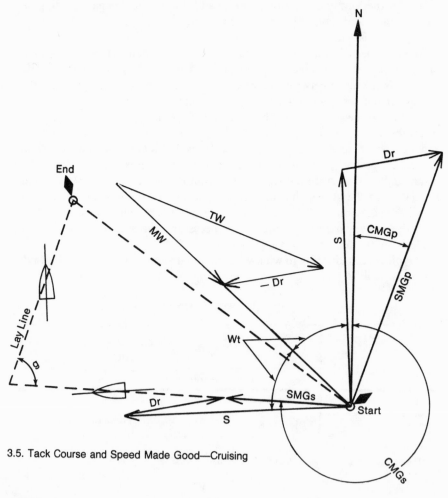

3.5. Tack Course and Speed Made Good—Cruising

SMGs and **SMGp,** which incorporate the effects of the current. These are asymmetric with respect to **MW.**

A vessel that departs on the starboard tack, with tacking angle *Wt,* first progresses, crabbing as a result of the current, along the speed-made-good vector **SMGs,** its direction being *CMGs.* When the vessel reaches the lay line, it changes its course made good by *g* degrees. In coming about to the port tack, it swings its bow through 2 × *Wt* degrees (not equal to *g*), thereby attaining a tacking angle with respect to the modified true wind that is equal to the tacking angle on the previous leg. At the same time, as has been shown, the angle of the course made good with respect to the wind changes, because of the differing effect of the current.

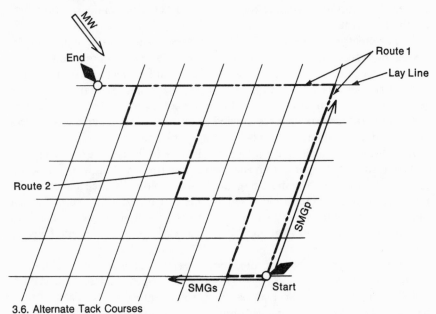

3.6. Alternate Tack Courses

This route is not the only one that could have been adopted for the journey in question. Figure 3.6 indicates the options available. The grid in the area between the start and the end of the journey consists of a set of courses made good, parallel to those the vessel was shown following in the preceding figure. Under the given conditions of wind and current, the course made good over the bottom must be confined to tracks in the same directions as these if the angle to the wind (*Wt* in figure 3.5) is to be kept uniform on both tacks. The vessel will move more slowly over the bottom on the starboard tack than on the port tack, and the respective courses made good over the bottom will not identically reflect the influence of the wind, because of the deflecting influence of the current. On any set of tacks paralleling the lines of this grid, the duration of the journey will be the same (except for the time lost in going from one tack to another).

Two sample routes are presented in figure 3.6. Route 1 shows a way of gaining the destination with only two tacks; the vessel sails on the port tack until the lay line is reached, and then maintains the starboard tack for the rest of the journey. Route 2, consisting of a series of tacks, will require the same amount of sailing time as Route 1.

The calculator can perform many functions during a windward passage like the one shown here. To begin with, given the necessary data on vessel speed and apparent wind, it can determine the speed and direction of the modified true wind. With this information, the tacking angle *(Wt)*, can be calculated from the wind and speed triangle of figure 3.2. If the wind speed and direction are assumed to be holding steady, the calculator can then supply the course to steer to obtain the same tacking angle, and the same sailing performance, on the next tack.

The calculator also displays course and speed made good over the bottom, taking into account the presence of current, so that progress toward the destination can be ascertained. Thus, for a selected tacking angle (to the wind) tactical problems (e.g., determining course to steer) and navigation problems (e.g., identifying course over the bottom) are solved by the same sequence of operations. If there are changes in wind or current, a new course to steer can be calculated, to maintain constant sailing performance.

In addition, the calculator displays the distance to the lay line on the present tack, and the time required to reach the lay line (information which makes it much easier to avoid overstanding); and it displays the distance and course to the mark at any selected time. Facts of this sort are especially useful when sailing in fog, or in other conditions of reduced visibility; they are always available to provide a navigational backup, as various tactics are employed to reach the destination.

The instructions for performing the necessary calculator operations are given in routines 3.1–3.4. They have been developed only for the HP-67, HP-97, and SR-52, for two reasons. First, since a great deal of data must be handled, the calculator employed must be one of those which can properly manage and process large amounts of information. These calculators have sufficient capacity, and the presence on each magnetic card of blanks to be used for specialized labeling of the uppermost row of keys greatly simplifies the entry of the proper data in the proper sequence.

Second, even under cruising conditions, there is no time for manually sequencing through endless steps of calculation; and certainly during a race, a harassed skipper is not likely to wait patiently while his navigator struggles through several hundred keystrokes, all the while wondering if he has reached the lay line! Making this sort of tactical decision is the territory of the programmable calculator with an external memory.

3.4.1 Cruising Navigation on the HP-67 and HP-97 For the HP-67 and HP-97, only a single program card and a single routine—routine 3.1—

160

are needed to provide all of the required navigational answers.* This single card is used on both port and starboard tacks; steps 6–8 are executed on the former, and steps 9–11 on the latter. Since compass deviation may be different on the port and starboard tacks, provision has been made in the routine to enter it twice—for the present tack at step 8 or step 11, and for the anticipated next tack at step 14. This second entry, made during a pause, while the display of true course is visible, allows the calculator to resume its computation and display the compass course to steer on the next tack. If deviation is not entered at this point, the calculator will just continue to display true course.

The distance to be traveled to reach the lay line is displayed at step 17; this is followed by the time needed to arrive at the lay line and the time needed to reach the mark from the lay line. The bearing and distance from the vessel to the mark are obtained after entry at step 18 of the time that has elapsed since the previous position calculation was made. In the calculations for the first leg of a journey, the bearing and distance to the mark are entered at steps 15 and 16; for subsequent legs, no such entry is required, since the initial values for bearing and distance have been automatically replaced by those calculated and displayed in step 19, at the end of the sequence.

When a vessel comes about to the next tack, on the course previously calculated and displayed at step 14, the values for vessel speed, apparent-wind direction and speed, and angle of heel should be the same as before, if the wind has not changed. However, they must be re-entered in the calculations for the new leg even though they have not altered.

When the wind does change—so that, say, the vessel is lifted, and can sail in a direction closer to the mark—the helmsman will alter course to take advantage of the new conditions; once the situation has steadied, a new round of instrument readings should be taken, and all the steps of routine 3.1 should be repeated to supply updated values for speed and course made good, course to steer on the next tack, and the time and distance to the new lay line.

*The equations and program developed by the author for this routine are utilized in "Beating to Windward" in Hewlett-Packard's Navigation Pac 1.

Routine 3.1 (HP-67/97)

		Btm Dm	ΔT	Dmark Btmark
AW S Wa H→MW,Wt	PORT Cc Var De→Wm	STBD Cc Var De→Wm	St Dr→ SMG,CMG,Ct	D1 ΔT1 ΔT2

CRUISE SAILING

Step	Procedure	Input Data/Units	Keys	Output Data/Units
1	Load program—both sides			
2	Enter speed of apparent wind	knots	A	
3	Enter vessel speed	knots	A	
4	Enter angle of apparent wind (between 0 and 180 degrees, measured from bow on either side)†	DDD.d	A	
5	Enter angle of heel (port or starboard),	DD.d	A	
·	Calculate and display speed of modified true wind (*MW*),			knots
·	Tacking angle (*Wt*) relative to modified true wind, and continue at step 6 or 9, as appropriate			DDD.d
▶	If on *port tack,*			
6	Enter compass course*	DDD.d	B	
7	Enter variation (+E,−W), even if 0	DD.d	B	
8	Enter deviation (+E,−W), even if 0,	DD.d	B	
·	Calculate and display direction of modified true wind (*Wm*), and continue at step 12			DDD.d
▶	If on *starboard tack,*			
9	Enter compass course*	DDD.d	C	
10	Enter variation (+E,−W), even if 0	DD.d	C	
11	Enter deviation (+E,−W), even if 0,	DD.d	C	
·	Calculate and display direction of modified true wind (*Wm*)			DDD.d
12	Enter set of current, even if 0	DDD.d	D	
13	Enter drift of current, even if 0,	knots	D	

†To take leeway into account, enter sum of apparent-wind and leeway angles.
*Correct for leeway; see table 2.2.

162

Step	Procedure	Input Data/Units	Keys	Output Data/Units
•	Calculate and display speed made good on this tack,			knots
•	True course made good on this tack,			DDD.d
•	True course to steer on next tack			DDD.d
14	After displaying *Ct* (in step 13), display will alternately flash and pause. During a pause, enter compass deviation (+E, −W) for that course,			
•	Calculate and display compass course to steer on next tack,**			DDD.d
•	Speed made good on next tack,			knots
•	True course made good on next tack			DDD.d
15	Enter true bearing from start to mark or way point (only at beginning of journey, or if changed)	DDD.d	f c	
16	Enter distance from start to mark or way point (only at beginning of journey, or if changed)	naut. mi.	f c	
17	Calculate and display distance (*D1*) from start of this tack to lay line,		E	naut. mi.
•	Time (Δ*T1*) required from start of this tack to reach lay line,			H.MS
•	Time (Δ*T2*) required from start of next tack to reach mark or way point (on a course parallel to or along lay line)			H.MS
18	Enter time (Δ*T*) that has already elapsed on present tack, or that will have elapsed at a future time for which a prediction of position is desired (e.g., the time at which the vessel is expected to steer a new course, or come about to a new tack, following the completion of calculations)	H.MS	f d	
19	Calculate and display distance to mark or way point at end of interval specified,		f e	naut. mi.
•	True bearing to mark or way point at end of interval specified			DDD.d

For changes in course, speed, set, or drift, repeat steps 2–14 and 17–19. The interval used in step 18 should begin with the time of the change. If mark or way point is changed, a new problem begins, with bearing and distance to mark (steps 15–16) measured from present position to new destination.

**Uncorrect for leeway; see table 2.2.

163

The application of these procedures is illustrated in figure 3.7. In this instance, the vessel is on a beat to windward, starting at 0800 and lasting until 1021. During that period a number of wind shifts occur, and—as a result of the boat's changing position, and of time passing—considerable alterations in current as well.

Since a great deal of information is processed and kept in view, it is recommended that a form patterned after table 3.2 be designed and utilized. This table consists of a succession of "Enter" and "Display" columns, which enable the user to organize the data obtained from the vessel's instruments and from the calculator displays, and to see clearly what step in the calculations is next. It can also serve as a log of previous events. Its usefulness will be apparent as the beat to windward is followed step by step. Many of the figures in the table are given to two decimal places; this is done simply to prevent round-off error from creating misleading numerical results. In practice, most values are recorded to the nearest degree for bearing or course, and to the nearest tenth of a knot or mile for speed or distance.

The movements of the vessel are shown in figure 3.7. When it starts on the port tack at 0800, the values for wind, vessel speed, and angle of heel are read from the instruments, recorded on the 0800 line of the first "Enter" column in the table, and entered at $\boxed{A}$, in steps 2–5 of routine 3.1. The calculator then displays a modified-true-wind speed of 12.0 knots, and a tacking angle to the wind of 46.0 degrees. The compass course being sailed, and variation and deviation, are entered at $\boxed{B}$ because the vessel is on the port tack ($\boxed{C}$ would have been used on the starboard tack). These steps result in the display of the direction of the modified true wind as 20.0°.

Next, the set and drift of the current are entered, and the calculator displays speed and course made good on the present tack, and the true course to steer on the next tack—assuming that the vessel is to be sailed at the same angle to the modified true wind, and that wind conditions will not change.

Table 3.2

		ENTER				DISPLAY		ENTER			DIS.	ENTER	
Tack	Time	App. Wind Speed AW	Vessel Speed S	App. Wind Angle Wa	Angle of Heel H	Mod. True Wind Speed MW	Tacking Angle Wt	Compass Course Cc	Compass Var. Var	Compass Dev. Dev	Mod. True Wind Dir. Wm	Set of Current St	Drift of Current Dr
PORT	0800	15.62	4.8	33.31	12.0	12.0	46.0	77.0	11 W	0	20.0	160	2.0
PORT	0830	17.90	5.2	33.25	14.0	14.0	45.0	56.0	11 W	0	000.0	175	1.5
STBD	0910	15.53	4.7	33.51	12.0	12.0	46.0	315.0	11 W	0	350.0	180	0.5
PORT	0955	15.53	4.7	33.51	12.0	12.0	46.0	47.0	11 W	0	350.0	250	0.3
STBD	1000	13.13	4.2	34.31	10.0	10.0	48.0	328.0	11 W	0	5.0	250	0.3
PORT	1009	13.13	4.2	34.31	10.0	10.0	48.0	64.0	11 W	0	5.0	250	0.3
	1021	ARRIVE AT MARK											

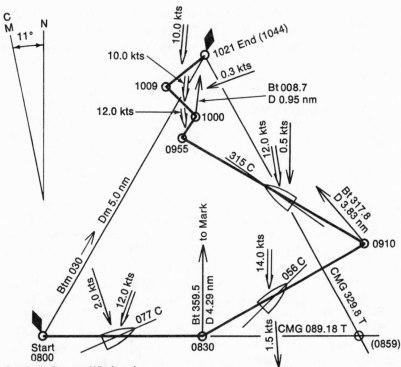

3.7. Cruising—Beat to Windward

The value of deviation for the next tack is then entered (even if it is equal to zero), and the compass course to steer on that tack, is displayed, along with the resulting speed and course to be made good.

The next step is the entry of the bearing and distance to the mark from the initial position. This is done only once, unless the destination is changed, or —after arrival at the original destination—a new one is selected. In the present

Cruising—Beat to Windward

DISPLAY			ENT.	DISPLAY			ENTER		DISPLAY			ENT.	DISPLAY	
Present Tack				Next Tack			Initial Bearing and Dist. to Mark		Dist. to Lay Line	Time to Lay Line	Time along Lay Line to Mark	Time on Preceding Tack	Dist. to Mark	Bearing to Mark
SMG1	CMG1	Ct2	Dev	Cc2	SMG2	CMG2	Btm	Dm	D1	ΔT1	ΔT2	ΔT	Dmark	Btmark
										h. m. s.	h. m. s.	m.		
5.07	89.18	334.0	0	345.0	2.82	329.8	30.0	5.0	4.98	0 58 58	1 44 55			
4.39	60.18	315.0	0	326.0	4.16	301.6			4.14	0 56 38	1 11 24	30	4.29	359.5
4.44	298.64	36.0	0	47.0	4.31	39.92			3.87	0 52 18	0 17 52	40	3.83	317.8
4.45	33.84	304.0	0	315.0	4.88	301.2			1.25	0 16 46	0 4 57	45	1.29	15.7
4.33	313.34	53.0	0	64.0	3.91	51.7			0.65	0 9 2	0 12 3	5	0.95	8.7
3.91	51.72								0.79	0 12 3	0	9	0.79	51.5

165

instance, the mark lies on a true bearing of 30.0° from the starting point, and is 5.0 nautical miles distant. When these values have been entered, the calculator displays the distance to the lay line (here, 4.98 nm), the time needed to reach the lay line (here, 58 minutes, 58 seconds), and the time needed to reach the mark along the lay line (here, 1 hour, 44 minutes, 55 seconds). This situation is illustrated in figure 3.7, where the lay line is shown to be at the end of a run along a course made good of 89.18°. If the vessel were to pursue this path, it would reach the lay line and come about at 0859, and move out on the starboard tack on a compass heading of 345°, making good 329.8° over the bottom, to reach the mark at 1044. This maneuver would result in a tacking angle of 46.0 degrees on each tack.

But the wind does not remain constant, and the helmsman must respond to changes. A shift at 0830 lifts the vessel and allows it to turn to port. When this has been done, the calculations must be updated at once. The procedure begins, at step 18, with entry of the amount of time that has passed since the start of the leg (here, 30 minutes); the calculator can then provide the new distance (4.29 nm) and true bearing (359.5°) to the mark. These values for elapsed time, distance, and bearing are the first to be recorded on the second line (marked 0830) of table 3.2. Once the vessel has steadied on its new heading —here, 56°C—the sequence of calculations is repeated, beginning with step 2. Measurements for wind, vessel speed, and angle of heel are obtained, and recorded in the 0830 line of the table, and fed to the calculator, which, in this instance, then shows that the modified true wind has picked up to 14.0 knots and the helmsman has steadied down to a tacking angle of 45.0 degrees relative to this wind. Compass course, variation, and deviation are next entered at B, once again, since the vessel is still on a port tack, and the calculator shows that the modified true wind is now at 000°, having shifted 20 degrees from its direction at 0800.

As before, values are entered in the table as they are obtained from the instruments and the calculator. The entries for the changed set and drift of current result in the display of the speed and course made good on the present tack, and the true course to steer on the next tack. Then, after the entry of the deviation on the next tack, the calculator provides the compass course to steer on that tack and the resulting speed and course made good. Steps 15 and 16 are omitted, since the values for distance and course to the mark found at 0830 remain in the calculator's memory. Next, pressing E yields the distance to the new lay line (4.14 nm), the time needed to reach it (56 minutes, 38 seconds), and the time needed to reach the mark along the new lay line (1 hour, 1 minute, 24 seconds).

At 0910, another wind shift occurs, and this time the helmsman elects to come onto the starboard tack. The lay line would have been reached at 0927; by turning onto the new tack he avoids the risk of overstanding, and begins to move closer to the mark. As the turn to starboard is being made, the time run on the present leg (from 0830 to 0910, or 40 minutes) is entered, and the vessel's position relative to the mark is calculated; the result being a distance of 3.83 nm and a true bearing of 317.8°. The calculation, display, and recording

166

of data then proceeds as before, except that since the vessel is now on the starboard tack, compass course, variation, and deviation are entered at $\boxed{\text{C}}$. Subsequently, the same procedures are repeated whenever the vessel's motion changes significantly—in response to shifts in wind or current, for example, or in order to avoid a hazard.

On the final leg of the journey, there is obviously no longer any need to obtain answers concerning the next tack. However, except—of course— for steps 15 and 16, all the steps of the routine must be executed, since they are necessary for calculation of the time of arrival. On the 1009 line of table 3.2, the distance to the "lay line"—in this case, the mark itself—is listed as 0.79 nm, and the time required to reach this point is 12 minutes, 3 seconds. Thus, the time of arrival will be 1021. The time needed to reach the mark along the lay line is displayed as zero because the mark is reached on the present tack.

An important feature of the HP-67 and HP-97 is the ability to record for future use the data stored in the memory. The procedure is simple. After step 19 of routine 3.1 has been performed, $\boxed{\text{f}}$ $\boxed{\text{W/DATA}}$ are pressed, and both sides of a magnetic data card are passed through the card handler. The calculator can then be turned off, with a consequent saving in power, until needed for the next sequence. Upon restarting, both this data card and the program card are inserted, and calculations can then be performed as if the unit had been running continuously. Of course, if the 12-volt power supply for the HP-67 (only) is in use, this procedure is unnecessary, since the calculator can then be left running without fear of discharging its batteries.

3.4.2 Cruising Navigation on the SR-52 Since the SR-52 has less sophisticated program and data capabilities than the HP-67 and HP-97, it requires three program cards and three routines (3.2, 3.3, and 3.4) to accomplish all that is done by routine 3.1, with one program card.* The procedures for the respective calculators differ in general arrangement, in the order in which data is entered, and in certain sign conventions (thus, in the sailing routines for the SR-52, variation and deviation are entered as positive if west, negative if east). However, the data required and the answers available—as recorded in table 3.2—are essentially the same, regardless of which calculator is employed. The user of the SR-52 may wish to change the order of the columns in his version of the table, so that they correspond to the sequence in which he enters data and obtains results. He may also wish to add columns for recording the distance from the start of the next tack to the mark, and the total time required to reach the mark from the start of the present tack, as displayed in steps 13 and 14 of routine 3.3.

The SR-52 is not equipped to record its stored data on a magnetic card. Therefore, it must be left running continuously.

*The programs for the SR-52 sailing routines (3.2–3.4, 3.11, and 3.19) were developed by Texas Instruments on the basis of equations supplied by the author. Except for routine 3.6, the SR-52 routines and programs presented in this chapter and in the corresponding section of the Appendix can also be found (the routines in slightly different form) in the Navigation Library (Program Manual NG1); some of them are also included in the manual on Marine Navigation for the TI-58 and TI-59.

Routine 3.2 (SR-52)

Var	Dr St		Cc;De→Wm	Dm Btm
Set Port	S	AW;H	Wa→Wt;MW	Set Stbd

MODIFIED WIND

Step	Procedure	Input Data/Units	Keys	Output Data/Units
	Before beginning, make sure D/R switch is set to D.			
1	Load program—both sides			
2	If on *port tack,* set for port calculations, and continue at step 4		A	
3	If on *starboard tack,* set for starboard calculations		E	
4	Enter variation ($+W, -E$),[1] even if 0	DD.d	2nd A'	
5	Enter drift of current, even if 0	knots	2nd B'	
6	Enter set of current, even if 0	DDD.d	2nd B'	
7	Enter distance from start to mark or way point (only at beginning of journey, or if changed)	naut. mi.	2nd E'	
8	Enter true bearing from start to mark or way point (only at beginning of journey, or if changed)	DDD.d	2nd E'	
9	Enter vessel speed	knots	B	
10	Enter speed of apparent wind	knots	C	
11	Enter angle of heel (port or starboard)	DD.d	RUN	
12	Enter angle of apparent wind (between 0 and 180 degrees, measured from bow on either side),†	DDD.d	D	
·	Calculate and display tacking angle (*Wt*) relative to modified true wind			DDD.d
13	Calculate and display speed of modified true wind (*MW*)		RUN	knots
14	Enter compass course*	DDD.d	2nd D'	
15	Enter deviation ($+W, -E$), even if 0,	DD.d	RUN	
·	Calculate and display direction of modified true wind (*Wm*)			DDD.d

For subsequent legs (following entry of present position in step 5 or 9 of routine 3.4), omit steps 7–8.

[1]The convention of using "plus" for westerly variation and deviation, and "minus" for easterly variation and deviation, conforms to the usage in the SR-52 and TI-59 navigation-program packages.
†To take leeway into account, enter sum of apparent-wind and leeway angles.
*Correct for leeway; see table 2.2.

Routine 3.3 (SR-52)

	PORT ΔT1 or 2 ;D1 or 2	ΔTmark	STBD ΔT2 or 1 ;D2 or 1	
PORT Ct;De→Cc	SMG;CMG		SMG;CMG	STBD Ct;De→Cc

SPEED MADE GOOD, COURSE MADE GOOD, TIME TO LAY LINE

Step	Procedure	Input Data/Units	Keys	Output Data/Units
1	After completion of routine 3.2 or 3.11, load program—both sides—and continue at step 2 or step 15, as appropriate			
▶	If on *port tack,*			
2	Calculate and display true course to steer on present tack		A	DDD.d
3	Enter deviation (+W, −E),[1] even if 0,	DD.d	RUN	
•	Calculate and display compass course to steer on present tack**			DDD.d
4	Calculate and display speed made good on present tack		B	knots
5	Calculate and display true course made good on present tack		RUN	DDD.d
6	Calculate and display true course to steer on next (starboard) tack		E	DDD.d
7	Enter deviation (+W, −E), even if 0,	DD.d	RUN	
•	Calculate and display compass course to steer on next (starboard) tack**			DDD.d
8	Calculate and display speed made good on next tack		D	knots
9	Calculate and display true course made good on next tack		RUN	DDD.d
10	Calculate and display time (Δ$T1$) required from start of this tack to reach lay line		2nd B'	H.MS
11	Calculate and display distance *(D1)* from start of this tack to lay line		RUN	naut. mi.
12	Calculate and display time (Δ$T2$) required from start of next tack to reach mark or way point (on a course parallel to or along lay line)		2nd D'	H.MS

[1]The convention of using "plus" for westerly variation and deviation, and "minus" for easterly variation and deviation, conforms to the usage in the SR-52 and TI-59 navigation-program packages.
**Un*correct for leeway; see table 2.2.

(CONTINUED)

Step	Procedure	Input Data/Units	Keys	Output Data/Units
13	Calculate and display distance (*D2*) from start of next tack to mark or way point		RUN	naut. mi.
14	Calculate and display total time (Δ *Tmark*) required from start of present tack to reach mark or way point		2nd C′	H.MS
▶	If on *starboard tack,*			
15	Calculate and display true course to steer on present tack		E	DDD.d
16	Enter deviation (+W,−E), even if 0,	DD.d	RUN	
·	Calculate and display compass course to steer on present tack**			DDD.d
17	Calculate and display speed made good on present tack		D	knots
18	Calculate and display true course made good on present tack		RUN	DDD.d
19	Calculate and display true course to steer on next (port) tack		A	DDD.d
20	Enter deviation (+W,−E), even if 0,	DD.d	RUN	
·	Calculate and display compass course to steer on next (port) tack**			DDD.d
21	Calculate and display speed made good on next (port) tack		B	knots
22	Calculate and display true course made good on next (port) tack		RUN	DDD.d
23	Calculate and display time (Δ *T1*) required from start of this tack to reach lay line		2nd D′	H.MS
24	Calculate and display distance (*D1*) from start of this tack to lay line		RUN	naut. mi.
25	Calculate and display time (Δ *T2*) required from start of next tack to reach mark or way point (on a course parallel to or along lay line)		2nd B′	H.MS
26	Calculate and display distance (*D2*) from start of next tack to mark or way point		RUN	naut. mi.
27	Calculate and display total time (Δ *Tmark*) required from start of present tack to reach mark or way point		2nd C′	H.MS

***Un*correct for leeway; see table 2.2.

170

Routine 3.4 (SR-52)

	PORT Dmark;Btmark	Update	STBD Dmark;Btmark	
	PORT ΔT		STBD ΔT	

DISTANCE AND BEARING TO MARK OR WAY POINT

Step	Procedure	Input Data/Units	Keys	Output Data/Units
1	After completion of routine 3.3 or 3.18, load program—both sides—and continue at step 2 or step 6, as appropriate			
▶	If on *port tack,*			
2	Enter time (ΔT) that has already elapsed on present tack, or that will have elapsed at a future time for which a prediction of position is desired (e.g., the time at which the vessel is expected to steer a new course or come about to a new tack following the completion of calculations)	H.MS	B	
3	Calculate and display distance to mark or way point at end of interval specified in step 2		2nd B'	naut. mi.
4	Calculate and display true bearing to mark or way point at end of interval specified in step 2		RUN	DDD.d
5	Update the calculator's memory of present position		2nd C'	
▶	If on *starboard tack,*			
6	Enter time (ΔT) that has already elapsed on present tack, or that will have elapsed at a future time for which a prediction of position is desired (e.g., the time at which the vessel is expected to steer a new course or come about to a new tack following the completion of calculations)	H.MS	D	
7	Calculate and display distance to mark or way point at end of interval specified in step 6		2nd D'	naut. mi.
8	Calculate and display true bearing to mark or way point at end of interval specified in step 6		RUN	DDD.d
9	Update the calculator's memory of present position		2nd C'	

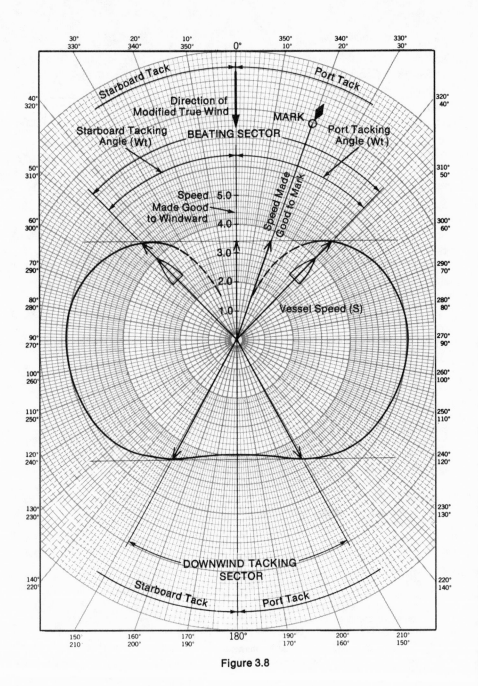

Figure 3.8

3.5 Optimum Speed to Windward—Racing

The calculator is especially useful in racing because in addition to performing the navigation functions described in the preceding sections, it can—if given the necessary data concerning wind speed and direction (taken from the vessel's instruments)—select the tacking angle that will maximize a vessel's speed made good to windward, and then display the values for the speed and direction of the apparent wind that should be achieved by the helmsman sailing with this tacking angle.

The calculator can perform this function because of its ability to store data concerning the speed through the water of a vessel sailing (with optimum trim and sheeting) at various angles to the wind and encountering various wind speeds. This data is obtained from a set of polar performance curves for the vessel, of the sort shown in figures 3.8 and 3.9.

In figure 3.8, the vessel's speed vector (S)—represented in each instance as a length marked off on a radius drawn from the center—is plotted for different tacking angles *(Wt)* to the modified true wind. The axis of the modified true wind is shown running from 000° to 180°, with the wind coming from 000°.

A vessel cannot sail directly into the wind—that is, in the sector extending about 30 degrees to either side of the wind, as indicated by the dotted lines in the figure; it then pinches for perhaps another 10 degrees, until it reaches a tacking angle of approximately 35 to 40 degrees. Tacking becomes unnecessary if the mark lies more than 45 to 50 degrees off the wind, since it can be reached by sailing directly. However, tacking downwind (discussed in detail in sections 3.6 and 3.6.4–3.6.6) may be desirable under certain circumstances when the mark lies within about 10–30 degrees of dead downwind.

When beating to windward—sailing to a mark that lies within the beating sector, up to 40 or 50 degrees to port or starboard of the modified true wind—a series of tacks will be used to reach the mark. On the chart, the speed made good to windward is shown as the projection on the wind axis of the tacking vessel's speed vector (S). In this example, a vessel on either tack at 45 degrees off the wind has a speed through the water of 4.8 knots, and is moving toward the wind at a speed of 3.4 knots. From the curve, it is evident that sailing at this angle to the wind results in a vector of maximum length for speed made good to windward. A vessel sailing closer to the wind would move more slowly. Sailing farther from the wind it would have increased speed through the water, but its speed in the direction of the wind would be reduced. Hence, in this instance 45 degrees is the optimum tacking angle, at which the vessel is moving as fast as it can toward the wind, and therefore toward any mark that lies within the beating sector.

The curve shown in figure 3.8 defines the vessel's speed performance for a *single* value of modified true wind—in this case, a speed of 10.0 knots. Figure 3.9 shows a family of curves for a particular vessel, for wind speeds of 4.0, 10.0, 16.0, and 22.0 knots. A line has been drawn from curve to curve joining the points of optimum speed to windward, which fall at tacking angles of 49

MW	So	Wto
4.0 kts	2.8 kts	49°
10.0	4.6	45
16.0	5.8	43
22.0	6.7	42.5

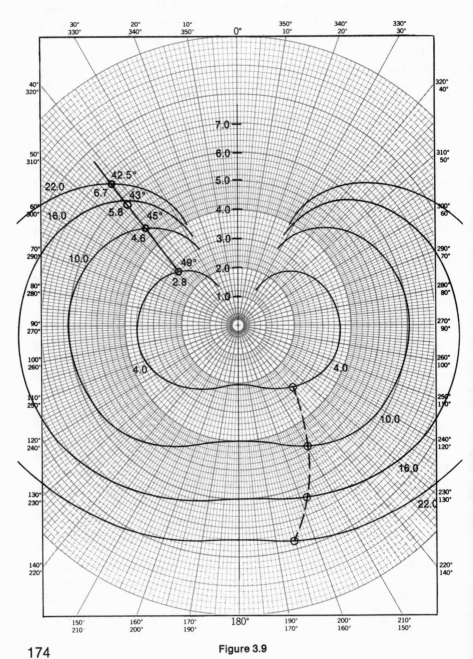

Figure 3.9

degrees, 45 degrees, 43 degrees, and 42.5 degrees. These points have values of 2.8, 4.6, 5.8, and 6.7 knots, respectively. Information of this sort provides the basis for two new curves (figure 3.10), showing optimum speed to windward *(So)* and optimum tacking angle *(Wto)*, each plotted with respect to the speed of the modified true wind. These curves can be stored in a programmable calculator, and then utilized in the calculation of the optimum vessel speed and tacking angle for a particular wind.

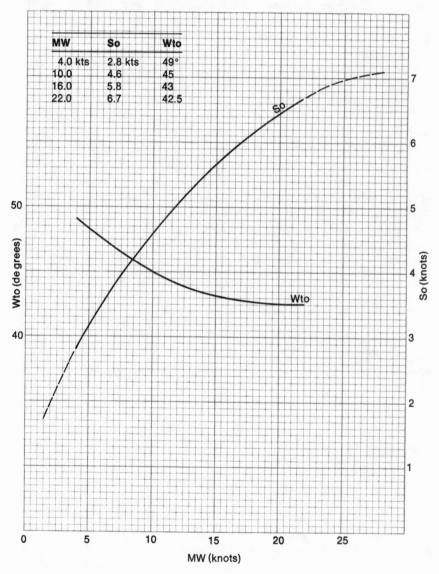

MW	So	Wto
4.0 kts	2.8 kts	49°
10.0	4.6	45
16.0	5.8	43
22.0	6.7	42.5

Figure 3.10. .

175

Obtaining the information required for this purpose involves firsthand observation aboard the vessel itself. The first step is to record—simultaneously, or nearly so—the speed and direction of the apparent wind, and the corresponding speed and angle of heel of the vessel, under a variety of circumstances. Data should be collected for winds that come from different directions and that have various speeds—ranging from those as light as 3 or 4 knots to those as heavy as are likely to be encountered when sailing under normal conditions. The readings should be taken when the vessel has been trimmed to make the fastest possible speed through the water for the heading in question, and is steady on course, so that the data obtained will represent optimum sailing conditions.

Ideally, during a time of constant wind, the vessel should be pointed and trimmed on a series of headings at intervals of approximately 5 degrees. But if the wind changes, readings can of course be taken for the new conditions, since observations under many different circumstances are required. If several combinations of sails are likely to be used (e.g., a variety of jibs, with and without spinnaker), separate data will have to be collected, and a separate set of polar curves prepared, for each suit of sails. In recording the data obtained on board the vessel, organized as shown in table 3.3, care should be taken to separate port-tack and starboard-tack values, since the calculations for MW and Wt cannot distinguish between the two tacks. Values of Wt calculated from data observed on the port tack will be entered in the last column of table 3.3 as calculated; values of Wt based on data observed on the starboard tack will have to be increased by 180 degrees before being listed in the table.

Table 3.3   Wind Speed and Tacking Angle

| Tack | Apparent Wind | | Vessel Speed S | Angle of Heel H | Speed of Modified True Wind MW | Tacking Angle Wt |
| | Speed AW | Angle Wa (with A added) | | | | |
	Data Collected on Board				Calculated Values	
Port						Port
Starboard						Starboard (+180°)

Any needed correction for leeway should be made just prior to entering the data in table 3.3. As figure 3.4 makes evident, the measurement of apparent wind will read low by the amount of leeway angle present at the time of the reading. This is true for both port and starboard tacks. Therefore, before a value for apparent-wind angle (Wa) is entered in the table, the correction for leeway (A) should be *added* to it.

176

Routine 3.5 (HP-67/97)

MW				
AW	S	Wa	H→MW,Wt	MWnom→Sc

POLAR PERFORMANCE CURVES

Step	Procedure	Input Data/Units	Keys	Output Data/Units
1	Load program—both sides			

For each line of data recorded in table 3.3, perform steps 2–5; then continue according to instructions preceding step 6.

Step	Procedure	Input Data/Units	Keys	Output Data/Units
2	Enter speed of apparent wind	knots	A	
3	Enter vessel speed	knots	B	
4	Enter angle of apparent wind (between 0 and 180 degrees, measured from bow on either side)†	DDD.d	C	
5	Enter angle of heel (port or starboard),	DD.d	D	
·	Calculate and display speed of modified true wind (*MW*),			knots
·	Tacking angle (*Wt*) relative to modified true wind, and record both as indicated in table 3.3			DDD.d

After rearranging calculated data as shown in table 3.4, and after choosing the nominal value of modified true wind for each of the polar curves to be constructed, proceed as follows (steps 6–8) for each value of speed in the table:

Step	Procedure	Input Data/Units	Keys	Output Data/Units
6	Enter value of vessel speed	knots	B	
7	Enter value of modified-true-wind speed (*MW*) adjacent (in table 3.4) to value of *S* entered in step 6	knots	f a	
8	Enter nominal value of *MW* that labels the column in table 3.4 in which the values entered in steps 6 and 7 are located,	knots	E	
·	Calculate and display corrected value of vessel speed (*Sc*), and record as indicated in table 3.4, for use in plotting polar curve for nominal *MW*			knots

†To take leeway into account, enter sum of apparent-wind and leeway angles.

Routine 3.6 (SR-52)

MW	MWnom→Sc			
S	AW	H	Wa→Wt	MW

POLAR PERFORMANCE CURVES

Step	Procedure	Input Data/Units	Keys	Output Data/Units
	Before beginning, make sure D/R switch is set to D.			
1	Load program—both sides			
	For each line of data recorded in table 3.3, perform steps 2–5; then continue according to instructions preceding step 6.			
2	Enter vessel speed	knots	A	
3	Enter speed of apparent wind	knots	B	
4	Enter angle of heel (port or starboard)	DD.d	C	
5	Enter angle of apparent wind (between 0 and 180 degrees, measured from bow on either side),†	DDD.d	D	
·	Calculate and display tacking angle (*Wt*) relative to modified true wind			DDD.d
6	Calculate and display speed of modified true wind (*MW*), and record both as indicated in table 3.3		E	knots
	After rearranging calculated data as shown in table 3.4, and after choosing the nominal value of modified true wind for each of the polar curves to be constructed, proceed as follows (steps 7–9) for each value of vessel speed in the table:			
7	Enter value of vessel speed	knots	A	
8	Enter value of modified-true-wind speed (*MW*) adjacent (in table 3.4) to value of *S* entered in step 7	knots	2nd A'	
9	Enter nominal value of *MW* that labels the column in table 3.4 in which the values entered in steps 7 and 8 are located,	knots	2nd B'	
·	Calculate and display corrected value of vessel speed (*Sc*), and record as indicated in table 3.4, for use in plotting polar curve for nominal *MW*			knots

†To take leeway into account, enter sum of apparent-wind and leeway angles.

178

Construction of the polar performance curves is aided by use of routine 3.5 for the HP-67 and HP-97, or routine 3.6 for the SR-52. In steps 1–5 of routine 3.5, and steps 1–6 of routine 3.6, the data assembled in table 3.3 is entered, and corresponding values for speed of the modified true wind *(MW)* and tacking angle *(Wt)* are obtained; these are recorded in the table. Next, the answers are rearranged as shown in table 3.4. Here, 2, 4, 8, 12, 16, and 22 knots have been chosen as the nominal, or label, values for a series of polar curves to be constructed in the style of figure 3.9. Three pieces of data from each line in table 3.3 are used—vessel speed *(S)*, speed of the modified true wind *(MW)*, and tacking angle *(Wt)*. The value of *S* is paired with the value of *MW* calculated for a particular *Wt*. Each value of *MW* selected for a column lies within the range specified at the head of that column, and the values of *S* and *MW* are arranged in ascending order of *Wt*. The corrected vessel speed *(Sc)* is then obtained by using routine 3.5 (steps 6–8) for the HP-67 and HP-97, or routine 3.6 (steps 7–9) for the SR-52. The input for this procedure consists of vessel speed, the actual speed of the modified true wind, and the nominal, or label, speed of the modified true wind, as shown in the top row of table 3.4. The corresponding corrected vessel speed *(Sc)* displayed by the calculator should in each instance be entered in the appropriate column, next to the values of *S* and *MW* from which it was calculated.

Table 3.4   Polar Performance Curves

minal MW	2			4			8			12			16			22		
ual MW	1.5–2.7			2.7–6.0			6.0–10.0			10.0–14.0			14.0–19.0			19.0–25.0		
Wt	S	MW	Sc	S	MW	Sc	S	MW	Sc	S	MW	Sc	S	MW	Sc	S	MW	Sc

If there are appreciable gaps in the table, the data is incomplete. For example, there should be good coverage of tacking angles in the beating sectors, from 35 to 50 degrees and from 310 to 325 degrees, as well as in the downwind tacking sector, from about 140 to 220 degrees. However, it is not necessary to obtain a value of *MW* for every nominal wind speed at every tacking angle.

When the table is complete, the figures obtained for *Wt* and *Sc* can be used in the preparation of a series of polar curves, one for each of the nominal values of *MW*. The curves should be plotted on a single sheet of polar graph paper.

179

For each value of *Wt* a radius is drawn from the center of the graph, the angle being measured clockwise through 360 degrees. Points at length *Sc* from the center are placed, as appropriate, on each radius, and all the points for one nominal value of *MW* are joined to make a smooth polar curve.

Table 3.5   Optimum Sailing to Windward

Nominal Speed of the Modified True Wind MW (x)	Optimum Speed to Windward So (y)	Optimum Tacking Angle Wto (y)

The next step is to locate and join the points of optimum speed to windward on the several curves, as shown in figure 3.9, and to tabulate the values of these points (table 3.5). This information serves as the basis for two curves, like those in figure 3.10, plotting *So* with respect to *MW,* and plotting *Wto* with respect to *MW.* The curves (which need not actually be drawn) are each stored in the form of the equation $y=ax^b$. The "Power" segment of routine 3.7 for the HP-67 and HP-97, and routine 3.8 for the SR-52, are used to obtain the necessary curve-fitting coefficients *(a)* and exponents *(b)* for the calculation of *So* and *Wto.* *

---

*Preprogrammed magnetic cards that can be employed for these routines are supplied by the manufacturers. For the HP-67 or HP-97, the "Curve Fitting" program, included in the Standard Pac, is used for the various segments of routine 3.7. It is reproduced in this volume by permission of Hewlett-Packard. For the SR-52 the equivalent material is in the Navigation Library (Program Manual NG1), and is reproduced by permission of Texas Instruments; the "Power Curve Fit" program in the Navigation Library corresponds to routine 3.8, the "Exponential Curve Fit" program to routine 3.12, and the "Logarithmic Curve Fit" program to routine 3.13.

Routine 3.7 (HP-67/97)

P?	LIN?	EXP?	LOG?	PWR?
$x_i \uparrow y_i(+)$	$x_i \uparrow y_i(-)$	$\rightarrow r^2, a, b$	$y \rightarrow \hat{x}$	$x \rightarrow \hat{y}$

CURVE FITTING

Step	Procedure	Input Data/Units	Keys	Output Data/Units
1	Load program—both sides			
2	For HP-97, select printing mode		f a	
	Optimum Speed to Windward (*So*)			
3	After completion of steps 1–2, select type of curve fitting—use "Power"		f e	

For each value of modified-true-wind speed (*MW*) in table 3.5, starting with the lowest, perform steps 4–5; then continue at step 6.

Step	Procedure	Input Data/Units	Keys	Output Data/Units
4	Enter *MW* that labels one of the polar performance curves	knots	ENTER	
5	Enter corresponding vessel speed at point of maximum speed to windward (*So*)	knots	A	
6	Set four decimal places		DSP 4	
7	Calculate and display coefficient of correlation (should be between 0.8 and 1.0),		C	n.nnnn
·	Coefficient (*a*) of curve-fitting equation $So = aMW^b$,			±n.nnnn
·	Exponent (*b*) of curve-fitting equation $So = aMW^b$			±n.nnnn

The values obtained for *a* and *b* are incorporated into the program for routine 3.9, in accordance with the instructions in the Appendix.

Optimum Tacking Angle While Beating to Windward (*Wto*)

Step	Procedure	Input Data/Units	Keys	Output Data/Units
8	After completion of steps 1–2, select type of curve fitting—use "Power"		f e	

For each value of modified-true-wind speed (*MW*) in table 3.5, starting with the lowest, perform steps 9–10; then continue at step 11.

Step	Procedure	Input Data/Units	Keys	Output Data/Units
9	Enter *MW* that labels one of the polar performance curves	knots	ENTER	

(CONTINUED)

Step	Procedure	Input Data/Units	Keys	Output Data/Units
10	Enter corresponding tacking angle at point of maximum speed to windward (*Wto*)	DDD.d	A	
11	Set four decimal places		DSP 4	
12	Calculate and display coefficient of correlation (should be between 0.8 and 1.0),		C	n.nnnn
·	Coefficient (*a*) of curve-fitting equation $Wto = aMW^b$,			±n.nnnn
·	Exponent (*b*) of curve-fitting equation $Wto = aMW^b$			±n.nnnn

The values obtained for *a* and *b* are incorporated into the program for routine 3.9, in accordance with the instructions in the Appendix.

Due-Downwind Speed (*Sd*)

Step	Procedure	Input Data/Units	Keys	Output Data/Units
13	After completion of steps 1–2, select type of curve fitting—use "Power"		f e	

For each value of modified-true-wind speed (*MW*), starting with the lowest, perform steps 14–15; then continue at step 16.

Step	Procedure	Input Data/Units	Keys	Output Data/Units
14	Enter *MW* that labels one of the polar performance curves	knots	ENTER	
15	Enter corresponding vessel speed due downwind, at a tacking angle of 180 degrees (*Sd*)	knots	A	
16	Set four decimal places		DSP 4	
17	Calculate and display coefficient of correlation (should be between 0.8 and 1.0),		C	n.nnnn
·	Coefficient (*a*) of curve-fitting equation $Sd = aMW^b$,			±n.nnnn
·	Exponent (*b*) of curve-fitting equation $Sd = aMW^b$			±n.nnnn

The values obtained for *a* and *b* are incorporated into the program for routine 3.16, in accordance with the instructions in the Appendix.

To calculate values of *Sd* for use in obtaining the ratio $\Delta S/Sd$, proceed as follows (step 18) for each of four values of *MW* in the range of 4–10 knots, starting with the lowest:

Step	Procedure	Input Data/Units	Keys	Output Data/Units
18	Enter *MW*,	knots	D	
·	Calculate and display corresponding *Sd*			knots

Optimum Downwind Tacking Speed (*Sdo*)

Step	Procedure	Input Data/Units	Keys	Output Data/Units
19	After completion of steps 1–2, select type of curve fitting—use "Power"		f e	

182

Step	Procedure	Input Data/Units	Keys	Output Data/Units
	For each value of modified-true-wind speed (*MW*), starting with the lowest, perform steps 20–21; then continue at step 22.			
20	Enter *MW* that labels one of the polar performance curves	knots	ENTER	
21	Enter corresponding vessel speed at optimum downwind tacking angle (*Sdo*)	knots	A	
22	Set four decimal places		DSP 4	
23	Calculate and display coefficient of correlation (should be between 0.8 and 1.0),		C	n.nnnn
·	Coefficient (*a*) of curve-fitting equation $Sdo = aMW^b$,			±n.nnnn
·	Exponent (*b*) of curve-fitting equation $Sdo = aMW^b$			±n.nnnn

The values obtained for *a* and *b* are incorporated into the program for routine 3.18, in accordance with the instructions in the Appendix.

To calculate values of *Sdo* for use in obtaining the ratio $\Delta S/Sd$, proceed as follows (step 24) for each of four values of *MW* in the range of 4–10 knots, starting with the lowest:

Step	Procedure	Input Data/Units	Keys	Output Data/Units
24	Enter *MW*,	knots	D	
·	Calculate and display corresponding *Sdo*			knots

Downwind Tacking Sector ($\Delta W/2$)

Step	Procedure	Input Data/Units	Keys	Output Data/Units
25	After completion of steps 1–2, select type of curve fitting—use "Exponential"		f c	

For each value of modified-true-wind speed (*MW*), starting with the lowest and continuing to a maximum of 16 knots, perform steps 26–27; then continue at step 28.

Step	Procedure	Input Data/Units	Keys	Output Data/Units
26	Enter *MW* that labels one of the polar performance curves	knots	ENTER	
27	Enter corresponding value for $\Delta W/2$— the angular interval between due downwind and the heading that produces optimum speed downwind	DDD.d	A	
28	Set four decimal places		DSP 4	
29	Calculate and display coefficient of correlation (should be between 0.8 and 1.0),		C	n.nnnn
·	Coefficient (*a*) of curve-fitting equation $\Delta W/2 = ae^{bMW}$,			±n.nnnn
·	Exponent (*b*) of curve-fitting equation $\Delta W/2 = ae^{bMW}$			±n.nnnn

The values obtained for *a* and *b* are incorporated into the programs for routines 3.16 and 3.18, in accordance with the instructions in the Appendix.

(CONTINUED)

Ratio $\Delta S/Sd$

Data for this sequence consists of values for $\Delta S/Sd$ for four values of MW in the range of 4–10 knots. As explained in the text, the method of obtaining this data is as follows: First, select four values of modified-true-wind speed (MW) in the range of 4–10 knots. Next, for each of the selected wind speeds calculate the corresponding due-downwind vessel speed (Sd) and optimum downwind tacking speed (Sdo), by means of steps 13–18 and steps 19–24 of this routine. Then, for each of the selected wind speeds subtract Sd from Sdo to obtain ΔS. And finally, for each of the selected wind speeds divide ΔS by Sd to obtain $\Delta S/Sd$.

Step	Procedure	Input Data/Units	Keys	Output Data/Units
30	After preparation of the data and completion of steps 1–2, select type of curve fitting—use "Logarithmic"		f d	

For each value of MW, starting with the lowest, perform steps 31–32; then continue at step 33.

Step	Procedure	Input Data/Units	Keys	Output Data/Units
31	Enter MW	knots	ENTER	
32	Enter corresponding value for $\Delta S/Sd$	n.nnnn	A	
33	Set four decimal places		DSP 4	
34	Calculate and display coefficient of correlation (should be between 0.8 and 1.0),		C	n.nnnn
·	Constant term (a) of curve-fitting equation $\Delta S/Sd=a+b\ln MW$,			$\pm$n.nnnn
·	Coefficient of natural logarithm term (b) of curve-fitting equation $\Delta S/Sd=a+b\ln MW$			$\pm$n.nnnn

The values obtained for a and b are incorporated into the program for routine 3.16, in accordance with the instructions in the Appendix.

Routine 3.8 (SR-52)

Delete	y→x′	x→y′	b	
Initialize	x_i	y_i	→a	→r²

POWER CURVE FIT

Step	Procedure	Input Data/Units	Keys	Output Data/Units
	Before beginning, make sure D/R switch is set to D.			
1	Load program—both sides			
2	Initialize		A	
3	Set four decimal places		2nd fix 4	
	Optimum Speed to Windward (So)			

Complete steps 1–3; then, for each value of modified-true-wind speed (MW) in table 3.5, starting with the lowest, perform steps 4–5. Then continue at step 6.

Step	Procedure	Input Data/Units	Keys	Output Data/Units
4	Enter MW that labels one of the polar performance curves	knots	B	
5	Enter corresponding vessel speed at point of maximum speed to windward (So)	knots	C	
6	Calculate and display coefficient (a) of curve-fitting equation $So=aMW^b$		D	±n.nnnn
7	Calculate and display exponent (b) of curve-fitting equation $So=aMW^b$		2nd D′	±n.nnnn
8	Calculate and display coefficient of correlation (should be between 0.8 and 1.0)		E	n.nnnn

The values obtained for *a* and *b* are incorporated into the program for routine 3.11, in accordance with the instructions in the Appendix.

Optimum Tacking Angle While Beating to
   Windward (Wto)

Complete steps 1–3; then, for each value of modified-true-wind speed (MW) in table 3.5, starting with the lowest, perform steps 9–10. Then continue at step 11.

Step	Procedure	Input Data/Units	Keys	Output Data/Units
9	Enter MW that labels one of the polar performance curves	knots	B	
10	Enter corresponding tacking angle at point of maximum speed to windward (Wto)	DDD.d	C	

(CONTINUED)

185

Step	Procedure	Input Data/Units	Keys	Output Data/Units
11	Calculate and display coefficient (a) of curve-fitting equation $Wto=aMW^b$		D	$\pm$n.nnnn
12	Calculate and display exponent (b) of curve-fitting equation $Wto=aMW^b$		2nd D'	$\pm$n.nnnn
13	Calculate and display coefficient of correlation (should be between 0.8 and 1.0)		E	n.nnnn

The values obtained for a and b are incorporated into the program for routine 3.11, in accordance with the instructions in the Appendix.

Due-Downwind Speed (Sd)

Complete steps 1–3; then, for each value of modified-true-wind speed (MW), starting with the lowest, perform steps 14–15. Then continue at step 16.

Step	Procedure	Input Data/Units	Keys	Output Data/Units
14	Enter MW that labels one of the polar performance curves	knots	B	
15	Enter corresponding vessel speed due downwind, at a tacking angle of 180 degrees (Sd)	knots	C	
16	Calculate and display coefficient (a) of curve-fitting equation $Sd=aMW^b$		D	$\pm$n.nnnn
17	Calculate and display exponent (b) of curve-fitting equation $Sd=aMW^b$		2nd D'	$\pm$n.nnnn
18	Calculate and display coefficient of correlation (should be between 0.8 and 1.0)		E	n.nnnn

The values obtained for a and b are incorporated into the program for routine 3.11, in accordance with the instructions in the Appendix.

To calculate values of Sd for use in obtaining the ratio $\Delta S/Sd$, proceed as follows (step 19) for each of four values of MW in the range of 4–10 knots, starting with the lowest:

Step	Procedure	Input Data/Units	Keys	Output Data/Units
19	Enter MW,	knots	2nd C'	
·	Calculate and display corresponding Sd			knots

Optimum Downwind Tacking Speed (Sdo)

Complete steps 1–3; then, for each value of modified-true-wind speed (MW), starting with the lowest, perform steps 20–21. Then continue at step 22.

Step	Procedure	Input Data/Units	Keys	Output Data/Units
20	Enter MW that labels one of the polar performance curves	knots	B	
21	Enter corresponding vessel speed at optimum downwind tacking angle (Sdo)	knots	C	
22	Calculate and display coefficient (a) of curve-fitting equation $Sdo=aMW^b$		D	$\pm$n.nnnn
23	Calculate and display exponent (b) of curve-fitting equation $Sdo=aMW^b$		2nd D'	$\pm$n.nnnn

Step	Procedure	Input Data/Units	Keys	Output Data/Units
24	Calculate and display coefficient of correlation (should be between 0.8 and 1.0)		E	n.nnnn

The values obtained for *a* and *b* are incorporated into the program for routine 3.11, in accordance with the instructions in the Appendix.

To calculate values of *Sdo* for use in obtaining the ratio $\Delta S/Sd$, proceed as follows (step 25) for each of four values of *MW* in the range of 4–10 knots, starting with the lowest:

Step	Procedure	Input Data/Units	Keys	Output Data/Units
25	Enter *MW,*	knots	2nd C'	
·	Calculate and display corresponding *Sdo*			knots

When the curve-fitting coefficients have been calculated, they are incorporated into the programs used in routine 3.9 for the HP-67 and HP-97, and routine 3.11 for the SR-52, as shown by the instructions for these programs in the Appendix. It is then possible to determine, for a particular suit of sails, the optimum course—resulting in minimum sailing time at the wind speed in question.

For the curves shown in figure 3.10, the equations are as follows:

$$So = 1.3836\ MW^{0.5147}$$
$$Wto = 55.0842\ MW^{-0.0865}$$

These figures may be used in a test program, as explained in the text accompanying the listings in the Appendix. But since the coefficients and exponents are different for each vessel, these should be used *only* for practice.

3.5.1 Optimum Sailing on the HP-67 and HP-97

A beat to windward during a race is described in this section. The initial data provided by the vessel's instruments serves as the basis for calculating the speed and direction of the modified true wind, in steps 1–8 (port tack) or steps 1–5 and 9–11 (starboard tack) of routine 3.9. The vessel need *not* be sailing with optimum trim when this data is obtained. The values for the modified true wind are stored by the calculator and used as input for the calculation of the optimum vessel speed, and the optimum speed and direction of the apparent wind, displayed in steps 12–14. For a vessel on the port tack, steps 15–16 then provide the compass course to steer to attain the optimum tacking angle; for a vessel on the starboard tack, steps 17–18 provide the same information. When a vessel is on that heading and is properly trimmed, the speed of the vessel and the speed and direction of the apparent wind, as shown on the helmsman's instruments, should be the same as the optimum values just calculated.

Routine 3.9 (HP-67/97)

Wao	PORT Cmo De→Cco	STBD Cmo De→Cco		
AW S Wa H→MW,Wt	PORT Cc Var De→Wm	STBD Cc Var De→Wm	So	AWo

BEATING TO WINDWARD—OPTIMUM COURSE AND SPEED

Step	Procedure	Input Data/Units	Keys	Output Data/Units
1	Load program—both sides			
2	Enter speed of apparent wind	knots	A	
3	Enter vessel speed	knots	A	
4	Enter angle of apparent wind (between 0 and 180 degrees, measured from bow on either side)†	DDD.d	A	
5	Enter angle of heel (port or starboard),	DD.d	A	
•	Calculate and display speed of modified true wind (MW),			knots
•	Tacking angle (Wt) relative to modified true wind, and continue at step 6 or 9, as appropriate			DDD.d
▶	If on *port tack*,			
6	Enter compass course*	DDD.d	B	
7	Enter variation (+E,−W), even if 0	DD.d	B	
8	Enter deviation (+E,−W), even if 0,	DD.d	B	
•	Calculate and display direction of modified true wind (Wm), and continue at step 12			DDD.d
▶	If on *starboard tack*,			
9	Enter compass course*	DDD.d	C	
10	Enter variation (+E,−W), even if 0	DD.d	C	
11	Enter deviation (+E,−W), even if 0,	DD.d	C	
•	Calculate and display direction of modified true wind (Wm)			DDD.d
12	Calculate and display optimum vessel speed to windward (So)		D	knots
13	Calculate and display optimum speed of apparent wind (AWo)		E	knots

†To take leeway into account, enter sum of apparent-wind and leeway angles.
*Correct for leeway; see table 2.2.

189

Step	Procedure	Input Data/Units	Keys	Output Data/Units
14	Calculate and display optimum angle of apparent wind (*Wao*),‡ and continue at step 15 or 17, as appropriate		f a	DDD.d
▶	If on *port tack*,			
15	Calculate and display optimum magnetic course to steer		f b	DDD.d
16	Enter deviation (+E, −W), even if 0,	DD.d	f b	
·	Calculate and display optimum compass course to steer**			DDD.d
▶	If on *starboard tack*,			
17	Calculate and display optimum magnetic course to steer		f c	DDD.d
18	Enter deviation (+E, −W), even if 0,	DD.d	f c	
·	Calculate and display optimum compass course to steer**			DDD.d

‡To take leeway into account, subtract the leeway angle.
**Uncorrect for leeway; see table 2.2.

If the wind changes, the altered data provided by the vessel's instruments must be used for recalculation of the speed and direction of the modified true wind. The subsequent sequence of calculations should be repeated as well, since the optimum values for vessel speed and for speed and direction of the apparent wind will also have changed.

Table 3

		ENTER				DISPLAY		ENTER			DISPLAY					ENT.	DIS.
Tack	Time	App. Wind Speed	Vessel Speed	App. Wind Angle	Angle of Heel	Mod. True Wind Speed	Tacking Angle	Compass Course	Compass Var.	Compass Dev.	Mod. True Wind Dir.	Opt. Vessel Speed	Opt. App. Wind Speed	Opt. App. Wind Angle	Opt. Mag. Course	Compass Dev.	Opt. Compass Course
		AW	S	Wa	H	MW	Wt	Cc	Var	Dev	Wm	So	AWo	Wao	Cmo	Dev	Cc
PORT	0800	14.38	4.6	31.97	9.0	10.81	45.0	87.0	14W	0	28.0	4.71	14.48	31.62	86.84	0	86.
STBD	0806	13.24	4.5	32.65	8.0	9.79	47.0	12.0	14W	0	45.0	4.48	13.30	31.43	13.78	0	13.
PORT	0848	15.36	4.7	31.78	10.0	11.69	44.0	80.0	14W	0	22.0	4.91	15.51	31.77	80.53	0	80.
PORT	0855	11.39	3.8	31.38	7.0	8.41	45.0	68.0	14W	0	9.0	4.14	11.65	31.09	68.82	0	68.
STBD	0905	11.84	3.9	31.56	8.0	8.79	45.0	336.6	14W	0	7.6	4.23	12.10	31.19	335.95	0	335.
PORT	0935	11.84	3.9	31.56	8.0	8.79	45.0	66.6	14W	0	7.6	4.23	12.10	31.19	67.25	0	67.
	0940	ARRIVE AT MARK															

190

Table 3.6, like table 3.2, for cruising, enables one to organize input data and to place calculated results in their proper order. The "Enter" columns are used for listing data obtained from the vessel's instruments and charts; the "Display" columns are used for the calculated results. Once again, many of the values are given to two decimal places—although these would probably not be used in practice—in order to eliminate misleading numerical results arising from round-off errors.

Deviation must be entered where called for, even if it is zero. The presence of leeway must of course be taken into account where necessary, as discussed in section 3.3.

The vessel movements, winds, and currents during this hypothetical leg of a race are illustrated in figure 3.11. The vessel starts the windward leg on the port tack at 0800. The entry of values for wind, vessel speed, and angle of heel taken at or just before this time results in the display of a modified-true-wind speed of 10.81 knots and a tacking angle of 45.0 degrees. Compass course, variation, and deviation are then entered, and the calculator displays not only the direction of the modified true wind (28.0°) but also the optimum values for the speed of the vessel (4.71 knots), the speed and direction of the apparent wind (14.48 knots and 31.62 degrees), and the magnetic course to steer (86.84°). Re-entry of deviation, still zero, yields the optimum compass course (86.84°).

These results show that the vessel is sailing on virtually its optimum heading; the initial speed through the water of 4.6 knots can be increased to 4.71 for a heading shift of less than a half degree (assuming that wind conditions remain stable). If the vessel had been sailing farther away from this optimum

acing—Beat to Windward

ENTER	DISPLAY			ENT.	DISPLAY			ENTER	DISPLAY			ENT.	DISPLAY	
Drift of Current	Present Tack				Next Tack			Initial Bearing and Dist. to Mark	Dist. to Lay Line	Time to Lay Line	Time along Lay Line to Mark	Time on Preceding Tack	Dist. to Mark	Bearing to Mark
Dr	SMG1	CMG1	Ct2	Dev	Cc2	SMG2	CMG2	Btm Dm	D1	ΔT1	ΔT2	ΔT	Dmark	Btmark
										h. m. s.	h. m. s.	m.		
2.0	5.51	93.56	343.17	0	357.17	2.80	352.53	30.0 5.0	3.10	0 33 44	1 37 45			
1.8	3.44	21.40	90.22	0	104.22	5.90	102.64		4.74	1 22 38	0 2 18	6	4.78	24.08
1.5	5.92	78.27	337.47	0	351.47	3.83	351.27		1.38	0 14 00	0 29 12	42	2.38	26.79
1.5	4.96	70.76	323.18	0	337.18	2.82	335.26		1.19	0 14 26	0 37 9	7	2.02	11.26
1.2	3.35	334.36	53.23	0	67.23	5.07	63.96		1.70	0 30 29	0 4 38	10	1.75	347.26
1.2	5.06	63.97	321.97	0	335.97	3.35	334.39		0.39	0 4 38	0 0 29	30	0.39	60.01

191

heading, or if it had not been trimmed for maximum speed, there would have been a greater difference between the actual values for vessel speed and speed and direction of the apparent wind and the optimum values calculated and displayed in steps 12–14.

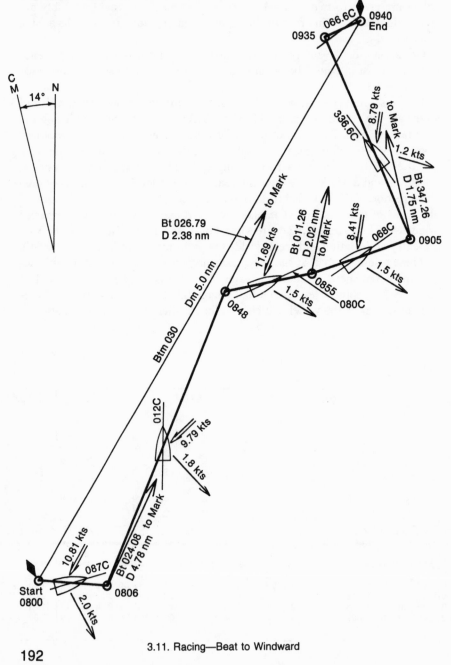

3.11. Racing—Beat to Windward

Routine 3.10 (HP-67/97)

	Btm Dm				
Set Stbd	St Dr SMG,CMG,Ct	D1 ΔT1 ΔT2	ΔT	Dmark Btmark

SPEED MADE GOOD, COURSE MADE GOOD, POSITION RELATIVE TO MARK

Step	Procedure	Input Data/Units	Keys	Output Data/Units
1	After completion of step 16 or 18 of routine 3.9, or step 16 or 18 of routine 3.18, load program—both sides			
2	If on *starboard tack,* set for starboard calculations		A	
3	Enter set of current, even if 0	DDD.d	B	
4	Enter drift of current, even if 0,	knots	B	
·	Calculate and display speed made good on this tack,			knots
·	True course made good on this tack,			DDD.d
·	True course to steer on next tack			DDD.d
5	After displaying *Ct* (in step 4), display will alternately flash and pause. During a pause, enter compass deviation (+E, −W) for that course,	DD.d		
·	Calculate and display compass course to steer on next tack,**			DDD.d
·	Speed made good on next tack,			knots
·	True course made good on next tack			DDD.d
6	Enter true bearing from start to mark or way point	DDD.d	f b	
7	Enter distance from start to mark or way point	naut. mi.	f b	
8	Calculate and display distance (*D1*) from start of this tack to lay line,		C	naut. mi.
·	Time (Δ*T1*) required from start of this tack to reach lay line,			H.MS
·	Time (Δ*T2*) required from start of next tack to reach mark or way point (on a course parallel to or along lay line)			H.MS

***Un*correct for leeway; see table 2.2.

(CONTINUED)

193

Step	Procedure	Input Data/Units	Keys	Output Data/Units
9	Enter time (ΔT) that has already elapsed on present tack, or that will have elapsed at a future time for which a prediction of position is desired (e.g., the time at which the vessel is expected to steer a new course, or come about to a new tack, following the completion of calculations)	H.MS	D	
10	Calculate and display distance to mark or way point at end of interval specified,		E	naut. mi.
•	True bearing to mark or way point at end of interval specified			DDD.d

For changes in course, speed, set, or drift, repeat routine 3.9 and steps 1–5 and 8–10 of routine 3.10. The interval used in step 9 of routine 3.10 should begin with the time of the change. If mark or way point is changed, a new problem begins, with bearing and distance to mark (steps 6–7) measured from present position to new destination.

The results thus far concern the attainment of maximum speed to windward. After step 16 of routine 3.9 has been completed, routine 3.10 is begun. The entry of values for set and drift of current (which must be included even if equal to zero) results in calculation of the vessel's speed (5.51 knots) and course made good over the bottom (93.56°) for the present—i.e., port—tack, and of the true course (343.17°) for the next tack, which will be to starboard. Then, with the entry of deviation—in this instance equal to zero—the compass course (357.17°), speed made good (2.80 knots), and course made good (352.53°) for the next tack are displayed. Thus, the calculated results define the grid, similar to the one shown in figure 3.6, of headings and courses made good enabling the vessel to sail at maximum speed to windward while tacking to the mark.

Next, values for the bearing and distance to the mark are entered. These steps are performed only once, since at the time of each course change, the vessel's new position relative to the mark will be calculated and stored, for use in the next round of calculations. After these entries have been made, the distance to the lay line that defines the end of the present tack, the time required to reach the lay line, and the time required to reach the mark from the lay line, are displayed by pressing $\boxed{C}$.

In the example in question, the selected course is maintained until—at 0806 —the wind shifts, heading the vessel so that it must come about to the starboard tack. As this is done, the navigator enters, at step 9, the amount of time spent on the tack just completed (six minutes) and then obtains the values for distance to the mark (4.78 nautical miles) and true bearing to the mark (24.08°) from the present position. These are stored in the calculator's memory, and

194

become input for the next such calculation. Thus, accumulation of the vessel's successive positions accounts for movement along each new course.

Once the vessel has settled down on its new heading, the sequence begins again. Wind and speed data are obtained from the instruments, and the navigator is able to give the helmsman the optimum course to steer and the values for speed and direction of the wind that his instruments will display when the vessel is indeed on this course. Since the wind has shifted, the compass heading required (13.78°) is different from the one originally predicted for the starboard tack (357.17°); the 16.61-degree change reflects the extent of the change in the direction of the modified true wind (from 28.0° to 45.0°, or 17 degrees). (The 0.39-degree discrepancy results from the revision at 0806 in the estimate of set and drift of current.)

The entry of data and the calculation and display of results proceeds until the distance and time to the new lay line have been determined, showing the limit not to be exceeded (assuming no further wind shifts) on the starboard tack.

The vessel is headed again at 0848, and comes about to the port tack. Calculation of the position relative to the mark after the 42-minute run just completed results in the display of a distance to the mark of 2.38 nm on a true bearing of 26.79°. At 0855 the vessel is lifted, the appropriate heading change is made, the vessel position at that time is calculated, and new optimum values for course and apparent wind are given to the helmsman, as before.

The sequences continue, following each tack. On the next-to-the-last tack, the time calculated for the run to reach the mark after turning onto the lay line is 4 minutes, 38 seconds. On the last tack, this same figure is specified as the time required to reach the lay line. These figures are identical because on this last tack, the vessel is finally sailing along the lay line—carrying out the starboard tack along the lay line which was calculated at 0905. Hence, the time needed to reach the "lay line" is in this instance actually the time needed to reach the mark. The fact that the time along the lay line to the mark calculated at 0935 turns out to be 29 seconds rather than zero, as would be expected, results from an accumulation of round-off errors.

3.5.2 Optimum Sailing on the SR-52 All of the procedures described in this chapter can also be carried out by means of the SR-52. Differences in capacity and organization between the SR-52 and the HP-67 and HP-97 result in differences in the sequence and content of the respective programs and routines, but the problems solved are the same.

On the SR-52, performance of the calculations required for optimum sailing involves the employment of a series of routines. Three of these—routines 3.2, 3.3, and 3.4—have already been mentioned in connection with cruising, in section 3.4.2. The fourth—routine 3.11—is used for determining optimum values for both beating and downwind sailing. Its program (in the Appendix), like that of routine 3.9 for the HP-67 and HP-97, incorporates the equations

195

Routine 3.11 (SR-52)

WINDWARD			DOWNWIND	
Wto	So	AWo;Wao	Sdo	Wto

OPTIMUM TACKING—TO WINDWARD AND DOWNWIND

Step	Procedure	Input Data/Units	Keys	Output Data/Units
1	After completion of routine 3.2, load program—both sides—and continue at step 2 or step 6, as appropriate			
▶	If tacking while *beating to windward*,			
2	Calculate and display optimum tacking angle (*Wto*)		A	DDD.d
3	Calculate and display optimum vessel speed (*So*)		B	knots
4	Calculate and display optimum speed of apparent wind (*AWo*)		C	knots
5	Calculate and display optimum angle of apparent wind (*Wao*)‡		RUN	DDD.d
▶	If tacking while *sailing downwind*,			
6	Calculate and display optimum tacking angle (*Wto*)		E	DDD.d
7	Calculate and display optimum downwind tacking speed (*Sdo*)		D	knots
8	Calculate and display optimum speed of apparent wind (*AWo*)		C	knots
9	Calculate and display optimum angle of apparent wind (*Wao*)		RUN	DDD.d

‡To take leeway into account, subtract the leeway angle.

representing optimum vessel speed *(So)* and tacking angle *(Wto)* which are drawn from polar performance curves. As noted in section 3.5, the necessary coefficients and exponents for these equations are obtained for the SR-52 by means of routine 3.8.

The sequence of routines used on the SR-52 in the calculations for optimum sailing is best seen in diagrammatic form.

START

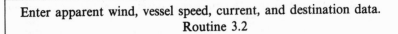

| Enter apparent wind, vessel speed, current, and destination data. |
| Routine 3.2 |

| Calculate optimum tack course, vessel speed, and apparent-wind speed and angle. |
| Routine 3.11 |

| Calculate speeds and courses made good, and time on tacks. |
| Routine 3.3 |

| Calculate distance and bearing to the mark. |
| Routine 3.4 |

Figure 3.11, along with the data in table 3.6, can be used to test the programs and routines for the SR-52. The order in which the data is entered in these routines is slightly different from the order in routine 3.9 for the HP-67 and HP-97, and the sign convention used for entering variation and deviation is just the reverse, but the answers provided by the two calculators are identical. The individual who is planning to use the SR-52 will of course find it convenient to make changes in his version of table 3.6, so that it corresponds to the presentation of the data in the routines for his calculator.

3.6 Downwind Sailing

A sailing vessel will usually make better time on a broad reach than on a dead run, especially in light airs. If the additional speed more than makes up for the additional distance sailed, tacking downwind is desirable. The calculator can be used to determine whether tacking downwind is faster than direct sailing in any particular instance, taking into account wind speed and direction, set and drift of current, course to the mark, and the vessel's downwind sailing performance. Also, it can indicate the tack courses which will result in maximum speed to the mark.

This is another of the situations in which the data embodied in a yacht's polar performance curves is used to obtain quantitative answers. For example, the yacht whose performance is shown in the curves of figure 3.9 has a speed directly downwind (i.e., at a tacking angle of 180 degrees) of 2.0 knots when the modified-true-wind speed is 4.0 knots; at a tacking angle of 138 (or 222) degrees the vessel's speed is 2.85 knots, or 1.43 times as great. The distance

197

traveled is 1.35 times as long on either of these tacks as on the direct course. Accordingly, the time required for the journey will be 1.35/1.43 of the time required for the direct course, for a saving of 6 percent. This is a slender difference, and an adverse current can more than offset it, making direct sailing faster.

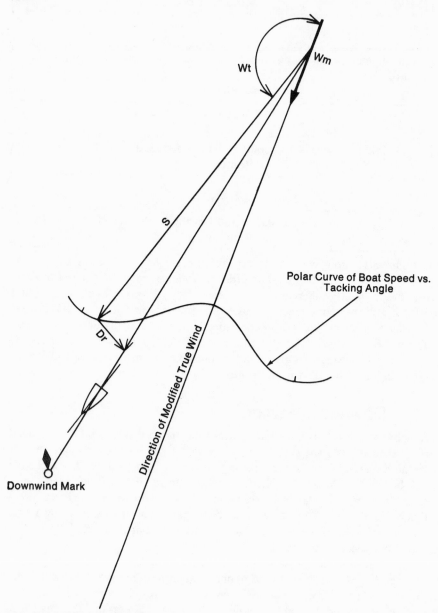

3.12. Sailing Directly Downwind

Furthermore, as shown in figure 3.9, the advantage gained by tacking downwind disappears at higher wind velocities. At a wind speed of 10.0 knots, the vessel's downwind speed when tacking is only slightly greater than its speed when sailing directly downwind; at 16.0 and 22.0 knots, the speed gained by tacking rather than sailing directly downwind is negligible.

3.6.1 Sailing Directly Downwind
Figure 3.12 illustrates the situation of a vessel sailing downwind in the presence of current, when the mark is somewhat off the wind. The navigation problem is to determine the course to be steered to make good the bearing of the mark, and the tactical problem is to forecast the elapsed time to the mark.

The matter is complicated by the fact that vessel speed varies with tacking angle in a complex fashion; figure 3.12 contains a section of a typical polar curve, like those of figures 3.8 and 3.9, showing the relationship between boat speed and tacking angle in the downwind tacking sector when a modified true wind of a particular speed is present. The navigation problem is solved by finding which vessel speed *(S)* and tacking angle *(Wt)* yield a vector that combines with the current vector in such a way that the resultant lies on the track from the vessel's starting position to the mark.

Before the calculator can be used to obtain this answer, some way must be found to store in its memory the polar curves in the downwind region, so that a curve can be reproduced for the value of modified true wind found to be present at the time in question. The curve that is needed is the one shown in figure 3.12—the smooth line that joins the end points of all of the possible speed vectors in the downwind sector; if this curve can be reproduced, it will be possible to test for the tacking angle that yields the correct result.

Figure 3.13 provides another view of this curve, this time labeled to show the quantities that must be measured and stored as a preliminary step toward reproducing it. These include the vessel speed going due downwind *(Sd)*, the vessel speed on the port and starboard tacks at the point of maximum speed projected in the downwind direction *(Sdo)*, and the angular shift from due downwind to the heading that produces this maximum speed ($\Delta W/2$). Also employed is $\Delta S/Sd$, a ratio showing the relationship to the due-downwind speed of the difference (ΔS) between vessel speed at the optimum tacking angle and vessel speed on a course due downwind; this ratio is obtained because its alterations as wind speed varies are more readily stored in the calculator's memory than are the changes in ΔS alone.

The curve and the quantities *Sd, Sdo,* $\Delta W/2$, and ΔS— defined as features of it—are shown for only a single value of modified true wind. Figure 3.9, which shows a number of curves, each for a different modified true wind, is a reminder that many such curves exist; it would be highly coincidental if the actual modified true wind encountered during a particular downwind sail were one for which a single polar curve had been constructed and stored.

Therefore, the next step is to determine the manner in which *Sd, Sdo,* $\Delta W/2$, and $\Delta S/Sd$ vary with the modified true wind. Figure 3.9 shows the

199

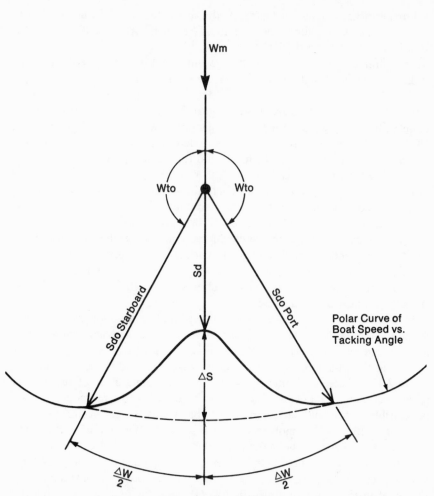

Wm

Wto   Wto

Sd

Sdo Starboard   Sdo Port

Polar Curve of
Boat Speed vs.
Tacking Angle

ΔS

$\frac{\Delta W}{2}$ $\frac{\Delta W}{2}$

3.13. Downwind-Speed Curve

point at which a vessel attains maximum downwind speed at each *MW*, so the values of *Sd, Sdo,* and $\Delta W/2$ for each curve can be found at their appropriate locations. To store these curves in the calculator memory, a process similar to the one used in optimized sailing to windward is employed, the curves being represented by the coefficients, exponents, and constants of four different equations. Three of the curves—for *Sd, Sdo,* and $\Delta W/2$—are based on the data in figure 3.9. The first table accompanying figure 3.14 shows this data for four different speeds of modified true wind.

With values like these as input, the equations for *Sd* and *Sdo* are obtained by means of the "Power" segment of routine 3.7 for the HP-67 and HP-97, or by means of routine 3.8 for the SR-52; similarly, the values for $\Delta W/2$ taken from the polar curves are utilized in the "Exponential" segment of routine 3.7 or in routine 3.12 for the SR-52. The resulting equations are representative of curves like those shown for *Sd, Sdo,* and $\Delta W/2$ in figure 3.14.

200

**INPUT DATA, OBTAINED FROM
POLAR PERFORMANCE CURVES**

MW	Sdo	Sd	△W/2
4 kts	2.85 kts	2.0 kts	42°
10	4.9	4.0	32
16	6.4	6.0	22
22	7.7	7.4	15

Curve-Fitting Equations Based on the Input Data,
Obtained by Routine 3.7 or Routines 3.8 and 3.12
1. $Sd = 0.6804MW^{0.7741}$ (Power Curve Fit)
2. $Sdo = 1.2735MW^{0.5828}$ (Power Curve Fit)
3. $\triangle W/2 = 53.0025e^{-.0539\,MW}$ (Exponential Curve Fit, 4–16 kts)

VALUES PROVIDED BY EQUATIONS 1 AND 2

MW	Sdo	Sd	△S	△S/Sd
4 kts	2.8567	1.9951	0.8616	0.4319
6	3.6181	2.7329	0.8852	0.3239
8	4.2786	3.4165	0.8621	0.2523
10	4.8728	4.0624	0.8104	0.1995

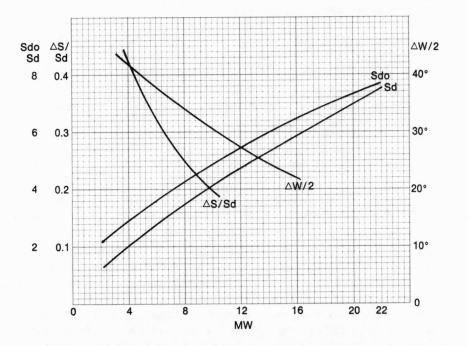

Curve-Fitting Equation Based on Calculated Values of △S/Sd,
Obtained by Routine 3.7 or 3.13
$\triangle S/Sd = 0.7819 - 0.2541\ln MW$ (Logarithmic Curve Fit)

3.14. Downwind Performance Factors

Routine 3.12 (SR-52)

Delete	y→x'	x→y'	→b	
Initialize	x_i	y_i	→a	→r^2

EXPONENTIAL CURVE FIT (DOWNWIND TACKING SECTOR—$\Delta W/2$)

Step	Procedure	Input Data/Units	Keys	Output Data/Units
	Before beginning, make sure D/R switch is set to D.			
1	Load program—both sides			
2	Initialize		A	
	For each value of modified-true-wind speed (*MW*), starting with the lowest and continuing to a maximum of 16 knots, perform steps 3—4; then continue at step 5.			
3	Enter *MW* that labels one of the polar performance curves	knots	B	
4	Enter corresponding value for $\Delta W/2$— the angular interval between due downwind and the heading that produces optimum speed downwind	DDD.d	C	
5	Calculate and display coefficient (*a*) of curve-fitting equation $\Delta W/2 = ae^{bMW}$		D	±n.nnnn
6	Calculate and display exponent (*b*) of curve-fitting equation $\Delta W/2 = ae^{bMW}$		2nd D'	±n.nnnn
7	Calculate and display coefficient of correlation (should be between 0.8 and 1.0)		E	n.nnnn

The values obtained for *a* and *b* are incorporated into the program for routine 3.11, in accordance with the instructions in the Appendix.

The next step is to determine ΔS (the difference between *Sdo* and *Sd*) for wind speeds of 4.0, 6.0, 8.0, and 10.0 knots. Though used in the earlier calculations, values for wind speeds above 10 knots are unnecessary here, since for most sailboats the change in vessel speed resulting from a shift in tacking angle becomes insignificant once the wind reaches 10–14 knots. The necessary values of *Sdo* and *Sd* can be calculated by means of the coefficients and exponents obtained in routine 3.7 or routine 3.8. Next, *Sd* at each of the four

Routine 3.13 (SR-52)

Delete	y→x'	x→y'	→b	
Initialize	x_i	y_i	→a	→r^2

LOGARITHMIC CURVE FIT (RATIO ΔS/SD)

Step	Procedure	Input Data/Units	Keys	Output Data/Units

Data for this sequence consists of values for $\Delta S/Sd$ for four values of MW in the range of 4–10 knots. As explained in the text, the method of obtaining this data is as follows: First, select four values of modified-true-wind speed (MW) in the range of 4–10 knots. Next, for each of the selected wind speeds calculate the corresponding due-downwind vessel speed (Sd) and optimum downwind tacking speed (Sdo), by means of steps 14–19 and steps 20–25 of routine 3.8. Then, for each of the selected wind speeds subtract Sd from Sdo to obtain ΔS. And finally, for each of the selected wind speeds divide ΔS by Sd to obtain $\Delta S/Sd$.

Before beginning, make sure D/R switch is set to D.

Step	Procedure	Input Data/Units	Keys	Output Data/Units
1	After preparation of the data, load program—both sides			
2	Initialize		A	

For each value of MW, starting with the lowest, perform (steps 3–4); then continue at step 5.

Step	Procedure	Input Data/Units	Keys	Output Data/Units
3	Enter MW	knots	B	
4	Enter corresponding value for $\Delta S/Sd$	n.nnnn	C	
5	Calculate and display constant term (a) of curve-fitting equation $\Delta S/Sd = a + b\ln MW$		D	±n.nnnn
6	Calculate and display coefficient of the natural logarithm term (b) of curve-fitting equation $\Delta S/Sd = a + b\ln MW$		2nd D'	±n.nnnn
7	Calculate and display coefficient of correlation (should be between 0.8 and 1.0)		E	n.nnnn

The values obtained for a and b are incorporated into the program for routine 3.11, in accordance with the instructions in the Appendix.

203

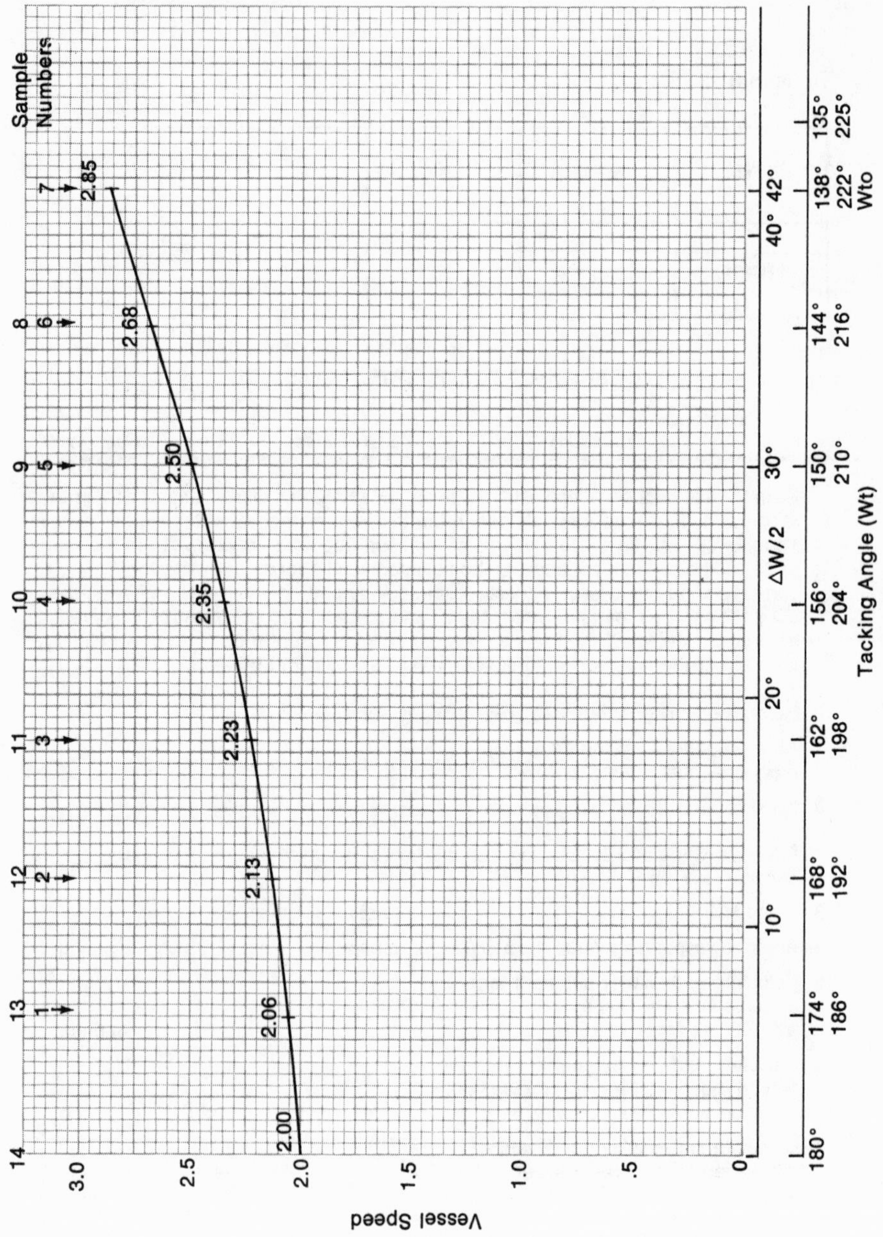

Sample Numbers

Vessel Speed

2.00 2.06 2.13 2.23 2.35 2.50 2.68 2.85

3.0   2.5   2.0   1.5   1.0   .5   0

Tacking Angle (Wt)

180°   10°   20°   ΔW/2   30°   40° 42°

174°   168°   162°   156°   150°   144°   138°   135°
186°   192°   198°   204°   210°   216°   222°   225°
                                              Wto

2.15 Boat Speed Versus Tacking Angle

204

wind speeds specified is divided into ΔS, and the values for $\Delta S/Sd$ are recorded, as shown in the right-hand column of the second table accompanying figure 3.14. These serve as input to the "Logarithmic" segment of routine 3.7 for the HP-67 and HP-97, or to routine 3.13 for the SR-52, both of which supply the necessary constant (0.7819, in this instance) and coefficient (-0.2541, in this instance). The corresponding curve is shown in figure 3.14.

The constants, coefficients, and exponents provided by these routines are incorporated as needed into the programs for routines 3.16 (Direct-Downwind Sailing) and 3.18 (Downwind Tacking) on the HP-67 and HP-97, and for routine 3.11 (Optimum Tacking) on the SR-52. Instructions for inserting the values into the respective programs are given in the Appendix.

When all this information has been stored, the calculator has available, for utilization in the downwind routines, all the necessary data for a particular vessel concerning the variation of the sailing parameters with changes in wind speed. What remains to be supplied is the actual shape of the downwind polar performance curve; this is accomplished by calculating and storing the Fourier series coefficients for one such curve.

A curve of the type required is shown in figure 3.15. This is the downwind sector of the polar performance curve in figure 3.9 for a wind speed of 4.0 knots. Actually, only half of the curve is constructed—from a tacking angle of 180 degrees (dead downwind) to the optimum downwind tacking angle (in this instance 138 degrees); the other half is simply a mirror image of this one. The curve is then marked at a series of points equidistant along the tacking-angle axis, the minimum number of points being six for the SR-52 and seven for the HP-67 and HP-97; since the total number of points (for both halves of the curve) is double this amount, there will be at least twelve or fourteen

Table 3.7   Samples for Calculation of Fourier Coefficients

	Sample Number	Boat Speed (S)	Sample Value (S−Sd)
Samples taken from figure 3.15	1	2.06	.06
	2	2.13	.13
	3	2.23	.23
	4	2.35	.35
	5	2.50	.50
	6	2.68	.68
	7	2.85	.85
Repeat of samples 6 through 1	8	2.68	.68
	9	2.50	.50
	10	2.35	.35
	11	2.23	.23
	12	2.13	.13
	13	2.06	.06
Sample at start (and end) of interval of curve	14	2.00	.00

samples altogether, and the total will be—as it must for these calculations—an even number. It is perfectly acceptable for the interval between the tacking angles sampled to be nonintegral. For instance, if *Sd* and *Sdo* are separated by 53 degrees, and if seven samples are to be taken from the half curve, the interval will be 7.6 degrees. In the curve in figure 3.15, the angular interval of the downwind tacking sector ($\Delta W/2$) is 42 degrees; dividing that interval into seven parts of 6 degrees each provides fourteen samples across the whole curve. For each of the tacking angles chosen, the boat speed is recorded, along with the difference between that speed and the speed *(Sd)* at the central tacking angle (180 degrees)—in this instance 2.0 knots. The results are arranged as shown in table 3.7.

The calculation of the Fourier-series coefficients is done by routine 3.14 for the HP-67 and HP-97 or routine 3.15 for the SR-52.* For the HP-67 and HP-97, seven coefficients are obtained, while for the SR-52, with its more limited memory capacity, six coefficients are found. These coefficients are then incorporated into the programs for the direct-downwind routines (3.17 and 3.19). The program listed in the Appendix for routine 3.17 contains the following Fourier coefficients, which apply to the downwind section of the 4.0-knot polar curve in figure 3.9:

$a_0/2$ 0.3393 (from a_0—0.6786—as supplied by the routine)
a_1 −0.3546
a_2 0.0639
a_3 −0.0442
a_4 0.0155
a_5 −0.0183
a_6 0.0063

The program listed for routine 3.19 contains the coefficients for a_1–a_5 and $a_0/2$, as specified just above. These values can be used in testing the programs and routines—for example, in solving the problems, described in section 3.6.6, involving the comparison of direct sailing with downwind tacking.

*The programs for these two routines were developed by the manufacturers. For the HP-67 and HP-97 the "Fourier Series" program, in the E E Pac, is used. It is reproduced in this volume by permission of Hewlett-Packard. For the SR-52 the "Discrete Fourier Series" program, in the Navigation Library (Program Manual NG1), is used. It is reproduced by permission of Texas Instruments.

Routine 3.14 (HP-67/97)

Start			Polar	
N↑ #Freq's	J	Y_k	Rect	t→f(t)

FOURIER SERIES

Step	Procedure	Input Data/Units	Keys	Output Data/Units
1	Load program—both sides			
2	Initialize		f a	
3	Enter total number of samples (an even number greater than 12)	nn	ENTER	
4	Enter number of output coefficients required (7)	n	A	
5	Enter order of first coefficient	0	B	
6	Enter value of first sample	n.nn	C	
7	Repeat this operation for each of the other samples, and continue with step 8 or steps 9–10, as appropriate		C	
8	On the HP-97, calculate and display Fourier coefficients (normally a_0–a_6)		D	±n.nnnn
9	On the HP-67, calculate and display the first Fourier coefficient (normally a_0)		D	±n.nnnn
10	Calculate and display the remaining Fourier coefficients (normally a_1–a_6); this step must be repeated for each coefficient		R/S	±n.nnnn

The values obtained for a_0–a_6 are utilized in the program for routine 3.16, and are incorporated into the program for routine 3.17, in accordance with the instructions in the Appendix. The values for a_1–a_6 are used as calculated; a_0 must be converted into $a_0/2$.

207

Routine 3.15 (SR-52)

$C_j;C_{j+1}$	$C_{j+2};C_{j+3}$	$C_{j+4};C_{j+5}$	$C_{j+6};C_{j+7}$	$a_0/2$
N,J	Y_k	Sin Coef	1 Coef	Initialize

FOURIER SERIES

Step	Procedure	Input Data/Units	Keys	Output Data/Units
1	Load program—both sides			
2	Set D/R switch to R; if this is not done, the display will flash when step 3 is performed			
3	Initialize		E	
4	Enter total number of samples (an even number greater than 10)	nn	A	
5	Enter order of first coefficient	1	A	
6	Enter value of first sample		B	
7	Repeat this operation for each of the other samples		B	
8	Calculate and display Fourier coefficient a_1		2nd A′	±n.nnnn
9	Calculate and display Fourier coefficient a_2		RUN	±n.nnnn
10	Calculate and display Fourier coefficient a_3		2nd B′	±n.nnnn
11	Calculate and display Fourier coefficient a_4		RUN	±n.nnnn
12	Calculate and display Fourier coefficient a_5		2nd C′	±n.nnnn
13	Calculate and display Fourier coefficient $a_0/2$		2nd E′	±n.nnnn

The values obtained for a_1-a_5 and $a_0/2$ are utilized in the program for routine 3.11, and are incorporated into the program for routine 3.19, in accordance with the instructions in the Appendix.

208

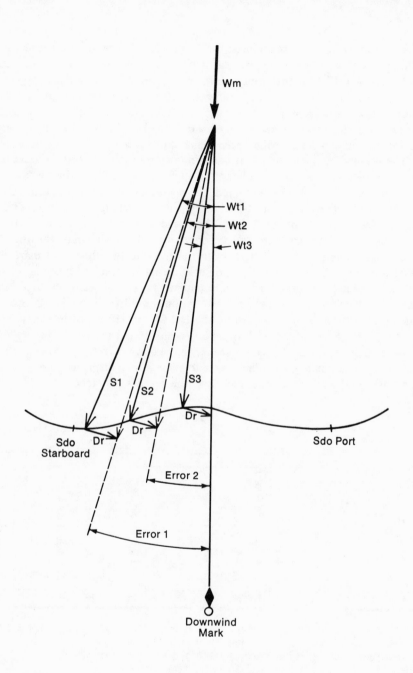

Wm

Wt1

Wt2

Wt3

S1 S2 S3

Dr

Sdo
Starboard

Dr

Dr

Sdo Port

Error 2

Error 1

Downwind
Mark

3.16. Determining Course to Steer Downwind

209

The Fourier coefficients are used by the programs to reproduce the downwind polar diagram for one particular wind speed—4.0 knots in the instance just discussed. If the actual wind speed, as calculated during the preliminary steps of the downwind routine, is different, compensating adjustments in the overall downwind curve are made automatically. The calculator is then able to compute the vessel speed at any heading within the downwind tacking sector, for the particular wind speed being experienced.

The method of calculation that yields a course to steer to reach the mark in the presence of current is illustrated in figure 3.16. Once the necessary programs and data have been entered, the operations required are performed automatically. The process starts, arbitrarily, at the tacking angle corresponding to *Sdo* on the starboard tack. The speed vector at this angle **(S1)** is combined with the current vector to produce a resultant, shown by the dotted line, whose difference in direction from the track to the downwind mark is labeled *Error 1.* A second trial is automatically made, for a new heading, with the speed vector **S2,** producing a resultant with a smaller error in direction *(Error 2).* The trial-and-error process continues until the error has been reduced to less than 0.5 of a degree on the HP-67 and HP-97, or less than 1.0 degree on the SR-52—i.e, until there has been located the speed vector **(S3** in the example shown) which combines with the current vector to produce the required course made good. The course to steer is then displayed, along with the time required to reach the mark and the speed made good.

Table

		ENTER				DISPLAY		ENTER			DISPLAY					ENT.	DIS
		App. Wind Speed	Vessel Speed	App. Wind Angle	Angle of Heel	Mod. True Wind Speed	Tacking Angle	Compass Course	Compass Var.	Compass Dev.	Mod. True Wind Dir.	Opt. Vessel Speed	Opt. App. Wind Speed	Opt. App. Wind Angle	Opt. Mag. Course	Compass Dev.	
Tack	Time	AW	S	Wa	H	MW	Wt	Cc	Var	Dev	Wm	Sdo	AWo	Wao	Cmo	Dev	C
PORT	0800	2.20	1.8	180	0	4.0	180	197.0	12W	0	5.0	2.86	2.72	91.73	154.28	0	15
DIRECT	0800	2.20	1.8	180	0	4.0	180	197.0	12W	0	5.0						199
PORT	0800	2.20	1.8	180	0	4.0	180	197.0	12W	0	5.0	2.86	2.72	91.73	154.28	0	15
DIRECT	0800	2.20	1.8	180	0	4.0	180	197.0	12W	0	5.0						175

210

3.6.2 Direct-Downwind Sailing on the HP-67 and HP-97

Even when no current is present, as in the case illustrated in figure 3.17, the Fourier-series representation of the downwind polar curve is used in the calculations to determine the course to steer and the speed made good in the direction of the mark. The data for this problem, and the calculated results, are shown in the second line of table 3.8.

Routines 3.16 and 3.17 are used to obtain the solution on the HP-67 and HP-97.

The initial conditions are set, and the preliminary calculations are performed, by means of routine 3.16. The entry of values for wind, vessel speed, and angle of heel, obtained from measurements made on board, results in the display of a value for the speed of the modified true wind (here, 4.0 knots) and a tacking angle (here, 180 degrees). Next, the vessel's compass course, and variation and deviation, are entered, at either $\boxed{B}$ or $\boxed{C}$, and the direction of the modified true wind (5.0°) is displayed. The entry of values for set and drift of current, and for true bearing and distance to the mark, followed by the pressing of $\boxed{E}$, completes routine 3.16.

...wnwind Sailing

...TER		DISPLAY			ENT.	DISPLAY			ENTER		DISPLAY¹			
Set of Current	Drift of Current	Present Tack				Next Tack			Initial Bearing and	Dist. to Mark	Dist. to Lay Line	Time to Lay Line	Time along Lay Line to Mark	Total Time to Mark
...t	Dr	SMG1	CMG1	Ct2	Dev	Cc2	SMG2	CMG2	Btm	Dm	D1	ΔT1	ΔT2	Total T
												h. m. s.	h. m. s.	h. m. s.
0		2.86	142.28	227.72	0	239.72	2.86	227.72	187.0	3.0	1.96	0 41 14	0 44 29	[1 25 43]
0		2.01							187.0	3.0				1 29 32
1.0		1.97	153.38	227.72	0	239.72	3.30	244.49	187.0	3.0	2.53	1 17 8	0 30 11	[1 47 19]
1.0		1.71							187.0	3.0				1 45 8

¹The values in brackets, obtained by adding ΔT1 and ΔT2, are not displayed.

211

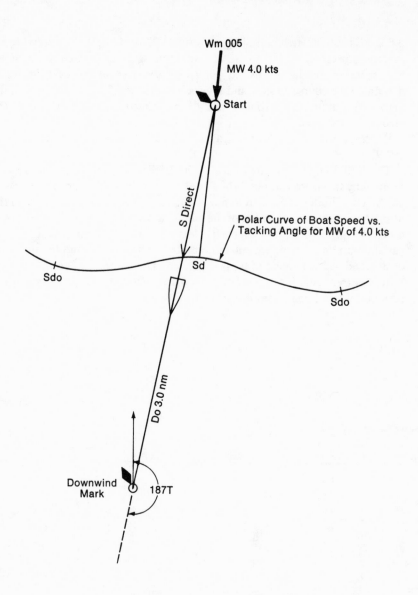

Wm 005

MW 4.0 kts

Start

S Direct

Polar Curve of Boat Speed vs.
Tacking Angle for MW of 4.0 kts

Sdo

Sd

Sdo

Do 3.0 nm

Downwind
Mark

187T

3.17. Direct-Downwind Sailing—No Current

Routine 3.16 (HP-67/97)

St Dr				
AW S Wa H→MW,Wt	PORT Cc Var De→Wm	STBD Cc Var De→Wm	Btm Dm	Calculate

DIRECT-DOWNWIND SAILING I

Step	Procedure	Input Data/Units	Keys	Output Data/Units
1	Load program—both sides			
2	Enter speed of apparent wind	knots	A	
3	Enter vessel speed	knots	A	
4	Enter angle of apparent wind (between 0 and 180 degrees, measured from bow on either side)	DDD.d	A	
5	Enter angle of heel (port or starboard),	DD.d	A	
·	Calculate and display speed of modified true wind (*MW*),			knots
·	Tacking angle (*Wt*) relative to modified true wind, and continue at step 6 or 9, as appropriate			DDD.d
▶	If on *port tack,*			
6	Enter compass course	DDD.d	B	
7	Enter variation (+E, −W), even if 0	DD.d	B	
8	Enter deviation (+E, −W), even if 0,	DD.d	B	
·	Calculate and display direction of modified true wind (*Wm*), and continue at step 12			DDD.d
▶	If on *starboard tack,*			
9	Enter compass course	DDD.d	C	
10	Enter variation (+E, −W), even if 0	DD.d	C	
11	Enter deviation (+E, −W), even if 0,	DD.d	C	
·	Calculate and display direction of modified true wind (*Wm*)			DDD.d
12	Enter set of current, even if 0	DDD.d	f a	
13	Enter drift of current, even if 0	knots	f a	
14	Enter true bearing from start of downwind leg to downwind mark	DDD.d	D	

(CONTINUED)

213

Step	Procedure	Input Data/Units	Keys	Output Data/Units
15	Enter true distance from start of downwind leg to downwind mark	naut. mi.	D	
16	Start calculation		E	

Continue calculations by means of routine 3.17.

Routine 3.17 (HP-67/97)

ΔTmark	Cc	SMG		

DIRECT-DOWNWIND SAILING II

Step	Procedure	Input Data/Units	Keys	Output Data/Units
1	After completion of routine 3.16, load program—both sides			
2	Calculate and display total time required to reach mark by direct-downwind sailing. The display will periodically pause; the number displayed is the angular error between trial course made good and required course made good. When this is reduced to less than 0.5 of a degree, the total time required for the downwind leg will be continuously displayed		A	H.MS
3	Calculate and display compass course to steer		B	DDD.d
4	Calculate and display speed made good to downwind mark		C	knots

214

The program for routine 3.17 is then loaded, and when $\boxed{\text{A}}$ has been pressed, the iterative calculation of vessel speed along various headings is automatically performed, until the heading is found that results in a course lying within 0.5 of a degree of the bearing to the mark (here, within 0.5 of a degree of 187°). At this point, the calculator displays the time required to reach the mark (1 hour, 29 minutes, 32 seconds). The display of compass course to steer (199.32°) is then obtained by pressing $\boxed{\text{B}}$, and that of speed made good (2.01 knots) by pressing $\boxed{\text{C}}$. In the table, the listings for these last two items are to be found toward the center of the row.

The process of repeated calculation is fairly lengthy. In this particular case, the time required to obtain an answer at step 2 of routine 3.16 is 2 minutes, 14 seconds, on the HP-97 and 2 minutes, 9 seconds, on the HP-67.

The same procedures are followed when current is present, as shown in figure 3.18 and in the fourth line of table 3.8. In this instance, the set (300°) and drift (1.0 knots) of current are entered at steps 12 and 13 of routine 3.16. The time required to reach the downwind mark turns out to be 1 hour, 45 minutes, 8 seconds; the course to steer is 175.44°; and the speed made good is 1.71 knots.

3.6.3 Direct-Downwind Sailing on the SR-52

Routine 3.19 is used for the calculation of course to steer and time and speed to the mark in direct-downwind sailing. It is part of a sequence also involving other routines, which is described in section 3.6.7.

3.6.4 Downwind Tacking

Tacking downwind is the counterpart of tacking on optimum courses while beating to windward. Figure 3.19 shows a vessel reaching the mark by taking first a starboard and then a port tack, each on the heading that provides maximum projected speed in the downwind direction. The current vector is added to the speed vector on each tack, and the resultant track over the bottom is shown—along the speed-made-good vector on the starboard tack, and along the lay line on the port tack. As in beating to windward, instead of the two long tacks, many shorter ones could be made; the time to the mark would be the same (not counting the time required to come about to the new tack) provided all of the tacks were parallel to one or the other of those shown here.

3.6.5 Downwind Tacking on the HP-67 and HP-97 The process of calculating the course to steer on each tack, and the corresponding course and speed made good, is identical in downwind tacking with that used in beating to windward. In fact, routine 3.10, the second of the two routines by means of which these calculations are performed for the beat to windward, is employed here as well. The preliminary calculations are carried out by means of routine 3.18, the counterpart of routine 3.9.

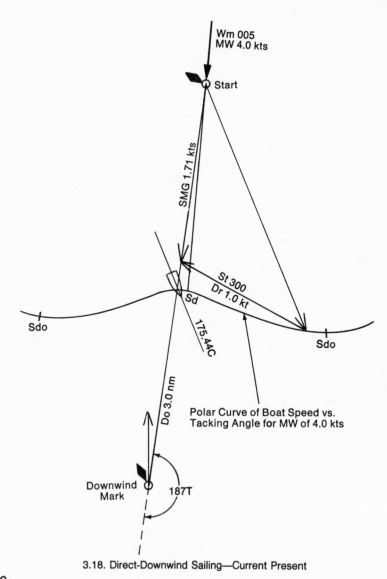

3.18. Direct-Downwind Sailing—Current Present

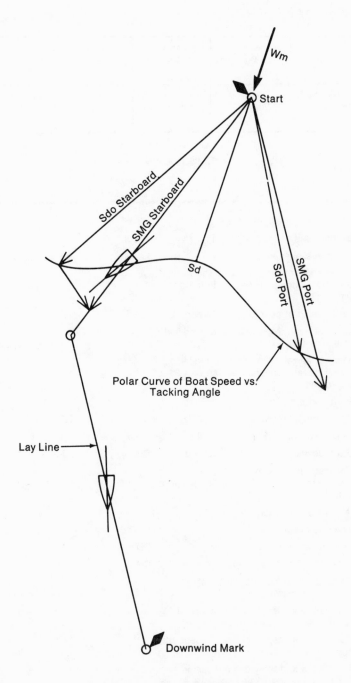

Wm

Start

Sdo Starboard

SMG Starboard

Sd

Sdo Port

SMG Port

Polar Curve of Boat Speed vs.
Tacking Angle

Lay Line

Downwind Mark

3.19. Tacking Downwind, with Current

217

Routine 3.18 (HP-67/97)

Wao	PORT Cmo De→Cco	STBD Cmo De→Cco		
AW S Wa H→MW,Wt	PORT Cc Var De→Wm	STBD Cc Var De→Wm	Sdo	AWo

TACKING DOWNWIND

Step	Procedure	Input Data/Units	Keys	Output Data/Units
1	Load program—both sides			
2	Enter speed of apparent wind	knots	A	
3	Enter vessel speed	knots	A	
4	Enter angle of apparent wind (between 0 and 180 degrees, measured from bow on either side)	DDD.d	A	
5	Enter angle of heel (port or starboard),	DD.d	A	
·	Calculate and display speed of modified true wind (MW),			knots
·	Tacking angle (Wt) relative to modified true wind, and continue at step 6 or 9, as appropriate			DDD.d
▶	If on *port tack,*			
6	Enter compass course	DDD.d	B	
7	Enter variation (+E,−W), even if 0	DD.d	B	
8	Enter deviation (+E,−W), even if 0,	DD.d	B	
·	Calculate and display direction of modified true wind (Wm), and continue at step 12			DDD.d
▶	If on *starboard tack,*			
9	Enter compass course	DDD.d	C	
10	Enter variation (+E,−W), even if 0	DD.d	C	
11	Enter deviation (+E,−W), even if 0,	DD.d	C	
·	Calculate and display direction of modified true wind (Wm)			DDD.d
12	Calculate and display optimum vessel speed downwind (Sdo)		D	knots
13	Calculate and display optimum speed of apparent wind (AWo)		E	knots
14	Calculate and display optimum angle of apparent wind (Wao) and continue at step 15 or 17, as appropriate		f a	DDD.d

218

Step	Procedure	Input Data/Units	Keys	Output Data/Units
▶	If on *port tack*,			
15	Calculate and display optimum magnetic course to steer		f b	DDD.d
16	Enter deviation (+E, −W), even if 0,	DD.d	f b	
·	Calculate and display optimum compass course to steer			DDD.d
▶	If on *starboard tack*,			
17	Calculate and display optimum magnetic course to steer		f c	DDD.d
18	Enter deviation (+E, −W), even if 0,	DD.d	f c	
·	Calculate and display optimum compass course to steer			DDD.d

Two different problems involving downwind tacking have been solved. In the first case, shown in figure 3.20, no current is present. The data for this case is given on the first line of table 3.8. Routine 3.18 is used to provide the optimum vessel speed and the speed and angle of the apparent wind (steps 12–14) and the compass course to steer to attain these values (step 16). Routine 3.10 then provides the rest of the information needed. After set and drift of current (zero in this case) have been entered, speeds and course made good on the present tack and true course on the next tack are shown. Then entry of deviation (also zero) results in the display of the compass course and course and speed made good on the next tack; and entry of the initial bearing and distance to the mark is followed by the display of distance to the lay line and of time to the lay line and along the lay line to the mark, which, added together, give the time to the mark from the starting position—in this instance, 1 hour, 25 minutes, 43 seconds. When necessary, distance and bearing to the mark (not listed in table 3.8) can be obtained by means of the last step in the routine.

219

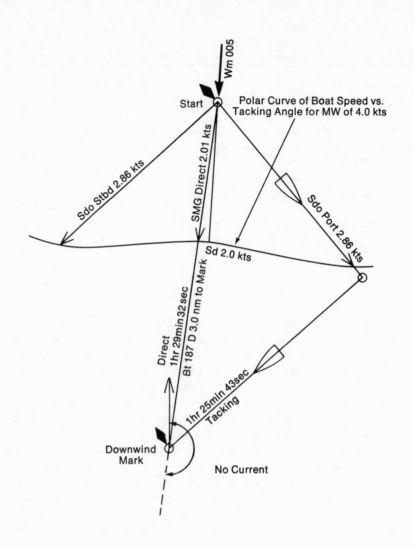

Wm 005

Start
Polar Curve of Boat Speed vs.
Tacking Angle for MW of 4.0 kts

Sdo Stbd 2.86 kts

SMG Direct 2.01 kts

Sdo Port 2.86 kts

Sd 2.0 kts

Direct
1hr 29min 32sec
Bt 187 D 3.0 nm to Mark

1hr 25min 43sec
Tacking

Downwind
Mark

No Current

3.20. Tacking Downwind Versus Direct Sailing—Tacking Faster

220

In the second case, shown in figure 3.21, current is present. The procedures for entering and calculating the information (recorded on the third line of table 3.8) are much the same. In this instance, of course, values of 300° and 1.0 knot are entered for current in steps 3 and 4 of routine 3.10. The total sailing time turns out to be 1 hour, 47 minutes, 19 seconds.

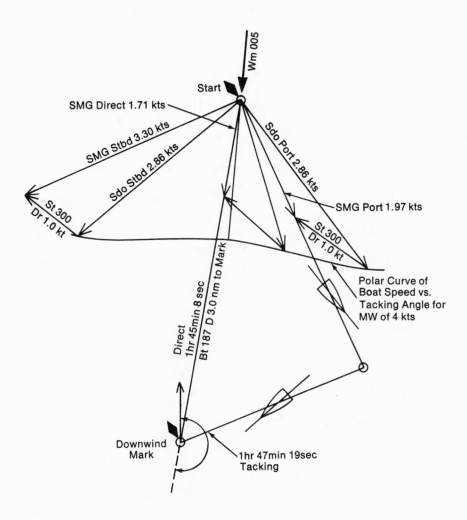

3.21. Tacking Downwind Versus Direct Sailing—Direct Faster

221

3.6.6 Comparison of Direct Sailing with Downwind Tacking
The downwind routines make it possible to determine whether under particular conditions tacking or sailing directly to the mark will be faster. A comparison of the first two lines in table 3.8 indicates that in this case, in which no current is present, tacking is faster. The speed made good of 2.86 knots on each downwind tack results in a shorter total time to the mark than does the speed made good of 2.01 knots for direct sailing, even though on the tack courses the total distance is greater, as shown in figure 3.20.

The next case, illustrated in figure 3.21, introduces current into the situation, and direct sailing becomes quicker, as indicated by the third and fourth lines of table 3.8. In this example, the vessel must steer a course that heads into the current. A compass course of 175.44° (i.e., a true course of 163.44°) is necessary to offset the effect of the current and enable the vessel to reach a mark that bears 187° true. In other words, because of the current, the vessel must sail away from the mark, onto a faster heading, 22 degrees off dead downwind (185°), in order to make good a course directly to the mark. The vessel's speed (as measured from the polar performance curve) increases from 2.01 to 2.31 knots in consequence; the speed made good (reflecting the adverse current) is 1.71 knots.

The speed increase resulting from the faster heading is enough to make the sailing time on the direct course less than it would be on the two tacks at the optimum speed for downwind progress. Tacking requires the longer journey, and in this case, the longer time to reach the mark. Direct sailing takes 1 hour, 45 minutes, 8 seconds; tacking—as we have seen—takes 1 hour, 47 minutes, 19 seconds.

3.6.7 Downwind Tacking and Direct Sailing on the SR-52
The sequence of routines used on the SR-52 in the calculations for downwind sailing—like the sequence for optimum sailing to windward—is best shown diagrammatically.

Four of the routines listed here have been discussed in earlier sections: routines 3.2, 3.3, and 3.4 are used also for both cruising and optimum sailing to windward, and routine 3.11 is used to provide optimum tack courses and speeds for beating as well as for downwind sailing. The data incorporated into the single program for routine 3.11 (all derived from the polar performance curves for a particular vessel, as explained in section 3.5) is the same as that used in the separate programs for several routines on the HP-67 and HP-97. As throughout, the specific instructions for using the program for the routine are to be found in the Appendix.

Routine 3.19, since it is concerned with sailing directly downwind, requires a program that can reconstruct the polar curve of the vessel in the downwind sector. As was shown in section 3.6.1, the Fourier-series coefficients required for this purpose—four-decimal-place numbers—are obtained by means of

222

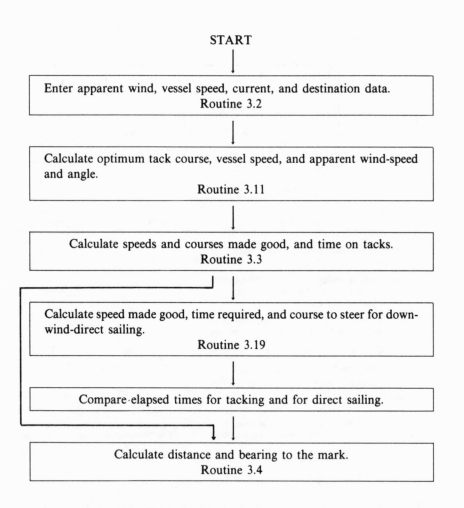

START

Enter apparent wind, vessel speed, current, and destination data.
Routine 3.2

Calculate optimum tack course, vessel speed, and apparent wind-speed and angle.
Routine 3.11

Calculate speeds and courses made good, and time on tacks.
Routine 3.3

Calculate speed made good, time required, and course to steer for down-wind-direct sailing.
Routine 3.19

Compare elapsed times for tacking and for direct sailing.

Calculate distance and bearing to the mark.
Routine 3.4

routine 3.15; the instructions for incorporating them into the program for routine 3.19 are given in the Appendix.

Once the programs for routines 3.11 and 3.19 embody the data for the vessel in question, the sequence of five routines is ready for use in attaining optimum sailing both to windward and downwind.

The data recorded in table 3.8, for the downwind examples shown in figures 3.20 and 3.21, can be employed to test the reader's own programs for this sequence of routines. For routines 3.11 and 3.19, test program cards incorporating the constants derived from the curves of figure 3.9 will of course be necessary. As in the beating routines, there are minor differences in the order in which data is entered for the respective calculators. Also, the signs employed for variation and deviation are reversed. Essentially, however, the entry and use of data is the same in the SR-52 as in the HP-67 and HP-97.

Routine 3.19 (SR-52)

	/	SMG;ΔTmark	Ct;De→Cc	

DIRECT-DOWNWIND SAILING

Step	Procedure	Input Data/Units	Keys	Output Data/Units
1	After completion of routine 3.3, load program—both sides			
2	Calculate and display speed made good to downwind mark (this may take up to two minutes of calculation time)		C	knots
3	Calculate and display total time required to reach mark by direct-downwind sailing		RUN	H.MS
4	Calculate and display true course to steer		D	DDD.d
5	Enter deviation (+W,−E),[1] even if 0,	DD.d	RUN	
·	Calculate and display compass course to steer			DDD.d

[1]The convention of using "plus" for westerly variation and deviation, and "minus" for easterly variation and deviation, conforms to the usage in the SR-52 and TI-59 navigation-program packages.

There are also some minor differences between the results obtained on the SR-52 and those obtained on the HP-67 and HP-97. The elapsed time for sailing directly downwind shown on the SR-52 is 1 hour, 45 minutes, 11 seconds—three seconds more than the time shown on the Hewlett-Packard models—when current is present. This difference results from the fact that the greater memory capacity of the HP-67 and HP-97 permits the use of a seventh term (a_6) in the Fourier series, which the SR-52 cannot accommodate. Also, as has been mentioned, the HP-67 and HP-97 calculate a course to steer that is less than 0.5 of a degree off the mark; the SR-52 calculates this course to the nearest degree.

4

Celestial Navigation

ABBREVIATIONS Used in the Routines of Chapter 4

B bearing
Cc compass course
Ct true course
Day day of month (1–31)
DD.d, DDD.dd degrees and decimal parts of a degree
DD.MM degrees and minutes
DDMM.m degrees, minutes, and tenths of a minute
DD.MMSS degrees, minutes, and seconds
De deviation
Dec declination
DR dead reckoning
E east
EP estimated position
GHA Greenwich hour angle
GMT Greenwich mean time
H sextant altitude
Hmax maximum sextant altitude
H.MS hour(s), minute(s), and second(s)
HP horizontal parallax
Hs observed sextant altitude (corrected for index error)
L latitude
LAN local apparent noon
Lo longitude
LoDR dead-reckoning longitude
Mo month of year (1–12)
1stMo first month

2ndMo second month
N north
naut. mi. nautical miles
S vessel speed; south
SD semidiameter
SHA sidereal hour angle
T time
Thmax time of maximum sextant altitude
Ts time of sextant observation
Var variation
W west
Y year
↑ following a data-entry item indicates that it is entered by pressing [ENTER] instead of a letter key.
→ following a data-entry item indicates that its entry initiates (without further keyboard activity) the calculation and display of one or more results.
+ indicates that the item (e.g., north declination) is entered simply by pressing the appropriate numerical keys.
− indicates that the item is entered by pressing the appropriate numerical keys followed by [CHS].

4.1   Introduction

The programmable scientific calculator is extraordinarily useful as a means of solving celestial-navigation problems. It enables one to convert sextant and time readings directly to the latitude and longitude of one's position—entirely without employing almanacs, sight-reduction tables, or plotting sheets. The calculator can also be used to smooth and make more accurate the observations taken on rough seas, thereby increasing the accuracy of the final position determinations.

Elimination of the almanac is possible because, given the necessary data, the calculator itself computes the positions of the celestial bodies involved. The method is applicable regardless of which bodies are used. Fixes may be derived with the aid of the calculator from observations on the sun or stars, the planets, or the moon. A new publication issued by the U.S. Naval Observatory, *Almanac for Computers,* * provides data that can be stored on the magnetic cards of the HP-67 or HP-97; when this data is used in the routines presented in the following sections, the position of the celestial object in question is freshly computed as part of the sight reduction. After the loading of the appropriate data card or cards, calculation of celestial lines of position requires only the entry of a few easily observed data items. When two lines of position have been calculated, the latitude and longitude of the fix are obtained by means of a short additional routine.

If readings are being made in rough seas, the employment of regression techniques to smooth sextant-altitude observations is desirable. The linear form of regression is used for observations on an object not at or near meridian passage; the parabolic form is used for observations on the sun at local noon. In both types of regression, readings taken over an interval of many minutes are fitted by the calculator to a smooth curve. An altitude selected from this smoothed data then becomes input to the appropriate routine for sight reduction or, in the case of the noon sun, the immediate calculation of a fix.

Since the reader is assumed to possess a working knowledge of celestial navigation, the basic principles and definitions will not be repeated here. The subject is covered in many books, written at many levels. The most authoritative and comprehensive treatment of celestial navigation is found in the latest

---

*LeRoy E. Doggett, George H. Kaplan, and P. Kenneth Seidelmann, *Almanac for Computers* (Washington, D.C.: Nautical Almanac Office, United States Naval Observatory). This volume, which is to be published each year, can be purchased directly from the Nautical Almanac Office, Washington, D.C. 20390. The price in 1978 is $3.00

edition of "Bowditch"—*American Practical Navigator,* vol. 1 (Defense Mapping Agency Hydrographic Center, 1977), pp. 341–640.

The routines in this chapter are designed for the HP-67 and HP-97 only.

4.2 Regression for Accuracy Improvement

The application of regression methods to sextant-altitude measurements makes possible significant improvement in the over-all accuracy of celestial navigation. The principal reason for using these techniques is, of course, to reduce the effect of random, fluctuating disturbances in a sequence of sextant observations. Whatever the cause of these disturbances—the rising or falling of the height of eye of an observer on the bridge of a rolling ship, or the physical battering that bounces the sextant up and down while the "horizon" skips from nearby to distant wave tops—regression methods can smooth the results, revealing the underlying trend in the data.

The use of these methods involves the repeated observation of a celestial body, with the values for successive altitude–time pairs noted and entered into the calculator. If a number of observations are made—say five, six, or seven —over a two- or three-minute interval, the calculator routine will provide the best estimate of the altitudes that would have been observed under ideal circumstances, with the sequence of changes over time corresponding to a smooth curve (straight line or parabola). The employment of linear regression to smooth visual bearings made on charted objects was explained in section 2.2.2, and illustrated in figure 2.1. The same technique enables one to smooth most observations on celestial objects. Indeed, the celestial application of the method is even simpler than the coastwise in that no provision need be made in the program for a sequence which includes both the highest numerical values (near 360°) and the lowest (near 000°); sextant angles are never higher than 140° (values in excess of 90° can be encountered when taking backsights).

Linear regression can be used for a series of sextant altitudes observed relatively close to the time of meridian transit—provided the interval over which the observations are made is not too long. If five to seven observations are completed within three to five minutes, the result obtained with linear regression will be quite accurate for a sequence of observations as close as seven to ten minutes from the time of meridian transit. However, if observations are made both before and after meridian transit, the variation in sextant altitude with the passage of time is best represented by a parabola. The method of parabolic regression—not applicable in coastwise navigation—fits such a curve to the observed data. Once the parabola has been computed, its point of maximum altitude can be given by the calculator, for use in calculating the vessel's position. The employment of parabolic regression at meridian passage of the sun, with particular attention to the problem of obtaining the most accurate value possible for longitude, is discussed in sections 4.6–4.9.

Routine 4.1 (HP-67/97)

Hs	Ts	Calculate	T→H	Clear

CELESTIAL LINEAR REGRESSION

Step	Procedure	Input Data/Units	Keys	Output Data/Units
1	Load program—both sides			
2	Clear; this step *must* be performed		E	
3	Enter sequence of altitude-time pairs; for each pair, enter observed sextant altitude (corrected for index error), followed by	DDMM.m	A	
4	*GMT* of observation of altitude	H.MS	B	

If an error is noted in the entry of altitude or time data before the corresponding letter key (A or B) is pressed, eliminate the incorrect data by pressing CLx ; if the error is noted after the letter key has been pressed, clear the calculator by pressing E , and re-enter all data, starting at step 3.

5	Calculate regression coefficients		C	
6	Enter *GMT* for which sextant altitude is required,	H.MS	D	
·	Calculate and display sextant altitude corresponding to time entered in preceding step, in degrees, minutes, and *seconds*			DD.MMSS
7	Clear, to start a new problem		E	

The function of routine 4.1 is to provide smoothed values for celestial observations by means of the linear-regression method. The altitude–time pairs are entered at A and B, and calculation of the regression coefficients follows when C is pressed. Next, the time for which a sextant altitude is required is entered at D. Display of the calculated altitude follows automatically. An illustration of the use of linear regression for observations on the sun will be found in the top segment of table 4.2. This can be used to test the program; entry of the values listed for observed sextant altitude and time should yield the values for calculated altitude shown in the right-hand column.

229

4.3 Prerecorded Almanac Data Cards

All sight-reduction methods require knowledge of the positions of celestial objects at the moment of the sextant observations. Traditionally, this information was obtained from almanacs. Not long ago, techniques were developed which made it possible to generate these positions in the calculator itself—after the loading of the necessary preliminary data—by entering the date and Greenwich Mean Time *(GMT)* of each observation. However, these methods were applicable only to sun and star observations; for observations of the moon or the planets, reference to the almanac was still required.

By contrast, the programs developed for this volume can accept observations on *all* bodies; the traditional almanac is completely replaced by a series of magnetic data cards incorporating information supplied by the *Almanac for Computers.* Thus, the moon, which is often visible during daylight hours, can be used as conveniently as the sun for daytime celestial fixes. During dusk or dawn observations, the four bright and conspicuous planets—Saturn, Venus, Jupiter, and Mars—can be given treatment uniform with that accorded the stars and the moon.

Table 4.1   Data Cards for One Year of Celestial Navigation

Bodies	Time Interval Covered on One Card (Two Sides)	Number of Cards per Year
Sun	2 months	6
Planets	2 months (per planet)	6 (per planet)
Moon	6 days	61
Stars (*GHA* Aries)	4 months	3
Stars (*SHA* and *Dec*)		
Apparent Places[1]	1 year (16 stars)	4 (to cover 64 stars)
Mean Places[2]	1 month (16 stars)	48 (to cover 64 stars)

[1]For accuracy to ± 1.3 minutes of arc.
[2]For accuracy to ± 0.5 minutes of arc.

The data cards should be prerecorded and kept ready for use. The number of cards required for a whole year of celestial navigation is shown in table 4.1. For the sun and each of the planets, one side of a magnetic card can accommodate the data for a month, so the year is covered by six cards, to be changed once every two months (a total of thirty cards for the sun and four planets). The moon requires a larger number of cards, which must therefore be changed more frequently. Each moon data card covers six days, so altogether sixty-one cards are needed for an entire year. This number can be reduced by recording moon cards only for periods when they will actually be required.

Data for the Greenwich hour angle *(GHA)* of Aries for two months is contained on one side of a card; hence, the year is covered by three cards, which need to be changed only once every four months. Stars also require a

230

set of cards recording data concerning sidereal hour angle *(SHA)* and declination *(Dec)*. If values with an accuracy of ±1.3 minutes of arc are acceptable, only the tabulated apparent place *for the entire year* need be used for each star. Since eight such entries (with the stars assigned identification numbers 1–8) can be contained on one side of one card, probably no more than three or four star data cards (covering forty-eight or sixty-four stars) will suffice for most navigational purposes. However, if somewhat greater accuracy is required (to ±0.5 minutes of arc), a separate data card is made for each month, with each side once again holding the data for eight stars. These cards must, of course, be changed each month, and for sixty-four stars, four cards per month—for a total of forty-eight per year—will be required.

The stars most commonly used for celestial navigation are included in a group of fifty-seven. They are identified in the 1978 edition of the *Almanac for Computers;* in section F, "Stellar Tables," which gives the names and numbers of stars, along with their almanac parameters, the navigation stars are those that are numbered in the "NAV" column.

Routine 4.2 (HP-67/97)

Clear	Mo	Moon Date	Moon Clear	Finalize

CELESTIAL DATA CARDS

Step	Procedure	Input Data/Units	Keys	Output Data/Units
1	Load program			
2	Clear; this step *must* be performed		A	1
	Star Data Card (Eight Apparent Yearly Places per Side)			
	After completion of steps 1–2, proceed as follows (steps 3–4) for each of eight stars:			
3	Enter apparent *SHA*, from the stellar tables in the *Almanac for Computers* (section F in 1978 edition)	DDD.dddd	ENTER	
4	Enter apparent declination $(+N,-S)$, from the *Almanac* (section F in 1978 edition)	DD.dddd	R/S	2–9
5	Finalize		E	CRD
6	Record star data card, first side, and label with star names and corresponding numbers (1–8)			CRD
7	Clear		CL*x*	
	For eight additional entries, repeat steps 3–5 and record star data card, second side.			
	Sun or Planet Data Card (One Month per Side)			
8	After completion of steps 1–2, enter month number	1–12	B	0
9	Enter coefficients 0–5 for *GHA*, from the appropriate sun or planet columns in the *Almanac* (pp. C1–C6 in 1978 edition), pressing $\boxed{R/S}$ following entry of each coefficient	a_0–a_5	R/S	1,2,3,4,5,0
10	Enter coefficients 0–5 for *Dec*, from the appropriate sun or planet columns in the *Almanac* (pp. C1–C6 in 1978 edition),			

232

Step	Procedure	Input Data/Units	Keys	Output Data/Units
	pressing $\boxed{R/S}$ following entry of each coefficient	$b_0–b_5$	R/S	1,2,3,4,5,0
11	*For sun only*, enter coefficients 0 and 1 for *SD*, from the *Almanac* (pp. C1–C6 in 1978 edition), pressing $\boxed{R/S}$ following entry of each coefficient	$d_0–d_1$	R/S	1,2
12	Finalize		E	CRD
13	Record sun/planet data card, one side, and label with appropriate name and date interval.			CRD
14	Clear		CLx	

For an additional month of sun or planet data, repeat steps 8–13 and record sun/planet data card, second side.

GHA Aries Data Card (Two One-Month Intervals per Side)

Step	Procedure	Input Data/Units	Keys	Output Data/Units
15	After completion of steps 1–2, enter month number for first monthly interval	1–12	B	0
16	Enter month number for second monthly interval	1–12	B	0
17	Enter coefficients 0–5 for *GHA* Aries for first monthly interval, from the appropriate columns in the *Almanac* (pp. C1–C6 in 1978 edition), pressing $\boxed{R/S}$ following entry of each coefficient	$a_0–a_5$	R/S	1,2,3,4,5,0
18	Enter coefficients 0–5 for *GHA* Aries for second monthly interval, from the appropriate columns in the *Almanac* (pp. C1–C6 in 1978 edition), pressing $\boxed{R/S}$ following entry of each coefficient	$a_1–a_5$	R/S	1,2,3,4,5,0
19	Finalize		E	CRD
20	Record *GHA* Aries card, first side, and label with the two time intervals covered			CRD
21	Clear		CLx	

For entries covering an additional two months of *GHA* Aries, repeat steps 15–19, and record GHA Aries card, second side.

Moon Data Card (Six Days per Card, Requiring Both Sides)

Step	Procedure	Input Data/Units	Keys	Output Data/Units
22	After completion of steps 1–2, enter month number of first day of time interval	1–12	ENTER	
23	Enter date of first day of time interval	1–31	ENTER	
24	Enter year of first day of time interval (last two digits)	00–99	C	0
25	Enter coefficients 0–5 for moon *GHA* for the six-day time interval, from the *Almanac* (pp. C7–C27 in 1978 edition),			

(CONTINUED)

Step	Procedure	Input Data/Units	Keys	Output Data/Units
	pressing [R/S] following entry of each coefficient	a_0–a_5	R/S	1,2,3,4,5,0
26	Enter coefficients 0–5 for moon *Dec* for the six-day time interval, from the *Almanac* (pp. C7–C27 in 1978 edition), pressing [R/S] following entry of each coefficient	b_0–b_5	R/S	1,2,3,4,5,0
27	Finalize		E	CRD
28	Record moon data card, first side, and label with dates of the six-day interval and with identification as first side			CRD
29	Clear		CL*x* D	0
30	Enter coefficients 0–5 for moon *HP* for the six-day time interval, from the *Almanac* (pp. C7–C27 in 1978 edition), pressing [R/S] following entry of each coefficient	c_0–c_5	R/S	1,2,3,4,5,0
31	Enter coefficients 0–5 for moon *SD* for the six-day time interval, from the *Almanac* (pp. C7–C27 in the 1978 edition), pressing [R/S] following entry of each coefficient	d_0–d_5	R/S	1,2,3,4,5,0
32	Finalize		E	CRD
33	Record moon data card, second side, and label as second side			CRD
34	Clear		CL*x*	

Routine 4.2 provides the instructions for recording all of the data cards employed in sight reduction except for the monthly star data cards used when accuracy better than ± 1.3 minutes of arc is required. These are prepared as shown in routine 4.3.

The reader who wishes to check the accuracy of his program listings by working out the examples discussed in the following sections will find the necessary data from the 1978 *Almanac for Computers* in table 4.9, at the end of this chapter.

Routine 4.3 (HP-67/97)

Mo	Mean	Coefficients		Finalize

MONTHLY STAR DATA CARD

Step	Procedure	Input Data/Units	Keys	Output Data/Units
1	Load program			
2	Enter month number	1–12	A	

For each of eight stars, proceed as follows (steps 3–12), obtaining all input data from the stellar tables in the *Almanac for Computers* (section F in 1978 edition):

3	Enter mean *SHA*	DDD.dddd	B	

For *SHA*, proceed as follows (steps 4–7):

4	Enter *H*	±0.dddd	ENTER	
5	Enter *R*	±0.dddd	ENTER	
6	Enter *S*	±0.dddd	ENTER	
7	Enter *C*	±0.dddd	C	
8	Enter mean declination (+N,−S)	DD.dddd	B	

For *Dec*, proceed as follows (steps 9–12):

9	Enter *H*	±0.dddd	ENTER	
10	Enter *R*	±0.dddd	ENTER	
11	Enter *S*	±0.dddd	ENTER	
12	Enter *C*	±0.dddd	C	
13	Finalize		E	CRD
14	Record monthly star data card, first side, and label with month and with star names and corresponding numbers (1–8)			CRD
15	Clear		CLx	

For eight additional entries, repeat entire routine and record monthly star data card, second side.

4.4 Sight Reduction

Routine 4.4 (for the sun, stars, and planets) and routine 4.5 (for the moon only) provide the azimuth and intercept of a line of position. Either routine can be used ahead of the other. Information concerning the position co-ordinates of the celestial object is loaded from the appropriate data cards, and entries are made specifying the date and time, the latitude and longitude of the vessel's dead-reckoning or estimated position, height of eye, and the observed altitude of the object above the horizon. In the calculation of the second line of position required for a fix, the course made good and speed made good of the vessel (maintained—or averaged—between observations) are entered in place of latitude and longitude. These values can be calculated by means of routine 2.22. Where the two observations are simultaneous, course and speed are entered as zero in these steps.

If routine 4.4 or routine 4.5 must be repeated—as might be the case if some of the data originally entered turns out to be erroneous—it is *essential* to reload the necessary data card or cards (for star, Aries, sun, moon, or planet). Failure to do so will result in the display of incorrect results for the azimuth and intercept of the line of position.

Routine 4.4 (HP-67/97)

STARS StarNo Day↑Ts(1stMo)	STARS Day↑Ts(2ndMo)	SUN PLANETS Day↑Ts	L↑Lo	CMG↑SMG

SIGHT REDUCTION—SUN, STARS, AND PLANETS

Step	Procedure	Input Data/Units	Keys	Output Data/Units
1	Load program—both sides			
	Reducing Star Observations			
2	After completion of step 1, load star data card—one side			
3	Clear		CLx	
4	Enter star number	1–8	A	
5	Load Aries data card—one side			
6	Clear		CLx	
7	Enter day of month, corresponding to *GMT* to be entered in step 8 or 9	1–31	ENTER	
8	If data is in first month on Aries card, enter time of day (*GMT*)	H.MS	A	
9	If data is on second month on Aries card, enter time of day (*GMT*)	H.MS	B	
	For first line of position, proceed as follows (steps 10–11):			
10	Enter vessel's DR or EP latitude (+N, −S)	DD.MMSS	ENTER	
11	Enter vessel's DR or EP longitude (+W, −E),	DD.MMSS	D	
•	Calculate and display azimuth of line of position, and continue at step 14			DDD.dd
	For second line of position, repeat steps 2–9, and continue at step 12. If vessel is stationary between observations, or fix is to be calculated from a single DR or estimated position, enter course and speed as 0 in steps 12–13.			
12	Enter true course made good between observations	DDD.d	ENTER	
13	Enter speed made good between observations,	knots	E	
•	Calculate and display azimuth of line of position			DDD.dd

(CONTINUED)

237

Step	Procedure	Input Data/Units	Keys	Output Data/Units
14	Calculate and display calculated altitude of star		R/S	DD.dd
15	Enter height of eye of observer	feet	ENTER	
16	Enter observed sextant altitude (corrected for index error), in degrees, minutes, and *seconds,*	DD.MMSS	R/S	
·	Calculate and display intercept of line of position (+ away, − toward)			naut. mi.

Reducing Sun or Planet Observations

Step	Procedure	Input Data/Units	Keys	Output Data/Units
17	After completion of step 1, load sun or planet data card–one side			
18	Clear		CL*x*	
19	Enter day of month, corresponding to *GMT* to be entered in step 20	1–31	ENTER	
20	Enter time of day (*GMT*)	H.MS	C	

For first line of position, proceed as follows (steps 21–22):

Step	Procedure	Input Data/Units	Keys	Output Data/Units
21	Enter vessel's DR or EP latitude (+N, −S)	DD.MMSS	ENTER	
22	Enter vessel's DR or EP longitude (+W, −E),	DD.MMSS	D	
·	Calculate and display azimuth of line of position, and continue at step 25			DDD.dd

For second line of position repeat steps 17–20 and continue at step 23. If vessel is stationary between observations, or fix is to be calculated from a single DR or estimated position, enter course and speed as 0 in steps 23–24.

Step	Procedure	Input Data/Units	Keys	Output Data/Units
23	Enter true course made good between observations	DDD.d	ENTER	
24	Enter speed made good between observations,	knots	E	
·	Calculate and display azimuth of line of position			DDD.dd
25	Calculate and display calculated altitude of sun or planet		R/S	DD.dd

For planet, continue at step 28; for sun, perform step 26 or step 27, as appropriate, and then continue at step 28.

Step	Procedure	Input Data/Units	Keys	Output Data/Units
26	Set flag for upper-limb observation of sun		f STF 1	
27	Set flag for lower-limb observation of sun		f STF 2	
28	Enter height of eye of observer	feet	ENTER	
29	Enter observed sextant altitude (corrected for index error), in degrees, minutes, and *seconds,*	DD.MMSS	R/S	
·	Calculate and display intercept of line of position (+ away, − toward)			naut. mi.

238

Routine 4.5 (HP-67/97)

Day↑Ts	Dec		L↑Lo	CMG↑SMG

SIGHT REDUCTION—MOON

Step	Procedure	Input Data/Units	Keys	Output Data/Units
1	Load program—both sides			
2	Load moon data card—first side			
3	Clear		CLx	
4	Enter day of month, corresponding to *GMT* to be entered in step 5	1–31	ENTER	
5	Enter time of day (*GMT*)	H.MS	A	
6	Load moon data card—second side			
7	Calculate and display declination		CLx B	±DD.dddd
	For first line of position, proceed as follows (steps 8–9):			
8	Enter vessel's DR or EP latitude (+N, −S)	DD.MMSS	ENTER	
9	Enter vessel's DR or EP longitude (+W, −E),	DD.MMSS	D	
·	Calculate and display azimuth of line of position, and continue at step 12			DDD.dd

For second line of position, repeat steps 2–7, and continue at step 10. If vessel is stationary between observations, or fix is to be calculated from a single DR or estimated position, enter course and speed as 0 in steps 10–11.

10	Enter true course made good between observations	DDD.d	ENTER	
11	Enter speed made good between observations,	knots	E	
·	Calculate and display azimuth of line of position			DDD.dd
12	Calculate and display calculated altitude		R/S	DD.dd

Perform step 13 or step 14, as appropriate, and then continue at step 15.

13	Set flag for upper-limb observation		f STF 1	
14	Set flag for lower-limb observation		f STF 2	
15	Enter height of eye of observer	feet	ENTER	(CONTINUED)

239

Step	Procedure	Input Data/Units	Keys	Output Data/Units
16	Enter observed sextant altitude (corrected for index error), in degrees, minutes, and *seconds,*	DD.MMSS	R/S	
·	Calculate and display intercept of line of position (+away, −toward)			naut. mi.

Routine 4.6 (HP-67/97)

Calculate				

FIX FROM CELESTIAL LINES OF POSITION

Step	Procedure	Input Data/Units	Keys	Output Data/Units
	This routine is used following the calculation of two lines of position, by means of routine 4.4 and/or routine 4.5; since this data is retained by the calculator, no further input is necessary.			
1	Load program			
2	Calculate and display latitude of fix from two lines of position (for time of second observation),		A	±DD.MMSS
·	Longitude of fix			±DD.MMSS
3	To obtain fix for time of first observation, calculate and display latitude of fix,		R/S	±DD.MMSS
·	Longitude of fix			±DD.MMSS

240

The results supplied by the Sight Reduction routines are retained by the calculator. When two lines of position have been obtained—whether the observations were simultaneous, separated by a few minutes, or separated by hours —routine 4.6 can be used without additional keyboard entries to calculate the latitude and longitude of the fix.

As explained in section 4.2, the values for sextant altitude to be entered in the Sight Reduction routines may be obtained by regression methods, with linear regression used when the body observed is not at or near meridian transit, and parabolic regression used when the sun is observed both before and after meridian transit.

Table 4.2   Sun Line of Position, with Linear Regression

Linear Regression (Routine 4.1)

Observed Sextant Altitude	GMT	Calculated Sextant Altitude
52°02.5'	17 08 28	52°02'43"
51°55.9'	17 10 17	51°55'18"
51°48.6'	17 11 37	51°49'51"
51°46.0'	17 12 56	51°44'29"
51°37.5'	17 14 29	51°38'09"

Sight Reduction (Routine 4.4)

DATA	
Date	January 27, 1978
GMT	17 11 37
Latitude	18°17'49"N
Longitude	64°55'05"W
Limb	lower
Height of Eye	6 feet
Sextant Altitude	51°49'51" (from regression, above)
CALCULATED RESULTS	
Azimuth of Line of Position	195.20°
Altitude of Sun	52.05°
Intercept of Line of Position	−0.14nm

Table 4.2 illustrates the employment of routines 4.1 and 4.4 to obtain an accurate line of position even though the sextant observations, on the sun, have been made under very difficult conditions. The data in table 4.2 was obtained from sightings taken by an individual sitting on the deck of a twenty-six-foot sailboat pounded by five-foot seas. The values of latitude and longitude, for entry in steps 10–11 of the Sight Reduction routine, were obtained by taking a series of vessel bearings on a buoy and lighthouse in the vicinity, and therefore represent the vessel's actual position. The displayed value of altitude

241

intercept, −0.14 nautical miles, indicates that the line of position calculated in this routine passes that distance away from the true position. If the sextant altitude actually observed at 17 11 37 had been used, instead of the value calculated by regression methods, the altitude intercept displayed in the Sight Reduction routine would have been 0.91 nautical miles. This is an example of how the use of regression rather than a single observation can result in a considerable reduction in error.

Table 4.3   Fix on Two Celestial Objects

Sight Reduction

DATA

	First Observation (Routine 4.4)	Second Observation (Routine 4.5)
Body	Kochab	moon
Date	January 27, 1978	January 27, 1978
GMT	10 57 00 (morning)	11 01 00
DR Latitude	18°20′08″N	
DR Longitude	64°47′50″W	
CMG		50°
SMG		6.0 knots
Limb		lower
Height of Eye	10 feet	10 feet
Sextant Altitude	34°08′33″	25°23′39″

Fix (Routine 4.6)

CALCULATED RESULTS	
Latitude	18°20′21″N
Longitude	64°47′35″W

Table 4.4   Running Fix, with Sun Lines of Position

Sight Reduction (Routine 4.4)

DATA

	First Observation	Second Observation
Date	January 15, 1978	January 15, 1978
GMT	13 35 00	17 15 00
DR Latitude	42°35′00″N	
DR Longitude	64°50′00″W	
CMG		78°
SMG		6.0 knots
Limb	lower	lower
Height of Eye	10 feet	10 feet
Sextant Altitude	14°36′27″	25°06′05″

Fix (Routine 4.6)

CALCULATED RESULTS	
Latitude	42°39′38″N
Longitude	64°20′44″W

242

Table 4.3 shows the type of information required (in addition to the data entered by loading the appropriate magnetic cards) for a typical two-body fix, with the star Kochab as the first body and the moon as the second. No further data entries are needed for the actual fix calculation. When routine 4.4 and 4.5 have been completed, and the program for routine 4.6 has been loaded, one need only press $\boxed{A}$ to obtain the latitude and longitude of the two-body fix.

If three or more bodies are observed, the data is utilized for a series of two-body fixes. A cluster of fixes will be obtained; when the navigator has plotted these points on a chart, he will normally be able to estimate the most probable position. (Fixes resulting from poor or questionable observations can usually be eliminated at this time.)

Table 4.4 exemplifies the data required to calculate a running fix from two successive sun lines of position by means of routines 4.4 and 4.6. As always, regression methods can be used to obtain the sextant altitudes. Since there is no transit of the meridian, routine 4.1 would be appropriate here. There is a large time interval—approximately four hours—between the observations, so that the two lines of position will cross at a fairly wide angle, yielding a reasonably "strong" fix; the azimuth of the morning sun line is 138.45° and that of the afternoon line is 192.42°, for a difference of 54 degrees. As in all running fixes, the accuracy of the result is heavily dependent upon exact knowledge of the vessel's course and speed made good between the two observations—that is, knowledge not only of the true course being steered and the speed being maintained, but of the set and drift of any currents that may be interfering with the vessel's movement. When the time interval between observations is long, as it usually is when sun lines are to be crossed, uncertainties concerning vessel course and speed, and the set and drift of current, can give rise to significant errors in the final result.

The uncertainties in a running fix with a long time interval between observations can be largely avoided by the substitution of a multibody fix, with the celestial readings taken simultaneously or nearly so.

4.5 Observations at Local Apparent Noon

Many navigators use observations of the sun as it crosses the meridian as an important part of their daily navigation routine. A line of position drawn for the sun at local apparent noon *(LAN)* is a line of latitude. The time of meridian crossing can be converted directly into longitude east or west of Greenwich by simple arithmetic.

However, there may be problems in obtaining accurate values for the line of position and the time of meridian crossing. One source of error, as in coastwise navigation, is fluctuation in the observed bearings, such as that caused by the movements of a small vessel in rough seas. In particular, observations at *LAN* may result in erroneous values for longitude because the position of the sun in longitude relative to an observer changes rapidly; it

moves steadily east to west at 15 degrees per hour. (By contrast, since the sun literally hangs in the sky at *LAN,* its altitude, and hence the observer's latitude can be easily measured.) The sun's motion makes identification of the *moment* of maximum altitude difficult, especially when there are fluctuations in the observed data; and if this moment is not correctly determined, the corresponding value for longitude will be incorrect. Another source of error is the northward or southward movement of a vessel during the time of meridian passage. This movement, which of course is most significant when the vessel speed is relatively high, results in a small change in latitude and therefore affects the observed sextant altitude of the sun.

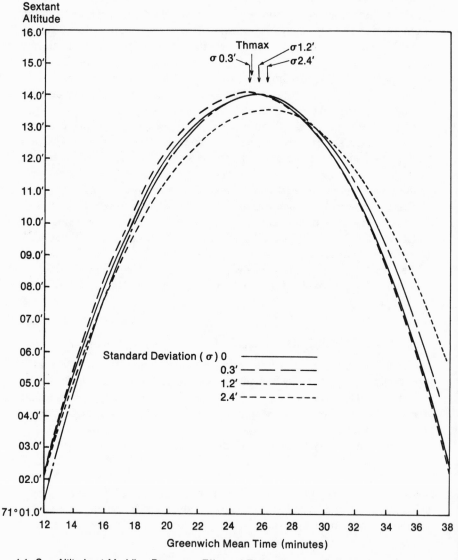

4.1. Sun Altitude at Meridian Passage—Effect of Fluctuations on Calculated Latitude and Longitude

244

The procedures described in the following sections and embodied in routines 4.7 and 4.8, while they cannot eliminate all of these problems—especially as regards the determination of longitude—do minimize them, to facilitate achievement of the maximum accuracy possible.

4.5.1 Parabolic Regression to Reduce the Effects of Fluctuations during the Noon Sight

The advantage of regression methods lies, as we know, in their ability to reduce the effects of fluctuations in the observed sextant angles. A representative situation is illustrated in figure 4.1, which shows the curves calculated by regression methods for the four sets of observations of the noon sun presented in table 4.5. One of the curves is based on observations with no fluctuations; for the other three, the standard deviations

Table 4.5 Effect of Fluctuations in Measurements
of Sun Altitude at Meridian Passage

DATA
Date   June 21, 1978
Limb   lower
Height of Eye   10 feet
Bearing to Sun south

GMT	Sextant Altitude			
	No Fluctuations	Standard Deviation 0.3'	Standard Deviation 1.2'	Standard Deviation 2.4'
16 12 10	71° 02.0'	71° 02.4'	71° 02.1'	71° 03.8'
16 14 00	71 05.1	71 05.1	71 03.1	71 04.3
16 15 55	71 07.9	71 08.0	71 06.8	71 04.9
16 18 12	71 10.5	71 10.5	71 11.6	71 09.4
16 21 05	71 12.7	71 13.0	71 13.9	71 16.5
16 23 12	71 13.7	71 14.2	71 13.1	71 13.0
16 25 15	71 14.0	71 14.1	71 14.0	71 09.4
16 27 06	71 13.7	71 14.0	71 14.5	71 15.0
16 28 48	71 13.1	71 13.0	71 12.9	71 11.4
16 31 00	71 11.6	71 11.5	71 09.1	71 14.8
16 34 06	71 08.5	71 08.0	71 10.6	71 09.6
16 35 54	71 06.0	71 05.8	71 08.7	71 09.6
16 37 06	71 04.3	71 04.5	71 04.0	71 05.2

CALCULATED RESULTS

	No Fluctuations	Standard Deviation 0.3'	Standard Deviation 1.2'	Standard Deviation 2.4'
GMT of Maximum Alt.	16 25 15	16 25 09 [16 sec early]	16 25 43 [34 sec late]	16 26 13 [58 sec late]
Maximum Alt.	71°14'00"	71°14'04"	71°14'00"	71°13'33"
Latitude [Error]	42°00'00"N	41°59'53"N [00°00'07"]	41°59'57"N [00°00'03"]	42°00'24"N [00°00'24"]
Longitude [Error]	65°53'53"W	65°52'23"W [00°01'30"]	66°00'51"W [00°06'58"]	66°08'25"W [00°14'32"]

are, respectively, 0.3, 1.2, and 2.4 minutes of sextant altitude. The first of these three represents the situation on a calm day on a small vessel; the other two typify the results that may be obtained under conditions when nearby wave tops may be mistaken for the horizon, or when the heaving of the deck upsets the observer's ability to read. The values shown represent instances in which the navigator still expects to obtain fairly accurate results. The situation could, of course, get much worse; fluctuations of many minutes of arc at the sextant are possible.

Two principal conclusions can be drawn from figure 4.1. First of all, even when there are fairly severe fluctuations, the method of parabolic regression can extract the sun's maximum altitude with reasonable accuracy. This is evident from the fact that for the parabolas showing standard deviations of 0, 0.3, and 1.2 minutes, the values for maximum altitude *(Hmax)* cluster within a narrow range. Even the curve for the greatest level of fluctuation (with the standard deviation of 2.4 minutes) results in a calculated latitude only 24 seconds from the true value. By contrast, if latitude at *LAN* were to be calculated on the basis of observations made just at the peak of sun altitude, and if the fluctuations at the sextant were severe enough to yield a standard deviation of 2.4 minutes, the resulting latitude error would have a high probability of being equal to or exceeding 2 minutes, or 2 nautical miles. That is, it would be five times as great as the error accompanying the use of parabolic regression. Hence, the general conclusion should be drawn that regression methods enable one to calculate maximum sun altitude, and therefore latitude, with sustained accuracy even in the face of fairly severe fluctuations in observed sextant altitudes.

At the same time, however, as indicated by the calculated results shown in table 4.5, these fluctuations severely degrade the calculations of longitude. As the fluctuations increase, the shift in the calculated time of maximum altitude also tends to increase; the error in this case may be as large as a minute (58 seconds for the standard deviation of 2.4 minutes). Longitude calculated from this data would be in error by 14 minutes, 32 seconds.

In general, if the observed sextant altitudes are such that the standard deviation of the data is 0.5 minutes or less, longitude errors will probably be less than 3 to 4 minutes of arc; if the standard deviation is approximately twice that amount, longitude errors of up to 10 minutes or more can be expected —translating to position errors of 5 to 7 nautical miles in the middle latitudes, and up to 10 miles at the equator.

The parabolic regression technique, with its property of smoothing and making a mathematical best fit to the observed data, is about as useful as any method of curve fitting in the face of uncertainty. Any other technique, such as the one that requires values for equal sun altitudes observed before and after noon, will not provide better results. Hence, when fluctuations become very severe—with sextant altitudes that can vary from reading to reading by more than 3 or 4 minutes of arc—it is probably useless to try to calculate longitude from a noon sight.

246

4.5.2 Shift in Time of Local Apparent Noon Due to Vessel Motion If a vessel is not stationary, the effect of any northward or southward component in its motion at the time of meridian passage must be considered when longitude is computed from the time of *LAN*. For example, in the Northern Hemisphere, it will be found that if a vessel is moving south, the time of maximum altitude of the sun will be later than it would otherwise have been; if the vessel is moving north, the time of maximum altitude will be earlier. In both cases, the observed altitude at *LAN* will be greater than it would be if measured from a stationary vessel in the same position at that time. The vessel's motion thus

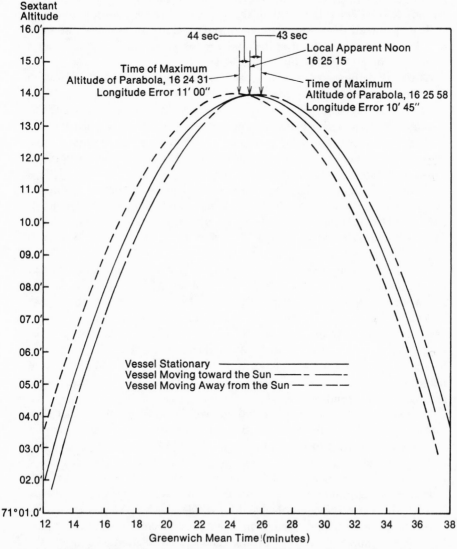

4.2. Longitude Error Resulting from Movement Toward or Away from the Sun at Local Apparent Noon

247

results in a shift both in the value of the sun's maximum altitude and in the *time* at which the maximum occurs. The former—as we know—affects the calculated latitude, and the latter the longitude.

Figure 4.2 illustrates these effects. Three parabolic curves have been constructed, based on the calculated behavior of the sun as it would have been observed at an approximate latitude of 42 degrees north on June 21, 1978, under three conditions: from a stationary vessel at latitude 42°00′00″N and longitude 65°53′53″W (solid line); from a vessel moving due north at 6.0 knots and passing through latitude 42°00′00″N at the *LAN* for this longitude (broken line); and from a vessel moving due south at 6.0 knots and passing through latitude 42°00′00″N at the *LAN* for this longitude (alternating short and long dashes). From all three vessels the noon sun would be observed on the same meridian at the same latitude at the same time, so the latitudes and longitudes calculated for all three should be the same.

As the figure indicates, the curve of observed sun altitude with respect to time for the northward-moving vessel actually reaches its maximum 44 seconds in advance of meridian passage. A regression parabola employed to obtain the time of meridian passage would reflect this error, and the longitude would be calculated as 65°42′53″W, for a position incorrect by 11 minutes east. At a northward speed of 6.0 knots, this would result in a position error of 8.2 nautical miles.

Correspondingly, on the southward-moving vessel the observed time of maximum altitude is 43 seconds later than meridian passage (the difference of one second between the two cases is due to rounding errors in the calculation). The resulting longitude of 66°04′38″W is in error by 10 minutes, 45 seconds west, for a position error of 8.0 nautical miles.

On the other hand, the calculations of latitude are only minimally affected by the movement of the vessels. In the 43- or 44-second interval, errors of only 2 or 3 seconds of arc result from the movement of the vessels and the change in declination of the sun between the time of maximum altitude of the parabola and the time of *LAN*. The error might be slightly larger at certain times of the year—for example, the vernal and autumnal equinoxes, when the sun's declination changes most rapidly. Also, if a vessel is moving north or south at higher speed, the latitude shift at the time of maximum sun altitude will be proportionately greater.

Even so, the error in calculated latitude will be substantially smaller than that in calculated longitude under the same conditions. The latter error is significant even at the moderate vessel speed of 6.0 knots, and of course will be proportionately larger for vessels going north or south at higher speeds. If in addition there are significant fluctuations in the observations of sun altitudes, introducing further uncertainty about the time the maximum altitude is reached, the error in the calculated longitude will be even greater.

However, although the calculation of longitude from a noon sight should be understood to be much less precise than the calculation of latitude, the errors in both latitude and longitude *due to vessel motion* can be virtually eliminated by introduction of the necessary correction factors. These factors

248

DATA

	Away from Sun	Toward Sun
Deviation	0	0
Variation	−20°(W)	−20°(W)
Compass Course	020°(000°T)	200°(180°T)
Speed	6.0 knots	6.0 knots
Date	June 21, 1978	June 21, 1978
Limb	lower	lower
Height of Eye	10 feet	10 feet
Bearing to Sun	south	south

GMT	Sextant Altitude		
	Stationary	Ct 000°	Ct 180°
16 12 10	71° 02.0′	71° 03.6′	71° 00.7′
16 14 00	71 05.1	71 06.2	71 04.0
16 15 55	71 07.9	71 08.8	71 06.9
16 18 12	71 10.5	71 11.2	71 09.8
16 21 05	71 12.7	71 13.2	71 12.3
16 23 12	71 13.7	71 13.9	71 13.5
LAN 16 25 15	71 14.0	71 14.0	71 14.0
16 27 06	71 13.7	71 13.5	71 13.9
16 28 48	71 13.1	71 12.7	71 13.4
16 31 00	71 11.6	71 11.1	71 12.2
16 34 06	71 08.5	71 07.6	71 09.4
16 35 54	71 06.0	71 05.0	71 07.1
16 37 06	71 04.3	71 03.0	71 05.3

CALCULATED RESULTS

	Stationary	Away from Sun		Toward Sun	
		Not Corrected	Corrected	Not Corrected	Corrected
GMT of Maximum Alt.	16 25 15	16 24 31 [44 sec early]	16 25 14 [1 sec early]	16 25 58 [43 sec late]	16 25 15 [correct]
Maximum Alt.	71°14′00″	71°13′59″	71°13′57″	71°14′00″	71°13′58″
Latitude [Error]	42°00′00″N	41°59′58″N [00°00′02″]	42°00′00″N [none]	41°59′57″N [00°00′03″]	41°59′59″N [00°00′01″]
Longitude [Error]	65°53′53″W	65°42′53″W [00°11′00″]	65°53′36″W [00°00′17″]	66°04′38″W [00°10′45″]	65°53′50″W [00°00′03″]

have been incorporated into the program for routine 4.7.* Their effectiveness is evident from table 4.6, which presents the data from which the three parabolas shown in figure 4.2 were constructed, with comparisons of the positions obtained from parabolic regression without corrections and from parabolic regression with corrections (by means of routine 4.7, used in conjunction with routine 4.8).

4.5.3 Routines for the Noon Fix

The use of the calculator routine for parabolic regression is a substitute for the method of plotting altitudes of the sun on graph paper in order to establish its maximum altitude and the time when it reaches that maximum. Drawing a smooth parabolic curve by eye is replaced by the automatic curve fitting of the regression technique. If data concerning course and speed of the vessel is entered, corrections are made automatically for any inherent error in calculated longitude due to motion of the vessel.

The calculator computes the elements of a parabola that makes the best fit to the observed data; it then displays the maximum sextant altitude and the time *(GMT)* at which this maximum occurs. These results can be utilized in routine 4.8 for the calculation of the vessel's position. All of the remarks in the preceding sections concerning fluctuation in observed sextant angles, and its effect on the accuracy, should of course be given consideration—especially the fact that the latitude calculated by these methods is probably more precise than the longitude. Nevertheless, routines 4.7 and 4.8 are useful; there is no need for almanacs, since a data card prepared by means of routine 4.2 is employed, and the user need not remember any of the complicated rules about combining corrected sextant altitude with declination, since the procedures for converting sun altitude to latitude and time into longitude are built into the program.

When routine 4.7 is begun, care should be taken to press $\boxed{f}\,\boxed{a}$ to make sure that the calculator's memory registers are empty. If the vessel is moving, entry

---

*The program is formulated so that the correction factors are used as shown in the following equations:

$$T_{LAN} = T_M - \frac{S}{2C}$$

and

$$H_{LAN} = H_M + \frac{S^2}{4C}$$

where T_{LAN} = corrected time of local apparent noon,
   T_M = time of the vertex of the regression parabola,
   H_{LAN} = corrected sun altitude at *LAN*,
   H_M = sun altitude at the vertex of the regression parabola,
   S = speed, in degrees of latitude change per hour (+ if away from the sun, − if toward the sun),
   C = coefficient of the second-order term of the regression parabola, in units of degrees per hour squared, and always negative.

From these equations, it is evident that the correction to the *time* of *LAN* can be either positive or negative, to compensate for the shift in time of maximum altitude resulting from a vessel's movement away from or toward the sun. The correction to sun altitude itself is always negative, because the effect of motion in either direction is to increase the observed altitude at *LAN* as compared to that seen from a stationary vessel at the same latitude and longitude at the same time.

Routine 4.7 (HP-67/97)

Clear	De Var	Compass Course		S
		Toward Sun	Away from Sun	
Hs	Ts	LAN Hmax	Day	

PARABOLIC REGRESSION

Step	Procedure	Input Data/Units	Keys	Output Data/Units
1	Load program—both sides			
2	Clear; this step *must* be performed		f a	
	If vessel is stationary, continue at step 7.			
3	Enter deviation (+E,−W), even if 0	DD.d	f b	
4	Enter variation (+E,−W), even if 0	DD.d	f b	
5	If vessel is moving *toward* the sun (on any true course from 270° through 90° when the sun is *north* of the vessel, or from 90° through 270° when the sun is *south* of the vessel), enter compass course*	DDD.d	f c	
6	If vessel is moving *away* from the sun (on any true course from 90° through 270° when the sun is *north* of the vessel, or from 270° through 90° when the sun is *south* of the vessel), enter compass course*	DDD.d	f d	
7	Enter vessel speed; if vessel is stationary, enter speed as 0	knots	f e	
8	Enter sequence of altitude-time pairs; for each pair, enter observed sextant altitude (corrected for index error), followed by	DDMM.m	A	
9	*GMT* of observation of altitude	H.MS	B	

If an error is noted in the entry of altitude or time data before the corresponding letter key (A or B) is pressed, eliminate the incorrect data by pressing CLx ; if the error is noted after the letter key has been pressed, clear the calculator by pressing f a , and re-enter all data, starting at step 3.

| 10 | Calculate and display *GMT* of local apparent noon (corrected for vessel's motion), | | C | H.MS |

*Correct for leeway; see table 2.2.

(CONTINUED)

Step	Procedure	Input Data/Units	Keys	Output Data/Units
·	Corresponding (i.e., maximum) sextant altitude, in degrees, minutes, and *seconds*			DD.MMSS
11	If routine 4.8 is to be used next, enter day of month, corresponding to *GMT* displayed in step 10	1–31	D	

of deviation and variation follows, and then the compass course is entered either at step 5 (with keys $\boxed{f}\boxed{c}$) or at step 6 (with keys $\boxed{f}\boxed{d}$), depending on whether the course is toward or away from the sun. Steps 3–6 are omitted for a stationary vessel, but step 7—entry of vessel speed—is always performed, with speed being set equal to zero if the vessel is not in motion.

Input of the altitude–time pairs is next, with sextant altitude in the form of degrees, minutes, and tenths of minutes, as read on the instrument, and the time of each observation in hours, minutes, and seconds. Pressing $\boxed{C}$ then results in calculation and display of the time of *LAN* and the corresponding sextant altitude. The last step is entry of the day of the month. This is necessary for the use of the sun data card in routine 4.8, for the noon fix.

Once the program for routine 4.8, and the sun data card, have been loaded, and the calculator has been cleared, pressing $\boxed{A}$ results in utilization of the almanac in the calculation of the Greenwich hour angle and declination of the sun at *LAN* at the time and date specified in steps 10–11 of routine 4.7.

Two questions next arise: has the upper or lower limb of the sun been observed, and is the sun north or south of the vessel? The first is answered by pressing $\boxed{B}$ (for upper limb) or $\boxed{C}$ (for lower limb) when height of eye is entered; the second, by pressing $\boxed{D}$ (if the sun is to the south) or $\boxed{E}$ (if the sun is to the north) to display the calculated latitude.

Routine 4.8 can also be used independently of routine 4.7, when the navigator relies upon traditional methods to obtain the sun's altitude at *LAN*. All that is necessary is to enter sextant altitude, date, and *GMT* of the observation, as shown in steps 2–5, before loading the sun data card. The remainder of the routine can then be performed.

After the latitude has been displayed, the calculated longitude can be obtained by pressing $\boxed{f}\boxed{e}$. However, as noted in section 4.5.1, unless the exact time of meridian passage can be determined (to a precision of a few seconds), the resulting longitude will not be accurate enough to be of use. By contrast, for the calculation of latitude alone any value within a few minutes of the actual time of meridian passage is acceptable; the sun's declination will change by only a few seconds of arc in that period, and the effect on the accuracy of the computed latitude will therefore be negligible.

The data in tables 4.6 and 4.9 can be employed to check the accuracy of the user's program.

252

Routine 4.8 (HP-67/97)

Hs Day Ts				Longitude
GHA Dec	Height of Eye Upper Limb	Lower Limb	Latitude B to Sun, S	B to Sun, N

NOON FIX

Step	Procedure	Input Data/Units	Keys	Output Data/Units
1	Load program—both sides			
	If routine 4.7 has just been completed, continue at step 5. If routine 4.7 has not just been completed, proceed as follows (steps 2–13):			
2	Enter observed sextant altitude (corrected for index error) at time of meridian passage, in degrees, minutes, and *seconds*	DD.MMSS	f a	
3	Enter day of month, corresponding to *GMT* to be entered in step 4	1–31	f a	
4	Enter *GMT* of observation of altitude entered in step 2	H.MS	f a	
5	Load sun data card—one side		CRD	
6	Clear		CL*x*	
7	Calculate *GHA* and declination of sun (these values are not displayed)	A		
8	If upper-limb observation has been made, enter height of eye	feet	B	
9	If lower-limb observation has been made, enter height of eye	feet	C	
	If bearing to sun has been south during observations, proceed as follows (steps 10–11):			
10	Calculate and display vessel's latitude		D	±DD.MMSS
11	Calculate and display vessel's longitude		f e	±DD.MMSS
	If bearing to sun has been north during observations, proceed as follows (steps 12–13):			
12	Calculate and display vessel's latitude		E	±DD.MMSS
13	Calculate and display vessel's longitude		f e	±DD.MMSS

253

4.5.4 Predicting the Time of Local Apparent Noon

It is important to be able to predict the time of meridian passage, especially when using regression methods, since observation of the sun must begin five or ten minutes *before* it actually crosses the meridian. The normal way to make this prediction is to consult the nautical almanac, and by interpolation, find the time at which the Greenwich hour angle of the sun is equal to the DR longitude of the observer's meridian. However, if the vessel is moving, and the observer's meridian is constantly changing, additional calculation becomes necessary. This whole procedure, including any use of the almanac, can be avoided by employing routine 4.9.

A sun data card for the appropriate interval is necessary. In most respects the procedure in this routine is straightforward. It should be emphasized, however, that as part of the input, a dead-reckoning longitude for a time earlier than local apparent noon is required. If the time (as entered in step 5) is later than *LAN*, the result displayed in step 11 will represent the approximate time of *LAN* on the *following day* at the dead-reckoning longitude which has just been entered.

The data for the example given in tables 4.7 and 4.9 can be employed to test the user's program.

Table 4.7   Time of Local Apparent Noon

DATA	
Date	June 21, 1978
GMT	15 00 00
Compass Course	45°
Variation	−10°(W)
Deviation	+2°(E)
Speed	8.0 knots
DR Longitude	60°30′W
CALCULATED RESULT	
Time of LAN	16 03 18

254

Routine 4.9 (HP-67/97)

Day GMT	GHA	Cc Var De	S	LoDR→LAN

TIME OF LOCAL APPARENT NOON

Step	Procedure	Input Data/Units	Keys	Output Data/Units
1	Load program—both sides			
2	Load sun data card—one side			CRD
3	Clear		CLx	
4	Enter day of month, corresponding to *GMT* to be entered in step 5	1–31	A	
5	Enter time of day (*GMT*) for which DR position is available; this must be earlier than local apparent noon	H.MS	A	
6	Calculate *GHA* of sun (this value is not displayed)		B	
7	Enter compass course*	DDD.d	C	
8	Enter variation (+E, −W), even if 0	DD.d	C	
9	Enter deviation (+E, −W), even if 0	DD.d	C	
10	Enter vessel speed	knots	D	
11	Enter vessel's DR longitude at time entered in step 5 (+W, −E),	DD.MMSS	E	
·	Calculate and display *GMT* of local apparent noon (if the value displayed is earlier than the value entered in step 5, it refers to the local apparent noon of the following day)			H.MS

*Correct for leeway; see table 2.2.

4.6 Planning Star Observations

Routine 4.11 provides the reader with a convenient method of planning star observations at dusk or dawn, at any place on the earth, without having to resort to the almanac for any data relating to Aries or to the sidereal hour angle of forty-two stars. The prerecording of a data card, as shown in routine 4.10, is required.* This must be done only once, since in this instance annual updating of the data is not necessary. In routine 4.11, once the data card has been loaded, and the necessary particulars concerning the vessel's approximate position and the date and time have been entered, a list is supplied showing which of the forty-two are above the user's horizon at the place and time specified, and including for each of these the number of the star (for identification), its altitude in degrees and minutes (although this figure can be assumed to be accurate only to the nearest degree), and its azimuth to the nearest tenth of a degree.

---

*Routine 4.10 and routine 4.11 (with its accompanying program) were developed by Hewlett-Packard and are included as "SHA Star Data Card" and "Star Sight Planner" in Navigation Pac 1. They are reproduced in this volume by permission of Hewlett-Packard.

Routine 4.10 (HP-67/97)

```
┌─────────────────────────────────────────────────────────────────┐
│                                                                   │
│                      Star Planning Data Card                      │
│                                                                   │
└─────────────────────────────────────────────────────────────────┘
```

STAR PLANNING DATA CARD

Step	Procedure	Input Data/Units	Keys	Output Data/Units
1	Set decimal point of display		DSP 9	
	Enter the following numbers (steps 2–12):			
2	0.339372100		STO 1	
3	18941.60088		STO 2	
4	81717.37302		STO 3	
5	72264.47856		STO 4	
6	22270.41177		STO 5	
7	54476.24512		STO 6	
8	46256.79618		STO 7	
9	59588.47426		STO 8	
10	34622.74119		STO 9	
11	82118.25485		STO A	
12	44888.67166		STO B	
13	Shift to secondary storage		f p⟷s	
	Enter the following numbers (steps 14–23):			
14	89094.55238		STO 0	
15	43536.15781		STO 1	
16	41856.59664		STO 2	
17	85192.19148		STO 3	
18	56337.23035		STO 4	
19	39743.84219		STO 5	
20	9228.353662		STO 6	
21	64772.70977		STO 7	
22	43175.28825		STO 8	
23	64907.45486		STO 9	
24	Prepare to record data card		f W/DATA	CRD
25	Record data card—both sides			CRD

257

Routine 4.11 (HP-67/97)

Print?				
L↑Lo	Y↑Mo↑Day	GMT→List	DAWN Y↑Mo↑Day→List	DUSK Y↑Mo↑Day→List

STAR SIGHT PLANNER

Step	Procedure	Input Data/Units	Keys	Output Data/Units
1	Load program—both sides			
2	Load star planning data card—both sides			
3	For HP-97, instruct calculator to print (repeat step if necessary until "1" is diplayed)		f a	1
4	Enter DR or approximate latitude at time observations are to be made (+N,−S)	DD.MMSS	ENTER	
5	Enter DR or approximate longitude at time observations are to be made (+W, −E)	DD.MMSS	A	
6	Enter year	19nn	ENTER	
7	Enter month	1–12	ENTER	

For a list of stars visible at a specified time, proceed as follows (steps 8–9):

Step	Procedure	Input Data/Units	Keys	Output Data/Units
8	Enter day of month, corresponding to *GMT* to be entered in step 9	1–31	B	
9	Enter time of day (*GMT*) for which list is to be displayed or printed,	H.MS	C	
·	For each star above horizon at place and time specified, calculate and display star number,			0–56
·	Altitude,			DD.MM
·	Azimuth			DDD.d

For a list of stars visible at dawn, proceed as follows (step 10):

Step	Procedure	Input Data/Units	Keys	Output Data/Units
10	Enter day of month, corresponding to *GMT* of dawn,	1–31	D	
·	Calculate and display *GMT* of middle of nautical dawn,			H.M
·	For each star above horizon at dawn at place specified, calculate and display star number,			0–56
·	Altitude,			DD.MM
·	Azimuth			DDD.d

258

Step	Procedure	Input Data/Units	Keys	Output Data/Units
	For a list of stars visible at dusk, proceed as follows (step 11):			
11	Enter day of month, corresponding to GMT of dusk,	1–31	E	
·	Calculate and display *GMT* of middle of nautical dusk,			H.M
·	For each star above horizon at dusk at place specified, calculate and display star number,			0–56
·	Altitude,			DD.MM
·	Azimuth			DDD.d

The routine can be used in several ways. If a list of stars for a particular time of day is desired, the day of the month is entered at B in step 8, and the *GMT* is entered at C in step 9; the calculator then lists the stars above the horizon at that time. If a list of stars visible at dawn is required, the day of the month is ented at D in step 10, and the list of stars for the middle of nautical dawn is provided without further keyboard activity. For the list of stars visible at dusk, the day of the month is entered at E, in step 11.

Table 4.8   Star Sight Planning

DATA			
Latitude	40°00′00″N		
Longitude	75°00′00″W		
Year	1978		
Month	August		
Day	28		
CALCULATED RESULTS			
Middle of			
Nautical	0958		
Dawn			
Star Number	54.	18.	7.
Altitude	6.58	18.51	9.20
Azimuth	277.2	133.6	188.7
	53.	16.	6.
	18.10	45.52	63.23
	314.1	129.5	237.6
	40.	12.	4.
	24.18	71.42	18.51
	3.7	63.0	224.5
	32.	11.	3.
	12.28	37.36	56.33
	22.6	151.1	313.9
	27.	10.	1.
	26.07	63.11	45.26
	29.3	149.6	272.9
	21.	9.	0.
	39.13	79.33	40.00
	83.9	344.7	360.0
	20.	8.	
	26.08	52.49	
	106.6	197.1	

Table 4.8, illustrating the procedure for obtaining a list of stars visible at dawn, can be employed to test the user's program and data card.

Table 4.9 Almanac Data for 1978[1]

Sun and Aries, January 15 and 27

DAYS 1 THRU 32   JD 2443509.5 TO 2443541.5   DATES JAN 1 THRU FEB 1

A = 16.00000000   B = -1.06250000

POWERS OF TIME COEFFICIENTS

	ARIES GHA	SUN GHA	SUN DEC	SUN S D
	0	0	0	0
0	6236.0627	6297.5195	-20.8507	0.2717
1	5775.7708	5758.6564	3.0968	0.0
2	-0.0036	0.3829	0.8462	0.0
3	-0.0029	0.0441	-0.0642	0.0
4	-0.0031	-0.0206	-0.0058	0.0
5	0.0027	0.0013	0.0044	0.0

Sun, June 21

DAYS 152 THRU 183   JD 2443660.5 TO 2443692.5   DATES JUNE 1 THRU JULY 2

A = 16.00000000   B = -10.50000000

POWERS OF TIME COEFFICIENTS

	ARIES GHA	SUN GHA	SUN DEC	SUN S D
	0	0	0	0
0	6024.8941	5939.8385	23.3613	0.2633
1	5775.7686	5759.1417	0.5232	0.0
2	0.0001	-0.0375	-0.8772	0.0
3	0.0043	-0.0599	-0.0043	0.0
4	-0.0001	-0.0018	0.0048	0.0
5	-0.0027	0.0010	-0.0016	0.0

(CONTINUED)

Moon, January 27

DAYS 25 THRU 30   JD 2443533.5 TO 2443539.5   DATES JAN 25 THRU JAN 30

A = 3.00000000   B = -9.33333333

POWERS OF TIME COEFFICIENTS

	MOON GHA	MOON DEC	MOON H P	MOON S D
	0	0	0	0
0	1397.3389	2.7633	0.9333	0.2543
1	1046.7636	-11.8904	0.0257	0.0070
2	-0.5113	-0.8233	0.0039	0.0011
3	-0.6102	0.7265	-0.0011	-0.0003
4	-0.0849	0.0530	-0.0005	-0.0001
5	0.0263	0.0063	0.0009	0.0002

Kochab, January 27

ID	NAV	NAME	MAG/SP		MEAN PLACE	H	R	S	C	APPT PLACE
					0	0	0	0		0
113	39	ALPHA-2 LIB ZUBENELGENUBI	2.9 A3	SHA	137.5854	-0.0014	-0.0123	-0.0047	0.0032	137.5746
				DEC	-15.9514	0.0014	-0.0035	-0.0014	0.0009	-15.9526
114	40	BETA UMI KOCHAB	2.2 K5	SHA	137.3113	0.0066	0.0009	-0.0165	0.0115	137.3068
				DEC	74.2453	0.0014	-0.0035	-0.0032	-0.0047	74.2496
115		BETA LUP	2.8 B2	SHA	135.7292	-0.0027	-0.0147	-0.0060	0.0044	135.7147
				DEC	-43.0464	0.0015	-0.0034	0.0003	0.0029	-43.0495

[1]LeRoy E. Doggett, George H. Kaplan, and P. Kenneth Seidelmann, *Almanac for Computers* (Washington, D.C.: Nautical Almanac Office, United States Naval Observatory, 1978), extracts from pp. C1, C3, C8, and F6.

5
Loran

ABBREVIATIONS Used in the Routines of Chapter 5

Bt true bearing from vessel to destination

Btdest true bearing from reference point to destination

Btstart true bearing from reference point to vessel at first fix

Btv true bearing from calibration or reference point to vessel

Cc compass course

Cm magnetic course

CMG true course made good

D distance from vessel to destination

DD.d, DDD.d degrees and tenths of a degree

Ddest distance from reference point to destination

DD.MMSS degrees, minutes, and seconds

De deviation

DMG distance made good

Dr drift of current

Dstart distance from reference point to vessel at first fix

Dv distance from calibration or reference point to vessel

E east

EP estimated position

H.MS hour(s), minute(s), and second(s)

L latitude

La latitude of A slave

Lb latitude of B slave

Lcp latitude of calibration point

Lfix latitude of fix

Lm latitude of master

Lo longitude

Loa longitude of A slave

Lob longitude of B slave

Locp longitude of calibration point

Lofix longitude of fix

Lom longitude of master

Loref longitude of reference point

Lostart longitude of vessel at previous fix

Lref latitude of reference point

Lstart latitude of vessel at previous fix

mmmm microseconds

mmmmm.m microseconds and tenths of microseconds

N north

naut. mi. nautical miles

S vessel speed; south

SMG speed made good

St set of current

ΔT time required to reach destination

T1 time of previous fix

T2 time of present fix

TDa A-slave time difference

TDacp A-slave time difference at calibration point

TDb B-slave time difference

TDbcp B-slave time difference at calibration point

Var variation

W west

↑ following a data-entry item indicates that it is entered by pressing ENTER instead of a letter key.

→ following a data-entry item indicates that its entry initiates (without further keyboard activity) the calculation and display of one or more results.

+ indicates that the item (e.g., east variation or north latitude) is entered simply by pressing the appropriate numerical keys.

− indicates that the item is entered by pressing the appropriate numerical keys followed by CHS.

5.1 Introduction

This chapter describes the use of the HP-67 and HP-97 in converting received loran signals into position co-ordinates. The method is equally effective in handling Loran A and Loran C signals; also, time-difference readings based on Loran A signals may be converted into the equivalent readings that would be obtained from a Loran C receiver, and vice versa. In addition, it is possible to predict the loran time differences that would be recorded at a location of known latitude and longitude, such as a vessel's dead-reckoning or estimated position. This procedure helps to identify the signals when they are received, and is particularly useful where high levels of radio interference are present.

The chapter is not intended to serve as a primary reference on the principles governing the operation of loran systems. A basic knowledge of these principles is assumed, and the discussion focuses on the utilization of the calculator in loran navigation. For a fuller explanation of loran, the reader is encouraged to consult such standard texts as *Dutton's Navigation and Piloting* (Annapolis, Naval Institute Press, 1969), chapter 32, and "Bowditch"—*American Practical Navigator, vol. 1* (Defense Mapping Agency Hydrographic Center, 1977), pp. 991–1002.

The calculator is especially useful in dealing with loran because it enables one to combine position fixing with planning and the determination of estimated position. To make accurate estimates of position, one must take into account currents, leeway, and other factors (including possible errors in the speed and compass readings that have been obtained) which can interfere with achieving the desired or expected track made good over the bottom. These factors will be reflected in the values for set and drift of "current" obtained on the basis of successive loran fixes. And since repeated loran fixes can be made, updated information on this current is continuously available, to serve as input for the calculation of courses to steer and estimated position. This chapter discusses a set of integrated programs and routines by means of which repeated readouts of vessel position, based upon loran data, may be obtained.

At present, both Loran A and Loran C systems are being actively maintained, with considerable overlap in their coverage. Loran A, however, will be phased out during the next few years. Many mariners and navigators rely upon previously determined position locations known only in terms of their Loran A co-ordinates, and conversion to the new Loran C time-difference values will be necessary if this information is to continue to be of use after Loran A transmissions cease. A method for making the conversion is described in this

chapter. Routine 5.5 first converts Loran A time differences into the latitude and longitude of the location in question, and then, without further keyboard input, displays the predicted Loran C time differences for the same location.

Instructions in this chapter have been supplied only for the HP-67 and HP-97, because at this writing no other hand-held models have program and data memories large enough to require only one or two program cards for the completion of a sequence. This situation will most assuredly change in the future, and programs and routines will be written for new calculators as they become available.

5.2 Accuracy of the Loran A and Loran C Systems

Generally speaking, when used within the accepted limits of coverage, Loran A fixes range in accuracy from a few tenths of a mile to three to five miles, depending on the location of the vessel within the coverage area. One reason Loran C is replacing Loran A is that the Loran C system is inherently more accurate; it can provide fixes correct to within tenths of a mile throughout the ground-wave coverage area. This system is superior in part because it is instrumented to make possible time-difference readings of a precision of tenths of microseconds (compared to microseconds in Loran A). Also, it operates at a lower radio frequency (100 kilohertz, as opposed to 2,000 kilohertz in Loran A), and therefore permits exploitation of the more stable propagation of low-frequency waves. Since the method depends entirely on measurement of the time of arrival of shaped pulses of radio energy, this stability is essential. Loran C can utilize ground-wave signals transmitted over longer distances—up to 1,000 or 1,500 miles. Reflecting objects have not more than one-twentieth as much effect on the longer, lower-frequency waves of Loran C. Furthermore, because of the stability of transmission, and the receiver's ability to measure differential timing between signals with high accuracy, the repeatability of Loran C is high; that is to say, the time differences at a particular location will remain uniform over a long period of time.

The calculator methods described in the following sections will work equally well for either system. However, the results will reflect the inherent accuracy of the time-difference readings upon which they are based, and since more precise readings are available from Loran C, the positions determined by Loran C will be more exact.

The routines presented in this chapter utilize a method of local calibration which compensates for anomalies or distortions in the time of arrival of the pulses received. The input for this calibration includes the latitude and longitude of a place and the time-difference readings obtained at that place from two pairs of loran stations.

In many cases, the useful coverage area of a Loran A calibration will be smaller than that of a Loran C calibration made in the same vicinity, because at the higher frequencies of Loran A, propagation anomalies and distortions

266

change more rapidly with respect to distance. Since, to preserve accuracy, the area relying on a single calibration point will be smaller with Loran A than with Loran C, more calibration points may be necessary.

It is difficult to lay down a hard and fast rule covering the location of calibration points, but it is safe to say that the number of these points can be reduced as the distance from shore lines and harbors is increased. In coastal waters, calculations involving a calibration point will yield precise results if the vessel is in the vicinity of the calibrated location. Calibrations made out at sea, far from coastlines and buildings, can cover much larger areas. For example, with Loran C a calibration made at sea might easily provide accuracy of $\pm$ 0.25 of a nautical mile throughout the area covered by a radius extending up to two hundred miles from the calibration point. Table 5.1 provides rough guidelines, applicable within the ground-wave coverage area of two or more Loran C pairs.

Table 5.1 Loran Calibration Coverage

Required Accuracy in Position Location	Radius of Coverage of a Single Calibration[1]
$\pm$ 80 yards	1 mile
$\pm$ 200 yards	5 miles
$\pm$ 500 yards	50 miles

[1]The radius of usefulness of a single calibration should be checked by actual test observations, since different localities will possess different characteristics.

The crossing angle of Loran C lines of position will also affect position accuracy, and should not be much less than 60 degrees. Also, automatic-tracking Loran C receivers will provide performance superior to that of manual-setting receivers, especially in high-interference or low-signal-strength areas.

Since the effective coverage of a single calibration point does vary from one place to another, the user should make his own survey to determine the accuracy obtainable in the area in question, and hence the frequency with which one calibration point should be exchanged for the next. In some cases, accuracy of $\pm$ 80 yards can be obtained from a single calibration over many miles; in others, it will be apparent that for this degree of accuracy the more stringent limits of a 1-mile radius of coverage, as specified in the table, should be observed.

Once made, a calibration will be useful over long periods of time. Surveys of the stability of Loran C transmissions over many weeks indicate that shifts in the designation of positions due to transmitter mistiming or short-term weather effects are almost always less than 30 yards. There may be observable shifts from one season of the year to the next, but these will probably have only a small effect on the level of performance as predicted in table 5.1. With Loran A, the propagation anomalies change somewhat more rapidly, over time. In every case, the navigator should make his own assessment of the need to recalculate calibration, and act accordingly.

5.3 Preparation of Loran Calibrations

Calibrations for both the Loran A and the Loran C systems are made by means of routine 5.1, the Loran Calibrator routine. The resulting data cards are subsequently used in routine 5.2, the Loran Locator routine. The initial input data for routine 5.1 consists of the latitude and longitude co-ordinates for three loran transmitter stations—two slaves (arbitrarily designated A and B) and their master. Further input data, in later steps, consists of the latitude and longitude for the selected calibration point, and of the time-difference readings obtained at that point from the signals of the two slave stations. These readings are designated time-difference A *(TDa)* and time-difference B *(TDb)*.

Routine 5.1 (HP-67/97)

La↑Loa	Lb↑Lob	La↑Lom		Lcp↑Locp↑ TDacp↑TDbcp

LORAN CALIBRATOR

Step	Procedure	Input Data/Units	Keys	Output Data/Units
1	Load program—both sides			
2	Enter latitude of A slave (+N,−S)	DD.MMSS	ENTER	
3	Enter longitude of A slave (+W,−E)	DD.MMSS	A	
4	Enter latitude of B slave (+N,−S)	DD.MMSS	ENTER	
5	Enter longitude of B slave (+W,−E)	DD.MMSS	B	
6	Enter latitude of master (+N,−S)	DD.MMSS	ENTER	
7	Enter longitude of master (+W,−E)	DD.MMSS	C	
8	Record data card, both sides, and label with names of A slave, B slave, and master		f W/DATA	
9	Enter latitude of calibration point (+N, −S)	DD.MMSS	ENTER	
10	Enter longitude of calibration point (+W, −E)	DD.MMSS	ENTER	
11	Enter A-slave time difference at calibration point	mmmmm.m	ENTER	
12	Enter B-slave time difference at calibration point	mmmmm.m	E	CRD

Where Loran A time differences are involved, care should be taken in steps 11–12 to enter negative values when necessary, as explained in the text, p. 271.

13 Record calibration data card, both sides, and label with names of A slave, B slave, master, and calibration point

To make a card for a different calibration point, using the same A slave, B slave, and master, load data card recorded in step 8, and repeat steps 9–13 for the new calibration point.

269

When the calibration is being done for a Loran C system, the master will be the station officially functioning as the master of the chain from which the stations are selected. For example, for the 9930 chain, the master station, whose co-ordinates would be entered at steps 6 and 7 of the routine, is at Carolina Beach, North Carolina. There are four slaves in this chain—the W, at Jupiter, Florida; the X, at Cape Race, Newfoundland; the Y, at Nantucket, Massachusetts; and the Z, at Dana, Indiana. However, only two would be used in this routine; the X station could be designated A, and the Z station designated B, with their time differences labeled respectively *TDa* and *TDb*.

When the calibration is being done for a Loran A system, the situation is more complicated, since the stations are normally grouped as pairs, each consisting of one master and one slave, rather than as chains. To obtain the necessary configuration, similar to that found in Loran C, two of these pairs are chosen which have one station in common. The common station is regarded as the master of that group, whether or not it is the official master (shown in capital letters in the list that follows) in either of the pairs. Almost all of the Loran A station pairs can be used in this fashion. For example, the following station pairs in the North Atlantic area are suitable:

Station Pairs	*Rates*
Battle Harbour, Labrador; FREDERICKSDAL, Greenland	1L 2
Battle Harbour, Labrador; BONAVISTA, Newfoundland	1L 3
DEMING, Nova Scotia; Port-aux-Basques, Newfoundland	1H 1
DEMING, Nova Scotia; Baccaro, Nova Scotia	1H 2
Baccaro, Nova Scotia; DEMING, Nova Scotia	1H 2
Baccaro, Nova Scotia; SIASCONSET, Nantucket I., Mass.	1H 3
SIASCONSET, Nantucket I., Mass.; Baccaro, Nova Scotia	1H 3
SIASCONSET, Nantucket I., Mass.; Marshall Point, Maine	1H 7
SIASCONSET, Nantucket I., Mass.; Baccaro, Nova Scotia	1H 3
Siasconset, Nantucket I., Mass.; SANDY HOOK, N.J.	3H 5
SIASCONSET, Nantucket I., Mass.; Baccaro, Nova Scotia	1H 3
SIASCONSET, Nantucket I., Mass.; Cape Hatteras, N.C.	3H 4
SIASCONSET, Nantucket I., Mass.; Cape Hatteras, N.C.	3H 4
Siasconset, Nantucket I., Mass.; SANDY HOOK, N.J.	3H 5
SIASCONSET, Nantucket I., Mass.; Marshall Point, Maine	1H 7
SIASCONSET, Nantucket I., Mass.; Cape Hatteras, N.C.	3H 4
SIASCONSET, Nantucket I., Mass.; Marshall Point, Maine	1H 7
Siasconset, Nantucket I., Mass.; SANDY HOOK, N.J.	3H 5
Cape Hatteras, N.C.; SIASCONSET, Nantucket I., Mass.	3H 4
Cape Hatteras, N.C., FOLLY I., S.C.	3H 6

FOLLY I., S.C.; Cape Hatteras, N.C.,	3H 6
FOLLY I., S.C.; Jupiter, Fla.	3L 1
Jupiter, Fla.; FOLLY I., S.C.	3L 1
Jupiter, Fla.; SAN SALVADOR, B.W.I.	3L 5
CAPE SAN BLAS, Fla., Venice, Fla.	3H 0
CAPE SAN BLAS, Fla., Grande Isla, La.	3H 1
Grande Isle, La.; CAPE SAN BLAS, Fla.	3H 1
Grande Isle, La.; GALVESTON, Texas	3H 2
South Caicos, B.W.I.; CAPE SAN JUAN, P.R.	3L 2
South Caicos, B.W.I.; SAN SALVADOR, B.W.I.	3L 3
SAN SALVADOR, B.W.I.; South Caicos, B.W.I.	3L 3
SAN SALVADOR, B.W.I.; Jupiter, Fla.	3L 5
Orssuiagssuag, Greenland; SANDUR, Iceland	1L 4
Orssuiagssuag, Greenland; KUTDLEK, Greenland	1L 5
Porto Santo, Madeira I.; SAGRES PT., Portugal	1S 5
Porto Santo, Madeira I.; SANTA MARIA, Azores	1S 6
SANTA MARIA, Azores; Porto Santo, Madeira I.	1S 6
SANTA MARIA, Azores; Flores, Azores	1S 7

In the case of Loran C, signals from the slave station are always transmitted later than those from the master, and the values for all time differences are therefore regarded as positive. However, in the case of Loran A, the situation varies, depending on whether or not the master of the group of three is also the official master in the two pairs involved. For example, for rates 1H 3 and 1H 7, the common station, Siasconset, is also the one designated master in the official list, and all time-difference readings are therefore regarded as positive. But for rates 1H 3 and 3H 5, the common station—again Siasconset—is master in one pair and slave in the other. Hence, the time-difference readings from 1H 3 will be positive, and those from 3H 5 will be negative. For rates 3L 2 and 3L 3, where the common station (South Caicos, B.W.I.) is officially the slave in both pairs, both time-difference readings will be negative.

After the latitude and longitude co-ordinates of the three stations have been entered, in steps 2–7 of routine 5.1, they are recorded on a data card, in step 8. This card can be preserved permanently, for use whenever the particular set of three stations is to be employed in a calibration procedure. That the same three stations will be used for several different calibrations is very likely, since they may provide coverage for thousands of square miles, while a calibration is valid for a much smaller area. (Note that in preparing the data card, after a latitude is entered, just the "Enter" key is pressed. The letter key— $\boxed{A}$ for the first location, $\boxed{B}$ for the second, and $\boxed{C}$ for the third—is pressed in each

instance only after the entry of the longitude in question.) The actual calibration is made by entering, in steps 9–12, the latitude and longitude of the particular point that has been chosen, and the time-difference readings *(TDa* and *TDb)* obtained there. Care must, of course, be taken to label the master and slave stations correctly, and to make the time-difference readings negative where necessary. When ⌐E⌐ has been pressed in step 12, and processing is complete, "CRD" appears in the display. A data card is then passed through the calculator (step 13), and it records all of the input information—the locations of the three stations, the location of the calibration point, and the time-difference readings at that point. The corners of this card, and of the card prepared in step 8, should be clipped to prevent accidental erasure or overwriting. This second card provides the initial data for the Loran Locator routine (routine 5.2). It can be used repeatedly—whenever the vessel is in the vicinity of the calibration point.

Wherever possible, time-difference data for a calibration point should be obtained by direct measurements at the place in question. These measurements are of course most desirable for calibrations in areas where the greatest accuracy is needed—in harbors and pilot waters, for example. If, at the same time that loran readings are taken, accurate position fixing can be accomplished by means of a round of compass bearings on visible, fixed, charted objects, or by means of horizontal sextant angles obtained for these objects, then exact calibrations can be made. For restricted waters, where the highest precision in fixing is needed, a number of calibration data cards should be prepared.

One advantage of this calculator method is that fixes can be obtained where there is no loran chart coverage. At this writing, loran lines of position do not appear on charts of larger scale than 1 to 80,000, so they are not present on the large-scale (small-area) charts most useful for inner harbors. But as will be evident in section 5.5, once a calibration for a point in a harbor has been calculated, a fix can be completed without these lines, and the latitude and longitude co-ordinates obtained can be plotted directly on a large-scale harbor chart.

Out at sea, where the best method of position fixing other than loran may be celestial navigation—customarily resulting in position uncertainties greater than some tenths of a mile—it is probably sufficient to utilize calibration data taken from loran charts instead of from direct readings. A calibration point is selected, say, in the middle of the chart, and the corresponding time differences at that place are read from the chart. Since the accuracy of the calibration will depend on the accuracy of the chart, and on the accuracy with which time differences and latitudes and longitudes are read from the chart, an effort should be made to employ the largest-scale chart available (that is, the one covering the smallest area) that contains the necessary loran lines of position. Latitude, longitude, and time differences can then be read with the greatest possible precision. On a chart of the scale of 1 to 80,000, it should be possible to measure latitude and longitude to a tenth of a minute of arc and time

272

differences to a tenth of a microsecond. With calibration from such a chart, a fixing accuracy of close to $\pm$ 0.25 of a nautical mile is probably available. This may not suffice in a harbor, but it is adequate in the open sea.

5.4 Use of Loran Sky-Wave Signals

Sky-wave signals are used frequently in Loran A, less often in Loran C. They tend to reduce accuracy, since the resulting time differences are less stable and predictable than those obtained with ground waves. However, under some circumstances, it may be necessary to use sky waves, and it is possible to produce calibrations for cases where, for example, ground-wave signals are received from the master and sky-wave signals from one or both of the slaves. When a calibration of this sort is used for position fixing, the receiving conditions must duplicate those under which the calibration was produced— so that, in this instance, the time-difference readings would once again involve ground-wave signals from the master and sky-wave signals from the slave or slaves, as was the case when the calibration was made. Even the master can be a sky-wave signal if the calibration was made that way.

5.5 Position Location

Routine 5.2 is employed to convert time-difference readings into position fixes. It offers two modes—direct and relative. For the direct mode, the input data is provided by the calibration data card and by time-difference readings obtained at the vessel's present position. The fix is supplied in terms of latitude and longitude, and may also be obtained in terms of distance and bearing to the vessel from the calibration point or from a reference point of specified latitude and longitude. For the relative mode, a data card is prepared (in steps 17–21) which provides not only the location data and time-difference readings for a nearby calibration point, but also the time-difference readings for a selected reference point. The relative position fix is calculated in terms of distance and bearing from this point.

Routine 5.2 (HP-67/97)

TDa	TDb→ Lfix,Lofix	Lref↑Loref	Set Relative Mode	Dv Btv

LORAN LOCATOR

Step	Procedure	Input Data/Units	Keys	Output Data/Units
1	Load program—both sides Direct Mode			
2	After completion of step 1, if calibration and reference-point data have been recorded on a card during a preceding operation of this routine (step 13), load this card, and continue with steps 4–7 and/or 14–16, as desired			
3	Load calibration data card for A slave, B slave, master, and calibration point in question, as recorded in step 13 of routine 5.1			
4	Enter A-slave time difference observed at vessel's position	mmmmm.m	A	
5	Enter B-slave time difference observed at vessel's position,	mmmmm.m	B	
·	Calculate and display latitude of fix,			±DD.MMSS
·	Longitude of fix			±DD.MMSS
6	To review latitude		x↔y	±DD.MMSS
7	To review longitude		x↔y	±DD.MMSS

To measure distance and bearing from calibration point, proceed as follows (steps 8–10):

Step	Procedure	Input Data/Units	Keys	Output Data/Units
8	Calculate and display distance from calibration point to vessel,		E	naut. mi.
·	True bearing from calibration point to vessel			DDD.d
9	To review distance		x↔y	naut. mi.
10	To review bearing		x↔y	DDD.d

274

Step	Procedure	Input Data/Units	Keys	Output Data/Units
	To measure distance and bearing from a reference point, proceed as follows (steps 11–16):			
11	Enter latitude of reference point (+N, −S)	DD.MMSS	ENTER	
12	Enter longitude of reference point (+W, −E)	DD.MMSS	C	
13	If repeated fixes are to be made with respect to this reference point, record the calibration and reference-point data on a data card, both sides		f W/DATA	
14	Calculate and display distance from reference point to vessel,		E	naut. mi.
·	True bearing from reference point to vessel			DDD.d
15	To review distance		x⟷y	naut. mi.
16	To review bearing		x⟷y	DDD.d
	Relative Mode—Preparation of Calibration Card			
17	After completion of step 1, load calibration data card for A slave, B slave, master, and calibration point in question, as recorded in step 13 of routine 5.1			
18	Enter A-slave time difference at reference point for which calibration is to be made	mmmmm.m	A	
19	Enter B-slave time difference at reference point for which calibration is to be made,	mmmmm.m	B	
·	Calculate and display latitude of reference point,			
·	Longitude of the reference point			
	The values displayed in this step are to be ignored.			
20	Set calculator to record relative-mode calibration data card		D	CRD
21	Record relative-mode calibration data card, both sides, and label card with names of A slave, B slave, master, calibration point, and reference point			
	Relative Mode—Fixing			
22	After completion of step 1, load relative-mode calibration data card recorded in step 21			
23	Enter A-slave time difference observed at vessel's position	mmmmm.m	A	

(CONTINUED)

Step	Procedure	Input Data/Units	Keys	Output Data/Units
24	Enter B-slave time difference observed at vessel's position,	mmmmm.m	B	
·	Calculate and display latitude of fix,			
·	Longitude of fix			
	The values displayed in this step are to be ignored.			
25	Calculate and display distance from reference point to vessel,		E	naut. mi.
·	True bearing from reference point to vessel			DDD.d

In using routine 5.2, care should be taken to enter time-difference readings in a manner consistent with the calibration procedure completed in routine 5.1; for instance, if a particular station was designated as A during calibration, the time difference *(TDa)* now measured between this station and the master should be entered at A.

Examples of the various uses of routine 5.2 are given in figure 5.1 and figure 5.2.

Figure 5.1 illustrates the *direct mode.* The calibration information used in this illustration is taken from a chart containing Loran C lines of position. After the loading of the Loran Locator program, and of a calibration data card (prepared by routine 5.1, for a calibration point at latitude 40°25'N and longitude 73°45'W), time-difference readings observed at the vessel's position are entered at A and B. Calculation begins when B is pressed, and the vessel's latitude and longitude (40°21'36"N and 73°42'57"W) are sequentially displayed. Also, the distance from the calibration point is seen to be 3.74 nm, and the true bearing is 155.38°. This situation is illustrated in figure 5.1 at the fix for 08 19 57.

The latitude and longitude of a reference, or way, point can also be inserted, as shown in steps 11 and 12 in routine 5.2, and the calculated position will then be expressed in terms of distance and bearing from this reference point. In figure 5.1, the vessel's destination serves also as the reference point. The distance and true bearing from this point turn out to be 4.0775 nm and 213.496°. This calculation is purely geometric; it does not involve further use of loran time differences.

276

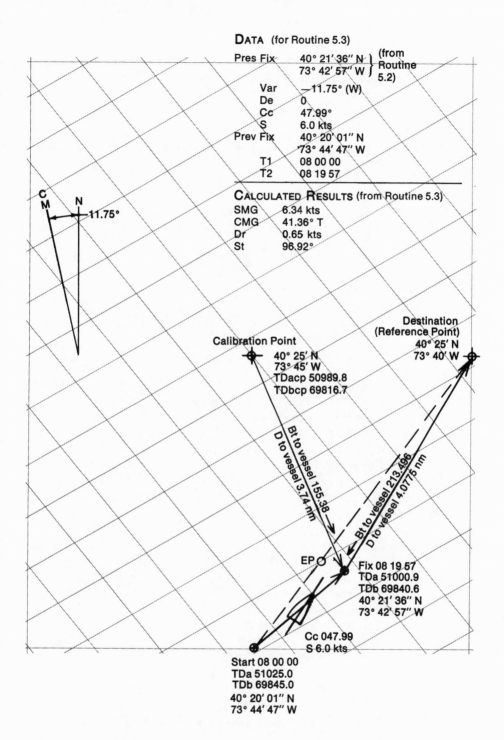

DATA (for Routine 5.3)

Pres Fix 40° 21′ 36″ N } (from Routine 5.2)
73° 42′ 57″ W

Var −11.75° (W)
De 0
Cc 47.99°
S 6.0 kts
Prev Fix 40° 20′ 01″ N
73° 44′ 47″ W
T1 08 00 00
T2 08 19 57

CALCULATED RESULTS (from Routine 5.3)
SMG 6.34 kts
CMG 41.36° T
Dr 0.65 kts
St 96.92°

C M
N
−11.75°

Calibration Point
40° 25′ N
73° 45′ W
TDacp 50989.8
TDbcp 69816.7

Destination
(Reference Point)
40° 25′ N
73° 40′ W

Bt to vessel 155.38
D to vessel 3.74 nm

Bt to vessel 213.496
D to vessel 4.0775 nm

EP

Fix 08 19 57
TDa 51000.9
TDb 69840.6
40° 21′ 36″ N
73° 42′ 57″ W

Cc 047.99
S 6.0 kts

Start 08 00 00
TDa 51025.0
TDb 69845.0
40° 20′ 01″ N
73° 44′ 47″ W

5.1. Loran Position Location, Direct Mode, and Loran Current Calculation

277

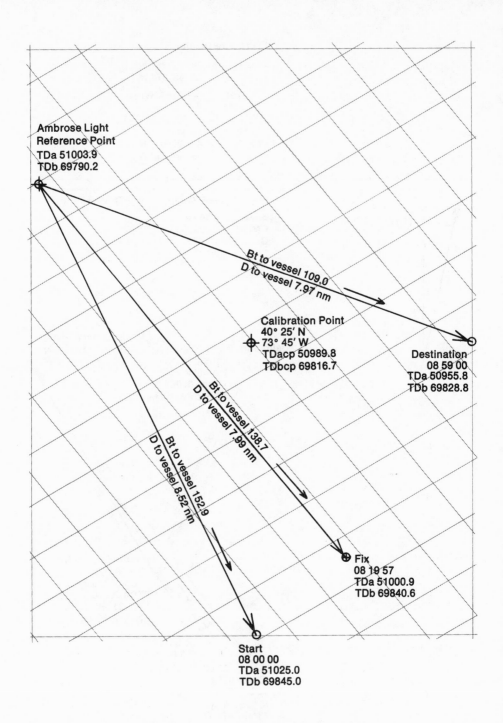

Ambrose Light
Reference Point
TDa 51003.9
TDb 69790.2

Bt to vessel 109.0
D to vessel 7.97 nm

Calibration Point
40° 25' N
73° 45' W
TDacp 50989.8
TDbcp 69816.7

Destination
08 59 00
TDa 50955.8
TDb 69828.8

Bt to vessel 138.7
D to vessel 7.99 nm

Bt to vessel 152.9
D to vessel 8.52 nm

Fix
08 19 57
TDa 51000.9
TDb 69840.6

Start
08 00 00
TDa 51025.0
TDb 69845.0

5.2. Loran Position Location, Relative Mode

278

Figure 5.2 illustrates the *relative mode*. This method requires a data card prepared according to the instructions in routine 5.2. It differs from the card used in the direct mode in that time-difference readings obtained at the reference point are entered, instead of its latitude and longitude. Hence, the relative mode is useful for navigating to or from locations whose latitude and longitude are not known.

Once the reference-point data card has been prepared, it can be used repeatedly. In figure 5.2, the results of three successive calculations are shown, giving the vessel's distance and true bearing from Ambrose Light at 08 00 00 (8.52 nm, 152.9°), 08 19 57 (7.99 nm, 138.7°), and 08 59 00 (7.97 nm, 109.0°).

The accuracy achieved in position finding by the methods described depends on the vessel's distance from the calibration point when the direct mode is used, and from the reference point when the relative mode is used. In most cases, a high degree of accuracy can be attained.

5.6   Navigation with Loran Position Fixes

While knowledge of a vessel's present position is often important in itself, it is also important as an aid in planning a safe passage to the next destination. Whenever a vessel is subjected to unknown or imperfectly known currents, when there may be compass errors, speed uncertainties, or unanticipated leeway, the journey from a known position to a way point or destination may be hazardous. To avoid danger, it is not sufficient to know the present position; the courses steered must take into proper account even those quantities that are imperfectly known.

If a navigation aid such as loran or radar is available, the accurate information which it provides concerning previous positions can be used for the measurement of *all* the forces affecting the movement of the vessel over the bottom. Knowledge of the vessel's speed and heading on top of the water, as indicated by its instruments, in combination with the knowledge of course and speed made good over the bottom that can be obtained with the aid of loran, makes possible calculation of the unknowns that affect the motion of the vessel. The results of computing the set and drift of a "current"—obtained by determining the difference between the vector for the vessel's motion on top of the water and the vector for motion over the bottom between the fixes—will also reflect the effects of inaccurate knowledge of vessel speed, heading, or leeway, and will therefore provide a basis for correcting the vessel's course. (Where this current is changeable, as in tidal waters, the process may have to be repeated several times during a journey.) Thus, the advantages of loran position finding can be utilized in planning and course prediction, to aid in effecting a safe passage to the destination.

Two routines have been developed to accomplish this purpose, the first employing latitude and longitude co-ordinates, the second operating in terms of distance and bearing.

Routine 5.3 (HP-67/97)

Var	De	T2	Select Dest	Load
Cc S	Lstart Lostart	T1	SMG CMG Dr St	Clear

LORAN CURRENT CALCULATOR (LATITUDE AND LONGITUDE)

Step	Procedure	Input Data/Units	Keys	Output Data/Units
	This procedure can be used only when a position fix *in terms of latitude and longitude* remains in the calculator, as a result of completion of step 5 of routine 5.2.			
1	Load program—both sides			
2	Enter variation (+E,−W), even if 0	DD.d	f a	
3	Enter deviation (+E,−W), even if 0	DD.d	f b	
4	Enter compass course of vessel between fixes*	DDD.d	A	
5	Enter vessel speed between fixes	knots	A	
6	Enter latitude of vessel at previous fix (+N,−S)	DD.MMSS	B	
7	Enter longitude of vessel at previous fix (+W,−E)	DD.MMSS	B	
8	Enter time of previous fix (*T1*)	H.MS	C	
9	Enter time of present fix (*T2*)	H.MS	f c	
10	Calculate and display speed made good between fixes,		D	knots
·	True course made good between fixes,			DDD.d
·	Drift of current between fixes,			knots
·	Set of current between fixes			DDD.d
	To obtain a course to steer, taking into account the current just calculated, proceed as follows:			
	If destination co-ordinates are on a data card,			
11	Load data card			
12	Enter identification number corresponding to destination co-ordinates (an even number from 0 to 20), and continue at step 15	0–20	f d	

*Correct for leeway; see table 2.2.

280

Step	Procedure	Input Data/Units	Keys	Output Data/Units
	If destination co-ordinates are not on a data card,			
13	Enter destination latitude (+N,−S)	DD.MMSS	ENTER	
14	Enter destination longitude (+W,−E), but *do not press* ENTER	DD.MMSS		
15	Load destination co-ordinates into memory		f e	
16	Load program for the Planning routine— either routine 2.17 (chart factor) or routine 2.18 (mid-latitude)			

If destination co-ordinates are not on a data card and the chart-factor routine is being used, care must be taken to enter the chart factor (step 24 of routine 2.17). Calculation then continues at step 28 of routine 2.17 or step 27 of routine 2.18.

Routine 5.3, the Loran Current Calculator, was designed to be integrated with routines 2.17 and 2.18 (the chart-factor and mid-latitude Planning routines). The current calculated from successive loran fixes is held in the calculator's memory, for use in calculating a plan to reach the destination.

An example of this use is shown in figure 5.1. In this case, the starting position is determined by loran (steps 1–5 of routine 5.2), and the initial plan for reaching the destination is developed—by means of routine 2.18 rather than 2.17, since no chart factor is specified—under the assumption that no current is acting on the vessel.

Once a vessel is on the planned compass course (in this instance, 47.99°), its estimated position at a future time (08 19 57) is calculated by means of routine 2.20 or 2.21, as appropriate. When that time is reached, routine 5.2 is used for a second loran fix. The resulting latitude and longitude co-ordinates, designating the vessel's present position, are retained by the calculator, and need not be re-entered for use in routine 5.3 and for subsequent use in the Planning routine.

Similarly, the set and drift which are calculated in routine 5.3 (in this instance, 96.92° and 0.65 knots) are automatically retained, and need not be re-entered for the next use of the Planning routine. Compass variation is also retained, and vessel speed must be re-entered only if it will change on the new run. The last steps in routine 5.3 involve entry of the destination co-ordinates. Hence, only the time of start of the new run remains to be entered when the Planning routine is begun once again, and after loading the program for routine 2.17 or 2.18 and entering the chart factor if necessary (step 24 of routine 2.17), one can proceed directly to step 28 of routine 2.17 or step 27 of routine 2.18.

Routine 5.4 (HP-67/97)

Load Present Fix	T1 T2	Set Next Start	Btstart Dstart	PLAN Cm Cc SMG ΔT
Cc Var De	S	Btdest Ddest	DMG CMG Dr St	EP D Bt

LORAN DISTANCE AND BEARING NAVIGATION

Step	Procedure	Input Data/Units	Keys	Output Data/Units
1	Load program—both sides			

If present position is in the calculator display, as it is after use of routine 5.2 in the relative mode, continue at step 4. If present position is not in the calculator display,

2	Enter distance from reference point to vessel	naut. mi.	ENTER	
3	Enter true bearing from reference point to vessel	DDD.d		
4	Load present fix		f a	

Steps 5–8, following, can be omitted after the first round of calculations provided the values are unchanged.

5	Enter compass course of vessel between fixes*	DDD.d	A	
6	Enter variation (+E,−W), even if 0	DD.d	A	
7	Enter deviation (+E,−W), even if 0	DD.d	A	
8	Enter speed of vessel between fixes	knots	B	
9	Enter time of previous fix (T1)	H.MS	f b	
10	Enter time of present fix (T2)	H.MS	f b	

Steps 11–14, following, can be omitted after the first round of calculations.

11	Enter true bearing from reference point to destination	DDD.d	C	
12	Enter distance from reference point to destination	naut. mi.	C	

If reference point and destination are identical, enter 0 in steps 11 and 12.

13	Enter true bearing from reference point to vessel at *first* fix	DDD.d	f d	
14	Enter distance from reference point to vessel at *first* fix	naut. mi.	f d	

*Correct for leeway; see table 2.2

282

Step	Procedure	Input Data/Units	Keys	Output Data/Units
	To change destination, proceed as follows (steps 15–16):			
15	Enter true bearing from reference point to new destination	DDD.d	C	
16	Enter distance from reference point to new destination	naut. mi.	C	
17	Calculate and display distance made good between fixes,		D	naut. mi.
·	True course made good between fixes,			DDD.d
·	Drift of current between fixes,			knots
·	Set of current between fixes			DDD.d
	To calculate estimated position, proceed as follows (steps 18–22):			
18	Enter time of present fix (as in step 10)	H.MS	f b	
19	For estimated position at a future time, enter time for which position is required, and continue at step 21	H.MS	f b	
20	For estimated position at the present time, re-enter time of present fix (as in step 18)	H.MS	f b	
21	For the time selected in step 19 or step 20, calculate and display distance from vessel to destination,		E	naut. mi.
·	True bearing from vessel to destination			DDD.d
22	Set next starting position		f c	

As a result of the preceding step, the values displayed in step 21 are transferred to serve as the previous fix in the next calculation of distance and course made good and drift and set.

If deviation is 0 on all headings, continue at step 30. If deviation is not 0 at all headings,

Step	Procedure	Input Data/Units	Keys	Output Data/Units
23	Enter vessel compass course as 0	0	A	
24	Enter variation (+E, −W), even if 0	DD.d	A	
25	Enter deviation as 0	0	A	
26	Calculate and display magnetic course to steer,		f e	DDD.d
·	Speed made good,			knots
·	Time required to reach destination			H.MS

If deviation is 0 on the magnetic course displayed in step 26, continue at step 30. If deviation is not 0 on this magnetic course,

Step	Procedure	Input Data/Units	Keys	Output Data/Units
27	Enter vessel compass course as 0	0	A	
28	Enter variation (+E, −W), even if 0	DD.d	A	
29	Enter deviation (+E, −W)	DD.d	A	

(CONTINUED)

283

Step	Procedure	Input Data/Units	Keys	Output Data/Units
30	To change vessel speed during run being planned, enter new vessel speed	knots	B	
	To change estimate of current during run being planned, proceed as follows (steps 31–32):			
31	Enter new set of current	DDD.d	STO A	
32	Enter new drift of current	knots	STO B	
33	Calculate and display compass course to steer,**		f e	DDD.d
·	Speed made good,			knots
·	Time required to reach destination			H.MS
	To calculate estimated position at a future time, proceed as follows (steps 34–36):			
34	Enter time of start of leg or run	H.MS	f b	
35	Enter time for which position is required	H.MS	f b	
36	For the time selected in step 35, calculate and display distance from vessel to destination,		E	naut. mi.
·	True bearing from vessel to destination			DDD.d

For the next estimated position, the time of start (step 34) is the time previously used in step 35, and the time for which the new estimated position is required is entered in step 35.

Step	Procedure	Input Data/Units	Keys	Output Data/Units
37	If a loran fix is to be obtained, by means of routine 5.2, record contents of data memory on both sides of an unclipped card		f W/DATA	
38	After obtaining new position fix (with distance and bearing still in the calculator's display and memory), load program for routine 5.4			
39	Load data card produced in step 37, and continue at step 4			

If the reference point is to be changed, the calculations must be handled as a completely new operation, starting at step 1.

**Uncorrect for leeway; see table 2.2.

In routine 5.4, a single program is employed to provide values for current, estimated position, course to steer, time required to reach the destination, and speed made good, based on successive loran position fixes. Because the fixing data is expressed in terms of distance and bearing from a known position (the reference point), this routine can be adapted for use with positions obtained by means of radar.

To provide the necessary data in relation to the reference point, the Loran Locator routine (5.2) must be used in conjunction with routine 5.4, in the relative mode; therefore, the calibration data card, prepared in advance, must include the time differences observed at the reference point (or taken from a loran chart, if somewhat degraded accuracies can be tolerated).

The instructions for routine 5.4 have been written in great detail to cover a number of possibilities—among them a change in destination, and alterations in speed, course, or set or drift of current.

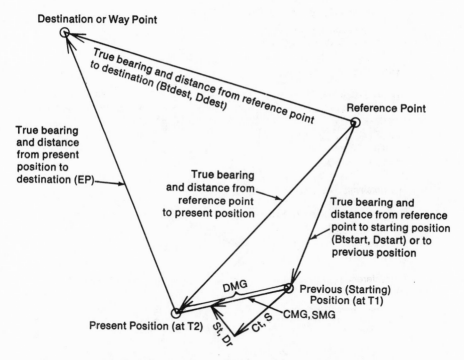

5.3. Positions and Relations Involved in Loran Navigation

The various positions and relations involved in these calculations are shown in figure 5.3. The positions are the reference point (as used in the relative mode of the Loran Locator routine), the vessel's previous position (defined by the fix obtained just before the present fix), the vessel's present position, and the destination or way point. If, as sometimes occurs, the vessel's destination is the reference point itself, the bearing and distance from the reference point to the destination will be set equal to zero.

285

5.4. Loran Distance and Bearing Navigation

286

Once steps 1–17 have been completed, the estimated position of the vessel en route to its destination can be calculated for any future time, by means of steps 34–36. Provided the data as originally entered remains unchanged, steps 1–17 need not be repeated. The estimated-position sequence is followed by a procedure (step 37) for preserving necessary information when routine 5.4 must be interrupted for operation of the Loran Locator routine. Pressing [f] [W/DATA] and passing an unclipped magnetic card through the card handler results in storage of the contents of the calculator's memory for use when routine 5.4 is resumed.

The routine also provides for the repeated calculation of current from a pair of successive fixes. The information produced by this method concerns the current affecting the vessel in the recent past (that is, up to the moment of the second of the fixes). Where currents are constant over long periods of time, one such calculation will have considerable predictive value. But since currents tend to vary with time and location—being affected, for example, by tidal action, in coastal waters—extrapolation is likely to be misleading. Instead, frequent recalculations must be made to keep track of the changes in the current and the consequent changes required in the vessel's course.

This situation is illustrated in figure 5.4, which shows the passage of a vessel from Long Island Sound into Block Island Sound, through the Race, at a time when tidal currents are swift, and are changing in both set and drift within fairly short distances.

Table 5.2 contains all of the data attendant on this passage. The example can be used to test the programs and rehearse the procedures required for use of routines 5.1, 5.2, and 5.4. The data presented in figure 5.4 includes the time differences at a reference point in the Race. Since these time-difference values, as well as those used to represent the readings taken on the vessel, were drawn from a Loran C chart of the area, they may be less accurate than readings obtained by on-the-spot measurements.

The journey begins at 0800, and the vessel's initial position in relation to the reference point is calculated by means of routine 5.2. At 0820, as the vessel approaches the Race, a second fix is taken. The program for routine 5.4 is then loaded (step 1), and data concerning the vessel's position, course, and speed is entered (steps 2–8), making possible calculation of the current present during this first leg (steps 9–17). The current turns out to have had a drift of 1.81 knots and a set of 236.73°. On the basis of this information, and present vessel speed, a plan will be calculated for reaching the reference point at the Race, which thus serves also as the destination.

An important feature of routine 5.4 is its ability to accommodate the time that is required to make the loran measurements, alter the destination, if necessary, calculate the current and the new course to steer, and change the vessel's heading and settle it down on the new course. As shown, in steps 18–21, immediately after each loran position fix and current calculation, a sequence is included to determine the estimated position which the vessel will

Table 5.2

Time	Measured Loran Time Differences		Position Measured from Reference Point to Vessel		Vessel Motion				Time Interval of Run		From Reference Point to Destination	
	TDa	TDb	Distance	Bearing	Cc	Var	De	S	T1	T2	Distance	Bearing
0800	50013.4	69774.3	5.6315	261.2089								
0820	49999.3	69778.4	4.1871	257.7917	94.71	−13.5(W)	0	6.0	0800	0820	0	•
									0820	0825		
0825												
									0825	0830		
									0830	0840		
									0840	0850		
0850	49967.0	69775.8	1.9704	298.1528					0825	0850		
									0850	0855		
0855												
									0855	0905		
0905	49959.1	69779.1	1.1190	312.3208					0855	0905		
									0905	0910		
0910												
									0910	0915		
									0915	0925		
									0925	0935		
0935	49954.0	69787.9	0.5276	141.7415					0910	0935	1.5	121.00
									0935	0940		
0940												
									0940	0945		
									0945	0950		
									0950	0955		
0955	49947.8	69792.5	1.4952	125.7338					0940	0955		
									0955	0955		

reach if it continues on its previous course, affected by the current just calculated, for a specified time (in this instance five minutes) following the loran fix. This estimated position then becomes the position fix for the start of the new leg, planned in steps 23–33, and is also retained (step 22) to serve eventually as the starting reference—the previous fix, at $T1$ —for the next calculation of distance and course made good, and of the accompanying current.

In the example just described, the second loran fix is made at 0820, and since the first subsequent estimated position is for 0825, this is the position that will be used as the starting reference in the next calculation of current. In the interim, by means of steps 34–36 successive estimated positions are calculated at 0830, 0840, and 0850. The contents of the data memory is next recorded for later use (step 37), and at 0850 another fix is made. It is then apparent that the current has turned out to be not as predicted, for the position of the vessel at 0850 is considerably to the north of the estimated position for the same time. Accordingly, the current is recalculated, with the 0825 position serving as the previous fix: After the loading of the program for routine 5.4 and the data card prepared in step 37, the 0850 position is loaded (step 4); and steps 9–10 and 17 are then performed. There is no need to repeat steps 5–8 and 11–14. This

288

During Run			Plan to Destination		ΔT		Estimated Position Measured from Vessel to Destination		Comments
CMG	St	Dr	Cc	SMG	min	sec	Distance	Bearing	1.The reference point (*TDa* 49955.0, *TDb* 69785.0) is in the Race, halfway between Valiant Rock and Race Point.
90.96	1.81	236.73							2.The reference point serves also as the initial destination.
							3.83	76.54	3.After the fix at 0820, the EP is obtained for 0825, to give time for calculations and maneuvers. The plan is then initiated from the 0825 EP.
			84.18	4.27	53	50			
							3.47	76.54	
							2.76	76.54	
							2.05	76.54	4.A data card is recorded after the 0850 EP.
47.49	2.55	339.47							
							1.86	134.00	5.As before, after the fix at 0850, the vessel's EP is obtained for a time five minutes in the future, to provide an interval in which a new plan can be calculated.
			158.02	3.60	31	3			
							1.26	134.00	
136.52	1.69	346.07							
							0.75	130.23	
			153.24	4.55	9	52			6.The EP at 9025 indicates that the vessel has passed beyond the Race.
							0.37	130.23	
							0.39	310.24	
							1.15	310.24	
134.99	2.97	324.61							7.Following the fix at 0935, a new destination is established, at a distance of 1.5 nm and a bearing of 121° from the reference point at the Race. All subsequent EP's are calculated with respect to the new destination.
							0.80	102.92	
			135.67	3.44	13	56			
							0.51	102.92	
							0.23	102.92	
							0.06	282.90	
110.25	3.05	314.19							
							0.10	33.00	

calculation indicates that the current has speeded up (to 2.55 knots) and has shifted northward (from 236.73° to 339.47°); it is probably about to shift even farther in the same direction, following the contours of the passage through the Race.

When the current has been calculated, an estimated position is obtained once again for a time five minutes in the future (i.e., 0855), by means of steps 18–22, and a new course is planned (steps 23–33). This course is modified at 0910, the calculation of an estimated position at 0905 being followed once again by the preparation of a data card, the use of routine 5.2 to calculate a fix, the recalculation of the current, and the corresponding alteration of the planned course and speed. Successive estimated positions are then obtained.

Once the vessel has passed through the Race, a new destination is chosen, 1.5 nm away from the initial destination (and reference point) in the Race, on a bearing 121° away from this point. The change in destination is entered by means of steps 15–16. These are performed after a fix is made (by means of routine 5.2), routine 5.4 is begun again, and the times of the previous fix and the present fix—in this instance, 0910 and 0935—are entered. The destination is changed just before the recalculation of the current.

The sequence then proceeds as before. The new current is calculated, the estimated position at a time five minutes in the future (i.e., 0940) with respect to the new destination is determined, successive estimated positions are found, a final fix is made at 0955, followed by a last calculation of current, and one more estimated position is then calculated. Because at this point the position at 0955 (rather than five minutes later) is desired, the time of the present fix is entered twice, as shown in step 20.

One option open to the navigator is not exercised in the example just discussed. When set and drift are calculated, he can accept the values shown, or he can substitute other values, which he has reason to believe will be more accurate. The calculated values for current always reflect conditions in the immediate past. But if shoreline or bottom configurations indicate that the current will change as a new area is entered, or if the current is changing rapidly with time, values for set and drift based on previous vessel motion are not very useful. In these circumstances, the navigator, exercising his judgment, can enter his best estimate of what the current will be. The operation is performed during the planning segment of routine 5.4, as shown in steps 31–32. It is also possible at this point to change the value for vessel speed (step 30).

One entry that is not easily changed is the reference point. If this must be shifted for some reason, calculation must be started anew, at step 1.

5.7 Conversion of Loran A to Loran C Time Differences

At this writing, Loran A is gradually being phased out; it will have been entirely discontinued within a few years. Many mariners have accumulated Loran A time-difference co-ordinates for a large number of points, but do not have precise knowledge of their geographic locations. If this information is to continue to be of use, the Loran A time differences will have to be converted into their equivalents in the Loran C system.

Routine 5.5 has been prepared to accomplish this conversion. Its use requires two calibration data cards, prepared as shown in routine 5.1, one for Loran A transmitter stations and a calibration point in the vicinity of the location in question, the second for Loran C stations, and a similarly located calibration point. Data cards on which reference-point time differences have been recorded can *not* be used for this purpose.

The conversion procedure is simple. The program and the Loran A calibration data card are loaded, the Loran A time differences *(TDa* and *TDb)* are entered, and the Loran C calibration card is loaded. When $\boxed{E}$ is pressed, the corresponding Loran C time differences are displayed.

For maximum accuracy, precautions concerning the distance from the calibration points and the use of sky waves, as discussed sections 5.2 and 5.4 of this chapter, should be observed.

Routine 5.5 (HP-67/97)

TDa	TDb			L↑Lo→TDa,TDb

LORAN PREDICTOR

Step	Procedure	Input Data/Units	Keys	Output Data/Units
1	Load program—both sides			
	Predicting Loran Readings			
2	After completion of step 1, load calibration data card for area of interest, as recorded in step 13 of routine 5.1. A card recording any reference-point data is *not acceptable*.			
3	Enter latitude of location for which time differences are required (+N,−S)	DD.MMSS	ENTER	
4	Enter longitude of location for which time differences are required (+W,−E),	DD.MMSS	E	
·	Calculate and display time difference predicted for A-slave station listed on card loaded in step 2,			mmmmm.m
·	Time difference predicted for B-slave station listed on card loaded in step 2			mmmmm.m
	Converting from Loran A to Loran C			
5	After completion of step 1, load Loran A calibration data card for area of interest, as recorded in step 13 of routine 5.1. A card recording any reference-point data is *not acceptable*.			
6	Enter A-slave Loran A time difference at location for which conversion is required	mmmm	A	
7	Enter B-slave Loran A time difference at location for which conversion is required,	mmmm	B	
·	Calculate and display latitude of location,			
·	Longitude of location			
	The values displayed in this step are to be ignored.			

(CONTINUED)

Step	Procedure	Input Data/Units	Keys	Output Data/Units
8	Load Loran C calibration data card for area of interest, as recorded in step 13 of routine 5.1. A card recording any reference-point data is *not acceptable*.			
9	Calculate and display A-slave Loran C time difference at location in question,		E	mmmmm.m
·	B-slave Loran C time difference at location in question			mmmmm.m

Converting from Loran C to Loran A

To convert from Loran C to Loran A, perform the operations shown in steps 5–9, but reverse the roles of Loran A and Loran C: load the Loran C card in step 5, and enter Loran C time differences in steps 6 and 7; then load the Loran A card in step 8, and calculate and display Loran A time differences in step 9.

5.8 Prediction of Loran Time-Difference Readings

Routine 5.5 can also be used to predict the loran time-difference readings that would be obtained at a given location of known latitude and longitude. The Loran Predictor program is loaded, along with a suitable calibration data card (without any reference-point data); then the latitude and longitude of the place in question are entered, at ENTER and E ; and the time differences are displayed. This routine can be used for either Loran A or Loran C, as long as the appropriate calibration data card is employed. It is of value when there may be a problem in distinguishing the signals received. For example, when a manual loran receiver is in use, reception may be hampered by excessive noise or interference. If the vessel's dead-reckoning or estimated position is known —and consequently its approximate latitude and longitude—the expected loran time differences can be obtained through the routine. This information will help in recognizing the signals despite the noise or interference. It can also be used for resolving 1-microsecond ambiguities in Loran C, distinguishing between ground waves and sky waves, and properly setting the .10-microsecond, cycle-match differences in Loran C. The latter are especially useful if a manual, nontracking loran receiver is in use.

Appendix
Programs

The Appendix contains all of the programs required for the routines presented in the text. Using his own calculator, the reader can record on magnetic cards the programs which he will be needing. Each program has the same number as the routine for which it is required. The Appendix also includes a discussion of some special topics that relate to the recording or use of program cards; these include recording procedures, customized programs, setting decimals and trigonometric mode on the HP-67 and HP-97, and nonprint displays.

Recording Procedures

Complete instructions for recording and preserving programs on magnetic cards on the HP-67, HP-97, and SR-52 are provided in the manufacturers' manuals for the calculators. These should be studied carefully and relied upon completely. This appendix does not repeat the standard information that must be understood when programs are to be recorded, such as the meaning of ERROR or CRD in the display of the HP-67 or HP-97, or of flashing zeros in the display of the SR-52.

The listings for the HP-67 and HP-97 programs were printed on an HP-97 calculator. For each step, they show the step number, the label of each key depressed in the performance of the step, and the corresponding numerical key code. (This code applies *only* to the HP-97. Because the HP-67 has a keyboard arrangement different from that of the HP-97, its key codes are different; however, the HP-97 equivalents can be found in the translation table in the HP-67 manual. Also, where the instructions specify the key PRINTx on the HP-97, the user of an HP-67 substitutes f -X- .)

In the listings for the SR-52 programs, the key label is shown at right and the corresponding key code at left. The step number for every tenth step has been inserted at the far left. In their inclusion of key labels these listings are different from those obtainable with the standard PC-100A printer, which provides just step numbers and key codes; a table in the SR-52 manual shows how to translate the key codes into key labels.

A number of different methods are available for checking the correctness of a program that has been copied. If the HP-97 or the PC-100A printer for the SR-52 is being used, one can simply load the program and compare the printout with the listing in the Appendix. If the SR-52 is being used without the printer, one can single-step through the program and compare each displayed key code with the key code printed in the listing. On the HP-67 too, one can single-step through the program. As has been noted, the displayed key codes will be different from those shown in the listing in the Appendix, but

with practice, the process of translation into the HP-97 equivalents becomes almost automatic, and the comparison between the newly recorded version and the master copy can be made easily and quickly. Another way to test a program—previously mentioned in chapter 1—is to run through the corresponding routine, using as input the data supplied in the illustrative example in the text. Correct answers will provide further evidence of the accuracy of the program copy.

If mistakes are found in the entry of some steps in a program, the needed revision can be done by means of the editing functions of the calculator, used in accordance with the manufacturer's instructions. These enable one to make changes, deletions, or additions to the program.

When the cards have been completely recorded and tested, they should be protected against inadvertent erasure in accordance with the manufacturer's instructions. For example, the corner of a Hewlett-Packard card should be clipped.

The labeling of the front of the magnetic card is best done with a fine-line pen, with ink formulated for writing on plastic. A lead pencil, with the lead made for lettering on plastic drafting film, can also be used, but the results are less clear and less permanent than those obtained with ink.

Customized Programs

Because not all calculators, and not all vessels, are identical, certain programs require numerical data which is different for each user. The insertion of this data in place of the illustrative values used in the program listings in this appendix results in customized programs. Instructions for replacing data within a program are provided in the manufacturers' manuals for the various calculators. In the HP-67 and HP-97, a change of this sort is made most easily by displaying the *last* digit of the sequence that is to be changed, then making a number of deletions equal to the number of digits to be replaced, and then entering the digits that are to be used, in their normal order. In all calculators, if the full program (224 steps) has been used, care must be taken not to introduce any extra digits when the program is customized, since doing so will result in obliteration of the last steps of the program. If a new value is longer than the one it replaces, the least significant digit (farthest to the right of the decimal point) should be eliminated.

Customizing is desirable in the programs for the Tracking routines of chapter 2. Routines 2.5, 2.20, and 2.21 incorporate a continuous-running feature, with the display of position repeated at the end of each cycle of computation. The time required for this cycle is different on the HP-67 and HP-97 and also varies from calculator to calculator. Therefore, the timing constants shown in the programs for these routines should be replaced by constants determined in the user's own calculator.

Each of the three routines provides for a self-timing adjustment that establishes the proper value of the loop time to be used in the program. This is done by means of the routine steps specified in the accompanying table.

Program and Routine	Routine Steps Used for Timing Adjustment	Program Steps Where Original Timing Constants Are Located	Register Where Timing Constants Are Located
2.5	12–13	28–33	6
2.20	15–16	214–218	S2
2.21	15–16	213–217	S2

After completion of the timing adjustment, the loop time is recalled from the calculator memory: pressing RCL 6 will display it for routine 2.5, and pressing f p↔s RCL 2 f p↔s will display it for routine 2.20 or 2.21. This data should be copied to the number of decimal places used in the program. Next, the original contents of the program memory, at the program steps shown in the table, should be displayed. These are the values to be deleted and replaced by those just calculated. Once this substitution has been made, a new program card should be recorded, with the proper loop time.

Customizing is also necessary for a number of the programs for chapter 3, which require numerical data—coefficients, constants, and exponents—defining the characteristic performance of a *particular vessel;* the use of this data is a way of customizing the programs, which then provide results applicable only to that specific vessel.

At the points where this numerical data is required, the program listings now contain the values needed to work out the illustrative examples discussed in the chapter. Once this has been done, the user should replace the illustrative data, with the corresponding values for his own vessel, obtained by the methods described in chapter 3. The accompanying table indicates the places where the customizing data is to be inserted.

Program and Routine	Program Step	Present Content	Name or Use of Data
3.9	101	.	
	102	5	Exponent (*b*) of the curve-fitting equation
	103	1	$So = a\ MW^b$
	104	4	(displayed in step 7 of routine 3.7)
	105	7	
	107	1	
	108	.	Coefficient (*a*) of the curve-fitting equation
	109	3	$So = a\ MW^b$
	110	8	(displayed in step 7 of routine 3.7)
	111	3	
	112	6	
	120	.	
	121	0	Exponent (*b*) of the curve-fitting equation
	122	8	$Wto = a\ MW^b$
	123	6	(displayed in step 12 of routine 3.7)
	124	5	
	125	CHS	
	127	5	
	128	5	Coefficient (*a*) of the curve-fitting equation
	129	.	$Wto = a\ MW^b$
	130	0	(displayed in step 12 of routine 3.7)
	131	8	
	132	4	
	133	2	

Program and Routine	Program Step	Present Content	Name or Use of Data
3.11	6	5	
	7	5	Coefficient (a) of the curve-fitting equation
	8	.	$Wto = a\ MW^b$
	9	0	(displayed in step 11 of routine 3.8)
	10	8	
	11	4	
	12	2	
	18	.	
	19	0	Exponent (b) of the curve-fitting equation
	20	8	$Wto = a\ MW^b$
	21	6	(displayed in step 12 of routine 3.8)
	22	5	
	23	$+/-$	
	31	1	
	32	.	Coefficient (a) of the curve-fitting equation
	33	3	$So = a\ MW^b$
	34	8	(displayed in step 6 of routine 3.8)
	35	3	
	36	6	
	42	.	
	43	5	Exponent (b) of the curve-fitting equation
	44	1	$So = a\ MW^b$
	45	4	(displayed in step 7 of routine 3.8)
	46	7	

Program and Routine	Program Step	Present Content	Name or Use of Data
	101	·	
	102	6	Coefficient (*a*) of the curve-fitting equation
	103	8	$Sd = a\,MW^b$
	104	0	(displayed in step 16 of routine 3.8)
	105	4	
	111	·	
	112	7	Exponent (*b*) of the curve-fitting equation
	113	7	$Sd = a\,MW^b$
	114	6	(displayed in step 17 of routine 3.8)
	115	1	
	122	·	
	123	7	Constant term (*a*) of the curve-fitting equation
	124	8	$\frac{\Delta S}{Sd} = a + b \ln MW$
	125	1	(displayed in step 5 of routine 3.13)
	126	9	
	133	·	
	134	2	Coefficient (*b*) of the curve-fitting equation
	135	5	$\frac{\Delta S}{Sd} = a + b \ln MW$
	136	4	(displayed in step 6 of routine 3.13)
	137	1	
	138	$+/-$	

Program and Routine	Program Step	Present Content	Name or Use of Data
	141	·	Difference between speed in the direction of optimum down-wind tacking and the direct-downwind speed, obtained, for
	142	8	this purpose only, from evaluation of Fourier-series coeffi-cients: the sum of the absolute values of all the Fourier
	143	3	coefficients, as provided by routine 3.15, minus the sum of the algebraic values of the same coefficients. (The absolute
	144	4	value is the numerical value—considered as positive even if preceded by a minus sign.)
	145	2	$$\left|\frac{a_0}{2}\right| + \sum_1^5 \left|a_n\right| \; - \; \frac{a_0}{2} + \sum_1^5 a_n$$
	154	·	
	155	0	Exponent (b) of the curve-fitting equation
	156	5	$$\frac{\Delta W}{2} = a\,e^{b\,MW}$$
	157	3	(displayed in step 6 of routine 3.12)
	158	9	
	159	+/−	
	164	5	
	165	3	Coefficient (a) of the curve-fitting equation
	166	·	$$\frac{\Delta W}{2} = a\,e^{b\,MW}$$
	167	0	(displayed in step 5 of routine 3.12)
	168	0	
	169	2	
	170	5	
	198	1	
	199	·	Coefficient (a) of the curve-fitting equation
	200	2	$$Sdo = a\,MW^b$$
	201	7	(displayed in step 22 of routine 3.8)
	202	3	
	203	5	

Program and Routine	Program Step	Present Content	Name or Use of Data
	209	·	
	210	5	Exponent (*b*) of the curve-fitting equation
	211	8	$Sdo = a\,MW^b$
	212	2	(displayed in step 23 of routine 3.8)
	213	8	
3.16	127	·	
	128	7	Exponent (*b*) of the curve-fitting equation
	129	7	$Sd = a\,MW^b$
	130	6	(displayed in step 17 of routine 3.7)
	131	1	
	133	·	
	134	6	Coefficient (*a*) of the curve-fitting equation
	135	8	$Sd = a\,MW^b$
	136	0	(displayed in step 17 of routine 3.7)
	137	4	
	140	·	
	141	7	Constant term (*a*) of the curve-fitting equation
	142	8	$\frac{\Delta S}{Sd} = a + b \ln MW$
	143	1	(displayed in step 34 of routine 3.7)
	144	9	
	147	·	
	148	2	Coefficient (*b*) of the curve-fitting equation
	149	5	$\frac{\Delta S}{Sd} = a + b \ln MW$
	150	4	(displayed in step 34 of routine 3.7)
	151	1	

Program and Routine	Program Step	Present Content	Name or Use of Data
	156	·	
	157	0	Exponent (*b*) of the curve-fitting equation
	158	5	$\frac{\Delta W}{2} = a\,e^{b\,MW}$
	159	3	(displayed in step 29 of routine 3.7)
	160	9	
	161	CHS	
	163	5	
	164	3	Coefficient (*a*) of the curve-fitting equation
	165	·	$\frac{\Delta W}{2} = a\,e^{b\,MW}$
	166	0	(displayed in step 29 of routine 3.7)
	167	0	
	168	2	
	169	5	
	192	·	Difference between speed in the direction of optimum down-wind tacking and the direct-downwind speed, obtained, for this purpose only, from evaluation of Fourier-series coefficients: the sum of the absolute values of all the Fourier coefficients, as provided by routine 3.14, minus the sum of the algebraic values of the same coefficients. (The absolute value is the numerical value—considered as positive even if preceded by a minus sign.)
	193	8	
	194	3	
	195	4	
	196	2	$\left\lvert \dfrac{a_0}{2} \right\rvert + \overset{6}{\underset{1}{\Sigma}} \lvert a_n \rvert \; - \; \dfrac{a_0}{2} + \overset{6}{\underset{1}{\Sigma}} a_n$
3.17	4	·	
	5	3	One-half of a_0, the 0th-order coefficient (DC term) of the Fourier series (displayed in step 8 or 9 of routine 3.14).
	6	3	
	7	9	
	8	3	

Program and Routine	Program Step	Present Content	Name or Use of Data
	15	·	
	16	3	First-order term (a_1) of the Fourier series (second coefficient displayed in step 8 of routine 3.14, or the first displayed in step 10)
	17	5	
	18	4	
	19	6	
	20	CHS	
	31	·	
	32	0	Second-order term (a_2) of the Fourier series (third coefficient displayed in step 8 of routine 3.14, or the second displayed in step 10)
	33	6	
	34	3	
	35	9	
	46	·	
	47	0	Third-order term (a_3) of the Fourier series (fourth coefficient displayed in step 8 of routine 3.14, or the third displayed in step 10)
	48	4	
	49	4	
	50	2	
	51	CHS	
	62	·	
	63	0	Fourth-order term (a_4) of the Fourier series (fifth coefficient displayed in step 8 of routine 3.14, or the fourth displayed in step 10)
	64	1	
	65	5	
	66	5	

304

Program and Routine	Program Step	Present Content	Name or Use of Data
	77	·	
	78	0	Fifth-order term (a_5) of the Fourier series (sixth coefficient displayed in step 8 of routine 3.14, or the fifth displayed in step 10)
	79	1	
	80	8	
	81	3	
	82	CHS	
	93	·	
	94	0	Sixth-order term (a_6) of the Fourier series (seventh coefficient displayed in step 8 of routine 3.14, or the sixth displayed in step 10)
	95	0	
	96	6	
	97	3	
3.18	101	·	
	102	5	Exponent (b) of the curve-fitting equation
	103	8	$Sdo = a\,MW^b$
	104	2	(displayed in step 23 of routine 3.7)
	105	8	
	107	1	
	108	·	Coefficient (a) of the curve-fitting equation
	109	2	$Sdo = a\,MW^b$
	110	7	(displayed in step 23 of routine 3.7)
	111	3	
	112	5	

Program and Routine	Program Step	Present Content	Name or Use of Data
	119	.	
	120	0	Exponent (b) of the curve-fitting equation
	121	5	$$\frac{\Delta W}{2} = a\, e^{b\,MW}$$
	122	3	(displayed in step 29 of routine 3.7)
	123	9	
	124	CHS	
	127	5	
	128	3	Coefficient (a) of the curve-fitting equation
	129	.	$$\frac{\Delta W}{2} = a\, e^{b\,MW}$$
	130	0	(displayed in step 29 of routine 3.7)
	131	0	
	132	2	
	133	5	
3.19	143	.	
	144	3	First-order term (a_1) of the Fourier series (displayed in step 8 of routine 3.15)
	145	5	
	146	4	
	147	6	
	148	+/−	
	150	.	
	151	3	0th-order coefficient (DC term) of the Fourier series, divided by 2 ($a_0/2$, displayed in step 13 of routine 3.15)
	152	3	
	153	9	
	154	3	

306

Program and Routine	Program Step	Present Content	Name or Use of Data
	156	.	
	157	0	Second-order term (a_2) of the Fourier series (displayed in step 9 of routine 3.15)
	158	6	
	159	3	
	160	9	
	161	0	
	165	.	
	166	0	Third-order term (a_3) of the Fourier series (displayed in step 10 of routine 3.15)
	167	4	
	168	4	
	169	2	
	170	$+/-$	
	174	.	
	175	0	Fourth-order term (a_4) of the Fourier series (displayed in step 11 of routine 3.15)
	176	1	
	177	5	
	178	5	
	179	0	
	183	.	
	184	0	Fifth-order term (a_5) of the Fourier series (displayed in step 12 of routine 3.15)
	185	1	
	186	8	
	187	3	
	188	$+/-$	

Setting Decimals and Trigonometric Mode on the HP-67 and HP-97

The results displayed by the HP-67 and HP-97 reflect the state of flags and the decimal setting *as they were at the time that a program was recorded* on a magnetic card. Thus, if answers are to be shown to four decimal places, the keys $\boxed{\text{DSP}}$ $\boxed{4}$ should be pressed just before the program is recorded. For the programs presented in this volume, the display should always be set to this fixed-four state (that is, $\boxed{\text{DSP}}$ $\boxed{4}$ should be pressed) before recording begins.

The HP-67 and HP-97 also offer alternative trigonometric modes—degree, radian, or grad notation. For every program in this volume except one, the degree mode is employed. The exception is the program for the Fourier Series routine (3.14), for which the keys $\boxed{\text{f}}$ $\boxed{\text{RAD}}$ should be pressed.

None of the programs presented in this volume requires the presetting of any flags.

Nonprint Operation of the HP-97

When the three-way print switch of the HP-97 is set at NORM(al), every keyboard input and the result of every computation is shown in the printout. If the calculator is used for tracking (routines 2.5, 2.20, and 2.21), the output printing may be undesirable because of extensive paper use and battery drain. The programs can be modified to eliminate the printing of every calculated bearing, distance, and time, leaving just the visual display. The procedure is shown in the accompanying table.

Program and Routine	Program Step	Present Content	Change to
2.5	122	PRTx −14	f DEL
	130*	PRTx −14	f DEL
	143*	PRTx −14	f DEL
	145*	SPC 16−11	f DEL
2.20	103	PRTx −14	f PSE 16 51
	104	SPC 16−11	f DEL
	179*	PRTx −14	f PSE 16 51
	188*	PRTx −14	f PSE 16 51
	196*	RTN 24	R/S 51
2.21	093	PRTx − 14	f PSE 16 51
	178	PRTx −14	f PSE 16 51
	187	PRTx −14	f PSE 16 51
	195	RTN 24	R/S 51

*Original step number, before any deletion has been made.

Interrupting the Display Interval on the HP-67

The only significant difference between the actual programs for the HP-97 and those for the HP-67 is that where $\boxed{\text{PRINTx}}$ is used on the HP-97, $\boxed{\text{f}}$ $\boxed{\text{—X—}}$ is used on the HP-67. The latter causes the display to be retained for

five seconds, showing a flashing decimal-point to signify the halt. In most cases this five-second interval provides enough time to read the answer. However, if desired, the display on the HP-67 can be made to halt altogether, by substitution of [R/S] for [PRINTx] in the program. In that case, where the HP-97 would yield a sequence of printed output data, the HP-67 will stop upon display of the first result, and [R/S] will have to be pressed to obtain each subsequent display of a result in the sequence. For example, if the programming for step 33 of routine 5.4 has been handled in this manner, the method of performing the step will be as follows:

Step	Procedure	Input Data/Units	Keys	Output Data/Units
33	Calculate and display compass course to steer,		f e	DDD.d
.	Speed made good,		R/S	knots
.	Time required to reach destination		R/S	H.MS
34	Enter time of start of leg or run	H.MS	f b	

Two cautions are necessary. First, care must be taken not to press [R/S] too many times, for then the program may begin to run without appropriate *input* data in place, and will yield incorrect answers. Thus, in the preceding example [R/S] must not be pressed after the time has been displayed. At this point the user proceeds with the data entry specified in step 34. Second, this adjustment must not be made in the programs for routines 2.5, 2.20, and 2.21. When one of these routines is employed for tracking, the calculator runs continuously, providing repeated displays of distance, bearing, and time. If the display is stopped, as it is by use of the [R/S] key, the timing of the operation is thrown off, and subsequent displays of distance, bearing, and time will be meaningless.

Using the HP-41C

The compatibility features incorporated into the card-reader accessory of the HP-41C make it possible to use on this calculator data and program cards that have been prepared on the HP-67 or HP-97. The conditions that must be fulfilled when the HP-41C is to be employed in this manner are listed on page 13. In addition, certain specific procedures must be followed with respect to a few particular programs and routines. These are discussed here, chapter by chapter.

COASTWISE NAVIGATION

Page 43 (Routine 2.1)
The method of recalling speed, set, and drift on the HP-41C is as follows:

309

Item	Press	To Enter, Press
Speed	RCL 1 5	A
Set	RCL 1 6	A
Drift	RCL 1 7	A

These changes are necessary because in the HP-41C there is no distinction between primary and secondary storage, and hence no [p↔s] key. All registers on the HP-41C are addressed with two digits; for those corresponding to secondary registers on the HP-67 and HP-97, the first digit is 1, as in the preceding table.

Page 92 (Routine 2.15)

The following changes are necessary:

- All storage registers are adressed with two digits; for example, in step 1, STO 0 becomes STO 0 0.
- Step 11 is eliminated, since there is no [p↔s] key on the HP-41C. Registers corresponding to secondary registers on the HP-67 and HP-97 are now addressed with a two-digit number beginning with 1; for example, in step 12, STO 0 becomes STO 1 0.
- In steps 22–25, the lettered registers are replaced by numbered registers, as follows:

Original Register	New Register
STO A	STO 2 0
STO B	STO 2 1
STO D	STO 2 3
STO E	STO 2 4

- In step 26, the instruction f W/DATA is replaced by XEQ ALPHA W D T A ALPHA.

Pages 105, 108 (Routines 2.20 and 2.21)

No changes in the HP-67 and HP-97 programs are required unless an accessory printer is connected to the HP-41C. If a printer is used, the changes shown in the following table should be made in the program as it appears on the HP-41C printout. When a step is inserted, subsequent steps are renumbered automatically.

310

Program and Routine	Original Program Step	Original Content	Insert	New Program Step	New Content
2.20	112	7 PRTx	PSE	112	7 PRTx
	113	ADV		113	PSE
				114	ADV
	187	7 PRTx	PSE	188	7 PRTx
	188	x↔y		189	PSE
				190	x↔y
	194	7 PRTx	PSE	196	7 PRTx
	195	RTN		197	PSE
				198	RTN
2.21	102	7 PRTx	PSE	102	7 PRTx
	103	GTO 1 2		103	PSE
				104	GTO 1 2
	184	7 PRTx	PSE	185	7 PRTx
	185	x↔y		186	PSE
				187	x↔y
	191	7 PRTx	PSE	193	7 PRTx
	192	RTN		194	PSE
				195	RTN

These changes make it possible to stop the tracking during the display of time.

After these changes have been made, the loop-time constant in the program for routine 2.20 is found at step 226, and the loop-time constant in the program for routine 2.21 is found at step 223.

SAILING

Page 167

Instead of [f] [W/DATA], the keys [XEQ] [ALPHA] [W] [D] [T] [A] [ALPHA] are pressed on the HP-41C.

Pages 188 and 205-6

Customizing programs is accomplished on the HP-41C in the same manner as on the HP-67 and HP-97. However, the step numbers for the program segments involved are different. For the HP-67 and HP-97, the program step numbers of the coefficients and exponents to be changed are given in the tables on pages 298 and 302–6. For the HP-41C, the equivalent step numbers can be found by printing the program on the HP-41C and locating the illustrative coefficients and exponents in the printout. These can then be replaced with the proper customizing values by means of the normal deletion and insertion methods used for HP-41C programs.

CELESTIAL NAVIGATION

Pages 232, 235 (Routines 4.2 and 4.3)

Celestial and monthly star data cards prepared on the HP-67 or HP-97 by means of routine 4.2 or 4.3 can be used for celestial sight reduction on the HP-41C. However, these routines should *not* be used on the HP-41C for the

preparation of almanac data cards. If cards prepared in this manner are employed for sight reduction, the results displayed will be incorrect.

Page 257 (Routine 4.10)

As in routine 2.15, the following changes are necessary:

- All storage registers are addressed with two digits.
- The shift to secondary storage (step 13) is eliminated.
- The lettered registers ($\boxed{\text{STO}}$ $\boxed{\text{A}}$ and $\boxed{\text{STO}}$ $\boxed{\text{B}}$) are replaced by numbered registers ($\boxed{\text{STO}}$ $\boxed{2}$ $\boxed{0}$ and $\boxed{\text{STO}}$ $\boxed{2}$ $\boxed{1}$).
- In step 24, the instruction $\boxed{\text{f}}$ $\boxed{\text{W/DATA}}$ is replaced by $\boxed{\text{XEQ}}$ $\boxed{\text{ALPHA}}$ $\boxed{\text{W}}$ $\boxed{\text{D}}$ $\boxed{\text{T}}$ $\boxed{\text{A}}$ $\boxed{\text{ALPHA}}$.

LORAN

The instruction $\boxed{\text{f}}$ $\boxed{\text{W/DATA}}$ is replaced by $\boxed{\text{XEQ}}$ $\boxed{\text{ALPHA}}$ $\boxed{\text{W}}$ $\boxed{\text{D}}$ $\boxed{\text{T}}$ $\boxed{\text{A}}$ $\boxed{\text{ALPHA}}$ in the following routines: 5.1 (step 8), 5.2 (step 13), 5.4 (step 37).

PRERECORDED CARDS FOR THE HP-41C

Prerecorded data and program cards for the HP-41C are available for all of the Hewlett-Packard routines presented in this volume. These cards are ready to use; the changes and restrictions described in the preceding paragraphs do not apply to them, and the instructions in the routines in this volume —the keystroke sequences for data entry and the display of results—are followed without modification. As a further convenience, each answer is labeled with the appropriate unit, such as knots, degrees, or nautical miles.

The HP-41C data and program cards can be obtained from Barco-Navigation, 62 West 45th Street, New York, N.Y, 10036.

Program Listings—pages 313 to 412.

312

001	*LBLa	21 16 11	046	ST+9	35-55 09	091	RCLB	36 12
002	STOA	35 11	047	RTN	24	092	→R	44
003	RTN	24	048	*LBLB	21 12	093	ST-3	35-45 03
004	*LBLa	21 16 11	049	HMS→	16 36	094	X≠Y	-41
005	STOB	35 12	050	P≠S	16-51	095	ST-4	35-45 04
006	RTN	24	051	STO8	35 08	096	RCL4	36 04
007	*LBLb	21 16 12	052	P≠S	16-51	097	RCL3	36 03
008	STOC	35 13	053	RTN	24	098	→P	34
009	RTN	24	054	*LBLB	21 12	099	STO5	35 05
010	*LBLb	21 16 12	055	HMS→	16 36	100	X≠Y	-41
011	STOE	35 15	056	P≠S	16-51	101	STO6	35 06
012	RTN	24	057	STO9	35 09	102	P≠S	16-51
013	*LBLA	21 11	058	RCL8	36 08	103	RCL2	36 02
014	GSB0	23 00	059	-	-45	104	-	-45
015	P≠S	16-51	060	STO1	35 01	105	SIN	41
016	ST04	35 04	061	P≠S	16-51	106	RCL2	36 02
017	P≠S	16-51	062	RCL8	36 08	107	RCL3	36 03
018	RTN	24	063	X≠Y	-41	108	-	-45
019	*LBLA	21 11	064	×	-35	109	SIN	41
020	P≠S	16-51	065	ST+3	35-55 03	110	÷	-24
021	ST05	35 05	066	LSTX	16-63	111	P≠S	16-51
022	P≠S	16-51	067	RCL9	36 09	112	RCL5	36 05
023	→R	44	068	×	-35	113	×	-35
024	STO8	35 08	069	ST+4	35-55 04	114	ABS	16 31
025	X≠Y	-41	070	RTN	24	115	STOB	35 12
026	STO9	35 09	071	*LBLC	21 13	116	P≠S	16-51
027	P≠S	16-51	072	GSB0	23 00	117	RCL3	36 03
028	0	00	073	P≠S	16-51	118	P≠S	16-51
029	STO6	35 06	074	STO2	35 02	119	STOA	35 11
030	STO7	35 07	075	P≠S	16-51	120	RCLB	36 12
031	RCL5	36 05	076	RTN	24	121	PRTX	-14
032	P≠S	16-51	077	*LBLD	21 14	122	SPC	16-11
033	RTN	24	078	GSB0	23 00	123	RTN	24
034	*LBLA	21 11	079	P≠S	16-51	124	*LBLc	21 16 13
035	P≠S	16-51	080	STO3	35 03	125	RCLA	36 11
036	STO6	35 06	081	P≠S	16-51	126	P≠S	16-51
037	P≠S	16-51	082	RTN	24	127	RCL6	36 06
038	RTN	24	083	*LBL0	21 00	128	-	-45
039	*LBLA	21 11	084	RCLE	36 15	129	SIN	41
040	P≠S	16-51	085	+	-55	130	RCL7	36 07
041	STO7	35 07	086	RCLC	36 13	131	×	-35
042	P≠S	16-51	087	+	-55	132	RCL5	36 05
043	→R	44	088	RTN	24	133	÷	-24
044	ST+8	35-55 08	089	*LBLE	21 15	134	SIN⁻	16 41
045	X≠Y	-41	090	RCLA	36 11	135	P≠S	16-51

#	Inst	Code		#	Inst	Code		#	Inst	Code
136	RCLA	36 11		181	RTN	24		001	*LBLA	21 11
137	+	-55		182	*LBLd	21 16 14		002	DSP2	-63 02
138	P⇄S	16-51		183	DSP2	-63 02		003	STO0	35 00
139	STO4	35 04		184	0	00		004	RTN	24
140	P⇄S	16-51		185	STO3	35 03		005	*LBLA	21 11
141	RCLC	36 13		186	STO4	35 04		006	STO1	35 01
142	-	-45		187	RTN	24		007	→R	4
143	RCLE	36 15		188	*LBLd	21 16 14		008	STO2	35 02
144	-	-45		189	STOA	35 11		009	X⇄Y	-41
145	X<0?	16-45		190	STOB	35. 12		010	STO3	35 03
146	GSB1	23 01		191	RTN	24		011	RCLA	36 11
147	PRTX	-14		192	*LBLe	21 16 15		012	RCLB	36 12
148	P⇄S	16-51		193	RCLA	36 11		013	→R	44
149	RCL4	36 04		194	RCLB	36 12		014	ST+2	35-55 02
150	RCL5	36 05		195	→R	44		015	X⇄Y.	-41
151	P⇄S	16-51		196	X⇄Y	-41		016	ST+3	35-55 03
152	→R	44		197	RCL4	36 04		017	RCL3	36 03
153	STO8	35 08		198	RCL3	36 03		018	RCL2	36 02
154	X⇄Y	-41		199	R↓	-31		019	→P	34
155	STO9	35 09		200	-	-45		020	STO4	35 04
156	P⇄S	16-51		201	CHS	-22		021	X⇄Y	-41
157	RCL6	36 06		202	R↓	-31		022	STO5	35 05
158	RCL7	36 07		203	X⇄Y	-41		023	RTN	24
159	P⇄S	16-51		204	-	-45		024	*LBLB	21 12
160	→R	44		205	CHS	-22		025	STOE	35 15
161	ST+8	35-55 08		206	R↑	16-31		026	RTN	24
162	X⇄Y	-41		207	X⇄Y	-41		027	*LBLC	21 13
163	ST+9	35-55 09		208	→P	34		028	P⇄S	16-51
164	RCL9	36 09		209	PRTX	-14		029	STO0	35 00
165	RCL8	36 08		210	X⇄Y	-41		030	P⇄S	16-51
166	→P	34		211	1	01		031	RTN	24
167	PRTX	-14		212	8	08		032	*LBLC	21 13
168	RCLB	36 12		213	0	00		033	P⇄S	16-51
169	X⇄Y	-41		214	+	-55		034	STO6	35 06
170	÷	-24		215	PRTX	-14		035	P⇄S	16-51
171	→HMS	16 35		216	SPC	16-11		036	RTN	24
172	DSP4	-63 04		217	R/S	51		037	*LBLC	21 13
173	PRTX	-14		218	X⇄Y	-41		038	P⇄S	16-51
174	SPC	16-11		219	P⇄S	16-51		039	STO7	35 07
175	RTN	24		220	RCL1	36 01		040	P⇄S	16-51
176	*LBL1	21 01		221	P⇄S	16-51		041	RCL5	36 05
177	3	03		222	÷	-24		042	P⇄S	16-51
178	6	06		223	PRTX	-14		043	RCL6	36 06
179	0	00		224	RTN	24		044	-	-45
180	+	-55						045	SIN	41

046	RCL7	36 07	091	P⇄S	16-51		46.	LBL
047	x	-35	092	RCL4	36 04		15.	E
048	RCL0	36 00	093	X⇄Y	-41		48.	EXC
049	÷	-24	094	÷	-24		0.	0
050	P⇄S	16-51	095	P⇄S	16-51		0.	0
051	SIN⁻¹	16 41	096	STO2	35 02		42.	STO
052	RCL5	36 05	097	P⇄S	16-51		9.	9
053	+	-55	098	→HMS	16 35		9.	9
054	STO7	35 07	099	DSP4	-63 04		56.	RTN
055	RCLE	36 15	100	PRTX	-14	10	46.	LBL
056	-	-45	101	SPC	16-11		16.	A"
057	X<0?	16-45	102	RTN	24		44.	SUM
058	GSB1	23 01	103	*LBL1	21 01		6.	6
059	RTN	24	104	3	03		9.	9
060	*LBLD	21 14	105	6	06		81.	HLT
061	STOC	35 13	106	0	00		46.	LBL
062	-	-45	107	+	-55		17.	B"
063	X<0?	16-45	108	RTN	24		48.	EXC
064	GSB1	23 01	109	*LBLd	21 16 14		1.	1
065	STO6	35 06	110	RCLB	36 12		9.	9
066	SPC	16-11	111	RCLA	36 11	20	48.	EXC
067	PRTX	-14	112	R↑	16-31		1.	1
068	RTN	24	113	CLRG	16-53		8.	8
069	*LBLE	21 15	114	P⇄S	16-51		81.	HLT
070	RCL7	36 07	115	CLRG	16-53		46.	LBL
071	P⇄S	16-51	116	R↓	-31		18.	C"
072	RCL0	36 00	117	STOA	35 11		48.	EXC
073	P⇄S	16-51	118	R↓	-31		1.	1
074	→R	44	119	STOB	35 12		5.	5
075	STO8	35 08	120	CLX	-51	30	48.	EXC
076	X⇄Y	-41	121	RTN	24		1.	1
077	STO9	35 09	122	*LBLe	21 16 15		4.	4
078	P⇄S	16-51	123	RCL5	36 05		81.	HLT
079	RCL6	36 06	124	X<0?	16-45		46.	LBL
080	RCL7	36 07	125	GSB1	23 01		11.	A
081	P⇄S	16-51	126	PRTX	-14		37.	DMS
082	→R	44	127	RCL4	36 04		75.	-
083	ST+8	35-55 08	128	PRTX	-14		48.	EXC
084	X⇄Y	-41	129	P⇄S	16-51		1.	1
085	ST+9	35-55 09	130	RCL1	36 01		3.	3
086	RCL9	36 09	131	P⇄S	16-51	40	3.	3
087	RCL8	36 08	132	PRTX	-14		90.	IF0
088	→P	34	133	SPC	16-11		1.	1
089	P⇄S	16-51	134	RTN	24			
090	STO1	35 01	135	R/S	51			

	0.	0		7.	7		6.	6
	0.	0		15.	E		22.	INV
	95.	=		44.	SUM		44.	SUM
	42.	STD		1.	1	130	0.	0
	1.	1		6.	6		0.	0
	2.	2	90	81.	HLT		43.	RCL
	65.	×		46.	LBL		1.	1
50	43.	RCL		12.	B		6.	6
	1.	1		85.	+		75.	-
	5.	5		43.	RCL		43.	RCL
	95.	=		6.	6		1.	1
	15.	E		9.	9		7.	7
	43.	RCL		95.	=		95.	=
	1.	1		48.	EXC	140	22.	INV
	4.	4		0.	0		39.	P/R
	85.	+	100	1.	1		75.	-
	43.	RCL		48.	EXC		43.	RCL
60	6.	6		0.	0		0.	0
	9.	9		4.	4		4.	4
	95.	=		95.	=		95.	=
	39.	P/R		81.	HLT		32.	SIN
	44.	SUM		46.	LBL		65.	×
	1.	1		13.	C		15.	E
	7.	7		48..	EXC	150	55.	÷
	43.	RCL		0.	0		53.	(
	1.	1	110	7.	7		43.	RCL
	9.	9		48.	EXC		0.	0
70	65.	×		0.	0		4.	4
	43.	RCL		8.	8		75.	-
	1.	1		81.	HLT		43.	RCL
	2.	2		46.	LBL		0.	0
	95.	=		14.	D		1.	1
	15.	E		43.	RCL		54.	)
	44.	SUM		0.	0	160	32.	SIN
	1.	1		7.	7		95.	=
	6.	6	120	15.	E		40.	X²
	43.	RCL		43.	RCL		30.	√
80	1.	1		0.	0		15.	E
	8.	8		8.	8		43.	RCL
	39.	P/R		39.	P/R		0.	0
	44.	SUM		48.	EXC		1.	1
	1.	1		1.	1		75.	-

Program 2.3

	1.	1		46.	LBL			46.	LBL
170	8.	8		17.	B'			15.	E
	0.	0		48.	EXC			42.	STO
	95.	=		0.	0			6.	6
	80.	IF+		0.	0			9.	9
	1.	1		42.	STO			81.	HLT
	8.	8		0.	0			46.	LBL
	1.	1		9.	9		50	16.	A'
	85.	+		56.	RTN			43.	RCL
	3.	3	10	46.	LBL			9.	9
	6.	6		11.	A			9.	9
180	0.	0		42.	STO			94.	+/-
	95.	=		0.	0			17.	B'
	42.	STO		1.	1			43.	RCL
	9.	9		81.	HLT			9.	9
	8.	8		46.	LBL			8.	8
	81.	HLT		12.	B			39.	P/R
	46.	LBL		48.	EXC		60	42.	STO
	10.	E'		1.	1			1.	1
	25.	CLR	20	9.	9			4.	4
	47.	CMS		48.	EXC			43.	RCL
190	81.	HLT		1.	1			0.	0
				8.	8			4.	4
				81.	HLT			17.	B'
				46.	LBL			42.	STO
				13.	C			0.	0
				48.	EXC			8.	8
				0.	0		70	43.	RCL
				4.	4			0.	0
			30	48.	EXC			3.	3
				0.	0			39.	P/R
				3.	3			44.	SUM
				81.	HLT			1.	1
				46.	LBL			4.	4
				14.	D			43.	RCL
				48.	EXC			0.	0
				9.	9			8.	8
				9.	9		80	44.	SUM
				48.	EXC			0.	0
			40	9.	9			0.	0
				8.	8			43.	RCL
				81.	HLT			1.	1

	4.	4		3.	3		8.	8

Left column

```
      4.    4
     22.    INV
     39.    P/R
     80.    IF+
      0.    0
90    9.    9
      5.    5
     85.    +
      3.    3
      6.    6
      0.    0
     95.    =
     81.    HLT
     46.    LBL
     18.    C'
100  43.    RCL
      0.    0
      0.    0
     75.    -
     43.    RCL
      1.    1
      8.    8
     95.    =
     32.    SIN
     65.    ×
110  43.    RCL
      1.    1
      9.    9
     55.    ÷
     43.    RCL
      6.    6
      9.    9
     95.    =
     22.    INV
     32.    SIN
120  85.    +
     43.    RCL
      0.    0
      0.    0
     95.    =
     80.    IF+
      1.    1
```

Middle column

```
      3.    3
      2.    2
     85.    +
130   3.    3
      6.    6
      0.    0
     75.    -
     43.    RCL
      0.    0
      1.    1
     95.    =
     42.    STO
      1.    1
140   0.    0
     81.    HLT
     46.    LBL
     19.    D'
     42.    STO
      0.    0
      2.    2
     22.    INV
     44.    SUM
      1.    1
150   0.    0
     43.    RCL
      1.    1
      0.    0
     81.    HLT
     46.    LBL
     10.    E'
     43.    RCL
      1.    1
      9.    9
160  48.    EXC
      0.    0
      0.    0
     43.    RCL
      1.    1
      8.    8
     39.    P/R
     42.    STO
      0.    0
```

Right column

```
      8.    8
170  43.    RCL
      6.    6
      9.    9
     48.    EXC
      0.    0
      0.    0
     42.    STO
      0.    0
      7.    7
     43.    RCL
180   1.    1
      0.    0
     85.    +
     43.    RCL
      0.    0
      1.    1
     85.    +
     43.    RCL
      0.    0
      2.    2
190  95.    =
     39.    P/R
     44.    SUM
      0.    0
      8.    8
     43.    RCL
      0.    0
      7.    7
     44.    SUM
      0.    0
200   0.    0
     43.    RCL
      0.    0
      8.    8
     22.    INV
     39.    P/R
     43.    RCL
      0.    0
      9.    9
     55.    ÷
210  17.    B'
```

Program 2.4

#		#			#	
95.	=		46.	LBL		46.	LBL
22.	INV		11.	A		16.	A°
37.	DMS		42.	STO		37.	DMS
57.	FIX		1.	1		42.	STO
4.	4		0.	0		0.	0
81.	HLT		81.	HLT		6.	6
			46.	LBL		81.	HLT
			12.	B	50	46.	LBL
			42.	STO		17.	B°
		10	0.	0		37.	DMS
			1.	1		42.	STO
			81.	HLT		0.	0
			46.	LBL		7.	7
			13.	C		81.	HLT
			48.	EXC		46.	LBL
			0.	0		18.	C°
			2.	2		48.	EXC
			48.	EXC	60	0.	0
			0.	0		9.	9
		20	3.	3		48.	EXC
			81.	HLT		0.	0
			46.	LBL		8.	8
			14.	D		43.	RCL
			85.	+		0.	0
			43.	RCL		9.	9
			1.	1		42.	STO
			0.	0		0.	0
			85.	+	70	0.	0
			43.	RCL		43.	RCL
		30	0.	0		0.	0
			1.	1		8.	8
			95.	=		39.	P/R
			42.	STO		42.	STO
			0.	0		1.	1
			4.	4		3.	3
			81.	HLT		43.	RCL
			46.	LBL		0.	0
			15.	E	80	0.	0
			42.	STO		42.	STO
		40	0.	0		1.	1
			5.	5		4.	4
			81.	HLT		81.	HLT

(CONTINUED)

	46.	LBL		7.	7	42.	STO
	19.	D'		75.	−	1.	1
	43.	RCL	170	1.	1	
	0.	0		7.	7	
	5.	5		43.	RCL	
90	42.	STO	130	0.	0	0.	0

```
      46.    LBL          7.    7          42.   STO
      19.    D'          75.    -      170   1.    1
      43.    RCL         43.    RCL         7.    7
       0.    0      130   0.    0          43.   RCL
       5.    5           6.    6           0.    0
  90  42.    STO        95.    =           0.    0
       0.    0          49.    PRD        42.   STO
       0.    0           1.    1           1.    1
      43.    RCL         1.    1          81.   HLT
       0.    0          49.    PRD        85.   +
       4.    4           1.    1           3.    3
      39.    P/R         2.    2      180   6.    6
      42.    STO        43.    RCL         0.    0
       1.    1      140   1.    1          95.   =
       1.    1           1.    1          42.   STO
 100  43.    RCL        22.    INV         1.    1
       0.    0          44.    SUM         7.    7
       0.    0           1.    1          43.   RCL
      42.    STO         3.    3           0.    0
       1.    1          43.    RCL         0.    0
       2.    2           1.    1          42.   STO
      43.    RCL         2.    2      190   1.    1
       0.    0          22.    INV         8.    8
       2.    2      150   44.    SUM      81.   HLT
      42.    STO         1.    1          46.   LBL
 110   0.    0           4.    4          10.   E'
       0.    0          43.    RCL        43.   RCL
      43.    RCL         1.    1           1.    1
       0.    0           4.    4           7.    7
       3.    3          42.    STO        81.   HLT
      39.    P/R         0.    0
      44.    SUM         0.    0
       1.    1          43.    RCL
       1.    1      160   1.    1
      43.    RCL         3.    3
 120   0.    0          22.    INV
       0.    0          39.    P/R
      44.    SUM        22.    INV
       1.    1          80.    IF+
       2.    2           1.    1
      43.    RCL         7.    7
       0.    0           7.    7
```

Entries for steps 28–33 should
be replaced when the loop time
or the particular calculator has
been determined, as shown in
the discussion of customized
programs earlier in this appendix.

001	*LBLA	21 11
002	STOE	35 15
003	RTN	24
004	*LBLA	21 11
005	STOD	35 14
006	RTN	24
007	*LBLA	21 11
008	STOI	35 46
009	RTN	24
010	*LBLB	21 12
011	STOC	35 13
012	RTN	24
013	*LBLa	21 16 11
014	STOA	35 11
015	RTN	24
016	*LBLa	21 16 11
017	STOB	35 12
018	RTN	24
019	*LBLb	21 16 12
020	RTN	24
021	*LBLb	21 16 12
022	→R	44
023	CHS	-22
024	STO4	35 04
025	X⇄Y	-41
026	CHS	-22
027	STO5	35 05
028	.	-62
029	0	00
030	0	00
031	3	03
032	1	01
033	9	09
034	STO6	35 06
035	CLX	-51
036	RTN	24
037	*LBLc	21 16 13
038	HMS→	16 36
039	P⇄S	16-51

040	STO4	35 04
041	STO8	35 08
042	RCL5	36 05
043	P⇄S	16-51
044	X=0?	16-43
045	RTN	24
046	GSB0	23 00
047	RCL8	36 08
048	P⇄S	16-51
049	RCL4	36 04
050	RCL5	36 05
051	P⇄S	16-51
052	-	-45
053	x	-35
054	ST+4	35-55 04
055	LSTX	16-63
056	RCL9	36 05
057	x	-35
058	ST+5	35-55 05
059	GSB1	23 01
060	0	00
061	STO7	35 07
062	P⇄S	16-51
063	RCL4	36 04
064	→HMS	16 35
065	DSP4	-63 04
066	P⇄S	16-51
067	RTN	24
068	*LBLd	21 16 14
069	HMS→	16 36
070	P⇄S	16-51
071	STO5	35 05
072	RCL8	36 08
073	-	-45
074	STO6	35 06
075	P⇄S	16-51
076	GSB0	23 00
077	RCL8	36 08
078	P⇄S	16-51
079	RCL6	36 06
080	x	-35
081	P⇄S	16-51
082	ST+4	35-55 04
083	LSTX	16-63
084	RCL9	36 09
085	x	-35

086	ST+5	35-55 05
087	GSB1	23 01
088	P⇄S	16-51
089	RCL5	36 05
090	RCL4	36 04
091	P⇄S	16-51
092	-	-45
093	RCL7	36 07
094	÷	-24
095	STO6	35 06
096	P⇄S	16-51
097	RCL8	36 08
098	RCL6	36 06
099	+	-55
100	STO8	35 08
101	→HMS	16 35
102	DSP4	-63 04
103	P⇄S	16-51
104	RTN	24
105	*LBLC	21 13
106	GSB0	23 00
107	1	01
108	ST+7	35-55 07
109	RCL6	36 06
110	RCL8	36 08
111	x	-35
112	ST+4	35-55 04
113	RCL6	36 06
114	RCL9	36 09
115	x	-35
116	ST+5	35-55 05
117	RCL5	36 05
118	RCL4	36 04
119	→P	34
120	STO3	35 03
121	PSE	16 51
122	PRTX	-14
123	X⇄Y	-41
124	1	01
125	8	08
126	0	00
127	+	-55
128	STO2	35 02
129	PSE	16 51
130	PRTX	-14
131	P⇄S	16-51

#	Instr	Code	#	Instr	Code	#	Instr	Code
132	RCL4	36 04	177	+	-55	001	*LBLA	21 1
133	P⇄S	16-51	178	RCLI	36 46	002	F2?	16 23 0,
134	RCL7	36 07	179	+	-55	003	GTO1	22 0
135	RCL6	36 06	180	RCLC	36 13	004	RCLA	36 1
136	x	-35	181	→R	44	005	-	-4;
137	+	-55	182	STO8	35 08	006	*LBL0	21 00
138	P⇄S	16-51	183	X⇄Y	-41	007	RCLE	36 1;
139	STO8	35 08	184	STO9	35 09	008	÷	-2;
140	P⇄S	16-51	185	RCLA	36 11	009	8	0;
141	→HMS	16 35	186	RCLB	36 12	010	+	-5;
142	DSP4	-63 04	187	→R	44	011	FRC	16 4;
143	PRTX	-14	188	ST+8	35-55 08	012	RCLE	36 1;
144	PSE	16 51	189	X⇄Y	-41	013	x	-3;
145	SPC	16-11	190	ST+9	35-55 09	014	RTN	2;
146	DSP2	-63 02	191	RTN	24	015	*LBL1	21 0;
147	GTOC	22 13	192	*LBL1	21 01	016	P⇄S	16-5;
148	*LBLD	21 14	193	RCL5	36 05	017	CLRG	16-5;
149	R/S	51	194	RCL4	36 04	018	P⇄S	16-5;
150	RTN	24	195	→P	34	019	3	0;
151	*LBLe	21 16 15	196	STO3	35 03	020	6	0;
152	.	-62	197	X⇄Y	-41	021	0	0;
153	0	00	198	1	01	022	STOE	35 1;
154	0	00	199	8	08	023	2	0;
155	3	03	200	0	00	024	÷	-2;
156	1	01	201	+	-55	025	+	-5;
157	9	09	202	STO2	35 02	026	STOA	35 1;
158	STO6	35 06	203	RTN	24	027	LSTX	16-6;
159	0	00	204	*LBLE	21 15	028	SF2	16 21 0;
160	STO7	35 07	205	RCL3	36 03	029	RTN	2;
161	P⇄S	16-51	206	PRTX	-14	030	*LBLB	21 1;
162	STO5	35 05	207	RCL2	36 02	031	HMS→	16 3;
163	P⇄S	16-51	208	DSP1	-63 01	032	F2?	16 23 0;
164	RCL2	36 02	209	PRTX	-14	033	STOC	35 1;
165	RCL3	36 03	210	P⇄S	16-51	034	STOB	35 1;
166	→R	44	211	DSP4	-63 04	035	Σ+	5;
167	CHS	-22	212	RCL8	36 08	036	RTN	2;
168	STO4	35 04	213	→HMS	16 35	037	*LBLC	21 13
169	X⇄Y	-41	214	PRTX	-14	038	*LBLD	21 14
170	CHS	-22	215	SPC	16-11	039	RCL4	36 04
171	STO5	35 05	216	DSP2	-63 02	040	STO7	35 07
172	CLX	-51	217	P⇄S	16-51	041	RCL5	36 05
173	RTN	24	218	RTN	24	042	STO8	35 08
174	*LBL0	21 00	219	R/S	51	043	RCL6	36 06
175	RCLE	36 15				044	STO9	35 09
176	RCLD	36 14				045	RCLB	36 12

046	RCLC	36 13	091	÷	-24	136	P≷S	16-51
047	+	-55	092	STO0	35 00	137	RTN	24
048	2	02	093	→HMS	16 35	138	*LBLc	21 16 13
049	÷	-24	094	PRTX	-14	139	STOI	35 46
050	STO6	35 06	095	RCL0	36 00	140	RTN	24
051	→HMS	16 35	096	RCL7	36 07	141	*LBLc	21 16 13
052	PRTX	-14	097	x	-35	142	STO3	35 03
053	P≷S	16-51	098	RCL8	36 08	143	RTN	24
054	RCL8	36 08	099	+	-55	144	*LBL6	21 06
055	RCL4	36 04	100	GSB0	23 00	145	P≷S	16-51
056	RCL6	36 06	101	STO1	35 01	146	RCL0	36 00
057	x	-35	102	PRTX	-14	147	+	-55
058	RCL9	36 09	103	RCL0	36 00	148	RCLi	36 01
059	÷	-24	104	RCL4	36 04	149	+	-55
060	-	-45	105	x	-35	150	P≷S	16-51
061	RCL5	36 05	106	RCL5	36 05	151	RTN	24
062	RCL4	36 04	107	+	-55	152	*LBLd	21 16 14
063	X²	53	108	GSB0	23 00	153	RCL1	36 01
064	RCL9	36 09	109	STO2	35 02	154	GSB6	23 06
065	÷	-24	110	PRTX	-14	155	STO1	35 01
066	-	-45	111	SPC	16-11	156	RCL2	36 02
067	÷	-24	112	RCL2	36 02	157	GSB6	23 06
068	P≷S	16-51	113	RCL1	36 01	158	STO2	35 02
069	STO4	35 04	114	-	-45	159	RCLI	36 46
070	x̄	16 53	115	SIN	41	160	RCL2	36 02
071	RCL4	36 04	116	P≷S	16-51	161	-	-45
072	x	-35	117	STO2	35 02	162	SIN	41
073	-	-45	118	P≷S	16-51	163	P≷S	16-51
074	RCLA	36 11	119	RCL2	36 02	164	RCL2	36 02
075	+	-55	120	RTN	24	165	P≷S	16-51
076	STO5	35 05	121	*LBLa	21 16 11	166	÷	-24
077	RCL6	36 06	122	CLRG	16-53	167	RCL3	36 03
078	RCL4	36 04	123	P≷S	16-51	168	x	-35
079	x	-35	124	CLRG	16-53	169	ABS	16 31
080	+	-55	125	CLX	-51	170	STOD	35 14
081	GSB0	23 00	126	SF2	16 21 02	171	PRTX	-14
082	SF2	16 21 02	127	RTN	24	172	RCL1	36 01
083	PRTX	-14	128	*LBLb	21 16 12	173	PRTX	-14
084	SPC	16-11	129	P≷S	16-51	174	SPC	16-11
085	RTN	24	130	STO0	35 00	175	RTN	24
086	*LBLE	21 15	131	P≷S	16-51	176	*LBLe	21 16 15
087	RCL6	36 06	132	RTN	24	177	RCLI	36 46
088	RCL9	36 09	133	*LBLb	21 16 12	178	RCL1	36 01
089	+	-55	134	P≷S	16-51	179	-	-45
090	2	02	135	STO1	35 01	180	SIN	41

181	P⇄S	16-51		46.	LBL		42.	STO
182	RCL2	36 02		11.	A		0.	0
183	P⇄S	16-51		37.	DMS		9.	9
184	÷	-24		42.	STO		1.	1
185	RCL3	36 03		0.	0		42.	STO
186	x	-35		3.	3		0.	0
187	ABS	16 31		44.	SUM		6.	6
188	P⇄S	16-51		0.	0	50	81.	HLT
189	STO3	35 03		7.	7		46.	LBL
190	P⇄S	16-51	10	40.	X²		13.	C
191	PRTX	-14		44.	SUM		42.	STO
192	RCL2	36 02		0.	0		0.	0
193	PRTX	-14		8.	8		2.	2
194	SPC	16-11		81.	HLT		75.	-
195	RTN	24		46.	LBL		43.	RCL
				12.	B		0.	0
				85.	+		1.	1
				1.	1	60	95.	=
				8.	8		22.	INV
			20	0.	0		80.	IF+
				95.	=		10.	E'
				42.	STO		42.	STO
				0.	0		1.	1
				1.	1		0.	0
				1.	1		22.	INV
				8.	8		80.	IF+
				0.	0		19.	D'
				44.	SUM	70	42.	STO
				0.	0		1.	1
			30	4.	4		0.	0
				40.	X²		44.	SUM
				44.	SUM		0.	0
				0.	0		4.	4
				5.	5		40.	X²
				1.	1		44.	SUM
				8.	8		0.	0
				0.	0		5.	5
				65.	x	80	43.	RCL
				43.	RCL		1.	1
			40	0.	0		0.	0
				3.	3		65.	x
				95.	=		43.	RCL

	0.	0			15.	E		6.	6
	3.	3			43.	RCL	170	20.	1/X
	95.	=			0.	0		65.	×
	44.	SUM		130	9.	9		53.	(
	0.	0			75.	–		43.	RCL
90	9.	9			53.	(		0.	0
	1.	1			43.	RCL		4.	4
	44.	SUM			0.	0		75.	–
	0.	0			7.	7		43.	RCL
	6.	6			65.	×		1.	1
	43.	RCL			43.	RCL		2.	2
	0.	0			0.	0	180	65.	×
	2.	2			4.	4		43.	RCL
	81.	HLT		140	55.	÷		0.	0
	46.	LBL			43.	RCL		7.	7
00	10.	E'			0.	0		54.	)
	53.	(			6.	6		54.	)
	43.	RCL			54.	)		42.	STO
	0.	0			54.	)		1.	1
	2.	2			55.	÷		3.	3
	75.	–			53.	(		43.	RCL
	43.	RCL			43.	RCL	190	1.	1
	0.	0			0.	0		2.	2
	1.	1		150	8.	8		65.	×
	85.	+			75.	–		43.	RCL
10	3.	3			53.	(		1.	1
	6.	6			43.	RCL		1.	1
	0.	0			0.	0		85.	+
	54.	)			7.	7		43.	RCL
	41.	GTO			40.	X²		1.	1
	0.	0			55.	÷		3.	3
	6.	6			43.	RCL	200	85.	+
	3.	3			0.	0		43.	RCL
	81.	HLT		160	6.	6		0.	0
	46.	LBL			54.	)		1.	1
20	14.	D			54.	)		95.	=
	37.	DMS			54.	)		81.	HLT
	42.	STO			42.	STO		46.	LBL
	1.	1			1.	1		19.	D'
	1.	1			2.	2		53.	(
	81.	HLT			43.	RCL		43.	RCL
	46.	LBL			0.	0	210	1.	1

Program 2.8

0.	0	001	*LBLa	21 16 11	047	+	-5
85.	+	002	CLRG	16-53	048	RCLD	36 1
3.	3	003	P≵S	16-51	049	+	-5
6.	6	004	CLRG	16-53	050	RTN	2
0.	0	005	P≵S	16-51	051	*LBLD	21 1
54.	)	006	CLX	-51	052	HMS→	16 3
41.	GTO	007	RTN	24	053	RCL6	36 0
0.	0	008	*LBLb	21 16 12	054	TAN	4
6.	6	009	STOE	35 15	055	1/X	5
220 9.	9	010	RTN	24	056	X≵Y	-4

Program listing:

001 *LBLa 21 16 11
002 CLRG 16-53
003 P≵S 16-51
004 CLRG 16-53
005 P≵S 16-51
006 CLX -51
007 RTN 24
008 *LBLb 21 16 12
009 STOE 35 15
010 RTN 24
011 *LBLb 21 16 12
012 STOD 35 14
013 RTN 24
014 *LBLA 21 11
015 GSB0 23 00
016 STO0 35 00
017 RTN 24
018 *LBLA 21 11
019 →R 44
020 STO8 35 08
021 X≵Y -41
022 STO9 35 09
023 RTN 24
024 *LBLB 21 12
025 STO2 35 02
026 RTN 24
027 *LBLB 21 12
028 →R 44
029 ST+8 35-55 08
030 X≵Y -41
031 ST+9 35-55 09
032 RCL9 36 09
033 RCL8 36 08
034 →P 34
035 STO5 35 05
036 X≵Y -41
037 STO4 35 04
038 RTN 24
039 *LBLC 21 13
040 GSB0 23 00
041 RCL4 36 04
042 - -45
043 STO6 35 06
044 RTN 24
045 *LBL0 21 00
046 RCLE 36 15

047 + -5
048 RCLD 36 1
049 + -5
050 RTN 2
051 *LBLD 21 1
052 HMS→ 16 3
053 RCL6 36 0
054 TAN 4
055 1/X 5
056 X≵Y -4
057 Σ+ 5
058 RTN 2
059 *LBLe 21 16 1
060 HMS→ 16 3
061 STOC 35 1
062 RTN 2
063 *LBLE 21 1
064 P≵S 16-5
065 RCL8 36 0
066 RCL4 36 0
067 RCL6 36 0
068 x -3
069 RCL9 36 0
070 ÷ -2
071 - -4
072 RCL5 36 0
073 RCL4 36 04
074 X² 5
075 RCL9 36 0
076 ÷ -2
077 - -4
078 ÷ -2
079 P≵S 16-5
080 STOA 35 11
081 P≵S 16-5
082 RCL6 36 0
083 RCL9 36 09
084 ÷ -2
085 RCL4 36 04
086 RCL9 36 09
087 ÷ -2
088 P≵S 16-5
089 RCLA 36 11
090 x -3
091 - -4
092 STOB 35 12

#	Key	Code		#	Key	Code		#	Key	Code
093	RCLA	36 11		139	FRC	16 44		185	ABS	16 31
094	÷	-24		140	3	03		186	PRTX	-14
095	CHS	-22		141	6	06		187	SPC	16-11
096	STOI	35 46		142	0	00		188	RTN	24
097	RCLA	36 11		143	x	-35				
098	RCLC	36 13		144	DSP1	-63 01				
099	x	-35		145	PRTX	-14				
100	RCLB	36 12		146	SPC	16-11				
101	+	-55		147	RTN	24				
102	1/X	52		148	*LBL3	21 03				
103	TAN⁻	16 43		149	P⇄S	16-51				
104	P⇄S	16-51		150	RCL1	36 01				
105	STO1	35 01		151	1	01				
106	P⇄S	16-51		152	8	08				
107	RCLC	36 13		153	0	00				
108	RCLI	36 46		154	+	-55				
109	X≤Y?	16-35		155	STO1	35 01				
110	GSB3	23 03		156	P⇄S	16-51				
111	P⇄S	16-51		157	RTN	24				
112	RCL1	36 01		158	*LBL4	21 04				
113	P⇄S	16-51		159	3	03				
114	COS	42		160	6	06				
115	RCLC	36 13		161	0	00				
116	RCLI	36 46		162	+	-55				
117	-	-45		163	RTN	24				
118	RCL5	36 05		164	*LBL0	21 00				
119	x	-35		165	RCLD	36 14				
120	X⇄Y	-41		166	+	-55				
121	÷	-24		167	RCLE	36 15				
122	ABS	16 31		168	+	-55				
123	P⇄S	16-51		169	RTN	24				
124	STO0	35 00		170	*LBLd	21 16 14				
125	DSP2	-63 02		171	RCLI	36 46				
126	PRTX	-14		172	→HMS	16 35				
127	RCL1	36 01		173	DSP4	-63 04				
128	P⇄S	16-51		174	PRTX	-14				
129	RCL4	36 04		175	SPC	16-11				
130	+	-55		176	DSP2	-63 02				
131	X<0?	16-45		177	RTN	24				
132	GSB4	23 04		178	*LBLd	21 16 14				
133	3	03		179	P⇄S	16-51				
134	6	06		180	RCL0	36 00				
135	0	00		181	RCL1	36 01				
136	÷	-24		182	P⇄S	16-51				
137	8	08		183	SIN	41				
138	+	-55		184	x	-35				

Program 2.9

	46.	LBL		8.	8		95.	=
	13.	C		43.	RCL		42.	STO
	85.	+		0.	0		0.	0
	43.	RCL		8.	8		9.	9
	0.	0		81.	HLT		65.	×
	1.	1		46.	LBL	90	43.	RCL
	75.	-		16.	A'		0.	0
	43.	RCL	50	37.	DMS		4.	4
	9.	9		42.	STO		94.	+/-
10	8.	8		0.	0		85.	+
	95.	=		7.	7		43.	RCL
	34.	TAN		43.	RCL		0.	0
	20.	1/X		0.	0		3.	3
	44.	SUM		6.	6		95.	=
	0.	0		75.	-		55.	÷
	3.	3		43.	RCL	100	43.	RCL
	42.	STO		0.	0		0.	0
	1.	1	60	3.	3		8.	8
	8.	8		65.	×		95.	=
20	81.	HLT		43.	RCL		42.	STO
	46.	LBL		0.	0		1.	1
	14.	D		4.	4		0.	0
	37.	DMS		55.	÷		55.	÷
	44.	SUM		43.	RCL		43.	RCL
	0.	0		0.	0		0.	0
	4.	4		8.	8	110	9.	9
	49.	PRD		95.	=		95.	=
	1.	1	70	55.	÷		42.	STO
	8.	8		53.	(		1.	1
30	40.	X²		43.	RCL		1.	1
	44.	SUM		0.	0		85.	+
	0.	0		5.	5		43.	RCL
	5.	5		75.	-		0.	0
	43.	RCL		43.	RCL		7.	7
	1.	1		0.	0		95.	=
	8.	8		4.	4	120	65.	×
	44.	SUM		40.	X²		43.	RCL
	0.	0	80	55.	÷		9.	9
	6.	6		43.	RCL		9.	9
40	1.	1		0.	0		55.	÷
	44.	SUM		8.	8		53.	(
	0.	0		54.	)		43.	RCL

	0.	0		81.	HLT		19.	D'

```
      0.   0          81.   HLT         19.   D'
      9.   9      170  46.   LBL        43.   RCL
     65.   ×           17.   B'          1.   1
130  43.   RCL         19.   D'          1.   1
      0.   0           80.   IF+        85.   +
      7.   7           87.   1'         43.   RCL
     85.   +            1.   1           0.   0
     43.   RCL          8.   8           7.   7
      1.   1            0.   0          95.   =
      0.   0           85.   +      220   4.   4
     54.   )           46.   LBL        22.   INV
     20.   1/X     180  87.   1'         37.   DMS
     22.   INV         43.   RCL        56.   RTN
140  34.   TAN          1.   1
     42.   STO          2.   2
      1.   1           85.   +
      2.   2           43.   RCL
     33.   COS          9.   9
     95.   =            8.   8
     40.   X²          75.   -
     30.   ⌈           46.   LBL
     81.   HLT     190  88.   2'
     46.   LBL          3.   3
150  10.   E'           6.   6
     57.   FIX          0.   0
      4.   4           85.   +
     25.   CLR         22.   INV
     47.   CMS         80.   IF+
     46.   LBL         88.   2'
     11.   A            0.   0
     44.   SUM         95.   =
      0.   0       200  81.   HLT
      1.   1           46.   LBL
160  81.   HLT         18.   C'
     46.   LBL         43.   RCL
     12.   B            1.   1
     48.   EXC          1.   1
      9.   9           94.   +/-
      9.   9           22.   INV
     48.   EXC         37.   DMS
      9.   9           81.   HLT
      8.   8       210  46.   LBL
```

001	*LBLe	21 16 15	047	–	-45		46.	LBL
002	STOD	35 14	048	SIN	41		13.	C
003	RTN	24	049	RCL1	36 01		85.	+
004	*LBLe	21 16 15	050	RCL2	36 02		43.	RCL
005	STOE	35 15	051	–	-45		6.	6
006	RTN	24	052	SIN	41		5.	5
007	*LBLA	21 11	053	÷	-24		65.	×
008	GSB0	23 00	054	×	-35		1.	1
009	STO0	35 00	055	STO6	35 06		44.	SUM
010	RTN	24	056	RCL2	36 02	10	9.	9
011	*LBLB	21 12	057	SIN	41		9.	9
012	GSB0	23 00	058	×	-35		95.	=
013	STO1	35 01	059	RCL0	36 00		36.	IND
014	RTN	24	060	SIN	41		42.	STD
015	*LBLC	21 13	061	–	-45		9.	9
016	GSB0	23 00	062	RCL6	36 06		9.	9
017	STO2	35 02	063	RCL2	36 02		43.	RCL
018	RTN	24	064	COS	42		0.	0
019	*LBLa	21 16 11	065	×	-35		0.	0
020	HMS→	16 36	066	RCL0	36 00	20	44.	SUM
021	STO3	35 03	067	COS	42		9.	9
022	RTN	24	068	–	-45		9.	9
023	*LBLb	21 16 12	069	÷	-24		81.	HLT
024	HMS→	16 36	070	TAN⁻¹	16 43		46.	LBL
025	STO4	35 04	071	X<0?	16-45		14.	D
026	RTN	24	072	GSB1	23 01		37.	DMS
027	*LBLc	21 16 13	073	PRTX	-14		36.	IND
028	HMS→	16 36	074	SPC	16-11		42.	STD
029	STO5	35 05	075	RTN	24		9.	9
030	RTN	24	076	*LBL1	21 01	30	9.	9
031	*LBL0	21 00	077	3	03		43.	RCL
032	RCLD	36 14	078	6	06		0.	0
033	+	-55	079	0	00		0.	0
034	RCLE	36 15	080	+	-55		22.	INV
035	+	-55	081	RTN	24		44.	SUM
036	RTN	24					9.	9
037	*LBLD	21 14					9.	9
038	RCL5	36 05					43.	RCL
039	RCL4	36 04					9.	9
040	–	-45				40	9.	9
041	RCL4	36 04					81.	HLT
042	RCL3	36 03					46.	LBL
043	–	-45					15.	E
044	÷	-24						
045	RCL0	36 00						
046	RCL1	36 01						

330

	6.	6	2.	2	130 42.	STO
	42.	STO	43.	RCL	6.	6
	0.	0	6.	6	8.	8
	0.	0	90 7.	7	65.	×
	6.	6	75.	-	43.	RCL
	2.	2	43.	RCL	6.	6
50	42.	STO	6.	6	4.	4
	6.	6	6.	6	32.	SIN
	1.	1	95.	=	75.	-
	1.	1	55.	÷	43.	RCL
	44.	SUM	53.	(	140 6.	6
	1.	1	43.	RCL	2.	2
	9.	9	6.	6	32.	SIN
	43.	RCL	100 6.	6	95.	=
	1.	1	75.	-	55.	÷
	9.	9	43.	RCL	53.	(
60	42.	STO	6.	6	43.	RCL
	9.	9	5.	5	6.	6
	8.	8	54.	)	8.	8
	36.	IND	95.	=	65.	×
	43.	RCL	65.	×	150 43.	RCL
	9.	9	53.	(	6.	6
	8.	8	43.	RCL	4.	4
	36.	IND	110 6.	6	33.	COS
	42.	STO	2.	2	75.	-
	6.	6	75.	-	43.	RCL
70	1.	1	43.	RCL	6.	6
	1.	1	6.	6	2.	2
	44.	SUM	3.	3	33.	COS
	6.	6	54.	)	54.	)
	1.	1	32.	SIN	160 95.	=
	43.	RCL	55.	÷	22.	INV
	9.	9	53.	(	34.	TAN
	9.	9	120 43.	RCL	80.	IF+
	55.	÷	6.	6	1.	1
	3.	3	3.	3	7.	7
80	95.	=	75.	-	1.	1
	44.	SUM	43.	RCL	85.	+
	9.	9	6.	6	1.	1
	8.	8	4.	4	8.	8
	58.	DSZ	54.	)	170 0.	0
	0.	0	32.	SIN	95.	=
	6.	6	95.	=	44.	SUM

(CONTINUED)

	6.	6	9.	9	001 *LBLA	21 11
	9.	9	8.	8	002 STO0	35 00
	43.	RCL	81.	HLT	003 RTN	24
	9.	9			004 *LBLA	21 11
	9.	9			005 STO1	35 01
	55.	÷			006 RTN	24
	3.	3			007 *LBLa	21 16 11
180	75.	-			008 STOD	35 14
	43.	RCL			009 RTN	24
	1.	1			010 *LBLa	21 16 11
	9.	9			011 STOE	35 15
	95.	=			012 RTN	24
	22.	INV			013 *LBLB	21 12
	90.	IFO			014 GSB0	23 00
	15.	E			015 STO2	35 02
	43.	RCL			016 RTN	24
	6.	6			017 *LBLB	21 12
190	9.	9			018 GSB0	23 00
	55.	÷			019 STO3	35 03
	43.	RCL			020 RTN	24
	9.	9			021 *LBLB	21 12
	9.	9			022 HMS→	16 36
	65.	×			023 STOA	35 11
	3.	3			024 RTN	24
	95.	=			025 *LBLC	21 13
	81.	HLT			026 GSB0	23 00
	46.	LBL			027 STO4	35 04
200	12.	B			028 RTN	24
	44.	SUM			029 *LBLC	21 13
	6.	6			030 GSB0	23 00
	5.	5			031 STO5	35 05
	81.	HLT			032 RTN	24
	46.	LBL			033 *LBLC	21 13
	11.	A			034 HMS→	16 36
	47.	CMS			035 STOB	35 12
	42.	STO			036 RTN	24
	0.	0			037 *LBLc	21 16 13
210	0.	0			038 RCL3	36 03
	25.	CLR			039 RCL2	36 02
	42.	STO			040 -	-45
	9.	9			041 SIN	41
	9.	9			042 P≷S	16-51
	42.	STO			043 STO6	35 06
					044 P≷S	16-51
					045 RCL0	36 00
					046 RCL3	36 03

047	–	-45	093	X⇄Y	-41	139	RCL6	36 06
048	SIN	41	094	÷	-24	140	→P	34
049	RCL1	36 01	095	ABS	16 31	141	RCLB	36 12
050	x	-35	096	P⇄S	16-51	142	RCLA	36 11
051	X⇄Y	-41	097	STO1	35 01	143	–	-45
052	÷	-24	098	PRTX	-14	144	÷	-24
053	ABS	16 31	099	RCL7	36 07	145	STOI	35 46
054	P⇄S	16-51	100	P⇄S	16-51	146	PRTX	-14
055	STO0	35 00	101	RCL0	36 00	147	X⇄Y	-41
056	PRTX	-14	102	RCL4	36 04	148	X<0?	16-45
057	RCL6	36 06	103	–	-45	149	GSB1	23 01
058	P⇄S	16-51	104	SIN	41	150	STOC	35 13
059	RCL0	36 00	105	RCL1	36 01	151	PRTX	-14
060	RCL2	36 02	106	x	-35	152	SPC	16-11
061	–	-45	107	X⇄Y	-41	153	RTN	24
062	SIN	41	108	÷	-24	154	*LBL0	21 00
063	RCL1	36 01	109	ABS	16 31	155	RCLD	36 14
064	x	-35	110	P⇄S	16-51	156	+	-55
065	X⇄Y	-41	111	STO9	35 09	157	RCLE	36 15
066	÷	-24	112	P⇄S	16-51	158	+	-55
067	ABS	16 31	113	PRTX	-14	159	RTN	24
068	P⇄S	16-51	114	RCLB	36 12	160	*LBL1	21 01
069	STO8	35 08	115	→HMS	16 35	161	3	03
070	P⇄S	16-51	116	DSP4	-63 04	162	6	06
071	PRTX	-14	117	PRTX	-14	163	0	00
072	RCLA	36 11	118	SPC	16-11	164	+	-55
073	→HMS	16 35	119	DSP2	-63 02	165	RTN	24
074	DSP4	-63 04	120	RTN	24	166	*LBLb	21 16 12
075	PRTX	-14	121	*LBLD	21 14	167	GSB0	23 00
076	DSP2	-63 02	122	RCL2	36 02	168	P⇄S	16-51
077	SPC	16-11	123	P⇄S	16-51	169	STO2	35 02
078	RTN	24	124	RCL0	36 00	170	P⇄S	16-51
079	*LBLd	21 16 14	125	P⇄S	16-51	171	RTN	24
080	RCL5	36 05	126	→R	44	172	*LBLb	21 16 12
081	RCL4	36 04	127	STO6	35 06	173	P⇄S	16-51
082	–	-45	128	X⇄Y	-41	174	STO3	35 03
083	SIN	41	129	STO7	35 07	175	P⇄S	16-51
084	P⇄S	16-51	130	RCL4	36 04	176	RTN	24
085	STO7	35 07	131	P⇄S	16-51	177	*LBLE	21 15
086	P⇄S	16-51	132	RCL1	36 01	178	RCLC	36 13
087	RCL0	36 00	133	P⇄S	16-51	179	RCLI	36 46
088	RCL5	36 05	134	→R	44	180	→R	44
089	–	-45	135	ST-6	35-45 06	181	STO8	35 08
090	SIN	41	136	X⇄Y	-41	182	X⇄Y	-41
091	RCL1	36 01	137	ST-7	35-45 07	183	STO9	35 09
092	x	-35	138	RCL7	36 07	184	P⇄S	16-51

185	RCL2	36 02		46.	LBL		3.	3
186	RCL3	36 03		11.	A		75.	-
187	P‡S	16-51		44.	SUM		43.	RCL
188	→R	44		1.	1		0.	0
189	ST-8	35-45 08		5.	5		2.	2
190	X‡Y	-41		81.	HLT		54.	)
191	ST-9	35-45 09		46.	LBL	50	32.	SII
192	RCL9	36 09		12.	B		60.	IFI
193	RCL8	36 08		36.	IND		1.	1
194	→P	34	10	42.	STD		88.	2°
195	P‡S	16-51		1.	1		65.	×
196	ST04	35 04		4.	4		53.	(
197	P‡S	16-51		1.	1		43.	RCl
198	PRTX	-14		44.	SUM		0.	0
199	X‡Y	-41		1.	1		0.	0
200	X<0?	16-45		4.	4		75.	-
201	GSB1	23 01		81.	HLT	60	43.	RCI
202	PRTX	-14		46.	LBL		0.	0
203	SPC	16-11		13.	C		3.	3
204	RTN	24	20	85.	+		54.	)
205	*LBLe	21 16 15		43.	RCL		32.	SII
206	CLRG	16-53		1.	1		95.	=
207	P‡S	16-51		5.	5		40.	X²
208	CLRG	16-53		95.	=		30.	Γ
209	CLX	-51		41.	GTD		50.	STF
210	RTN	24		12.	B		1.	1
				46.	LBL	70	81.	HL
				14.	D		46.	LBI
				37.	DMS		88.	2°
			30	94.	+/-		65.	×
				42.	STD		53.	(
				1.	1		43.	RCl
				9.	9		0.	0
				81.	HLT		0.	0
				46.	LBL		75.	-
				15.	E		43.	RCl
				43.	RCL	80	0.	0
				0.	0		2.	2
				1.	1		54.	)
			40	55.	÷		32.	SII
				53.	(		95.	=
				43.	RCL		40.	X²
				0.	0		30.	Γ

334

	42.	STO	130	54.	)		48.	EXC

```
      42.   STO    130 54.   )          48.   EXC
       1.   1          32.   SIN         0.   0
       8.   8          95.   =          0.   0
  90  81.   HLT        40.   X²         48.   EXC
      46.   LBL        30.   Γ           0.   0
      16.   A'         50.   STF         3.   3
      41.   GTO         2.   2          39.   P/R
      13.   C          81.   HLT    180 75.   -
      46.   LBL        46.   LBL        43.   RCL
      17.   B'         89.   3'          1.   1
      37.   DMS    140 65.   ×           8.   8
      44.   SUM        53.   (          95.   =
       1.   1          43.   RCL        48.   EXC
 100   9.   9           0.   0           0.   0
      81.   HLT         0.   0           0.   0
      46.   LBL        75.   -          75.   -
      18.   C'         43.   RCL        43.   RCL
      43.   RCL         0.   0     190   0.   0
       0.   0           4.   4           3.   3
       1.   1          54.   )          95.   =
      55.   ÷      150 32.   SIN        48.   EXC
      53.   (          95.   =           0.   0
      43.   RCL        40.   X²          0.   0
 110   0.   0          30.   Γ          22.   INV
       5.   5          42.   STO        39.   P/R
      75.   -           1.   1          80.   IF+
      43.   RCL         7.   7           2.   2
       0.   0          81.   HLT    200   0.   0
       4.   4          46.   LBL         6.   6
      54.   )          19.   D'         85.   +
      32.   SIN    160 43.   RCL         3.   3
      60.   IFL         1.   1           6.   6
       2.   2           7.   7           0.   0
 120  89.   3'         42.   STO        95.   =
      65.   ×           0.   0          81.   HLT
      53.   (           0.   0          46.   LBL
      43.   RCL        43.   RCL        10.   E'
       0.   0           0.   0     210  43.   RCL
       0.   0           5.   5           0.   0
      75.   -          39.   P/R         0.   0
      43.   RCL    170 48.   EXC        55.   ÷
       0.   0           1.   1          43.   RCL
       5.   5           8.   8           1.   1
```

Program 2.14

	9.	9		46.	LBL		1.	1
	95.	=		19.	D'		7.	7
	81.	HLT		48.	EXC		81.	HLT
	46.	LBL		0.	0		46.	LBL
220	41.	GTO		0.	0		14.	D
	86.	RST		42.	STO		43.	RCL
	47.	CMS		9.	9	50	1.	1
	25.	CLR		9.	9		5.	5
	81.	HLT		56.	RTN		85.	+
			10	46.	LBL		43.	RCL
				11.	A		1.	1
				85.	+		7.	7
				81.	HLT		95.	=
				46.	LBL		19.	D'
				12.	B		43.	RCL
				95.	=		1.	1
				19.	D'	60	4.	4
				81.	HLT		85.	+
				46.	LBL		43.	RCL
			20	17.	B'		1.	1
				19.	D'		6.	6
				39.	P/R		95.	=
				42.	STO		22.	INV
				1.	1		39.	P/R
				4.	4		42.	STO
				19.	D'		9.	9
				42.	STO	70	8.	8
				1.	1		22.	INV
				5.	5		80.	IF+
			30	81.	HLT		87.	1'
				46.	LBL		81.	HLT
				13.	C		46.	LBL
				19.	D'		15.	E
				81.	HLT		43.	RCL
				46.	LBL		1.	1
				18.	C'		7.	7
				19.	D'	80	75.	-
				39.	P/R		43.	RCL
				42.	STO		1.	1
			40	1.	1		5.	5
				6.	6		95.	=
				19.	D'		19.	D'
				42.	STO		43.	RCL

Program 2.17

	1.	1	001	*LBLa	21 16 11	047	STO6	35 06
	6.	6	002	STOI	35 46	048	STO7	35 07
	75.	–	003	RCLi	36 45	049	P⇄S	16-51
90	43.	RCL	004	ISZI	16 26 46	050	RTN	24
	1.	1	005	RCLi	36 45	051	*LBLA	21 11
	4.	4	006	RTN	24	052	P⇄S	16-51
	95.	=	007	*LBLb	21 16 12	053	STO6	35 06
	22.	INV	008	STOI	35 46	054	P⇄S	16-51
	39.	P/R	009	R↓	-31	055	RTN	24
	22.	INV	010	RCLi	36 45	056	*LBLA	21 11
	80.	IF+	011	ISZI	16 26 46	057	P⇄S	16-51
	87.	1'	012	RCLi	36 45	058	STO7	35 07
	81.	HLT	013	RTN	24	059	P⇄S	16-51
100	46.	LBL	014	*LBLc	21 16 13	060	RTN	24
	10.	E'	015	R↑	16-31	061	*LBLB	21 12
	19.	D'	016	STO0	35 00	062	HMS→	16 36
	81.	HLT	017	P⇄S	16-51	063	P⇄S	16-51
	46.	LBL	018	STO0	35 00	064	STO8	35 08
	87.	1'	019	R↑	16-31	065	P⇄S	16-51
	85.	+	020	P⇄S	16-51	066	RTN	24
	3.	3	021	STO1	35 01	067	*LBLC	21 13
	6.	6	022	P⇄S	16-51	068	P⇄S	16-51
	0.	0	023	STO1	35 01	069	RCL1	36 01
110	95.	=	024	P⇄S	16-51	070	RCL0	36 00
	81.	HLT	025	R↑	16-31	071	P⇄S	16-51
			026	STO2	35 02	072	STO0	35 00
			027	R↑	16-31	073	R↓	-31
			028	STO3	35 03	074	STO1	35 01
			029	0	00	075	RCL3	36 03
			030	STO4	35 04	076	HMS→	16 36
			031	STO5	35 05	077	P⇄S	16-51
			032	STOC	35 13	078	RCL1	36 01
			033	P⇄S	16-51	079	P⇄S	16-51
			034	STO9	35 09	080	HMS→	16 36
			035	P⇄S	16-51	081	–	-45
			036	RTN	24	082	RCLD	36 14
			037	*LBLe	21 16 15	083	×	-35
			038	STOE	35 15	084	CHS	-22
			039	RTN	24	085	RCL2	36 02
			040	*LBLe	21 16 15	086	HMS→	16 36
			041	STOD	35 14	087	P⇄S	16-51
			042	RTN	24	088	RCL0	36 00
			043	*LBLA	21 11	089	HMS→	16 36
			044	P⇄S	16-51	090	P⇄S	16-51
			045	STO5	35 05	091	–	-45
			046	0	00	092	→P	34

093	6	06	139	ST+8	35-55 08	001	*LBLa	21 16 11
094	0	00	140	X≷Y	-41	002	STOI	35 46
095	x	-35	141	ST+9	35-55 09	003	RCLi	36 45
096	STOI	35 46	142	RCL9	36 09	004	ISZI	16 26 46
097	X≷Y	-41	143	RCL8	36 08	005	RCLi	36 45
098	STO7	35 07	144	→P	34	006	RTN	24
099	P≷S	16-51	145	RCLI	36 46	007	*LBLb	21 16 12
100	RCL6	36 06	146	X≷Y	-41	008	STOI	35 46
101	-	-45	147	÷	-24	009	R↓	-31
102	SIN	41	148	→HMS	16 35	010	RCLi	36 45
103	RCL7	36 07	149	P≷S	16-51	011	ISZI	16 26 46
104	x	-35	150	RCL8	36 08	012	RCLi	36 45
105	RCL5	36 05	151	→HMS	16 35	013	RTN	24
106	÷	-24	152	HMS+	16-55	014	*LBLc	21 16 13
107	SIN⁻¹	16 41	153	DSP4	-63 04	015	R↑	16-31
108	P≷S	16-51	154	0	00	016	STO0	35 00
109	RCL7	36 07	155	STO9	35 09	017	P≷S	16-51
110	+	-55	156	P≷S	16-51	018	STO0	35 00
111	P≷S	16-51	157	STO4	35 04	019	R↑	16-31
112	STO4	35 04	158	STO5	35 05	020	P≷S	16-51
113	P≷S	16-51	159	X≷Y	-41	021	STO1	35 01
114	RCLE	36 15	160	PRTX	-14	022	P≷S	16-51
115	-	-45	161	RTN	24	023	STO1	35 01
116	GSB0	23 00	162	*LBL0	21 00	024	P≷S	16-51
117	PRTX	-14	163	3	03	025	R↑	16-31
118	RTN	24	164	6	06	026	STO2	35 02
119	*LBLC	21 13	165	0	00	027	R↑	16-31
120	STOC	35 13	166	→R	44	028	STO3	35 03
121	-	-45	167	→P	34	029	0	00
122	GSB0	23 00	168	X≷Y	-41	030	STO4	35 04
123	PRTX	-14	169	X<0?	16-45	031	STO5	35 05
124	RTN	24	170	+	-55	032	STOC	35 13
125	*LBLD	21 14	171	RTN	24	033	P≷S	16-51
126	P≷S	16-51	172	*LBLE	21 15	034	STO9	35 09
127	RCL4	36 04	173	RCLI	36 46	035	P≷S	16-51
128	RCL5	36 05	174	DSP2	-63 02	036	RTN	24
129	P≷S	16-51	175	PRTX	-14	037	*LBLe	21 16 15
130	→R	44	176	RTN	24	038	STOE	35 15
131	STO8	35 08	177	*LBLE	21 15	039	RTN	24
132	X≷Y	-41	178	RCL7	36 07	040	*LBLA	21 11
133	STO9	35 09	179	GSB0	23 00	041	P≷S	16-51
134	P≷S	16-51	180	PRTX	-14	042	STO5	35 05
135	RCL6	36 06	181	SPC	16-11	043	0	00
136	RCL7	36 07	182	RTN	24	044	STO6	35 06
137	P≷S	16-51				045	STO7	35 07
138	→R	44				046	P≷S	16-51

047	RTN	24	093	RCLD	36 14	139	→R	44
048	*LBLA	21 11	094	x	-35	140	STO8	35 08
049	P⇄S	16-51	095	CHS	-22	141	X⇄Y	-41
050	STO6	35 06	096	RCL2	36 02	142	STO9	35 09
051	P⇄S	16-51	097	HMS→	16 36	143	P⇄S	16-51
052	RTN	24	098	P⇄S	16-51	144	RCL6	36 06
053	*LBLA	21 11	099	RCL0	36 00	145	RCL7	36 07
054	P⇄S	16-51	100	HMS→	16 36	146	P⇄S	16-51
055	STO7	35 07	101	P⇄S	16-51	147	→R	44
056	P⇄S	16-51	102	-	-45	148	ST+8	35-55 08
057	RTN	24	103	→P	34	149	X⇄Y	-41
058	*LBLB	21 12	104	6	06	150	ST+9	35-55 09
059	HMS→	16 36	105	0	00	151	RCL9	36 09
060	P⇄S	16-51	106	x	-35	152	RCL8	36 08
061	STO8	35 08	107	STOI	35 46	153	→P	34
062	P⇄S	16-51	108	X⇄Y	-41	154	RCLI	36 46
063	RTN	24	109	STO7	35 07	155	X⇄Y	-41
064	*LBLC	21 13	110	P⇄S	16-51	156	÷	-24
065	P⇄S	16-51	111	RCL6	36 06	157	→HMS	16 35
066	RCL1	36 01	112	-	-45	158	P⇄S	16-51
067	RCL0	36 00	113	SIN	41	159	RCL8	36 08
068	P⇄S	16-51	114	RCL7	36 07	160	→HMS	16 35
069	STO0	35 00	115	x	-35	161	HMS+	16-55
070	R↓	-31	116	RCL5	36 05	162	DSP4	-63 04
071	STO1	35 01	117	÷	-24	163	0	00
072	RCL2	36 02	118	SIN⁻¹	16 41	164	STO9	35 09
073	HMS→	16 36	119	P⇄S	16-51	165	P⇄S	16-51
074	P⇄S	16-51	120	RCL7	36 07	166	STO4	35 04
075	RCL0	36 00	121	+	-55	167	STO5	35 05
076	HMS→	16 36	122	P⇄S	16-51	168	X⇄Y	-41
077	-	-45	123	STO4	35 04	169	PRTX	-14
078	2	02	124	P⇄S	16-51	170	RTN	24
079	÷	-24	125	RCLE	36 15	171	*LBL0	21 00
080	RCL0	36 00	126	-	-45	172	0	00
081	HMS→	16 36	127	RTN	24	173	X≤Y?	16-35
082	P⇄S	16-51	128	*LBLC	21 13	174	GTO1	22 01
083	+	-55	129	STOC	35 13	175	3	03
084	COS	42	130	-	-45	176	6	06
085	STOD	35 14	131	GSB0	23 00	177	0	00
086	RCL3	36 03	132	PRTX	-14	178	P⇄S	16-51
087	HMS→	16 36	133	RTN	24	179	RCL4	36 04
088	P⇄S	16-51	134	*LBLD	21 14	180	P⇄S	16-51
089	RCL1	36 01	135	P⇄S	16-51	181	RCLE	36 15
090	P⇄S	16-51	136	RCL4	36 04	182	-	-45
091	HMS→	16 36	137	RCL5	36 05	183	RCLC	36 13
092	-	-45	138	P⇄S	16-51	184	-	-45

185	+	-55		46.	LBL	0.	0
186	DSP2	-63 02		11.	A	8.	8
187	RTN	24		48.	EXC	51.	SBR
188	*LBL1	21 01		1.	1	87.	1'
189	P⇄S	16-51		9.	9	43.	RCL
190	RCL4	36 04		48.	EXC	0.	0
191	P⇄S	16-51		1.	1	50 8.	8
192	RCLE	36 15		8.	8	75.	-
193	-	-45		81.	HLT	43.	RCL
194	RCLC	36 13	10	46.	LBL	0.	0
195	-	-45		12.	B	6.	6
196	DSP2	-63 02		42.	STO	95.	=
197	RTN	24		1.	1	65.	×
198	*LBLE	21 15		7.	7	6.	6
199	RCLI	36 46		81.	HLT	0.	0
200	DSP2	-63 02		46.	LBL	95.	=
201	PRTX	-14		13.	C	60 42.	STO
202	RTN	24		46.	LBL	0.	0
203	*LBLE	21 15		14.	D	0.	0
204	RCL7	36 07	20	37.	DMS	43.	RCL
205	X<0?	16-45		46.	LBL	0.	0
206	GT09	22 09		87.	1'	8.	8
207	PRTX	-14		48.	EXC	85.	+
208	SPC	16-11		0.	0	43.	RCL
209	RTN	24		5.	5	0.	0
210	*LBL9	21 09		48.	EXC	6.	6
211	3	03		0.	0	70 95.	=
212	6	06		6.	6	55.	÷
213	0	00		48.	EXC	2.	2
214	+	-55	30	0.	0	95.	=
215	PRTX	-14		7.	7	33.	COS
216	SPC	16-11		48.	EXC	65.	×
217	RTN	24		0.	0	53.	(
				8.	8	43.	RCL
				56.	RTN	0.	0
				46.	LBL	5.	5
				16.	A'	80 75.	-
				43.	RCL	43.	RCL
				0.	0	0.	0
			40	8.	8	7.	7
				51.	SBR	54.	)
				87.	1'	95.	=
				43.	RCL	65.	×

340

	6.	6	130	3.	3		8.	8
	0.	0		6.	6		54.	)
	95.	=		0.	0		32.	SIN
90	22.	INV		95.	=		95.	=
	39.	P/R		56.	RTN		40.	X²
	42.	STO		46.	LBL		30.	Γ
	1.	1		17.	B'		20.	1/X
	4.	4		94.	+/-	180	65.	×
	75.	-		85.	+		43.	RCL
	43.	RCL		43.	RCL		0.	0
	1.	1	140	1.	1		0.	0
	8.	8		0.	0		95.	=
	95.	=		95.	=		22.	INV
100	32.	SIN		42.	STO		37.	DMS
	65.	×		1.	1		81.	HLT
	43.	RCL		0.	0		46.	LBL
	1.	1		15.	E		19.	D'
	9.	9		81.	HLT	190	43.	RCL
	55.	÷		46.	LBL		1.	1
	43.	RCL		18.	C'		4.	4
	1.	1	150	57.	FIX		15.	E
	7.	7		4.	4		81.	HLT
	95.	=		43.	RCL		46.	LBL
110	22.	INV		1.	1		10.	E'
	32.	SIN		8.	8		43.	RCL
	85.	+		75.	-		0.	0
	43.	RCL		43.	RCL		0.	0
	1.	1		0.	0	200	81.	HLT
	4.	4		9.	9			
	95.	=		95.	=			
	42.	STO	160	32.	SIN			
	1.	1		65.	×			
	0.	0		43.	RCL			
120	42.	STO		1.	1			
	0.	0		7.	7			
	9.	9		55.	÷			
	46.	LBL		53.	(			
	15.	E		43.	RCL			
	80.	IF+		1.	1			
	1.	1		4.	4			
	3.	3	170	75.	-			
	3.	3		43.	RCL			
	85.	+		1.	1			

Entries for steps 214–18 should
be replaced when the loop time
for the particular calculator has
been determined, as shown in
the discussion of customized
programs earlier in this appendix.

001	*LBLₘ	21 11
002	RCLE	36 15
003	+	-55
004	RCLC	36 13
005	+	-55
006	P⇄S	16-51
007	ST04	35 04
008	P⇄S	16-51
009	RTN	24
010	*LBLA	21 11
011	P⇄S	16-51
012	ST05	35 05
013	0	00
014	ST07	35 07
015	P⇄S	16-51
016	RTN	24
017	*LBLA	21 11
018	P⇄S	16-51
019	ST06	35 06
020	P⇄S	16-51
021	RTN	24
022	*LBLA	21 11
023	P⇄S	16-51
024	ST07	35 07
025	P⇄S	16-51
026	RTN	24
027	*LBLB	21 12
028	SF2	16 21 02
029	RTN	24
030	*LBLc	21 16 13
031	HMS→	16 36
032	P⇄S	16-51
033	ST08	35 08
034	P⇄S	16-51
035	STOA	35 11
036	0	00
037	ST06	35 06
038	P⇄S	16-51
039	RCL9	36 09

040	P⇄S	16-51
041	X=0?	16-43
042	GT05	22 05
043	P⇄S	16-51
044	RCL8	36 08
045	RCL9	36 09
046	P⇄S	16-51
047	-	-45
048	STOI	35 46
049	GSB0	23 00
050	GSB1	23 01
051	P⇄S	16-51
052	RCL8	36 08
053	P⇄S	16-51
054	→HMS	16 35
055	RTN	24
056	*LBLd	21 16 14
057	HMS→	16 36
058	P⇄S	16-51
059	ST09	35 09
060	P⇄S	16-51
061	RCLA	36 11
062	-	-45
063	STOI	35 46
064	GSB0	23 00
065	GSB1	23 01
066	F2?	16 23 02
067	GT06	22 06
068	P⇄S	16-51
069	RCL9	36 09
070	RCL8	36 08
071	-	-45
072	P⇄S	16-51
073	RCL6	36 06
074	÷	-24
075	P⇄S	16-51
076	ST02	35 02
077	RCL9	36 09
078	P⇄S	16-51
079	STOA	35 11
080	*LBL6	21 06
081	→HMS	16 35
082	RTN	24
083	*LBLC	21 13
084	1	01
085	ST+6	35-55 06
086	GSB0	23 00

087	P⇄S	16-51
088	RCL2	36 02
089	P⇄S	16-51
090	STOI	35 46
091	GSB1	23 01
092	GSB3	23 03
093	P⇄S	16-51
094	RCL8	36 08
095	RCL2	36 02
096	P⇄S	16-51
097	RCL6	36 06
098	x	-35
099	+	-55
100	STOA	35 11
101	→HMS	16 35
102	DSP4	-63 04
103	PRTX	-14
104	SFC	16-11
105	GTOC	22 13
106	*LBL0	21 00
107	P⇄S	16-51
108	RCL4	36 04
109	RCL5	36 05
110	P⇄S	16-51
111	→R	44
112	ST08	35 08
113	X⇄Y	-41
114	CHS	-22
115	ST09	35 09
116	P⇄S	16-51
117	RCL6	36 06
118	RCL7	36 07
119	P⇄S	16-51
120	→R	44
121	ST+8	35-55 08
122	X⇄Y	-41
123	CHS	-22
124	ST+9	35-55 09
125	RTN	24
126	*LBL1	21 01
127	RCL8	36 08
128	RCLI	36 46
129	x	-35
130	ST+4	35-55 04
131	LSTX	16-63
132	RCL9	36 09
133	x	-35

134	RCLD	36 14	181	1	01	
135	÷	-24	182	8	08	
136	ST+5	35-55 05	183	0	00	
137	RCL5	36 05	184	+	-55	
138	GSB4	23 04	185	P⇄S	16-51	
139	→HMS	16 35	186	STO3	35 03	
140	RCL1	36 01	187	P⇄S	16-51	
141	HMS+	16-55	188	PRTX	-14	
142	P⇄S	16-51	189	RTN	24	
143	STO1	35 01	190	*LBL4	21 04	
144	P⇄S	16-51	191	6	06	
145	RCL4	36 04	192	0	00	
146	GSB4	23 04	193	÷	-24	
147	→HMS	16 35	194	RTN	24	
148	RCL0	36 00	195	*LBLD	21 14	
149	HMS+	16-55	196	RTN	24	
150	P⇄S	16-51	197	*LBLE	21 15	
151	STO0	35 00	198	GSB3	23 03	
152	P⇄S	16-51	199	RTN	24	
153	RTN	24	200	*LBLE	21 15	
154	*LBL3	21 03	201	P⇄S	16-51	
155	P⇄S	16-51	202	RCL0	36 00	
156	RCL0	36 00	203	P⇄S	16-51	
157	HMS→	16 36	204	DSP4	-63 04	
158	P⇄S	16-51	205	PRTX	-14	
159	RCL2	36 02	206	RTN	24	
160	HMS→	16 36	207	*LBLE	21 15	
161	-	-45	208	P⇄S	16-51	
162	P⇄S	16-51	209	RCL1	36 01	
163	RCL1	36 01	210	P⇄S	16-51	
164	HMS→	16 36	211	PRTX	-14	
165	P⇄S	16-51	212	RTN	24	
166	RCL3	36 03	213	*LBL5	21 05	
167	HMS→	16 36	214	.	-62	
168	-	-45	215	0	00	
169	RCLD	36 14	216	0	00	
170	x	-35	217	3	03	
171	CHS	-22	218	5	05	
172	X⇄Y	-41	219	P⇄S	16-51	
173	→P	34	220	STO2	35 02	
174	6	06	221	RCL8	36 08	
175	0	00	222	P⇄S	16-51	
176	x	-35	223	→HMS	16 35	
177	STO7	35 07	224	RTN	24	
178	DSP1	-63 01				
179	PRTX	-14				
180	X⇄Y	-41				

Entries for steps 213–17 should be replaced when the loop time for the particular calculator has been determined, as shown in the discussion of customized programs earlier in this appendix.

001	*LBLA	21 11
002	RCLE	36 15
003	+	-55
004	RCLC	36 13
005	+	-55
006	P⇄S	16-51
007	STO4	35 04
008	RTN	24
009	*LBLA	21 11
010	STO5	35 05
011	0	00
012	STO7	35 07
013	RTN	24
014	*LBLA	21 11
015	STO6	35 06
016	RTN	24
017	*LBLA	21 11
018	STO7	35 07
019	P⇄S	16-51
020	RTN	24
021	*LBLB	21 12
022	SF2	16 21 02
023	RTN	24
024	*LBLc	21 16 13
025	HMS→	16 36
026	P⇄S	16-51
027	STO8	35 08
028	P⇄S	16-51
029	STOA	35 11
030	0	00
031	STO6	35 06
032	P⇄S	16-51
033	RCL9	36 09
034	P⇄S	16-51
035	X=0?	16-43
036	GTO5	22 05
037	P⇄S	16-51
038	RCL8	36 08
039	RCL9	36 09

040	P≵S	16-51	087	RCL6	36 06	134	÷	-24
041	-	-45	088	x	-35	135	ST+5	35-55 05
042	STOI	35 46	089	+	-55	136	RCL5	36 05
043	GSB0	23 00	090	STOA	35 11	137	GSB4	23 04
044	GSB1	23 01	091	→HMS	16 35	138	→HMS	16 35
045	RTN	24	092	DSP4	-63 04	139	RCL1	36 01
046	*LBLd	21 16 14	093	PRTX	-14	140	HMS+	16-55
047	HMS→	16 36	094	GTOC	22 13	141	P≵S	16-51
048	P≵S	16-51	095	*LBL0	21 00	142	STO1	35 01
049	STO9	35 09	096	P≵S	16-51	143	P≵S	16-51
050	P≵S	16-51	097	RCL4	36 04	144	RCL4	36 04
051	RCLA	36 11	098	RCL5	36 05	145	GSB4	23 04
052	-	-45	099	P≵S	16-51	146	→HMS	16 35
053	STOI	35 46	100	→R	44	147	RCL0	36 00
054	GSB0	23 00	101	STO8	35 08	148	HMS+	16-55
055	GSB1	23 01	102	X≵Y	-41	149	P≵S	16-51
056	F2?	16 23 02	103	CHS	-22	150	STO0	35 00
057	GTO6	22 06	104	STO9	35 09	151	P≵S	16-51
058	P≵S	16-51	105	P≵S	16-51	152	RTN	24
059	RCL9	36 09	106	RCL6	36 06	153	*LBL3	21 03
060	RCL8	36 08	107	RCL7	36 07	154	P≵S	16-51
061	-	-45	108	P≵S	16-51	155	RCL0	36 00
062	P≵S	16-51	109	→R	44	156	HMS→	16 36
063	RCL6	36 06	110	ST+8	35-55 08	157	P≵S	16-51
064	÷	-24	111	X≵Y	-41	158	RCL2	36 02
065	P≵S	16-51	112	CHS	-22	159	HMS→	16 36
066	STO2	35 02	113	ST+9	35-55 09	160	-	-45
067	RCL9	36 09	114	RTN	24	161	P≵S	16-51
068	P≵S	16-51	115	*LBL1	21 01	162	RCL1	36 01
069	STOA	35 11	116	RCL8	36 08	163	HMS→	16 36
070	*LBL6	21 06	117	RCLI	36 46	164	P≵S	16-51
071	→HMS	16 35	118	x	-35	165	RCL3	36 03
072	RTN	24	119	ST+4	35-55 04	166	HMS→	16 36
073	*LBLC	21 13	120	RCL4	36 04	167	-	-45
074	1	01	121	1	01	168	RCLD	36 14
075	ST+6	35-55 06	122	2	02	169	x	-35
076	GSB0	23 00	123	0	00	170	CHS	-22
077	P≵S	16-51	124	÷	-24	171	X≵Y	-41
078	RCL2	36 02	125	RCL0	36 00	172	→P	34
079	P≵S	16-51	126	HMS→	16 36	173	6	06
080	STOI	35 46	127	+	-55	174	0	00
081	GSB1	23 01	128	COS	42	175	x	-35
082	GSB3	23 03	129	STOD	35 14	176	STO7	35 07
083	P≵S	16-51	130	RCLI	36 46	177	DSP1	-63 01
084	RCL8	36 08	131	RCL9	36 09	178	PRTX	-14
085	RCL2	36 02	132	x	-35	179	X≵Y	-41
086	P≵S	16-51	133	X≵Y	-41	180	1	01

344

181	8	08	001	*LBLa	21 16 11	047	P⇄S	16-51
182	0	00	002	STOI	35 46 •	048	STO5	35 05
183	+	-55	003	RCLi	36 45	049	P⇄S	16-51
184	P⇄S	16-51	004	ISZI	16 26 46	050	RTN	24
185	STO3	35 03	005	RCLi	36 45	051	*LBLC	21 13
186	P⇄S	16-51	006	RTN	24	052	P⇄S	16-51
187	PRTX	-14	007	*LBLb	21 16 12	053	STO6	35 06
188	RTN	24	008	STOI	35 46	054	P⇄S	16-51
189	*LBL4	21 04	009	R↓	-31	055	RTN	24
190	6	06	010	RCLi	36 45	056	*LBLC	21 13
191	0	00	011	ISZI	16 26 46	057	P⇄S	16-51
192	÷	-24	012	RCLi	36 45	058	STO7	35 07
193	RTN	24	013	RTN	24	059	P⇄S	16-51
194	*LBLD	21 14	014	*LBLc	21 16 13	060	RTN	24
195	RTN	24	015	R↑	16-31	061	*LBLD	21 14
196	*LBLE	21 15	016	STO0	35 00	062	DSP4	-63 04
197	GSB3	23 03	017	R↑	16-31	063	HMS→	16 36
198	RTN	24	018	STO1	35 01	064	P⇄S	16-51
199	*LBLE	21 15	019	R↑	16-31	065	STO8	35 08
200	P⇄S	16-51	020	STO2	35 02	066	P⇄S	16-51
201	RCL0	36 00	021	R↑	16-31	067	→HMS	16 35
202	P⇄S	16-51	022	STO3	35 03	068	RTN	24
203	DSP4	-63 04	023	0	00	069	*LBLE	21 15
204	PRTX	-14	024	STO4	35 04	070	HMS→	16 36
205	RTN	2	025	STO5	35 05	071	P⇄S	16-51
206	*LBLE	21 15	026	STOC	35 13	072	STO9	35 09
207	P⇄S	16-51	027	STOD	35 14	073	RCL4	36 04
208	RCL1	36 01	028	STO8	35 08	074	RCL5	36 05
209	P⇄S	16-51	029	STO9	35 09	075	P⇄S	16-51
210	PRTX	-14	030	RTN	24	076	→R	44
211	RTN	24	031	*LBLA	21 11	077	STO8	35 08
212	*LBL5	21 05	032	STOC	35 13	078	X⇄Y	-41
213	.	-62	033	RTN	24	079	STO9	35 09
214	0	00	034	*LBLA	21 11	080	P⇄S	16-51
215	0	00	035	STOE	35 15	081	RCL6	36 06
216	3	03	036	RTN	24	082	RCL7	36 07
217	5	05	037	*LBLB	21 12	083	P⇄S	16-51
218	P⇄S	16-51	038	RCLE	36 15	084	→R	44
219	STO2	35 02	039	+	-55	085	ST+8	35-55 08
220	RCL8	36 08	040	RCLC	36 13	086	X⇄Y	-41
221	P⇄S	16-51	041	+	-55	087	ST+9	35-55 09
222	→HMS	16 35	042	P⇄S	16-51	088	P⇄S	16-51
223	RTN	24	043	STO4	35 04	089	RCL9	36 09
224	R/S	51	044	P⇄S	16-51	090	RCL8	36 08
			045	RTN	24	091	-	-45
			046	*LBLB	21 12	092	P⇄S	16-51

(CONTINUED) 345

093	STOI	35 46	139	SPC	16-11	185	PRTX		-14
094	RCL8	36 08	140	RTN	24	186	SPC		16-11
095	x	-35	141	*LBLe	21 16 15	187	RTN		24
096	ST+4	35-55 04	142	RCL6	36 06	188	*LBLe	21	16 15
097	RCLI	36 46	143	RCL2	36 02	189	RCL5		36 05
098	RCL9	36 09	144	CHS	-22	190	RCL4		36 04
099	x	-35	145	HMS+	16-55	191	→P		34
100	ST+5	35-55 05	146	HMS→	16 36	192	STOB		35 12
101	RTN	24	147	P≷S	16-51	193	DSP2		-63 02
102	*LBLd	21 16 14	148	STO0	35 00	194	PRTX		-14
103	RCL4	36 04	149	P≷S	16-51	195	*LBLe	21	16 15
104	6	06	150	2	02	196	X≷Y		-41
105	0	00	151	÷	-24	197	3		03
106	÷	-24	152	RCL2	36 02	198	6		06
107	2	02	153	HMS→	16 36	199	0		00
108	÷	-24	154	+	-55	200	→R		44
109	→HMS	16 35	155	COS	42	201	→P		34
110	RCL0	36 00	156	STOA	35 11	202	X≷Y		-41
111	HMS+	16-55	157	P≷S	16-51	203	X<0?		16-45
112	HMS→	16 36	158	RCL0	36 00	204	+		-55
113	COS	42	159	P≷S	16-51	205	PRTX		-14
114	STOD	35 14	160	RCL7	36 07	206	P≷S		16-51
115	RCL4	36 04	161	RCL3	36 03	207	RCL9		36 09
116	6	06	162	CHS	-22	208	RCL8		36 08
117	0	00	163	HMS+	16-55	209	-		-45
118	÷	-24	164	HMS→	16 36	210	P≷S		16-51
119	→HMS	16 35	165	RCLA	36 11	211	RCLB		36 12
120	RCL0	36 00	166	x	-35	212	X≷Y		-41
121	HMS+	16-55	167	CHS	-22	213	÷		-24
122	DSP4	-63 04	168	X≷Y	-41	214	PRTX		-14
123	STO6	35 06	169	→P	34	215	SPC		16-11
124	PRTX	-14	170	6	06	216	RTN		24
125	RTN	24	171	0	00				
126	*LBLd	21 16 14	172	x	-35				
127	RCL5	36 05	173	P≷S	16-51				
128	6	06	174	STO1	35 01				
129	0	00	175	P≷S	16-51				
130	÷	-24	176	PRTX	-14				
131	RCLD	36 14	177	X≷Y	-41				
132	÷	-24	178	1	01				
133	CHS	-22	179	8	08				
134	→HMS	16 35	180	0	00				
135	RCL1	36 01	181	+	-55				
136	HMS+	16-55	182	P≷S	16-51				
137	STO7	35 07	183	STO2	35 02				
138	PRTX	-14	184	P≷S	16-51				

#			#			#		
	46.	LBL		48.	EXC		1.	1
	11.	A		0.	0		8.	8
	37.	DMS		0.	0		39.	P/R
	75.	-		44.	SUM	90	44.	SUM
	48.	EXC		0.	0		1.	1
	1.	1		3.	3		2.	2
	3.	3	50	44.	SUM		65.	×
	90.	IFO		0.	0		43.	RCL
	1.	1		6.	6		6.	6
10	1.	1		55.	÷		8.	8
	9.	9		2.	2		95.	=
	95.	=		95.	=		94.	+/-
	55.	÷		85.	+		44.	SUM
	6.	6		43.	RCL	100	0.	0
	0.	0		0.	0		5.	5
	95.	=		6.	6		48.	EXC
	42.	STO	60	95.	=		0.	0
	1.	1		33.	COS		0.	0
	5.	5		20.	1/X		44.	SUM
20	65.	×		42.	STO		0.	0
	43.	RCL		6.	6		6.	6
	1.	1		8.	8		44.	SUM
	7.	7		65.	×		0.	0
	95.	=		43.	RCL	110	3.	3
	48.	EXC		0.	0		81.	HLT
	0.	0		0.	0		46.	LBL
	0.	0	70	95.	=		12.	B
	43.	RCL		94.	+/-		48.	EXC
	1.	1		44.	SUM		0.	0
30	6.	6		0.	0		2.	2
	85.	+		5.	5		48.	EXC
	43.	RCL		43.	RCL		0.	0
	0.	0		1.	1		1.	1
	1.	1		5.	5	120	95.	=
	85.	+		65.	×		81.	HLT
	43.	RCL		43.	RCL		46.	LBL
	0.	0	80	1.	1		13.	C
	2.	2		9.	9		48.	EXC
	95.	=		95.	=		1.	1
40	39.	P/R		48.	EXC		9.	9
	44.	SUM		0.	0		48.	EXC
	1.	1		0.	0		1.	1
	2.	2		43.	RCL		8.	8

(CONTINUED) 347

130	81.	HLT		46.	LBL	001	*LBLa	21 16 11
	46.	LBL		16.	A"	002	STOI	35 46
	14.	D		43.	RCL	003	RCLi	36 45
	48.	EXC		0.	0	004	ISZI	16 26 46
	1.	1		3.	3	005	RCLi	36 45
	7.	7		42.	STO	006	RTN	24
	48.	EXC		0.	0	007	*LBLb	21 16 12
	1.	1	180	0.	0	008	STOI	35 46
	6.	6		43.	RCL	009	R↓	-31
	81.	HLT		1.	1	010	RCLi	36 45
140	46.	LBL		2.	2	011	ISZI	16 26 46
	15.	E		22.	INV	012	RCLi	36 45
	37.	DMS		39.	P/R	013	RTN	24
	48.	EXC		80.	IF+	014	*LBLc	21 16 13
	0.	0		1.	1	015	R↑	16-31
	5.	5		9.	9	016	STO0	35 00
	48.	EXC		4.	4	017	R↑	16-31
	0.	0	190	85.	+	018	STO1	35 01
	6.	6		3.	3	019	R↑	16-31
	81.	HLT		6.	6	020	STO2	35 02
150	46.	LBL		0.	0	021	R↑	16-31
	18.	C"		95.	=	022	STO3	35 03
	57.	FIX		42.	STO	023	0	00
	4.	4		9.	9	024	STO4	35 04
	43.	RCL		8.	8	025	STO5	35 05
	0.	0		81.	HLT	026	RTN	24
	6.	6		46.	LBL	027	*LBLe	21 16 15
	22.	INV	200	17.	B"	028	STOC	35 13
	37.	DMS		43.	RCL	029	RTN	24
	81.	HLT		0.	0	030	*LBLe	21 16 15
160	46.	LBL		0.	0	031	STOE	35 15
	19.	D"		65.	×	032	RTN	24
	43.	RCL		6.	6	033	*LBLe	21 16 15
	0.	0		0.	0	034	STOD	35 14
	5.	5		95.	=	035	RTN	24
	22.	INV		42.	STO	036	*LBLA	21 11
	37.	DMS		9.	9	037	GSB0	23 00
	81.	HLT	210	9.	9	038	P⇄S	16-51
	46.	LBL		81.	HLT	039	STO4	35 04
	10.	E"				040	RTN	24
170	25.	CLR				041	*LBLA	21 11
	47.	CMS				042	STO5	35 05
	81.	HLT				043	0	00
						044	STO7	35 07
						045	RCL4	36 04
						046	RCL5	36 05

#	Key	Code	#	Key	Code	#	Key	Code
047	P⇄S	16-51	093	RTN	24	139	RCL2	36 02
048	→R	44	094	*LBL0	21 00	140	HMS→	16 36
049	STO8	35 08	095	RCLE	36 15	141	+	-55
050	X⇄Y	-41	096	+	-55	142	P⇄S	16-51
051	STO9	35 09	097	RCLC	36 13	143	STO0	35 00
052	RTN	24	098	+	-55	144	P⇄S	16-51
053	*LBLA	21 11	099	RTN	24	145	→HMS	16 35
054	P⇄S	16-51	100	*LBLE	21 15	146	PRTX	-14
055	STO6	35 06	101	RCL0	36 00	147	RTN	24
056	RTN	24	102	HMS→	16 36	148	*LBLE	21 15
057	*LBLA	21 11	103	RCL2	36 02	149	X⇄Y	-41
058	STO7	35 07	104	HMS→	16 36	150	RCLD	36 14
059	P⇄S	16-51	105	--	-45	151	÷	-24
060	→R	44	106	ST+4	35-55 04	152	RCL3	36 03
061	ST+8	35-55 08	107	RCL3	36 03	153	HMS→	16 36
062	X⇄Y	-41	108	HMS→	16 36	154	+	-55
063	ST+9	35-55 09	109	RCL1	36 01	155	P⇄S	16-51
064	RTN	24	110	HMS→	16 36	156	STO1	35 01
065	*LBLB	21 12	111		-45	157	P⇄S	16-51
066	HMS→	16 36	112	RCLD	36 14	158	→HMS	16 35
067	RTN	24	113	x	-35	159	PRTX	-14
068	*LBLB	21 12	114	ST+5	35-55 05	160	SPC	16-11
069	HMS→	16 36	115	RCL5	36 05	161	RTN	24
070	X⇄Y	-41	116	RCL4	36 04	162	*LBLE	21 15
071	-	-45	117	→P	34	163	RCL3	36 03
072	6	06	118	STO6	35 06	164	HMS→	16 36
073	0	00	119	X⇄Y	-41	165	P⇄S	16-51
074	÷	-24	120	STOA	35 11	166	RCL1	36 01
075	STx8	35-35 08	121	P⇄S	16-51	167	P⇄S	16-51
076	STx9	35-35 09	122	RCL2	36 02	168	--	-45
077	RCL8	36 08	123	-	-45	169	RCLD	36 14
078	ST+4	35-55 04	124	SIN	41	170	x	-35
079	RCL9	36 09	125	RCL2	36 02	171	RCL2	36 02
080	ST+5	35-55 05	126	RCL3	36 03	172	HMS→	16 36
081	RTN	24	127	-	-45	173	P⇄S	16-51
082	*LBLC	21 13	128	SIN	41	174	RCL0	36 00
083	GSB0	23 00	129	÷	-24	175	P⇄S	16-51
084	P⇄S	16-51	130	P⇄S	16-51	176	-	-45
085	STO2	35 02	131	RCL6	36 06	177	→P	34
086	P⇄S	16-51	132	x	-35	178	6	06
087	RTN	24	133	P⇄S	16-51	179	0	00
088	*LBLD	21 14	134	RCL3	36 03	180	x	-35
089	GSB0	23 00	135	P⇄S	16-51	181	DSP1	-63 01
090	P⇄S	16-51	136	X⇄Y	-41	182	PRTX	-14
091	STO3	35 03	137	→R	44	183	SPC	16-11
092	P⇄S	16-51	138	CHS	-22	184	RTN	24

(CONTINUED) 349

185	*LBLd	21 16 14		001	*LBLa	21 16 11		047	X⇄Y	-4
186	R↓	-31		002	STOI	35 46		048	STO9	35 0
187	STOB	35 12		003	RCLi	36 45		049	RTN	2
188	X⇄Y	-41		004	ISZI	16 26 46		050	*LBLA	21 1
189	STOA	35 11		005	RCLi	36 45		051	P⇄S	16-5
190	R↑	16-31		006	RTN	24		052	STO6	35 0
191	STOI	35 46		007	*LBLb	21 16 12		053	RTN	2
192	P⇄S	16-51		008	STOI	35 46		054	*LBLA	21 1
193	0	00		009	R↓	-31		055	STO7	35 0
194	STO9	35 09		010	RCLi	36 45		056	P⇄S	16-5
195	P⇄S	16-51		011	ISZI	16 26 46		057	→R	4
196	RCLi	36 45		012	RCLi	36 45		058	ST+8	35-55 0
197	ISZI	16 26 46		013	RTN	24		059	X⇄Y	-4
198	RCLi	36 45		014	*LBLc	21 16 13		060	ST+9	35-55 0
199	RCLA	36 11		015	R↑	16-31		061	RTN	2
200	PRTX	-14		016	STO0	35 00		062	*LBLB	21 1
201	RCLB	36 12		017	R↑	16-31		063	HMS→	16 3
202	PRTX	-14		018	STO1	35 01		064	RTN	2
203	SPC	16-11		019	R↑	16-31		065	*LBLB	21 1
204	RTN	24		020	STO2	35 02		066	HMS→	16 3
205	R/S	51		021	R↑	16-31		067	X⇄Y	-4
				022	STO3	35 03		068	-	-4
				023	0	00		069	6	0
				024	STO4	35 04		070	0	0
				025	STO5	35 05		071	÷	-2
				026	RTN	24		072	STx8	35-35 0
				027	*LBLe	21 16 15		073	STx9	35-35 0
				028	STOC	35 13		074	RCL8	36 0
				029	RTN	24		075	ST+4	35-55 0
				030	*LBLe	21 16 15		076	RCL9	36 0
				031	STOE	35 15		077	ST+5	35-55 0
				032	RTN	24		078	RTN	2
				033	*LBLA	21 11		079	*LBLC	21 1
				034	GSB0	23 00		080	GSB0	23 0
				035	P⇄S	16-51		081	P⇄S	16-5
				036	STO4	35 04		082	STO2	35 0
				037	RTN	24		083	P⇄S	16-5
				038	*LBLA	21 11		084	RTN	24
				039	STO5	35 05		085	*LBLD	21 14
				040	0	00		086	GSB0	23 0
				041	STO7	35 07		087	P⇄S	16-5
				042	RCL4	36 04		088	STO3	35 0
				043	RCL5	36 05		089	P⇄S	16-5
				044	P⇄S	16-51		090	RTN	24
				045	→R	44		091	*LBL0	21 00
				046	STO8	35 08		092	RCLE	36 15

093	+	-55	139	P⇄S	16-51	185	0	00
094	RCLC	36 13	140	RCL3	36 03	186	x	-35
095	+	-55	141	P⇄S	16-51	187	DSP1	-63 01
096	RTN	24	142	X⇄Y	-41	188	PRTX	-14
097	*LBLE	21 15	143	→R	44	189	SPC	16-11
098	RCL0	36 00	144	CHS	-22	190	RTN	24
099	HMS→	16 36	145	RCL2	36 02	191	*LBLd	21 16 14
100	RCL2	36 02	146	HMS→	16 36	192	R↓	-31
101	HMS→	16 36	147	+	-55	193	STOB	35 12
102	-	-45	148	P⇄S	16-51	194	X⇄Y	-41
103	STOB	35 12	149	STO0	35 00	195	STOA	35 11
104	2	02	150	P⇄S	16-51	196	R↑	16-31
105	÷	-24	151	→HMS	16 35	197	STOI	35 46
106	RCL0	36 00	152	PRTX	-14	198	P⇄S	16-51
107	HMS→	16 36	153	RTN	24	199	0	00
108	+	-55	154	*LBLE	21 15	200	STO9	35 09
109	COS	42	155	X⇄Y	-41	201	P⇄S	16-51
110	STOD	35 14	156	RCLD	36 14	202	RCLi	36 45
111	RCLB	36 12	157	÷	-24	203	ISZI	16 26 46
112	ST+4	35-55 04	158	RCL3	36 03	204	RCLi	36 45
113	RCL3	36 03	159	HMS→	16 36	205	RCLA	36 11
114	HMS→	16 36	160	+	-55	206	PRTX	-14
115	RCL1	36 01	161	P⇄S	16-51	207	RCLB	36 12
116	HMS→	16 36	162	STO1	35 01	208	PRTX	-14
117	-	-45	163	P⇄S	16-51	209	SPC	16-11
118	RCLD	36 14	164	→HMS	16 35	210	RTN	24
119	x	-35	165	PRTX	-14	211	R/S	51
120	ST+5	35-55 05	166	SPC	16-11			
121	RCL5	36 05	167	RTN	24			
122	RCL4	36 04	168	*LBLE	21 15			
123	→P	34	169	RCL3	36 03			
124	STO6	35 06	170	HMS→	16 36			
125	X⇄Y	-41	171	P⇄S	16-51			
126	STOA	35 11	172	RCL1	36 01			
127	P⇄S	16-51	173	P⇄S	16-51			
128	RCL2	36 02	174	-	-45			
129	-	-45	175	RCLD	36 14			
130	SIN	41	176	x	-35			
131	RCL2	36 02	177	RCL2	36 02			
132	RCL3	36 03	178	HMS→	16 36			
133	-	-45	179	P⇄S	16-51			
134	SIN	41	180	RCL0	36 00			
135	÷	-24	181	P⇄S	16-51			
136	P⇄S	16-51	182	-	-45			
137	RCL6	36 06	183	→P	34			
138	x	-35	184	6	06			

	46.	LBL		90.	IFO		1.	1
	19.	D"		1.	1		8.	8
	48.	EXC		1.	1		39.	P/R
	0.	0		0.	0	90	44.	SUM
	0.	0		95.	=		1.	1
	56.	RTN		55.	÷		7.	7
	46.	LBL	50	6.	6		19.	D"
	16.	A"		0.	0		44.	SUM
	44.	SUM		95.	=		1.	1
10	6.	6		42.	STO		6.	6
	9.	9		1.	1		81.	HLT
	81.	HLT		2.	2		46.	LBL
	46.	LBL		65.	×		12.	B
	17.	B"		43.	RCL	100	85.	+
	48.	EXC		1.	1		43.	RCL
	1.	1		5.	5		6.	6
	9.	9	60	95.	=		9.	9
	48.	EXC		19.	D"		95.	=
	1.	1		43.	RCL		48.	EXC
20	8.	8		1.	1		0.	0
	81.	HLT		4.	4		1.	1
	46.	LBL		85.	+		48.	EXC
	18.	C"		43.	RCL		0.	0
	48.	EXC		6.	6	110	4.	4
	1.	1		9.	9		95.	=
	5.	5		95.	=		81.	HLT
	48.	EXC	70	39.	P/R		46.	LBL
	1.	1		44.	SUM		13.	C
	4.	4		1.	1		37.	DMS
30	81.	HLT		7.	7		48.	EXC
	46.	LBL		43.	RCL		0.	0
	10.	E"		1.	1		5.	5
	42.	STO		9.	9		48.	EXC
	1.	1		65.	×	120	0.	0
	1.	1		43.	RCL		6.	6
	81.	HLT		1.	1		48.	EXC
	46.	LBL	80	2.	2		0.	0
	11.	A		95.	=		7.	7
	37.	DMS		19.	D"		48.	EXC
40	75.	-		44.	SUM		0.	0
	48.	EXC		1.	1		8.	8
	1.	1		6.	6		81.	HLT
	3.	3		43.	RCL		46.	LBL

130	14.	D		95.	=		22.	INV
	57.	FIX		32.	SIN		37.	DMS
	4.	4		65.	×		81.	HLT
	43.	RCL		19.	D'			
	1.	1		55.	÷			
	6.	6		53.	(			
	85.	+		43.	RCL			
	43.	RCL	180	0.	0			
	0.	0		4.	4			
	8.	8		75.	-			
140	75.	-		43.	RCL			
	43.	RCL		0.	0			
	0.	0		1.	1			
	6.	6		54.	)			
	44.	SUM		32.	SIN			
	0.	0		95.	=			
	8.	8		40.	X²			
	95.	=	190	30.	Γ			
	19.	D'		94.	+/-			
	43.	RCL		19.	D'			
150	1.	1		43.	RCL			
	1.	1		0.	0			
	65.	×		1.	1			
	53.	(		39.	P/R			
	43.	RCL		55.	÷			
	0.	0		43.	RCL			
	5.	5		1.	1			
	75.	-	200	1.	1			
	43.	RCL		94.	+/-			
	0.	0		85.	+			
160	7.	7		43.	RCL			
	54.	)		0.	0			
	85.	+		6.	6			
	43.	RCL		44.	SUM			
	1.	1		0.	0			
	7.	7		0.	0			
	95.	=		43.	RCL			
	22.	INV	210	0.	0			
	39.	P/R		5.	5			
	75.	-		95.	=			
170	43.	RCL		46.	LBL			
	0.	0		15.	E			
	4.	4		19.	D'			

Program 2.27

	46.	LBL		6.	6	19.	D'
	19.	D'		0.	0	44.	SU
	48.	EXC		95.	=	1.	1
	0.	0		42.	STD	90 6.	6
	0.	0		1.	1	81.	HL
	56.	RTN		2.	2	46.	LB
	46.	LBL	50	65.	×	12.	B
	16.	A'		43.	RCL	85.	+
	44.	SUM		1.	1	43.	RC
10	6.	6		5.	5	6.	6
	9.	9		95.	=	9.	9
	81.	HLT		19.	D'	95.	=
	46.	LBL		43.	RCL	48.	EX
	17.	B'		1.	1	100 0.	0
	48.	EXC		4.	4	1.	1
	1.	1		85.	+	48.	EX
	9.	9	60	43.	RCL	0.	0
	48.	EXC		6.	6	4.	4
	1.	1		9.	9	95.	=
20	8.	8		95.	=	81.	HL
	81.	HLT		39.	P/R	46.	LB
	46.	LBL		44.	SUM	13.	C
	18.	C'		1.	1	37.	DM
	48.	EXC		7.	7	110 48.	EX
	1.	1		43.	RCL	0.	0
	5.	5		1.	1	5.	5
	48.	EXC	70	9.	9	48.	EX
	1.	1		65.	×	0.	0
	4.	4		43.	RCL	6.	6
30	81.	HLT		1.	1	48.	EX
	46.	LBL		2.	2	0.	0
	11.	A		95.	=	7.	7
	37.	DMS		19.	D'	48.	EX
	75.	-		44.	SUM	120 0.	0
	48.	EXC		1.	1	8.	8
	1.	1		6.	6	81.	HL
	3.	3	80	43.	RCL	46.	LB
	90.	IFO		1.	1	14.	D
	1.	1		8.	8	57.	FI
40	0.	0		39.	P/R	4.	4
	4.	4		44.	SUM	43.	RC
	95.	=		1.	1	1.	1
	55.	÷		7.	7	6.	6

Line	Code	Key	Line	Code	Key	Line	Code	Key
130	85.	+		4.	4		19.	D'
	43.	RCL		95.	=		22.	INV
	0.	0		32.	SIN		37.	DMS
	8.	8		65.	×		81.	HLT
	75.	-		19.	D'	220	46.	LBL
	43.	RCL		55.	÷		10.	E'
	0.	0		53.	(		47.	CMS
	6.	6	180	43.	RCL		25.	CLR
	44.	SUM		0.	0		81.	HLT
	0.	0		4.	4			
140	8.	8		75.	-			
	95.	=		43.	RCL			
	19.	D'		0.	0			
	43.	RCL		1.	1			
	0.	0		54.	)			
	8.	8		32.	SIN			
	55.	÷		95.	=			
	2.	2	190	40.	X^2			
	95.	=		30.	Γ			
	33.	COS		94.	+/-			
150	42.	STO		19.	D'			
	1.	1		43.	RCL			
	1.	1		0.	0			
	65.	×		1.	1			
	53.	(		39.	P/R			
	43.	RCL		55.	÷			
	0.	0		43.	RCL			
	5.	5	200	1.	1			
	75.	-		1.	1			
	43.	RCL		94.	+/-			
160	0.	0		85.	+			
	7.	7		43.	RCL			
	54.	)		0.	0			
	85.	+		6.	6			
	43.	RCL		44.	SUM			
	1.	1		0.	0			
	7.	7		0.	0			
	95.	=	210	43.	RCL			
	22.	INV		0.	0			
	39.	P/R		5.	5			
170	75.	-		95.	=			
	43.	RCL		46.	LBL			
	0.	0		15.	E			

355

Program 2.28

#	Code	#	Code	#	Code
46.	LBL	8.	8	1.	1
11.	A	51.	SBR	0.	0
46.	LBL	87.	1'	81.	HLT
12.	B	43.	RCL	90 46.	LBL
37.	DMS	0.	0	88.	2'
46.	LBL	8.	8	85.	+
87.	1'	50 75.	−	3.	3
48.	EXC	43.	RCL	6.	6
0.	0	0.	0	0.	0
10 5.	5	6.	6	95.	=
48.	EXC	95.	=	42.	STO
0.	0	42.	STO	1.	1
6.	6	0.	0	0.	0
48.	EXC	0.	0	100 81.	HLT
0.	0	43.	RCL	46.	LBL
7.	7	0.	0	16.	A'
48.	EXC	60 8.	8	43.	RCL
0.	0	85.	+	0.	0
8.	8	43.	RCL	0.	0
20 56.	RTN	0.	0	65.	×
46.	LBL	6.	6	6.	6
13.	C	95.	=	0.	0
37.	DMS	55.	÷	95.	=
42.	STO	2.	2	110 42.	STO
0.	0	95.	=	1.	1
9.	9	33.	COS	1.	1
81.	HLT	70 65.	×	81.	HLT
46.	LBL	53.	(	46.	LBL
14.	D	43.	RCL	17.	B'
30 37.	DMS	0.	0	43.	RCL
42.	STO	5.	5	0.	0
0.	0	75.	−	1.	1
1.	1	43.	RCL	75.	−
81.	HLT	0.	0	120 43.	RCL
46.	LBL	7.	7	0.	0
15.	E	54.	)	9.	9
43.	RCL	80 95.	=	95.	=
0.	0	22.	INV	42.	STO
8.	8	39.	P/R	1.	1
40 51.	SBR	22.	INV	2.	2
87.	1'	80.	IF+	43.	RCL
43.	RCL	88.	2'	1.	1
0.	0	42.	STO	1.	1

130	55.	÷	
	43.	RCL	
	1.	1	
	2.	2	
	95.	=	
	81.	HLT	
	46.	LBL	
	10.	E'	
	47.	CMS	
	25.	CLR	
140	86.	RST	
	81.	HLT	

001	*LBLA	21 11	046	RCL8	36 08	091	+	-55
002	STO7	35 07	047	÷	-24	092	GSB9	23 09
003	R/S	51	048	RCL5	36 05	093	STOA	35 11
004	*LBLA	21 11	049	÷	-24	094	RCL6	36 06
005	STO8	35 08	050	COS⁻	16 42	095	RTN	24
006	R/S	51	051	STO6	35 06	096	*LBL8	21 08
007	*LBLA	21 11	052	PRTX	-14	097	→R	44
008	STO9	35 09	053	RTN	24	098	R↓	-31
009	R/S	51	054	*LBLB	21 12	099	R↓	-31
010	*LBLA	21 11	055	*LBLC	21 13	100	→R	44
011	COS	42	056	STO2	35 02	101	X⇄Y	-41
012	X²	53	057	R/S	51	102	R↓	-31
013	STOA	35 11	058	*LBLB	21 12	103	+	-55
014	RCL9	36 09	059	*LBLC	21 13	104	R↓	-31
015	1	01	060	STO1	35 01	105	+	-55
016	→R	44	061	R/S	51	106	R↑	16-31
017	X²	53	062	*LBLB	21 12	107	→P	34
018	X⇄Y	-41	063	SF1	16 21 01	108	RTN	24
019	X²	53	064	GSB0	23 00	109	*LBLD	21 14
020	RCLA	36 11	065	-	-45	110	STO4	35 04
021	x	-35	066	GSB9	23 09	111	R/S	51
022	+	-55	067	STO3	35 03	112	*LBLD	21 14
023	√X	54	068	R/S	51	113	STOI	35 46
024	RCL7	36 07	069	*LBLC	21 13	114	RCLA	36 11
025	X⇄Y	-41	070	CF1	16 22 01	115	RCL8	36 08
026	÷	-24	071	GSB0	23 00	116	GSB8	23 08
027	STO7	35 07	072	+	-55	117	PRTX	-14
028	RCL9	36 09	073	GSB9	23 09	118	STOB	35 12
029	X⇄Y	-41	074	STO3	35 03	119	X⇄Y	-41
030	→R	44	075	PRTX	-14	120	GSB9	23 09
031	RCL8	36 08	076	RTN	24	121	PRTX	-14
032	-	-45	077	*LBL9	21 09	122	STOC	35 13
033	→P	34	078	3	03	123	RCL3	36 03
034	STO5	35 05	079	6	06	124	RCL6	36 06
035	PRTX	-14	080	0	00	125	F1?	16 23 01
036	RCL7	36 07	081	→R	44	126	CHS	-22
037	X²	53	082	→P	34	127	+	-55
038	RCL8	36 08	083	X⇄Y	-41	128	GSB9	23 09
039	X²	53	084	X<0?	16-45	129	STOE	35 15
040	-	-45	085	+	-55	130	PRTX	-14
041	RCL5	36 05	086	RTN	24	131	CF3	16 22 03
042	X²	53	087	*LBL0	21 00	132	*LBL7	21 07
043	-	-45	088	STO0	35 00	133	PSE	16 51
044	2	02	089	+	-55	134	F3?	16 23 03
045	÷	-24	090	RCL2	36 02	135	GTO0	22 00

136	GTO7	22 07	181	PRTX	-14		81.		HLT
137	*LBL0	21 00	182	RCLB	36 12		86.		RST
138	RCLE	36 15	183	÷	-24		46.		LBL
139	X⇌Y	-41	184	STO3	35 03		45.		Y×
140	STO0	35 00	185	→HMS	16 35		75.		-
141	-	-45	186	PRTX	-14		80.		1F+
142	RCL1	36 01	187	RCL0	36 00		34.		TAN
143	-	-45	188	RCLC	36 13		0.		0
144	GSB9	23 09	189	-	-45		85.		+
145	PRTX	-14	190	SIN	41	10	46.		LBL
146	RCLE	36 15	191	RCL9	36 09		34.		TAN
147	RCL8	36 08	192	X	-35		3.		3
148	RCL4	36 04	193	ABS	16 31		6.		6
149	RCLI	36 46	194	RCLD	36 14		0.		0
150	GSB8	23 08	195	÷	-24		95.		=
151	PRTX	-14	196	STO2	35 02		22.		INV
152	STOD	35 14	197	→HMS	16 35		80.		IF+
153	X⇌Y	-41	198	PRTX	-14		45.		Y×
154	GSB9	23 09	199	RTN	24		56.		RTN
155	STOE	35 15	200	*LBLe	21 16 15	20	46.		LBL
156	PRTX	-14	201	RCL1	36 01		11.		A
157	RTN	24	202	RCLC	36 13		1.		1
158	*LBLc	21 16 13	203	1	01		94.		+/-
159	P⇌S	16-51	204	8	08		42.		STO
160	STO0	35 00	205	0	00		0.		0
161	R/S	51	206	+	-55		5.		5
162	*LBLc	21 16 13	207	RCLB	36 12		57.		FIX
163	STO1	35 01	208	RCL3	36 03		1.		1
164	P⇌S	16-51	209	X	-35		56.		RTN
165	RTN	24	210	RCL0	36 00	30	46.		LBL
166	*LBLE	21 15	211	R↓	-31		15.		E
167	P⇌S	16-51	212	GSB8	23 08		1.		'
168	RCL1	36 01	213	STO1	35 01		42.		STO
169	RCLC	36 13	214	PRTX	-14		0.		0
170	RCLE	36 15	215	X⇌Y	-41		5.		5
171	-	-45	216	GSB9	23 09		57.		FIX
172	SIN	41	217	STO0	35 00		1.		1
173	÷	-24	218	PRTX	-14		56.		RTN
174	STO9	35 09	219	P⇌S	16-51		46.		LBL
175	RCLE	36 15	220	RTN	24		16.		A'
176	RCL0	36 00	221	*LBLd	21 16 14	40	16.		
177	-	-45	222	HMS→	16 36		42.		STO
178	SIN	41	223	STO3	35 03		1.		1
179	X	-35	224	RTN	24		6.		6
180	ABS	16 31							

	56.	RTN	14.	D	**130**	0.	0
	46.	LBL	42.	STO		22.	INV
	17.	B'	0.	0		39.	P/R
	48.	EXC	**90** 0.	0		51.	SBR
	0.	0	1.	1		45.	Y×
	7.	7	48.	EXC		42.	STO
50	48.	EXC	0.	0		0.	0
	0.	0	0.	0		8.	8
	6.	6	39.	P/R		9.	9
	56.	RTN	65.	×		98.	PRT
	46.	LBL	43.	RCL	**140** 56.	RTN
	10.	E'	1.	1		43.	RCL
	48.	EXC	9.	9		0.	0
	1.	1	**100** 33.	COS		0.	0
	0.	0	95.	=		42.	STO
	48.	EXC	22.	INV		0.	0
60	1.	1	39.	P/R		4.	4
	1.	1	42.	STO		98.	PRT
	56.	RTN	0.	0		86.	RST
	46.	LBL	0.	0		46.	LBL
	12.	B	43.	RCL	**150** 19.	D'
	42.	STO	0.	0		42.	STO
	0.	0	2.	2		1.	1
	1.	1	**110** 48.	EXC		7.	7
	56.	RTN	0.	0		56.	RTN
	46.	LBL	0.	0		94.	+/-
70	13.	C	39.	P/R		85.	+
	42.	STO	55.	÷		43.	RCL
	0.	0	43.	RCL		1.	1
	2.	2	1.	1		7.	7
	25.	CLR	9.	9	**160** 75.	-
	42.	STO	33.	COS		43.	RCL
	1.	1	95.	=		1.	1
	9.	9	**120** 48.	EXC		6.	6
	43.	RCL	0.	0		85.	+
	0.	0	0.	0		43.	RCL
80	2.	2	75.	-		0.	0
	56.	RTN	43.	RCL		5.	5
	42.	STO	0.	0		65.	×
	1.	1	1.	1		43.	RCL
	9.	9	95.	=	**170** 0.	0
	56.	RTN	48.	EXC		8.	8
	46.	LBL	0.	0		95.	=

(CONTINUED)

Program 3.3

51.	SBR		81.	HLT	0.	0
45.	Yˣ		86.	RST	0.	0
42.	STO		46.	LBL	46.	LBL
0.	0		16.	A'	13.	C
9.	9		75.	–	75.	–
98.	PRT		43.	RCL	80.	IF+
86.	RST		1.	1	50	34.	TAN
			0.	0	0.	0
			95.	=	85.	+
		10	32.	SIN	46.	LBL
			65.	×	34.	TAN
			43.	RCL	3.	3
			1.	1	6.	6
			1.	1	0.	0
			55.	÷	95.	=
			53.	(	22.	INV
			43.	RCL	60	80.	IF+
			1.	1	13.	C
			3.	3	98.	PRT
		20	75.	–	56.	RTN
			43.	RCL	85.	+
			1.	1	43.	RCL
			5.	5	1.	1
			54.	)	6.	6
			32.	SIN	85.	+
			95.	=	43.	RCL
			40.	x²	70	0.	0
			30.	Γ	0.	0
			56.	RTN	95.	=
		30	46.	LBL	13.	C
			11.	A	86.	RST
			25.	CLR	46.	LBL
			43.	RCL	15.	E
			0.	0	25.	CLR
			9.	9	43.	RCL
			85.	+	0.	0
			46.	LBL	80	9.	9
			30.	Γ	75.	–
			43.	RCL	41.	GTO
		40	0.	0	30.	Γ
			8.	8	46.	LBL
			95.	=	12.	B
			42.	STO	25.	CLR

	43.	RCL	**130**	1.	1	37.	DMS
	0.	0		2.	2	65.	×
	1.	1		43.	RCL	43.	RCL
90	48.	EXC		0.	0	1.	1
	0.	0		0.	0	2.	2
	0.	0		42.	STD	95.	=
	39.	P/R		1.	1	86.	RST
	42.	STD		3.	3	**180**	46.	LBL
	1.	1		86.	RST	19.	D'
	8.	8		46.	LBL	25.	CLR
	43.	RCL	**140**	14.	D	43.	RCL
	0.	0		12.	B	1.	1
	6.	6		56.	RTN	3.	3
00	48.	EXC		42.	STD	16.	A'
	0.	0		1.	1	55.	÷
	0.	0		4.	4	43.	RCL
	42.	STD		43.	RCL	1.	1
	1.	1		0.	0	**190**	4.	4
	7.	7		0.	0	51.	SBR
	43.	RCL		42.	STD	37.	DMS
	0.	0	**150**	1.	1	56.	RTN
	7.	7		5.	5	37.	DMS
	39.	P/R		86.	RST	65.	×
10	44.	SUM		46.	LBL	43.	RCL
	1.	1		17.	B'	1.	1
	8.	8		25.	CLR	4.	4
	43.	RCL		43.	RCL	95.	=
	1.	1		1.	1	**200**	86.	RST
	7.	7		5.	5	46.	LBL
	44.	SUM		16.	A'	18.	C'
	0.	0	**160**	55.	÷	17.	B'
	0.	0		43.	RCL	37.	DMS
	43.	RCL		1.	1	42.	STD
20	1.	1		2.	2	1.	1
	8.	8		46.	LBL	7.	7
	22.	INV		37.	DMS	19.	D'
	39.	P/R		95.	=	37.	DMS
	13.	C		57.	FIX	**210**	85.	+
	48.	EXC		4.	4	43.	RCL
	0.	0		22.	INV	1.	1
	0.	0	**170**	37.	DMS	7.	7
	56.	RTN		98.	PRT	41.	GTO
	42.	STD		56.	RTN	37.	DMS

Program 3.4

	46.	LBL		81.	HLT	43.	RCL
	10.	E'		86.	RST	1.	1
	48.	EXC		46.	LBL	1.	1
	1.	1		12.	B	48.	EXC
220	0.	0		53.	(	0.	0
	48.	EXC		24.	CE	0.	0
	1.	1		37.	DMS	50 42.	STO
	1.	1		65.	×	1.	1
	56.	RTN		43.	RCL	7.	7
			10	1.	1	43.	RCL
				2.	2	1.	1
				54.	)	0.	0
				57.	FIX	39.	P/R
				1.	1	44.	SUM
				56.	RTN	1.	1
				46.	LBL	8.	8
				14.	D	60 43.	RCL
				53.	(	1.	1
				24.	CE	7.	7
			20	37.	DMS	44.	SUM
				65.	×	0.	0
				43.	RCL	0.	0
				1.	1	43.	RCL
				4.	4	1.	1
				54.	)	8.	8
				57.	FIX	22.	INV
				1.	1	70 39.	P/R
				56.	RTN	46.	LBL
				46.	LBL	45.	'X
			30	17.	B'	85.	+
				94.	+/-	22.	INV
				42.	STO	80.	IF+
				0.	0	34.	TAN
				0.	0	0.	0
				43.	RCL	75.	-
				1.	1	46.	LBL
				3.	3	80 34.	TAN
				46.	LBL	3.	3
				52.	EE	6.	6
			40	39.	P/R	0.	0
				42.	STO	95.	=
				1.	1	22.	INV
				8.	8	80.	IF+

	45.	Yx	130 5.	5	001 *LBLA 21 11
	42.	STO	48.	EXC	002 ST07 35 07
	1.	1	1.	1	003 RTN 24
90	7.	7	4.	4	004 *LBLB 21 12
	43.	RCL	56.	RTN	005 ST08 35 08
	0.	0	46.	LBL	006 RTN 24
	0.	0	10.	E°	007 *LBLC 21 13
	42.	STO	48.	EXC	008 ST09 35 09
	1.	1	1.	1	009 RTN 24
	8.	8	0.	0	010 *LBLD 21 14
	99.	PHP	140 48.	EXC	011 P⇄S 16-51
	98.	PRT	1.	1	012 ST04 35 04
	56.	RTN	1.	1	013 P⇄S 16-51
100	43.	RCL	56.	RTN	014 COS 42
	1.	1	46.	LBL	015 X² 53
	7.	7	18.	C°	016 STOA 35 11
	98.	PRT	43.	RCL	017 RCL9 36 09
	99.	PHP	1.	1	018 1 01
	86.	RST	7.	7	019 →R 44
	46.	LBL	42.	STO	020 X² 53
	14.	D°	150 1.	1	021 X⇄Y -41
	94.	+/-	0.	0	022 X² 53
	42.	STO	43.	RCL	023 RCLA 36 11
110	0.	0	1.	1	024 x -35
	0.	0	8.	8	025 + -55
	43.	RCL	42.	STO	026 √X 54
	1.	1	1.	1	027 RCL7 36 07
	5.	5	1.	1	028 X⇄Y -41
	41.	GTO	0.	0	029 ÷ -24
	52.	EE	56.	RTN	030 ST07 35 07
	46.	LBL			031 RCL9 36 09
	11.	A			032 X⇄Y -41
	48.	EXC			033 →R 44
120	1.	1			034 RCL8 36 08
	3.	3			035 - -45
	48.	EXC			036 →P 34
	1.	1			037 ST05 35 05
	2.	2			038 PRTX -14
	56.	RTN			039 RCL7 36 07
	46.	LBL			040 X² 53
	15.	E			041 RCL8 36 08
	48.	EXC			042 X² 53
	1.	1			043 - -45
					044 RCL5 36 05
					045 X² 53

Program 3.6

046	–	-45		46.	LBL		14.	D	
047	2	02		45.	Y^x		57.	FIX	
048	÷	-24		75.	–		2.	2	
049	RCL8	36 08		80.	IF+		42.	STO	
050	÷	-24		34.	TAN		0.	0	
051	RCL5	36 05		0.	0		0.	0	
052	÷	-24		85.	÷	50	1.	1	
053	COS⁻¹	16 42		46.	LBL		48.	EXC	
054	STO6	35 06		34.	TAN		0.	0	
055	PRTX	-14	10	3.	3		0.	0	
056	RTN	24		6.	6		39.	P/R	
057	*LBLE	21 15		0.	0		65.	×	
058	STO4	35 04		95.	=		43.	RCL	
059	1	01		22.	INV		1.	1	
060	0	00		80.	IF+		9.	9	
061	X≤Y?	16-35		45.	Y^x		33.	COS	
062	GTO1	22 01		56.	RTN	60	95.	=	
063	RCL8	36 08		46.	LBL		22.	INV	
064	RCL4	36 04		11.	A		39.	P/R	
065	x	-35	20	42.	STO		42.	STO	
066	RCL5	36 05		0.	0		0.	0	
067	÷	-24		1.	1		0.	0	
068	STO0	35 00		56.	RTN		43.	RCL	
069	PRTX	-14		46.	LBL		0.	0	
070	RTN	24		12.	B		2.	2	
071	*LBL1	21 01		43.	STO		48.	EXC	
072	RCL8	36 08		0.	0	70	0.	0	
073	RCL4	36 04		2.	2		0.	0	
074	RCL5	36 05		25.	CLR		39.	P/R	
075	÷	-24	30	42.	STO		55.	÷	
076	√X	54		1.	1		43.	RCL	
077	x	-35		5.	4		1.	1	
078	STO0	35 00		43.	RCL		9.	9	
079	PRTX	-14		0.	0		33.	COS	
080	RTN	24		2.	2		95.	=	
081	*LBLa	21 16 11		56.	RTN		48.	EXC	
082	STO5	35 05		46.	LBL	80	0.	0	
083	RTN	24		13.	C		0.	0	
084	R/S	51		42.	STO		75.	–	
			40	1.	1		43.	RCL	
				5.	4		0.	0	
				56.	RTN		1.	1	
				46.	LBL		95.	=	

Program 3.7

	Col 1		Col 2		Col 3	
	48.	EXC	130 0.	0	001 *LBLa	21 16 11
	0.	0	1.	1	002 0	00
	0.	0	65.	×	003 F2?	16 23 02
90	22.	INV	43.	RCL	004 RTN	24
	39.	P/R	0.	0	005 1	01
	51.	SBR	3.	3	006 SF2	16 21 02
	45.	Y×	55.	÷	007 RTN	24
	42.	STO	43.	RCL	008 *LBLb	21 16 12
	0.	0	0.	0	009 CF0	16 22 00
	8.	8	0.	0	010 CF1	16 22 01
	99.	PAP	140 95.	=	011 P⇄S	16-51
	98.	PRT	42.	STO	012 CLRG	16-53
	56.	RTN	0.	0	013 P⇄S	16-51
100	46.	LBL	5.	5	014 1	01
	15.	E	98.	PRT	015 RTN	24
	43.	RCL	99.	PAP	016 *LBLc	21 16 13
	0.	0	81.	HLT	017 GSBb	23 16 12
	0.	0	46.	LBL	018 SF1	16 21 01
	42.	STO	32.	SIN	019 RTN	24
	0.	0	43.	RCL	020 *LBLd	21 16 14
	4.	4	150 0.	0	021 GSBb	23 16 12
	98.	PRT	3.	3	022 SF0	16 21 00
	81.	HLT	55.	÷	023 RTN	24
110	46.	LBL	43.	RCL	024 *LBLe	21 16 15
	16.	A'	0.	0	025 GSBd	23 16 14
	42.	STO	0.	0	026 SF1	16 21 01
	0.	0	95.	=	027 RTN	24
	0.	0	30.	F	028 *LBLA	21 11
	81.	HLT	65.	×	029 CF3	16 22 03
	46.	LBL	43.	RCL	030 *LBL8	21 08
	17.	B'	160 0.	0	031 F2?	16 23 02
	52.	FIX	1.	1	032 GSB9	23 09
	2.	2	95.	=	033 STOD	35 14
120	42.	STO	42.	STO	034 F1?	16 23 01
	0.	0	0.	0	035 LN	32
	3.	3	5.	5	036 X⇄Y	-41
	75.	-	98.	PRT	037 STOC	35 13
	1.	1	99.	PAP	038 F0?	16 23 00
	0.	0	81.	HLT	039 LN	32
	95.	=			040 F3?	16 23 03
	80.	IF+			041 GTO0	22 00
	32.	SIN			042 Σ+	56
	43.	RCL			043 *LBL7	21 07
					044 ENT↑	-21
					045 1	01
					046 +	-55

(CONTINUED) 367

047	RCLC	36 13	093	÷	-24	139	Yˣ	31
048	X⇄Y	-41	094	CHS	-22	140	x	-35
049	RCLD	36 14	095	RCL7	36 07	141	F2?	16 23 02
050	X⇄Y	-41	096	+	-55	142	GTO9	22 09
051	RTN	24	097	÷	-24	143	RTN	24
052	*LBL0	21 00	098	PRTX	-14	144	*LBL3	21 03
053	Σ-	16 56	099	RCL6	36 06	145	SPC	16-11
054	GTO7	22 07	100	RCL4	36 04	146	1	01
055	*LBL9	21 09	101	RCLB	36 12	147	CHS	-22
056	SPC	16-11	102	x	-35	148	PRTX	-14
057	X⇄Y	-41	103	-	-45	149	SF2	16 21 02
058	PRTX	-14	104	RCL9	36 09	150	R↓	-31
059	X⇄Y	-41	105	÷	-24	151	RTN	24
060	PRTX	-14	106	F1?	16 23 01	152	*LBLD	21 14
061	SF2	16 21 02	107	eˣ	33	153	STOE	35 15
062	RTN	24	108	STOA	35 11	154	RCLB	36 12
063	*LBLB	21 12	109	PRTX	-14	155	1/X	52
064	SF3	16 21 03	110	RCLB	36 12	156	RCLA	36 11
065	F2?	16 23 02	111	PRTX	-14	157	RCLE	36 15
066	GSB3	23 03	112	P⇄S	16-51	158	X⇄Y	-41
067	GTO8	22 08	113	RTN	24	159	F1?	16 23 01
068	*LBLC	21 13	114	*LBLE	21 15	160	GTO1	22 01
069	P⇄S	16-51	115	STOE	35 15	161	-	-45
070	SPC	16-11	116	RCLA	36 11	162	x	-35
071	RCL8	36 08	117	RCLB	36 12	163	F0?	16 23 00
072	RCL4	36 04	118	RCLE	36 15	164	eˣ	33
073	RCL6	36 06	119	F1?	16 23 01	165	F2?	16 23 02
074	x	-35	120	GTO1	22 01	166	GTO9	22 09
075	RCL9	36 09	121	F0?	16 23 00	167	RTN	24
076	÷	-24	122	LN	32	168	*LBL1	21 01
077	-	-45	123	x	-35	169	÷	-24
078	ENT↑	-21	124	+	-55	170	F0?	16 23 00
079	ENT↑	-21	125	F2?	16 23 02	171	GTO1	22 01
080	RCL4	36 04	126	GTO9	22 09	172	LN	32
081	X²	53	127	RTN	24	173	x	-35
082	RCL9	36 09	128	*LBL1	21 01	174	F2?	16 23 02
083	÷	-24	129	F0?	16 23 00	175	GTO9	22 09
084	RCL5	36 05	130	GTO2	22 02	176	RTN	24
085	X⇄Y	-41	131	x	-35	177	*LBL1	21 01
086	-	-45	132	eˣ	33	178	X⇄Y	-41
087	÷	-24	133	x	-35	179	Yˣ	31
088	STOB	35 12	134	F2?	16 23 02	180	F2?	16 23 02
089	x	-35	135	GTO9	22 09	181	GTO9	22 09
090	RCL6	36 06	136	RTN	24	182	RTN	24
091	X²	53	137	*LBL2	21 02	183	R/S	51
092	RCL9	36 09	138	X⇄Y	-41			

#	Code		#	Code		#	Code
46.	LBL		44.	SUM		43.	RCL
11.	A		0.	0		0.	0
47.	CMS		4.	4		7.	7
25.	CLR		1.	1	90	22.	INV
56.	RTN		46.	LBL		44.	SUM
46.	LBL		87.	1'		0.	0
12.	B	50	44.	SUM		4.	4
23.	LNX		0.	0		1.	1
42.	STO		0.	0		94.	+/-
10 0.	0		43.	RCL		41.	GTO
6.	6		0.	0		87.	1'
22.	INV		0.	0		46.	LBL
23.	LNX		56.	RTN		14.	D
56.	RTN		46.	LBL	100	43.	RCL
46.	LBL		16.	A'		0.	0
13.	C		23.	LNX		2.	2
23.	LNX	60	42.	STO		75.	-
42.	STO		0.	0		43.	RCL
0.	0		7.	7		0.	0
20 7.	7		22.	INV		1.	1
44.	SUM		44.	SUM		40.	X²
0.	0		0.	0		55.	-
3.	3		3.	3		43.	RCL
40.	X²		40.	X²	110	0.	0
44.	SUM		22.	INV		0.	0
0.	0		44.	SUM		35.	=
5.	5	70	0.	0		20.	1/X
43.	RCL		5.	5		42.	STO
0.	0		43.	RCL		1.	1
30 6.	6		0.	0		0.	0
44.	SUM		6.	6		65.	X
0.	0		22.	INV		53.	(
1.	1		44.	SUM		43.	RCL
49.	PRD		0.	0	120	0.	0
0.	0		1.	1		4.	4
7.	7		49.	PRD		75.	-
40.	X²	80	0.	0		43.	RCL
44.	SUM		7.	7		0.	0
0.	0		40.	X²		1.	1
40 2.	2		22.	INV		65.	X
43.	RCL		44.	SUM		43.	RCL
0.	0		0.	0		0.	0
7.	7		2.	2		3.	3

(CONTINUED) 369

130	55.	÷		0.	0		43.	RCL
	43.	RCL		9.	9		1.	1
	0.	0		95.	=		1.	1
	0.	0		35.	x≷Y		40.	X²
	54.	)		43.	RCL	220	95.	=
	42.	STD		0.	0		42.	STD
	1.	1		8.	8		1.	1
	1.	1	180	95.	=		2.	2
	95.	=		56.	RTN		56.	RTN
	42.	STD		46.	LBL			
140	0.	0		18.	C'			
	8.	8		45.	Y×			
	94.	+/-		43.	RCL			
	65.	×		0.	0			
	43.	RCL		8.	8			
	0.	0		65.	×			
	1.	1		43.	RCL			
	85.	+	190	0.	0			
	43.	RCL		9.	9			
	0.	0		95.	=			
150	3.	3		56.	RTN			
	95.	=		46.	LBL			
	55.	÷		15.	E			
	43.	RCL		43.	RCL			
	0.	0		1.	1			
	0.	0		0.	0			
	95.	=		65.	×			
	22.	INV	200	53.	(			
	23.	LNX		43.	RCL			
	42.	STD		0.	0			
160	0.	0		5.	5			
	9.	9		75.	-			
	56.	RTN		43.	RCL			
	46.	LBL		0.	0			
	19.	D'		3.	3			
	43.	RCL		40.	X²			
	0.	0		55.	÷			
	8.	8	210	43.	RCL			
	56.	RTN		0.	0			
	46.	LBL		0.	0			
170	17.	B'		54.	)			
	55.	÷		20.	1/X			
	43.	RCL		65.	×			

Entries for steps 101–5, 107–12, 120–25, and 127–33 are to be replaced as shown in the discussion of customized programs earlier in this appendix.

001	*LBLA	21 11	041	RCL8	36 08	087	X<0?	16-45
002	STO7	35 07	042	X²	53	088	+	-55
003	R/S	51	043	-	-45	089	RTN	24
004	*LBLA	21 11	044	RCL5	36 05	090	*LBL0	21 00
005	STO8	35 08	045	X²	53	091	STO0	35 00
006	R/S	51	046	-	-45	092	+	-55
007	*LBLA	21 11	047	2	02	093	RCL2	36 02
008	STO9	35 09	048	÷	-24	094	+	-55
009	R/S	51	049	RCL8	36 08	095	GSB9	23 09
010	*LBLA	21 11	050	÷	-24	096	STOA	35 11
011	P⇄S	16-51	051	RCL5	36 05	097	RCL6	36 06
012	STO4	35 04	052	÷	-24	098	RTN	24
013	P⇄S	16-51	053	COS⁻¹	16 42	099	*LBLD	21 14
014	COS	42	054	STO6	35 06	100	RCL5	36 05
015	X²	53	055	PRTX	-14	101	.	-62
016	STOA	35 11	056	RTN	24	102	5	05
017	RCL9	36 09	057	*LBLB	21 12	103	1	01
018	1	01	058	*LBLC	21 13	104	4	04
019	→R	44	059	STO2	35 02	105	7	07
020	X²	53	060	R/S	51	106	Yˣ	31
021	X⇄Y	-41	061	*LBLB	21 12	107	1	01
022	X²	53	062	*LBLC	21 13	108	.	-62
023	RCLA	36 11	063	STO1	35 01	109	3	03
024	x	-35	064	R/S	51	110	8	08
025	+	-55	065	*LBLB	21 12	111	3	03
026	√X	54	066	SF1	16 21 01	112	6	06
027	RCL7	36 07	067	GSB0	23 00	113	x	-35
028	X⇄Y	-41	068	-	-45	114	DSP2	-63 02
029	÷	-24	069	GSB9	23 09	115	PRTX	-14
030	STO7	35 07	070	STO3	35 03	116	STO8	35 08
031	RCL9	36 09	071	R/S	51	117	RTN	24
032	X⇄Y	-41	072	*LBLC	21 13	118	*LBLE	21 15
033	→R	44	073	CF1	16 22 01	119	RCL5	36 05
034	RCL8	36 08	074	GSB0	23 00	120	.	-62
035	-	-45	075	+	-55	121	0	00
036	→P	34	076	GSB9	23 09	122	8	08
037	STO5	35 05	077	STO3	35 03	123	6	06
038	PRTX	-14	078	PRTX	-14	124	5	05
039	RCL7	36 07	079	RTN	24	125	CHS	-22
040	X²	53	080	*LBL9	21 09	126	Yˣ	31
			081	3	03	127	5	05
			082	6	06	128	5	05
			083	0	00	129	.	-62
			084	→R	44	130	0	00
			085	→P	34	131	8	08
			086	X⇄Y	-41	132	4	04

133	2	02	178	*LBLa	21 16 11	001	*LBLA	21 11
134	x	-35	179	RCL9	36 09	002	CF1	16 22 01
135	STO6	35 06	180	PRTX	-14	003	RTN	24
136	RCL6	36 06	181	RTN	24	004	*LBL9	21 09
137	RCL5	36 05	182	*LBLb	21 16 12	005	3	03
138	→R	44	183	RCL3	36 03	006	6	06
139	RCL8	36 08	184	RCL6	36 06	007	0	00
140	+	-55	185	+	-55	008	→R	44
141	→P	34	186	GSB9	23 09	009	→P	34
142	STO7	35 07	187	STOA	35 11	010	X⇄Y	-41
143	RCL5	36 05	188	GSB6	23 06	011	X<0?	16-45
144	X²	53	189	GSB9	23 09	012	+	-55
145	RCL7	36 07	190	R/S	51	013	RTN	24
146	X²	53	191	*LBLb	21 16 12	014	*LBL0	21 00
147	-	-45	192	-	-45	015	STO0	35 00
148	RCL8	36 08	193	GSB9	23 09	016	+	-55
149	X²	53	194	PRTX	-14	017	RCL2	36 02
150	-	-45	195	RTN	24	018	+	-55
151	RCL7	36 07	196	*LBLc	21 16 13	019	GSB9	23 09
152	÷	-24	197	RCL3	36 03	020	STOA	35 11
153	RCL8	36 08	198	RCL6	36 06	021	RCL6	36 06
154	÷	-24	199	-	-45	022	RTN	24
155	2	02	200	GSB9	23 09	023	*LBL8	21 08
156	÷	-24	201	STOA	35 11	024	→R	44
157	CHS	-22	202	GSB6	23 06	025	R↓	-31
158	COS⁻¹	16 42	203	GSB9	23 09	026	R↓	-31
159	STO9	35 09	204	R/S	51	027	→R	44
160	RCL7	36 07	205	*LBLc	21 16 13	028	X⇄Y	-41
161	RCL9	36 09	206	-	-45	029	R↓	-31
162	COS	42	207	GSB9	23 09	030	+	-55
163	X²	53	208	PRTX	-14	031	R↓	-31
164	RCL9	36 09	209	RTN	24	032	+	-55
165	SIN	41	210	*LBL6	21 06	033	R↑	16-31
166	X²	53	211	RCL1	36 01	034	→P	34
167	P⇄S	16-51	212	-	-45	035	RTN	24
168	RCL4	36 04	213	RTN	24	036	*LBLB	21 12
169	P⇄S	16-51	214	R/S	51	037	STO4	35 04
170	COS	42				038	R/S	51
171	X²	53				039	*LBLB	21 12
172	x	-35				040	STOI	35 46
173	+	-55				041	RCLA	36 11
174	√X	54				042	RCL8	36 08
175	x	-35				043	GSB8	23 08
176	PRTX	-14				044	PRTX	-14
177	RTN	24				045	STOB	35 12

Step	Instr	Code		Step	Instr	Code		Step	Instr	Code
046	X≷Y	-41		091	P≷S	16-51		136	RCLB	36 12
047	GSB9	23 09		092	RTN	24		137	RCL3	36 03
048	PRTX	-14		093	*LBLC	21 13		138	x	-35
049	STOC	35 13		094	P≷S	16-51		139	RCL0	36 00
050	RCL3	36 03		095	RCL1	36 01		140	R↓	-31
051	RCL6	36 06		096	RCLC	36 13		141	GSB8	23 08
052	F1?	16 23 01		097	RCLE	36 15		142	STO1	35 01
053	CHS	-22		098	-	-45		143	PRTX	-14
054	+	-55		099	SIN	41		144	X≷Y	-41
055	GSB9	23 09		100	÷	-24		145	GSB9	23 09
056	STOE	35 15		101	STO9	35 09		146	STO0	35 00
057	PRTX	-14		102	RCLE	36 15		147	PRTX	-14
058	CF3	16 22 03		103	RCL0	36 00		148	P≷S	16-51
059	*LBL7	21 07		104	-	-45		149	RTN	24
060	PSE	16 51		105	SIN	41		150	*LBLD	21 14
061	F3?	16 23 03		106	x	-35		151	P≷S	16-51
062	GTO0	22 00		107	ABS	16 31		152	HMS→	16 36
063	GTO7	22 07		108	PRTX	-14		153	STO3	35 03
064	*LBL0	21 00		109	RCLB	36 12		154	P≷S	16-51
065	RCLE	36 15		110	÷	-24		155	RTN	24
066	X≷Y	-41		111	STO3	35 03		156	R/S	51
067	STO0	35 00		112	→HMS	16 35				
068	-	-45		113	PRTX	-14				
069	RCL1	36 01		114	RCL0	36 00				
070	-	-45		115	RCLC	36 13				
071	GSB9	23 09		116	-	-45				
072	PRTX	-14		117	SIN	41				
073	RCLE	36 15		118	RCL9	36 09				
074	RCL8	36 08		119	x	-35				
075	RCL4	36 04		120	ABS	16 31				
076	RCLI	36 46		121	RCLD	36 14				
077	GSB8	23 08		122	÷	-24				
078	PRTX	-14		123	STO2	35 02				
079	STOD	35 14		124	→HMS	16 35				
080	X≷Y	-41		125	PRTX	-14				
081	GSB9	23 09		126	P≷S	16-51				
082	STOE	35 15		127	RTN	24				
083	PRTX	-14		128	*LBLE	21 15				
084	RTN	24		129	P≷S	16-51				
085	*LBLb	21 16 12		130	RCL1	36 01				
086	P≷S	16-51		131	RCLC	36 13				
087	STO0	35 00		132	1	01				
088	R/S	51		133	8	08				
089	*LBLb	21 16 12		134	0	00				
090	STO1	35 01		135	+	-55				

Program 3.11

Entries for steps 6–12, 18–23, 31–36, 42–46, 101–5, 111–15, 122–26, 133–38, 141–45, 154–59, 164–70, 198–203, and 209–13 are to be replaced as shown in the discussion of customized programs earlier in this appendix.

	81.	HLT		3.	3		1.	1
	86.	RST		6.	6		8.	8
	46.	LBL		65.	×	80	39.	P/R
	11.	A		43.	RCL		65.	×
	25.	CLR		0.	0		43.	RCL
	5.	5	40	4.	4		1.	1
	5.	5		45.	Y×		9.	9
	93.	.		93.	.		33.	COS
	0.	0		5.	5		95.	=
10	8.	8		1.	1		22.	INV
	4.	4		4.	4		39.	P/R
	2.	2		7.	7		43.	RCL
	65.	×		95.	=	90	0.	0
	43.	RCL		42.	STO		0.	0
	0.	0		0.	0		98.	PRT
	4.	4	50	1.	1		56.	RTN
	45.	Y×		56.	RTN		43.	RCL
	93.	.		46.	LBL		1.	1
	0.	0		13.	C		8.	8
20	8.	8		43.	RCL		98.	PRT
	6.	6		0.	0		86.	RST
	5.	5		42.	STO		46.	LBL
	94.	+/-		0.	0	100	15.	E
	95.	=		0.	0		93.	.
	42.	STO	60	43.	RCL		6.	6
	0.	0		0.	0		8.	8
	8.	8		8.	8		0.	0
	56.	RTN		39.	P/R		4.	4
	46.	LBL		48.	EXC		65.	×
30	12.	B		0.	0		43.	RCL
	1.	1		0.	0		0.	0
	93.	.		85.	+		4.	4
	3.	3		43.	RCL	110	45.	Y×
	8.	8		0.	0		93.	.
			70	1.	1		7.	7
				95.	=		7.	7
				48.	EXC		6.	6
				0.	0		1.	1
				0.	0		95.	=
				22.	INV		42.	STO
				39.	P/R		9.	9
				42.	STO		8.	8
						120	65.	×

53.	(	
93.	.	
7.	7	
8.	8	
1.	1	
9.	9	
85.	+	
43.	RCL	
0.	0	
130 4.	4	
23.	LNX	
65.	×	
93.	.	
2.	2	
5.	5	
4.	4	
1.	1	
94.	+/-	
54.	)	
140 55.	÷	
93.	.	
8.	8	
3.	3	
4.	4	
2.	2	
95.	=	
42.	STO	
9.	9	
9.	9	
150 43.	RCL	
0.	0	
4.	4	
65.	×	
93.	.	
0.	0	
5.	5	
3.	3	
9.	9	
94.	+/-	
160 95.	=	
22.	INV	
23.	LNX	
65.	×	

5.	5	
3.	3	
93.	.	
0.	0	
0.	0	
2.	2	
170 5.	5	
95.	=	
42.	STO	
0.	0	
2.	2	
75.	-	
1.	1	
8.	8	
0.	0	
95.	=	
180 94.	+/-	
42.	STO	
0.	0	
8.	8	
56.	RTN	
46.	LBL	
14.	D	
1.	1	
8.	8	
0.	0	
190 55.	÷	
43.	RCL	
0.	0	
2.	2	
95.	=	
42.	STO	
0.	0	
3.	3	
1.	1	
93.	.	
200 2.	2	
7.	7	
3.	3	
5.	5	
65.	×	
43.	RCL	
0.	0	

4.	4	
45.	Yˣ	
93.	.	
210 5.	5	
8.	8	
2.	2	
8.	8	
95.	=	
42.	STO	
0.	0	
1.	1	
56.	RTN	
46.	LBL	
220 18.	C'	
42.	STO	
1.	1	
9.	9	
56.	RTN	

Program 3.12

#			#			#		
	46.	LBL		43.	RCL		2.	2
	10.	E'		0.	0		43.	RCL
	43.	RCL		7.	7		0.	0
	0.	0		44.	SUM	90	7.	7
	0.	0		0.	0		22.	INV
	56.	RTN		4.	4		44.	SUM
	46.	LBL	50	1.	1		0.	0
	11.	A		46.	LBL		4.	4
	47.	CMS		87.	?'		1.	1
10	25.	CLR		44.	SUM		94.	+/-
	56.	RTN		0.	0		41.	GTO
	46.	LBL		0.	0		87.	?'
	12.	B		10.	E'		46.	LBL
	42.	STO		56.	RTN	100	14.	D
	0.	0		46.	LBL		43.	RCL
	6.	6		16.	A'		0.	0
	56.	RTN	60	23.	LNX		2.	2
	46.	LBL		42.	STO		75.	-
	13.	C		0.	0		43.	RCL
20	23.	LNX		7.	7		0.	0
	42.	STO		22.	INV		1.	1
	0.	0		44.	SUM		40.	X²
	7.	7		0.	0		55.	÷
	44.	SUM		3.	3	110	10.	E'
	0.	0		40.	X²		95.	=
	3.	3		22.	INV		20.	1/x
	40.	X²	70	44.	SUM		42.	STO
	44.	SUM		0.	0		1.	1
	0.	0		5.	5		0.	0
30	5.	5		43.	RCL		65.	×
	43.	RCL		0.	0		53.	(
	0.	0		6.	6		43.	RCL
	6.	6		22.	INV		0.	0
	44.	SUM		44.	SUM	120	4.	4
	0.	0		0.	0		75.	-
	1.	1		1.	1		43.	RCL
	49.	PRD	80	49.	PRD		0.	0
	0.	0		0.	0		1.	1
	7.	7		7.	7		65.	×
40	40.	X²		40.	X²		43.	RCL
	44.	SUM		22.	INV		0.	0
	0.	0		44.	SUM		3.	3
	2.	2		0.	0		55.	÷

130	10.	E'	43.	RCL	40.	X²
	54.	)	0.	0	95.	=
	42.	STO	8.	8	42.	STO
	1.	1	95.	=	1.	1
	1.	1	56.	RTN	220 2.	2
	95.	=	46.	LBL	56.	RTN
	42.	STO	18.	C'		
	0.	0	180 65.	x		
	8.	8	43.	RCL		
	94.	+/-	0.	0		
140	65.	x	8.	8		
	43.	RCL	95.	=		
	0.	0	22.	INV		
	1.	1	23.	LNX		
	85.	+	65.	x		
	43.	RCL	43.	RCL		
	0.	0	0.	0		
	3.	3	190 9.	9		
	95.	=	95.	=		
	55.	÷	56.	RTN		
150	10.	E'	46.	LBL		
	95.	=	15.	E		
	22.	INV	43.	RCL		
	23.	LNX	1.	1		
	42.	STO	0.	0		
	0.	0	65.	x		
	9.	9	53.	(		
	56.	RTN	200 43.	RCL		
	46.	LBL	0.	0		
	19.	D'	5.	5		
160	43.	RCL	75.	-		
	0.	0	43.	RCL		
	8.	8	0.	0		
	56.	RTN	3.	3		
	46.	LBL	40.	X²		
	17.	B'	55.	÷		
	55.	÷	10.	E'		
	43.	RCL	210 54.	)		
	0.	0	20.	1/X		
	9.	9	65.	x		
170	95.	=	43.	RCL		
	23.	LNX	1.	1		
	55.	÷	1.	1		

Program 3.13

	46.	LBL		1.	1		22.	INV
	11.	A		46.	LBL		44.	SUM
	47.	CMS		87.	1°		0.	0
	25.	CLR		44.	SUM	90	4.	4
	56.	RTN		0.	0		1.	1
	46.	LBL		0.	0		94.	+/-
	12.	B	50	43.	RCL		41.	GTO
	42.	STO		0.	0		87.	1°
	0.	0		0.	0		46.	LBL
10	6.	6		56.	RTN		14.	D
	56.	RTN		46.	LBL		43.	RCL
	46.	LBL		16.	H°		0.	0
	13.	C		42.	STO		2.	2
	42.	STO		0.	0	100	75.	–
	0.	0		7.	7		43.	RCL
	7.	7		22.	INV		0.	0
	44.	SUM	60	44.	SUM		1.	1
	0.	0		0.	0		40.	X²
	3.	3		3.	3		55.	÷
20	40.	X²		40.	X²		43.	RCL
	44.	SUM		22.	INV		0.	0
	0.	0		44.	SUM		0.	0
	5.	5		0.	0		95.	=
	43.	RCL		5.	5	110	20.	1/X
	0.	0		43.	RCL		42.	STO
	6.	6		0.	0		1.	1
	23.	LNX	70	6.	6		0.	0
	44.	SUM		23.	LNX		65.	×
	0.	0		22.	INV		53.	(
30	1.	1		44.	SUM		43.	RCL
	49.	PRD		0.	0		0.	0
	0.	0		1.	1		4.	4
	7.	7		49.	PRD		75.	–
	40.	X²		0.	0	120	43.	RCL
	44.	SUM		7.	7		0.	0
	0.	0		40.	X²		1.	1
	2.	2	80	22.	INV		65.	×
	43.	RCL		44.	SUM		43.	RCL
	0.	0		0.	0		0.	0
40	7.	7		2.	2		3.	3
	44.	SUM		43.	RCL		55.	÷
	0.	0		0.	0		43.	RCL
	4.	4		7.	7	130	0.	0

	0.	0		5.	5	8.	8
	54.	)		75.	-	85.	÷
	42.	STO		43.	RCL	43.	RCL
	1.	1		0.	0	220 0.	0
	1.	1		3.	3	9.	9
	95.	=		40.	X²	95.	=
	42.	STO	180	55.	÷	56.	RTN
	0.	0		43.	RCL		
	8.	8		0.	0		
140	94.	+/-		0.	0		
	65.	×		54.	)		
	43.	RCL		20.	1/X		
	0.	0		65.	×		
	1.	1		43.	RCL		
	85.	+		1.	1		
	43.	RCL		1.	1		
	0.	0	190	40.	X²		
	3.	3		95.	=		
	95.	=		42.	STO		
150	55.	÷		1.	1		
	43.	RCL		2.	2		
	0.	0		56.	RTN		
	0.	0		46.	LBL		
	95.	=		17.	B'		
	42.	STO		75.	-		
	0.	0		43.	RCL		
	9.	9	200	0.	0		
	56.	RTN		9.	9		
	46.	LBL		95.	=		
160	19.	D'		55.	÷		
	43.	RCL		43.	RCL		
	0.	0		0.	0		
	8.	8		8.	8		
	56.	RTN		95.	=		
	46.	LBL		22.	INV		
	15.	E		23.	LNX		
	43.	RCL	210	56.	RTN		
	1.	1		46.	LBL		
	0.	0		18.	C'		
170	65.	×		23.	LNX		
	53.	(		65.	×		
	43.	RCL		43.	RCL		
	0.	0		0.	0		

Program 3.14

The keys f RAD should be pressed before this program is recorded.			043	ST+i	35-55 45	089	GTO3	22 03
			044	X⇄Y	-41	090	2	02
			045	DSZI	16 25 46	091	RCLE	36 15
			046	ST+i	35-55 45	092	÷	-24
001	*LBLa	21 16 11	047	RCLC	36 13	093	x	-35
002	CLRG	16-53	048	ENT↑	-21	094	X⇄Y	-41
003	P⇄S	16-51	049	DSZI	16 25 46	095	LSTX	16-63
004	CLRG	16-53	050	GTO1	22 01	096	x	-35
005	RAD	16-22	051	1	01	097	*LBL4	21 04
006	RTN	24	052	ST+0	35-55 00	098	X⇄Y	-41
007	*LBLA	21 11	053	RCLE	36 15	099	GSB5	23 05
008	2	02	054	RCL0	36 00	100	R↓	-31
009	x	-35	055	X≤Y?	16-35	101	GSB5	23 05
010	STOB	35 12	056	GTO0	22 00	102	F0?	16 23 00
011	X⇄Y	-41	057	9	09	103	SPC	16-11
012	STOE	35 15	058	1/X	52	104	DSZI	16 25 46
013	RTN	24	059	RTN	24	105	GTO2	22 02
014	*LBLB	21 12	060	*LBL0	21 00	106	RTN	24
015	STOD	35 14	061	R/S	51	107	*LBL3	21 03
016	1	01	062	GTOC	22 13	108	X⇄Y	-41
017	STO0	35 00	063	*LBLd	21 16 14	109	→P	34
018	RTN	24	064	SF1	16 21 01	110	2	02
019	*LBLC	21 13	065	RCLB	36 12	111	RCLE	36 15
020	STOC	35 13	066	STOI	35 46	112	÷	-24
021	RCLB	36 12	067	GTO2	22 02	113	x	-35
022	STOI	35 46	068	*LBLD	21 14	114	GTO4	22 04
023	*LBL1	21 01	069	CF1	16 22 01	115	*LBLE	21 15
024	CLX	-51	070	RCLB	36 12	116	CF2	16 22 02
025	RCL0	36 00	071	STOI	35 46	117	STO0	35 00
026	RCLI	36 46	072	*LBL2	21 02	118	RCLB	36 12
027	RCLB	36 12	073	RCLI	36 46	119	STOI	35 46
028	-	-45	074	RCLB	36 12	120	CLX	-51
029	2	02	075	-	-45	121	*LBL6	21 06
030	CHS	-22	076	2	02	122	RCLI	36 46
031	÷	-24	077	CHS	-22	123	RCLB	36 12
032	RCLD	36 14	078	÷	-24	124	-	-45
033	+	-55	079	RCLD	36 14	125	2	02
034	RCLE	36 15	080	+	-55	126	CHS	-22
035	÷	-24	081	FIX	-11	127	÷	-24
036	x	-35	082	DSP0	-63 00	128	RCLD	36 14
037	2	02	083	GSB5	23 05	129	+	-55
038	x	-35	084	DSP4	-63 04	130	X=0?	16-43
039	Pi	16-24	085	RCLi	36 45	131	SF2	16 21 02
040	x	-35	086	DSZI	16 25 46	132	2	02
041	X⇄Y	-41	087	RCLi	36 45	133	x	-35
042	→R	44	088	F1?	16 23 01	134	Pi	16-24

380

Program 3.15

135	x	-35
136	RCL0	36 00
137	x	-35
138	RCLE	36 15
139	÷	-24
140	1	01
141	F2?	16 23 02
142	GSB0	23 00
143	→R	44
144	RCLi	36 45
145	x	-35
146	X⇄Y	-41
147	DSZI	16 25 46
148	RCLi	36 45
149	x	-35
150	+	-55
151	RCLE	36 15
152	÷	-24
153	2	02
154	x	-35
155	+	-55
156	DSZI	16 25 46
157	GTO6	22 06
158	GSB5	23 05
159	F0?	16 23 00
160	SPC	16-11
161	RTN	24
162	*LBL0	21 00
163	CLX	-51
164	.	-62
165	5	05
166	RTN	24
167	*LBL5	21 05
168	F0?	16 23 00
169	PRTX	-14
170	F0?	16 23 00
171	RTN	24
172	R/S	51
173	RTN	24

	56.	RTN	
	46.	LBL	
	33.	COS	
	1.	1	
	44.	SUM	
	1.	1	
	0.	0	
	43.	RCL	
	1.	1	
10	2.	2	
	65.	x	
	43.	RCL	
	1.	1	
	0.	0	
	65.	x	
	43.	RCL	
	1.	1	
	3.	3	
	95.	=	
20	60.	IFL	
	1.	1	
	42.	STO	
	33.	COS	
	41.	GTO	
	46.	LBL	
	42.	STO	
	32.	SIN	
	46.	LBL	
	46.	LBL	
30	65.	x	
	43.	RCL	
	1.	1	
	1.	1	
	95.	=	
	56.	RTN	
	46.	LBL	
	12.	B	
	44.	SUM	
	1.	1	
40	4.	4	
	65.	x	
	43.	RCL	
	0.	0	

	0.	0	
	95.	=	
	42.	STO	
	1.	1	
	1.	1	
	51.	SBR	
50	33.	COS	
	44.	SUM	
	0.	0	
	1.	1	
	60.	IFL	
	0.	0	
	87.	1'	
	51.	SBR	
	33.	COS	
	44.	SUM	
60	0.	0	
	2.	2	
	51.	SBR	
	33.	COS	
	44.	SUM	
	0.	0	
	3.	3	
	51.	SBR	
	33.	COS	
	44.	SUM	
70	0.	0	
	4.	4	
	51.	SBR	
	33.	COS	
	44.	SUM	
	0.	0	
	5.	5	
	51.	SBR	
	33.	COS	
	44.	SUM	
	0.	0	
	6.	6	
	51.	SBR	
	33.	COS	
	44.	SUM	
80	0.	0	
	7.	7	

	51.	SBR		0.	0		0.	U
	33.	COS		9.	9		4.	-
	44.	SUM		56.	RTN		98.	PRT
90	0.	0		75.	-		56.	RTN
	8.	8		1.	1		46.	LBL
	8.	8		95.	=		18.	C'
	46.	LBL		42.	STO		43.	RCL
	52.	EE		1.	1	180	0.	0
	94.	+/-		0.	0		5.	5
	44.	SUM		85.	+		98.	PRT
	1.	1	140	1.	1		56.	RTN
	0.	0		95.	=		43.	RCL
	1.	1		56.	RTN		0.	0
100	44.	SUM		46.	LBL		6.	6
	1.	1		13.	C		56.	RTN
	3.	3		50.	STF		46.	LBL
	43.	RCL		1.	1		19.	D'
	1.	1		56.	RTN	190	43.	RCL
	3.	3		46.	LBL		0.	0
	56.	RTN		14.	D		7.	7
	46.	LBL	150	50.	STF		56.	RTN
	87.	I'		0.	0		43.	RCL
	1.	1		56.	RTN		0.	0
110	41.	GTO		46.	LBL		8.	8
	52.	EE		16.	A'		56.	RTN
	46.	LBL		43.	RCL		46.	LBL
	11.	A		0.	0		15.	E
	42.	STO		1.	1	200	47.	CMS
	0.	0		98.	PRT		1.	1
	9.	9		56.	RTN		42.	STO
	20.	1/x	160	43.	RCL		1.	1
	65.	x		0.	0		3.	3
	2.	2		2.	2		9.	9
120	65.	x		98.	PRT		0.	0
	42.	STO		56.	RTN		33.	COS
	0.	0		46.	LBL		20.	1/x
	0.	0		17.	B'		0.	0
	59.	π		43.	RCL	210	57.	FIX
	95.	=		0.	0		4.	4
	42.	STO		3.	3		86.	RST
	1.	1	170	98.	PRT		46.	LBL
	2.	2		56.	RTN		10.	E'
	43.	RCL		43.	RCL		43.	RCL

Program 3.16

Entries for steps 127–31, 133–37, 140–44, 147–51, 156–61, 163–69, and 192–96 are to be replaced as shown in the discussion of customized programs earlier in this appendix.

Step	Instr	Code
001	*LBLA	21 11
002	STO7	35 07
003	R/S	51
004	*LBLA	21 11
005	STO8	35 08
006	R/S	51
007	*LBLA	21 11
008	STO9	35 09
009	R/S	51
010	*LBLA	21 11
011	COS	42
012	X²	53
013	STOA	35 11
014	RCL9	36 09
015	1	01
016	→R	44
017	X²	53
018	X⇄Y	-41
019	X²	53
020	RCLA	36 11
021	x	-35
022	+	-55
023	√X	54
024	RCL7	36 07
025	X⇄Y	-41
026	÷	-24
027	STO7	35 07
028	RCL9	36 09
029	X⇄Y	-41
030	→R	44
031	RCL8	36 08
032	-	-45
033	→P	34
034	STO5	35 05
035	PRTX	-14
036	RCL7	36 07
037	X²	53
038	RCL8	36 08
039	X²	53
040	-	-45
041	RCL5	36 05
042	X²	53
043	-	-45
044	2	02
045	÷	-24
046	RCL8	36 08
047	÷	-24
048	RCL5	36 05
049	÷	-24
050	COS⁻¹	16 42
051	STO6	35 06
052	PRTX	-14
053	RTN	24
054	*LBLB	21 12
055	*LBLC	21 13
056	STO2	35 02
057	R/S	51
058	*LBLB	21 12
059	*LBLC	21 13
060	STO1	35 01
061	R/S	51
062	*LBLB	21 12
063	SF1	16 21 01
064	GSB0	23 00
065	-	-45
066	GSB9	23 09
067	1	01
068	8	08
069	0	00
070	+	-55
071	GSB9	23 09
072	STO6	35 06
073	1	01
074	8	08
075	0	00
076	-	-45
077	GSB9	23 09
078	PRTX	-14
079	R/S	51
080	*LBLC	21 13
081	CF1	16 22 01
082	GSB0	23 00
083	+	-55

#	Code		#	Code		#	Code	
084	GSB9	23 09	130	6	06	176	8	
085	1	01	131	1	01	177	0	
086	8	08	132	Yˣ	31	178	X⇄Y	-4
087	0	00	133	.	-62	179	÷	-2
088	+	-55	134	6	06	180	.	-6
089	GSB9	23 09	135	8	08	181	0	
090	STO6	35 06	136	0	00	182	1	
091	1	01	137	4	04	183	7	
092	8	08	138	x	-35	184	5	
093	0	00	139	STOB	35 12	185	x	-3
094	-	-45	140	.	-62	186	P⇄S	16-5
095	GSB9	23 09	141	7	07	187	STO9	35 0
096	PRTX	-14	142	8	08	188	P⇄S	16-5
097	RTN	24	143	1	01	189	RCLC	36 1
098	*LBL9	21 09	144	9	09	190	RCLB	36 1
099	3	03	145	RCL5	36 05	191	x	-3
100	6	06	146	LN	32	192	.	-6
101	0	00	147	.	-62	193	8	
102	→R	44	148	2	02	194	3	
103	→P	34	149	5	05	195	4	
104	X⇄Y	-41	150	4	04	196	2	
105	X<0?	16-45	151	1	01	197	÷	-2
106	+	-55	152	x	-35	198	STOE	35 1
107	RTN	24	153	-	-45	199	RTN	2
108	*LBL0	21 00	154	STOC	35 13	200	*LBLa	21 16 1
109	STO0	35 00	155	RCL5	36 05	201	R/S	5
110	+	-55	156	.	-62	202	*LBLa	21 16 1
111	RCL2	36 02	157	0	00	203	→R	4
112	+	-55	158	5	05	204	STO4	35 0
113	GSB9	23 09	159	3	03	205	X⇄Y	-4
114	STOA	35 11	160	9	09	206	STOI	35 4
115	RCL6	36 06	161	CHS	-22	207	RTN	2
116	RTN	24	162	x	-35	208	R/S	5
117	*LBLD	21 14	163	5	05			
118	P⇄S	16-51	164	3	03			
119	STO0	35 00	165	.	-62			
120	R/S	51	166	0	00			
121	*LBLD	21 14	167	0	00			
122	STO1	35 01	168	2	02			
123	P⇄S	16-51	169	5	05			
124	RTN	24	170	LN	32			
125	*LBLE	21 15	171	+	-55			
126	RCL5	36 05	172	eˣ	33			
127	.	-62	173	STO3	35 03			
128	7	07	174	RCL3	36 03			
129	7	07	175	1	01			

Entries for steps 4–8, 15–20, 31–35, 46–51, 62–66, 77–82, and 93–97 are to be replaced as shown in the discussion of customized programs earlier in this appendix.

001	*LBLA	21 11	039	RCL9	36 09	085	P⇄S	16-51
002	DSP4	-63 04	040	P⇄S	16-51	086	RCL9	36 09
003	RAD	16-22	041	RCL3	36 03	087	P⇄S	16-51
004	.	-62	042	x	-35	088	RCL3	36 03
005	3	03	043	3	03	089	x	-35
006	3	03	044	x	-35	090	6	06
007	9	09	045	COS	42	091	x	-35
008	3	03	046	.	-62	092	COS	42
009	P⇄S	16-51	047	0	00	093	.	-62
010	RCL9	36 09	048	4	04	094	0	00
011	P⇄S	16-51	049	4	04	095	0	00
012	RCL3	36 03	050	2	02	096	6	06
013	x	-35	051	CHS	-22	097	3	03
014	COS	42	052	x	-35	098	x	-35
015	.	-62	053	+	-55	099	+	-55
016	3	03	054	P⇄S	16-51	100	RCLE	36 15
017	5	05	055	RCL9	36 09	101	x	-35
018	4	04	056	P⇄S	16-51	102	RCLB	36 12
019	6	06	057	RCL3	36 03	103	+	-55
020	CHS	-22	058	x	-35	104	RCL6	36 06
021	x	-35	059	4	04	105	RCL3	36 03
022	+	-55	060	x	-35	106	+	-55
023	P⇄S	16-51	061	COS	42	107	X⇄Y	-41
024	RCL9	36 09	062	.	-62	108	DEG	16-21
025	P⇄S	16-51	063	0	00	109	→R	44
026	RCL3	36 03	064	1	01	110	RCL4	36 04
027	x	-35	065	5	05	111	+	-55
028	2	02	066	5	05	112	X⇄Y	-41
029	x	-35	067	x	-35	113	RCLI	36 46
030	COS	42	068	+	-55	114	+	-55
031	.	-62	069	P⇄S	16-51	115	X⇄Y	-41
032	0	00	070	RCL9	36 09	116	→P	34
033	6	06	071	P⇄S	16-51	117	STO2	35 02
034	3	03	072	RCL3	36 03	118	X⇄Y	-41
035	9	09	073	x	-35	119	X<0?	16-45
036	x	-35	074	5	05	120	GSB1	23 01
037	+	-55	075	x	-35	121	P⇄S	16-51
038	P⇄S	16-51	076	COS	42	122	RCL0	36 00
			077	.	-62	123	P⇄S	16-51
			078	0	00	124	-	-45
			079	1	01	125	.	-62
			080	8	08	126	5	05
			081	3	03	127	X>Y?	16-34
			082	CHS	-22	128	GTO2	22 02
			083	x	-35	129	X⇄Y	-41
			084	+	-55	130	PSE	16 51

(CONTINUED)   385

131	2	02	177	0	00				
132	÷	-24	178	-	-45				
133	ST-3	35-45 03	179	DSP2	-63 02				
134	GTOA	22 11	180	PRTX	-14				
135	*LBL2	21 02	181	RTN	24				
136	RCL2	36 02	182	*LBL4	21 04				
137	P⇄S	16-51	183	X⇄Y	-41				
138	RCL1	36 01	184	3	03	001	*LBLA	21 11
139	P⇄S	16-51	185	6	06	002	ST07	35 07
140	X⇄Y	-41	186	0	00	003	R/S	51
141	÷	-24	187	+	-55	004	*LBLA	21 11
142	→HMS	16 35	188	DSP2	-63 02	005	ST08	35 08
143	DSP4	-63 04	189	PRTX	-14	006	R/S	51
144	PRTX	-14	190	RTN	24	007	*LBLA	21 11
145	RTN	24	191	*LBLC	21 13	008	ST09	35 09
146	*LBL1	21 01	192	RCL2	36 02	009	R/S	51
147	3	03	193	PRTX	-14	010	*LBLA	21 11
148	6	06	194	SPC	16-11	011	P⇄S	16-51
149	0	00	195	RTN	24	012	ST04	35 04
150	+	-55				013	P⇄S	16-51
151	RTN	24				014	COS	42
152	*LBLB	21 12				015	X²	53
153	RCL6	36 06				016	STOA	35 11
154	RCL3	36 03				017	RCL9	36 09
155	+	-55				018	1	01
156	RCL1	36 01				019	→R	44
157	-	-45				020	X²	53
158	RCL0	36 00				021	X⇄Y	-41
159	-	-45				022	X²	53
160	3	03				023	RCLA	36 11
161	6	06				024	x	-35
162	0	00				025	+	-55
163	X≤Y?	16-35				026	√X	54
164	GTO3	22 03				027	RCL7	36 07
165	X⇄Y	-41				028	X⇄Y	-41
166	0	00				029	÷	-24
167	X>Y?	16-34				030	ST07	35 07
168	GTO4	22 04				031	RCL9	36 09
169	X⇄Y	-41				032	X⇄Y	-41
170	DSP2	-63 02				033	→R	44
171	PRTX	-14				034	RCL8	36 08
172	RTN	24				035	-	-45
173	*LBL3	21 03				036	→P	34
174	X⇄Y	-41				037	ST05	35 05
175	3	03				038	PRTX	-14
176	6	06				039	RCL7	36 07

Entries for steps 101–5, 107–12, 119–24, and 127–33 are to be replaced as shown in the discussion of customized programs earlier in this appendix.

040	X²		53	086	X⇄Y		-41	132	2		02
041	RCL8	36	08	087	X<0?	16	-45	133	5		05
042	X²		53	088	+		-55	134	LN		32
043	-		-45	089	RTN		24	135	+		-55
044	RCL5	36	05	090	*LBL0	21	00	136	eˣ		33
045	X²		53	091	ST00	35	00	137	1		01
046	-		-45	092	+		-55	138	8		08
047	2		02	093	RCL2	36	02	139	0		00
048	÷		-24	094	+		-55	140	X⇄Y		-41
049	RCL8	36	08	095	GSB9	23	09	141	-		-45
050	÷		-24	096	STOA	35	11	142	ST06	35	06
051	RCL5	36	05	097	RCL6	36	06	143	RCL6	36	06
052	÷		-24	098	RTN		24	144	RCL5	36	05
053	COS⁻¹	16	42	099	*LBLD	21	14	145	→R		44
054	ST06	35	06	100	RCL5	36	05	146	RCL8	36	08
055	PRTX		-14	101	.		-62	147	+		-55
056	RTN		24	102	5		05	148	→P		34
057	*LBLB	21	12	103	8		08	149	ST07	35	07
058	*LBLC	21	13	104	2		02	150	RCL5	36	05
059	ST02	35	02	105	8		08	151	X²		53
060	R/S		51	106	Yˣ		31	152	RCL7	36	07
061	*LBLB	21	12	107	1		01	153	X²		53
062	*LBLC	21	13	108	.		-62	154	-		-45
063	ST01	35	01	109	2		02	155	RCL8	36	08
064	R/S		51	110	7		07	156	X²		53
065	*LBLB	21	12	111	3		03	157	-		-45
066	SF1	16 21	01	112	5		05	158	RCL7	36	07
067	GSB0	23	00	113	x		-35	159	÷		-24
068	-		-45	114	DSP2	-63	02	160	RCL8	36	08
069	GSB9	23	09	115	PRTX		-14	161	÷		-24
070	ST03	35	03	116	ST08	35	08	162	2		02
071	R/S		51	117	RTN		24	163	÷		-24
072	*LBLC	21	13	118	*LBLE	21	15	164	CHS		-22
073	CF1	16 22	01	119	.		-62	165	COS⁻¹	16	42
074	GSB0	23	00	120	0		00	166	ST09	35	09
075	+		-55	121	5		05	167	RCL7	36	07
076	GSB9	23	09	122	3		03	168	RCL9	36	09
077	ST03	35	03	123	9		09	169	COS		42
078	PRTX		-14	124	CHS		-22	170	X²		53
079	RTN		24	125	RCL5	36	05	171	RCL9	36	09
080	*LBL9	21	09	126	x		-35	172	SIN		41
081	3		03	127	5		05	173	X²		53
082	6		06	128	3		03	174	P⇄S	16	-51
083	0		00	129	.		-62	175	RCL4	36	04
084	→R		44	130	0		00	176	P⇄S	16	-51
085	→P		34	131	0		00	177	COS		42

178	X²	53
179	x	-35
180	+	-55
181	√X	54
182	x	-35
183	PRTX	-14
184	RTN	24
185	*LBLa	21 16 11
186	RCL9	36 09
187	PRTX	-14
188	RTN	24
189	*LBLb	21 16 12
190	RCL3	36 03
191	RCL6	36 06
192	+	-55
193	GSB9	23 09
194	STOA	35 11
195	GSB6	23 06
196	GSB9	23 09
197	R/S	51
198	*LBLb	21 16 12
199	-	-45
200	GSB9	23 09
201	PRTX	-14
202	RTN	24
203	*LBLc	21 16 13
204	RCL3	36 03
205	RCL6	36 06
206	-	-45
207	GSB9	23 09
208	STOA	35 11
209	GSB6	23 06
210	GSB9	23 09
211	R/S	51
212	*LBLc	21 16 13
213	-	-45
214	GSB9	23 09
215	PRTX	-14
216	RTN	24
217	*LBL6	21 06
218	RCL1	36 01
219	-	-45
220	RTN	24

Entries for steps 143–48, 150–54, 156–61, 165–170, 174–79, and 183–88 are to be replaced as shown in the discussion of customized programs earlier in this appendix.

	81.	HLT
	86.	RST
	46.	LBL
	11.	A
	1.	1
	44.	SUM
	1.	1
	8.	8
	53.	(
10	43.	RCL
	1.	1
	8.	8
	65.	×
	43.	RCL
	0.	0
	3.	3
	65.	×
	43.	RCL
	0.	0
20	2.	2
	54.	)
	33.	COS
	56.	RTN
	46.	LBL
	12.	B
	75.	-
	80.	IF+
	34.	TAN
	0.	0
30	85.	+
	46.	LBL
	34.	TAN
	3.	3
	6.	6
	0.	0
	95.	=

	22.	INV
	80.	IF+
	12.	B
40	56.	RTN
	46.	LBL
	13.	C
	25.	CLR
	43.	RCL
	0.	0
	1.	1
	46.	LBL
	29.	X"
	42.	STO
50	0.	0
	0.	0
	1.	1
	8.	8
	0.	0
	85.	+
	43.	RCL
	0.	0
	9.	9
	85.	+
60	43.	RCL
	0.	0
	2.	2
	95.	=
	42.	STO
	0.	0
	5.	5
	39.	P/R
	42.	STO
	1.	1
70	8.	8
	43.	RCL
	0.	0
	6.	6
	48.	EXC
	0.	0
	0.	0
	42.	STO
	1.	1
	7.	7

Line	Code	Key		Line	Code	Key		Line	Code	Key
80	43.	RCL			98.	PRT			0.	0
	0.	0			86.	RST			4.	4
	7.	7			46.	LBL			4.	4
	39.	P/R			87.	1'			2.	2
	44.	SUM			85.	+		170	94.	+/-
	1.	1			1.	1			65.	×
	8.	8			95.	=			11.	A
	43.	RCL		130	55.	÷			85.	+
	1.	1			2.	2			93.	.
	7.	7			95.	=			0.	0
90	44.	SUM			94.	+/-			1.	1
	0.	0			44.	SUM			5.	5
	0.	0			0.	0			5.	5
	43.	RCL			2.	2			0.	0
	1.	1			0.	0		180	65.	×
	8.	8			42.	STO			11.	A
	22.	INV			1.	1			85.	+
	39.	P/R		140	8.	8			93.	.
	75.	-			11.	A			0.	0
	43.	RCL			65.	×			1.	1
100	1.	1			93.	.			3.	3
	0.	0			3.	3			3.	3
	95.	=			5.	5			94.	+/-
	12.	B			4.	4			65.	×
	75.	-			6.	6		190	11.	A
	1.	1			94.	+/-			95.	=
	95.	=			85.	+			65.	×
	80.	IF+		150	93.	.			43.	RCL
	87.	''			3.	3			9.	9
	43.	RCL			3.	3			9.	9
110	0.	0			9.	9			85.	+
	0.	0			3.	3			43.	RCL
	56.	RTN			85.	+			9.	9
	55.	-			93.	.			8.	8
	43.	RCL			0.	0		200	95.	=
	1.	1			6.	6			41.	GTO
	1.	1			3.	3			29.	X°
	95.	=		160	9.	9			46.	LBL
	20.	1/X			0.	0			14.	D
	22.	INV			65.	×			43.	RCL
120	37.	DMS			11.	A			0.	0
	57.	FIX			85.	+			5.	5
	4.	4			93.	.			12.	B

```
     57.     FIX
210   1.     1
     56.     RTN
     85.     +
     43.     RCL
      1.     1
      6.     6
     85.     +
     43.     RCL
      0.     0
      5.     5
220  95.     =
     12.     B
     98.     PRT
     99.     PAP
     86.     RST
```

	Program 4.1						Program 4.2	
001	*LBLA	21 11	047	X²	53	001	*LBLA	21 11
002	DSP2	-63 02	048	RCL9	36 09	002	9	09
003	→HMS	16 35	049	÷	-24	003	STO0	35 00
004	EEX	-23	050	-	-45	004	STOI	35 46
005	2	02	051	÷	-24	005	1	01
006	÷	-24	052	STOA	35 11	006	*LBLa	21 16 11
007	HMS→	16 36	053	RCL6	36 06	007	R/S	51
008	P≷S	16-51	054	RCL9	36 09	008	ISZI	16 26 46
009	STO3	35 03	055	÷	-24	009	X≷Y	-41
010	P≷S	16-51	056	RCL4	36 04	010	STOi	35 45
011	RTN	24	057	RCL9	36 09	011	R↓	-31
012	*LBLB	21 12	058	÷	-24	012	ISZI	16 26 46
013	HMS→	16 36	059	RCLA	36 11	013	STOi	35 45
014	RCLI	36 46	060	x	-35	014	R↓	-31
015	X=0?	16-43	061	-	-45	015	1	01
016	GTO1	22 01	062	STOE	35 15	016	+	-55
017	R↓	-31	063	P≷S	16-51	017	GTOa	22 16 11
018	RCLI	36 46	064	RTN	24	018	*LBLE	21 15
019	-	-45	065	*LBLE	21 15	019	P≷S	16-51
020	P≷S	16-51	066	CLRG	16-53	020	WDTA	16-61
021	STO0	35 00	067	P≷S	16-51	021	RTN	24
022	*LBL2	21 02	068	CLRG	16-53	022	*LBLB	21 12
023	RCL3	36 03	069	P≷S	16-51	023	P≷S	16-51
024	RCL0	36 00	070	CLX	-51	024	RCL0	36 00
025	P≷S	16-51	071	RTN	24	025	STOE	35 15
026	Σ+	56	072	*LBLD	21 14	026	R↓	-31
027	RTN	24	073	HMS→	16 36	027	1	01
028	*LBL1	21 01	074	RCLI	36 46	028	2	02
029	R↓	-31	075	-	-45	029	÷	-24
030	STOI	35 46	076	STOD	35 14	030	INT	16 34
031	0	00	077	RCLA	36 11	031	1	01
032	P≷S	16-51	078	x	-35	032	7	07
033	STO0	35 00	079	RCLE	36 15	033	X≷Y	-41
034	GTO2	22 02	080	+	-55	034	-	-45
035	RTN	24	081	STOB	35 12	035	STO0	35 00
036	*LBLC	21 13	082	→HMS	16 35	036	P≷S	16-51
037	P≷S	16-51	083	DSP4	-63 04	037	STO0	35 00
038	RCL8	36 08	084	PRTX	-14	038	*LBLD	21 14
039	RCL4	36 04	085	RTN	24	039	1	01
040	RCL6	36 06				040	0	00
041	x	-35				041	STOI	35 46
042	RCL9	36 09				042	0	00
043	÷	-24				043	*LBLb	21 16 12
044	-	-45				044	R/S	51
045	RCL5	36 05				045	ISZI	16 26 46
046	RCL4	36 04				046	STOi	35 45

(CONTINUED) 391

Program 4.3

047	CLX	-51	001	*LBLA	21 11	047	P⇄S	16-51
048	5	05	002	.	-62	048	WDTA	16-61
049	X⇄Y	-41	003	5	05	049	R/S	51
050	1	01	004	-	-45			
051	+	-55	005	1	01			
052	X>Y?	16-34	006	2	02			
053	0	00	007	÷	-24			
054	GTOb	22 16 12	008	STO0	35 00			
055	*LBLC	21 13	009	3	03			
056	STO1	35 01	010	6	06			
057	R↓	-31	011	0	00			
058	STOD	35 14	012	x	-35			
059	R↓	-31	013	SIN	41			
060	STO3	35 03	014	STO1	35 01			
061	3	03	015	LSTX	16-63			
062	0	00	016	COS	42			
063	STOI	35 46	017	STO2	35 02			
064	RCL3	36 03	018	9	09			
065	8	08	019	STOI	35 46			
066	÷	-24	020	1	01			
067	INT	16 34	021	RTN	24			
068	RCL3	36 03	022	*LBLB	21 12			
069	+	-55	023	ISZI	16 26 46			
070	2	02	024	STO4	35 04			
071	÷	-24	025	RTN	24			
072	FRC	16 44	026	*LBLC	21 13			
073	X≠0?	16-42	027	STO5	35 05			
074	ISZI	16 26 46	028	CLX	-51			
075	RCL3	36 03	029	RCL2	36 02			
076	2	02	030	STx5	35-35 05			
077	X≠Y?	16-32	031	CLX	-51			
078	GTOc	22 16 13	032	RCL1	36 01			
079	RCL1	36 01	033	x	-35			
080	4	04	034	ST+5	35-55 05			
081	÷	-24	035	CLX	-51			
082	FRC	16 44	036	RCL0	36 00			
083	X≠0?	16-42	037	x	-35			
084	DSZI	16 25 46	038	ST+5	35-55 05			
085	DSZI	16 25 46	039	CLX	-51			
086	*LBLc	21 16 13	040	RCL5	36 05			
087	RCLI	36 46	041	+	-55			
088	STOE	35 15	042	RCL4	36 04			
089	GTOD	22 14	043	+	-55			
090	R/S	51	044	STOi	35 45			
			045	RTN	24			
			046	*LBLE	21 15			

001	*LBLA	21 11	047	*LBLC	21 13	093	÷	-24
002	8	08	048	GSB0	23 00	094	RCL9	36 09
003	÷	-24	049	GSB4	23 04	095	TAN	43
004	FRC	16 44	050	ST09	35 09	096	RCL0	36 00
005	X=0?	16-43	051	R↓	-31	097	COS	42
006	GTOd	22 16 14	052	GSB3	23 03	098	ST04	35 04
007	1	01	053	ST08	35 08	099	x	-35
008	6	06	054	RTN	24	100	R↑	16-31
009	x	-35	055	*LBLD	21 14	101	÷	-24
010	8	08	056	HMS→	16 36	102	-	-45
011	+	-55	057	X≠Y	-41	103	x	-35
012	STOI	35 46	058	HMS→	16 36	104	→P	34
013	P≠S	16-51	059	GTOa	22 16 11	105	CLX	-51
014	RCLi	36 45	060	*LBLE	21 15	106	1	01
015	ISZI	16 26 46	061	P≠S	16-51	107	8	08
016	RCLi	36 45	062	RCL7	36 07	108	0	00
017	*LBLe	21 16 15	063	x	-35	109	+	-55
018	ST09	35 09	064	6	06	110	ST02	35 02
019	R↓	-31	065	0	00	111	R/S	51
020	ST08	35 08	066	÷	-24	112	RCL0	36 00
021	P≠S	16-51	067	→R	44	113	SIN	41
022	RTN	24	068	RCL0	36 00	114	RCL9	36 09
023	*LBLd	21 16 14	069	+	-55	115	SIN	41
024	RCLE	36 15	070	X≠Y	-41	116	x	-35
025	RCLI	36 46	071	RCL4	36 04	117	RCL4	36 04
026	GTOe	22 16 15	072	÷	-24	118	RCL9	36 09
027	*LBLB	21 12	073	RCL1	36 01	119	COS	42
028	GSB0	23 00	074	X≠Y	-41	120	x	-35
029	GSB4	23 04	075	-	-45	121	RCL8	36 08
030	GTOb	22 16 12	076	X≠Y	-41	122	COS	42
031	*LBLA	21 11	077	P≠S	16-51	123	x	-35
032	RCLE	36 15	078	*LBLa	21 16 11	124	+	-55
033	ST00	35 00	079	ST00	35 00	125	SIN⁻	16 41
034	R↓	-31	080	X≠Y	-41	126	R/S	51
035	GSB0	23 00	081	ST01	35 01	127	HMS→	16 36
036	GSB3	23 03	082	ST-8	35-45 08	128	X≠Y	-41
037	*LBLb	21 16 12	083	P≠S	16-51	129	√X	54
038	P≠S	16-51	084	RCL6	36 06	130	6	06
039	RCL8	36 08	085	P≠S	16-51	131	2	02
040	+	-55	086	ST06	35 06	132	÷	-24
041	RCL9	36 09	087	RCL8	36 08	133	-	-45
042	P≠S	16-51	088	SIN	41	134	P≠S	16-51
043	ST09	35 09	089	RCL0	36 00	135	F1?	16 23 01
044	R↓	-31	090	SIN	41	136	GSB9	23 09
045	ST08	35 08	091	RCL8	36 08	137	F2?	16 23 02
046	RTN	24	092	TAN	43	138	GSB9	23 09

139	ENT↑		-21	185	DSZI	16 25 46	001	*LBLA	21 11
140	TAN		43	186	RCLi	36 45	002	P⇄S	16-51
141	1/X		52	187	+	-55	003	GSB0	23 00
142	6		06	188	P⇄S	16-51	004	GSB4	23 04
143	0		00	189	RTN	24	005	STO9	35 03
144	÷		-24	190	*LBL0	21 00	006	RCL5	36 05
145	-		-45	191	HMS→	16 36	007	GSB3	23 03
146	-		-45	192	ENT↑	-21	008	STO8	35 08
147	6		06	193	P⇄S	16-51	009	P⇄S	16-51
148	0		00	194	RCL6	36 06	010	RTN	24
149	x		-35	195	-	-45	011	*LBLB	21 12
150	P⇄S		16-51	196	STO7	35 07	012	P⇄S	16-51
151	STO3		35 03	197	R↓	-31	013	RCL5	36 05
152	P⇄S		16-51	198	STO6	35 06	014	GSB4	23 04
153	RTN		24	199	2	02	015	STOE	35 15
154	*LBL3		21 03	200	4	04	016	RCL5	36 05
155	1		01	201	÷	-24	017	GSB3	23 03
156	6		06	202	+	-55	018	STOD	35 14
157	GTO1		22 01	203	P⇄S	16-51	019	RCL9	36 03
158	*LBL4		21 04	204	RCL0	36 00	020	RCL8	36 08
159	2		02	205	P⇄S	16-51	021	P⇄S	16-51
160	2		02	206	-	-45	022	STO8	35 08
161	*LBL1		21 01	207	1	01	023	R↓	-31
162	STOI		35 46	208	6	06	024	STO9	35 09
163	R↓		-31	209	÷	-24	025	RTN	24
164	ENT↑		-21	210	STO5	35 05	026	*LBLD	21 14
165	ENT↑		-21	211	P⇄S	16-51	027	HMS→	16 36
166	P⇄S		16-51	212	RTN	24	028	X⇄Y	-41
167	RCLi		36 45	213	*LBL9	21 09	029	HMS→	16 36
168	x		-35	214	RCL5	36 05	030	GTOa	22 16 11
169	DSZI		16 25 46	215	RCLE	36 15	031	*LBLE	21 15
170	RCLi		36 45	216	x	-35	032	P⇄S	16-51
171	+		-55	217	RCLD	36 14	033	RCL7	36 07
172	x		-35	218	+	-55	034	x	-35
173	DSZI		16 25 46	219	F1?	16 23 01	035	6	06
174	RCLi		36 45	220	CHS	-22	036	0	00
175	+		-55	221	+	-55	037	÷	-24
176	x		-35	222	CF1	16 22 01	038	→R	44
177	DSZI		16 25 46	223	RTN	24	039	RCL0	36 00
178	RCLi		36 45	224	R/S	51	040	+	-55
179	+		-55				041	X⇄Y	-41
180	x		-35				042	RCL4	36 04
181	DSZI		16 25 46				043	÷	-24
182	RCLi		36 45				044	RCL1	36 01
183	+		-55				045	X⇄Y	-41
184	x		-35				046	-	-45

394

047	X≷Y	−41	093	COS	42	139	ENT↑	−21
048	P≷S	16-51	094	x	−35	140	ENT↑	−21
049	*LBLa	21 16 11	095	+	−55	141	RCLi	36 45
050	ST00	35 00	096	SIN⁻¹	16 41	142	x	−35
051	X≷Y	−41	097	R/S	51	143	DSZI	16 25 46
052	ST01	35 01	098	HMS→	16 36	144	RCLi	36 45
053	ST-8	35-45 08	099	X≷Y	−41	145	+	−55
054	P≷S	16-51	100	√X	54	146	x	−35
055	RCL6	36 06	101	6	06	147	DSZI	16 25 46
056	P≷S	16-51	102	2	02	148	RCLi	36 45
057	ST06	35 06	103	÷	−24	149	+	−55
058	RCL8	36 08	104	−	−45	150	x	−35
059	SIN	41	105	ENT↑	−21	151	DSZI	16 25 46
060	RCL0	36 00	106	COS	42	152	RCLi	36 45
061	SIN	41	107	RCLD	36 14	153	+	−55
062	RCL8	36 08	108	x	−35	154	x	−35
063	TAN	43	109	+	−55	155	DSZI	16 25 46
064	÷	−24	110	F1?	16 23 01	156	RCLi	36 45
065	RCL9	36 09	111	GSB9	23 09	157	+	−55
066	TAN	43	112	F2?	16 23 02	158	x	−35
067	RCL0	36 00	113	GSB9	23 09	159	DSZI	16 25 46
068	COS	42	114	ENT↑	−21	160	RCLi	36 45
069	ST04	35 04	115	TAN	43	161	+	−55
070	x	−35	116	1/X	52	162	RTN	24
071	R↑	16-31	117	6	06	163	*LBL0	21 00
072	÷	−24	118	0	00	164	HMS→	16 36
073	−	−45	119	÷	−24	165	ENT↑	−21
074	x	−35	120	−	−45	166	ENT↑	−21
075	→P	34	121	−	−45	167	RCL6	36 06
076	CLX	−51	122	6	06	168	−	−45
077	1	01	123	0	00	169	ST07	35 07
078	8	08	124	x	−35	170	R↓	−31
079	0	00	125	ST03	35 03	171	ST06	35 06
080	+	−55	126	P≷S	16-51	172	2	02
081	ST02	35 02	127	RTN	24	173	4	04
082	R/S	51	128	*LBL3	21 03	174	÷	−24
083	RCL0	36 00	129	1	01	175	+	−55
084	SIN	41	130	6	06	176	RCLE	36 15
085	RCL9	36 09	131	GTO1	22 01	177	X≷Y	−41
086	SIN	41	132	*LBL4	21 04	178	RCLD	36 14
087	x	−35	133	2	02	179	−	−45
088	RCL4	36 04	134	2	02	180	X<0?	16-45
089	RCL9	36 09	135	*LBL1	21 01	181	+	−55
090	COS	42	136	STOI	35 46	182	3	03
091	x	−35	137	R↓	−31	183	−	−45
092	RCL8	36 08	138	ENT↑	−21	184	3	03

Program 4.6

185	÷	-24	001	*LBL1	21 01	047	x	-35
186	STO5	35 05	002	RCL2	36 02	048	RCL2	36 02
187	RTN	24	003	RCL3	36 03	049	TAN	43
188	*LBL9	21 09	004	6	06	050	1/X	52
189	RCLE	36 15	005	0	00	051	STOB	35 12
190	F1?	16 23 01	006	÷	-24	052	RCL8	36 08
191	CHS	-22	007	CHS	-22	053	x	-35
192	+	-55	008	→R	44	054	+	-55
193	CF1	16 22 01	009	RCL0	36 00	055	RCLA	36 11
194	RTN	24	010	+	-55	056	TAN	43
195	R/S	51	011	X⇄Y	-41	057	1/X	52
			012	RCL4	36 04	058	STOC	35 13
			013	÷	-24	059	RCL6	36 06
			014	RCL1	36 01	060	x	-35
			015	-	-45	061	-	-45
			016	CHS	-22	062	RCLB	36 12
			017	RTN	24	063	RCLC	36 13
			018	*LBLA	21 11	064	-	-45
			019	P⇄S	16-51	065	÷	-24
			020	RCL2	36 02	066	STOD	35 14
			021	STOA	35 11	067	RCL8	36 08
			022	RCL0	36 00	068	-	-45
			023	RCL1	36 01	069	RCLB	36 12
			024	P⇄S	16-51	070	x	-35
			025	STO1	35 01	071	RCL5	36 05
			026	R↓	-31	072	÷	-24
			027	STO0	35 00	073	RCL9	36 09
			028	GSB1	23 01	074	+	-55
			029	STO9	35 09	075	STOE	35 15
			030	R↓	-31	076	RCLD	36 14
			031	STO8	35 08	077	→HMS	16 35
			032	P⇄S	16-51	078	DSP4	-63 04
			033	GSB1	23 01	079	PRTX	-14
			034	P⇄S	16-51	080	RCLE	36 15
			035	STO7	35 07	081	→HMS	16 35
			036	R↓	-31	082	PRTX	-14
			037	STO6	35 06	083	RTN	24
			038	RCL8	36 08	084	R/S	51
			039	+	-55			
			040	2	02			
			041	÷	-24			
			042	COS	42			
			043	STO5	35 05			
			044	RCL7	36 07			
			045	RCL9	36 09			
			046	-	-45			

Program 4.7

#			#			#		
001	*LBLA	21 11	047	RTN	24	093	RCL2	36 02
002	→HMS	16 35	048	*LBLC	21 13	094	x	-35
003	EEX	-23	049	P⇄S	16-51	095	STO5	35 05
004	2	02	050	RCL9	36 09	096	-	-45
005	÷	-24	051	RCL5	36 05	097	RCL0	36 00
006	HMS→	16 36	052	x	-35	098	P⇄S	16-51
007	P⇄S	16-51	053	RCL4	36 04	099	RCL9	36 09
008	STO3	35 03	054	X²	53	100	RCL2	36 02
009	P⇄S	16-51	055	-	-45	101	x	-35
010	RTN	24	056	P⇄S	16-51	102	RCL5	36 05
011	*LBLB	21 12	057	STO0	35 00	103	X²	53
012	HMS→	16 36	058	P⇄S	16-51	104	-	-45
013	RCLI	36 46	059	RCL9	36 09	105	x	-35
014	X=0?	16-43	060	RCL1	36 01	106	P⇄S	16-51
015	GTO1	22 01	061	x	-35	107	RCL1	36 01
016	R↓	-31	062	RCL4	36 04	108	P⇄S	16-51
017	RCLI	36 46	063	RCL5	36 05	109	X²	53
018	-	-45	064	x	-35	110	-	-45
019	P⇄S	16-51	065	-	-45	111	÷	-24
020	STO0	35 00	066	P⇄S	16-51	112	P⇄S	16-51
021	*LBL2	21 02	067	STO1	35 01	113	STO6	35 06
022	3	03	068	P⇄S	16-51	114	P⇄S	16-51
023	Yˣ	31	069	RCL9	36 09	115	STO3	35 03
024	ST+1	35-55 01	070	RCL8	36 08	116	P⇄S	16-51
025	RCL0	36 00	071	x	-35	117	RCL2	36 02
026	4	04	072	RCL4	36 04	118	RCL1	36 01
027	Yˣ	31	073	RCL6	36 06	119	RCL6	36 06
028	ST+2	35-55 02	074	x	-35	120	x	-35
029	RCL0	36 00	075	-	-45	121	-	-45
030	X²	53	076	P⇄S	16-51	122	RCL0	36 00
031	RCL3	36 03	077	STO2	35 02	123	÷	-24
032	x	-35	078	P⇄S	16-51	124	STO7	35 07
033	P⇄S	16-51	079	RCL9	36 09	125	P⇄S	16-51
034	ST+3	35-55 03	080	P⇄S	16-51	126	RCL6	36 06
035	P⇄S	16-51	081	RCL3	36 03	127	P⇄S	16-51
036	RCL3	36 03	082	P⇄S	16-51	128	RCL6	36 06
037	RCL0	36 00	083	x	-35	129	P⇄S	16-51
038	P⇄S	16-51	084	RCL5	36 05	130	RCL5	36 05
039	Σ+	56	085	RCL6	36 06	131	x	-35
040	RTN	24	086	x	-35	132	-	-45
041	*LBL1	21 01	087	-	-45	133	P⇄S	16-51
042	R↓	-31	088	P⇄S	16-51	134	RCL7	36 07
043	STOI	35 46	089	RCL0	36 00	135	P⇄S	16-51
044	0	00	090	x	-35	136	RCL4	36 04
045	P⇄S	16-51	091	STO4	35 04	137	x	-35
046	GTO2	22 02	092	RCL1	36 01	138	-	-45

(CONTINUED) 397

139	RCL9	36 09	185	STO1	35 01	001	*LBLA	21 11
140	÷	-24	186	P⇄S	16-51	002	GSB0	23 00
141	P⇄S	16-51	187	→HMS	16 35	003	GSB4	23 04
142	STO8	35 08	188	PRTX	-14	004	STO9	35 09
143	RCL7	36 07	189	RTN	24	005	R↓	-31
144	RCL6	36 06	190	*LBLa	21 16 11	006	GSB3	23 03
145	2	02	191	CLRG	16-53	007	STO8	35 08
146	x	-35	192	P⇄S	16-51	008	RTN	24
147	÷	-24	193	CLRG	16-53	009	*LBL3	21 03
148	CHS	-22	194	CLX	-51	010	1	01
149	RCLI	36 46	195	RTN	24	011	6	06
150	+	-55	196	*LBLb	21 16 12	012	GTO1	22 01
151	STOB	35 12	197	RTN	24	013	*LBL4	21 04
152	RCLA	36 11	198	*LBLb	21 16 12	014	2	02
153	2	02	199	+	-55	015	2	02
154	÷	-24	200	RTN	24	016	*LBL1	21 01
155	P⇄S	16-51	201	*LBLc	21 16 13	017	STOI	35 46
156	RCL3	36 03	202	+	-55	018	R↓	-31
157	÷	-24	203	COS	42	019	ENT↑	-21
158	-	-45	204	ABS	16 31	020	ENT↑	-21
159	STO8	35 08	205	CHS	-22	021	P⇄S	16-51
160	P⇄S	16-51	206	RTN	24	022	RCLi	36 45
161	→HMS	16 35	207	*LBLd	21 16 14	023	x	-35
162	PRTX	-14	208	+	-55	024	DSZI	16 25 46
163	HMS→	16 36	209	COS	42	025	RCLi	36 45
164	RCLB	36 12	210	ABS	16 31	026	+	-55
165	RCLI	36 46	211	RTN	24	027	x	-35
166	-	-45	212	*LBLe	21 16 15	028	DSZI	16 25 46
167	STOD	35 14	213	x	-35	029	RCLi	36 45
168	X²	53	214	6	06	030	+	-55
169	RCL6	36 06	215	0	00	031	x	-35
170	x	-35	216	÷	-24	032	DSZI	16 25 46
171	RCLD	36 14	217	STOA	35 11	033	RCLi	36 45
172	RCL7	36 07	218	RTN	24	034	+	-55
173	x	-35	219	*LBLD	21 14	035	x	-35
174	+	-55	220	P⇄S	16-51	036	DSZI	16 25 46
175	RCL8	36 08	221	RCL8	36 08	037	RCLi	36 45
176	+	-55	222	P⇄S	16-51	038	+	-55
177	RCLA	36 11	223	→HMS	16 35	039	x	-35
178	X²	53	224	RTN	24	040	DSZI	16 25 46
179	4	04				041	RCLi	36 45
180	÷	-24				042	+	-55
181	P⇄S	16-51				043	P⇄S	16-51
182	RCL3	36 03				044	RTN	24
183	÷	-24				045	*LBL0	21 00
184	+	-55				046	HMS→	16 36

047	ENT↑		-21	093	RCL1	36 01	139	RCL9	36 09
048	P⇄S	16-51		094	X⇄Y	-41	140	ABS	16 31
049	RCL6	36 06		095	-	-45	141	P⇄S	16-51
050	-		-45	096	STO1	35 01	142	RCL2	36 02
051	STO7	35 07		097	CLX	-51	143	P⇄S	16-51
052	R↓		-31	098	P⇄S	16-51	144	9	09
053	STO6	35 06		099	F1?	16 23 01	145	0	00
054	2		02	100	GSB9	23 09	146	X⇄Y	-41
055	4		04	101	F2?	16 23 02	147	-	-45
056	÷		-24	102	GSB9	23 09	148	F0?	16 23 00
057	+		-55	103	P⇄S	16-51	149	CHS	-22
058	P⇄S	16-51		104	RCL1	36 01	150	STO1	35 01
059	RCL0	36 00		105	+	-55	151	ABS	16 31
060	P⇄S	16-51		106	ENT↑	-21	152	X≤Y?	16-35
061	-		-45	107	TAN	43	153	GTO8	22 08
062	1		01	108	1/X	52	154	RCL1	36 01
063	6		06	109	6	06	155	RCL9	36 09
064	÷		-24	110	0	00	156	+	-55
065	STO5	35 05		111	÷	-24	157	→HMS	16 35
066	P⇄S	16-51		112	-	-45	158	CF0	16 22 00
067	RTN		24	113	STO2	35 02	159	PRTX	-14
068	*LBL9	21 09		114	P⇄S	16-51	160	RTN	24
069	RCL5	36 05		115	RTN	24	161	*LBL8	21 08
070	RCLE	36 15		116	*LBLD	21 14	162	RCL9	36 09
071	X		-35	117	RCL9	36 09	163	RCL1	36 01
072	RCLD	36 14		118	X>0?	16-44	164	+	-55
073	+		-55	119	GTOc	22 16 13	165	→HMS	16 35
074	F1?	16 23 01		120	GTOd	22 16 14	166	PRTX	-14
075	CHS		-22	121	RTN	24	167	RTN	24
076	+		-55	122	*LBLc	21 16 13	168	*LBLE	21 15
077	CF1	16 22 01		123	RCL9	36 09	169	RCL9	36 09
078	RTN		24	124	P⇄S	16-51	170	SF0	16 21 00
079	*LBLB	21 12		125	RCL2	36 02	171	CHS	-22
080	SF1	16 21 01		126	P⇄S	16-51	172	X>0?	16-44
081	GSB7	23 07		127	9	09	173	GTOc	22 16 13
082	RTN		24	128	0	00	174	GTOd	22 16 14
083	*LBLC	21 13		129	X⇄Y	-41	175	RTN	24
084	SF2	16 21 02		130	-	-45	176	*LBLe	21 16 15
085	GSB7	23 07		131	F0?	16 23 00	177	RCL8	36 08
086	RTN		24	132	CHS	-22	178	1	01
087	*LBL7	21 07		133	+	-55	179	→R	44
088	√X		54	134	→HMS	16 35	180	→P	34
089	6		06	135	PRTX	-14	181	X⇄Y	-41
090	2		02	136	CF0	16 22 00	182	X<0?	16-45
091	÷		-24	137	RTN	24	183	GSB2	23 02
092	P⇄S	16-51		138	*LBLd	21 16 14	184	GTO5	22 05

(CONTINUED) 399

185	*LBLb	21 16 12	001	*LBLA	21 11	047	DSZI	16 25 46
186	→HMS	16 35	002	RTN	24	048	RCLi	36 45
187	PRTX	-14	003	*LBLA	21 11	049	+	-55
188	RTN	24	004	STOE	35 15	050	x	-35
189	*LBL2	21 02	005	RTN	24	051	DSZI	16 25 46
190	3	03	006	*LBLB	21 12	052	RCLi	36 45
191	6	06	007	GSB0	23 00	053	+	-55
192	0	00	008	GSB4	23 04	054	P⇄S	16-51
193	+	-55	009	STO9	35 09	055	RTN	24
194	RTN	24	010	R↓	-31	056	*LBL0	21 00
195	*LBL5	21 05	011	GSB3	23 03	057	HMS→	16 36
196	ENT↑	-21	012	1	01	058	ENT↑	-21
197	ENT↑	-21	013	→R	44	059	P⇄S	16-51
198	1	01	014	→P	34	060	RCL6	36 06
199	8	08	015	X⇄Y	-41	061	-	-45
200	0	00	016	STO8	35 08	062	STO7	35 07
201	-	-45	017	→HMS	16 35	063	R↓	-31
202	X<0?	16-45	018	PRTX	-14	064	STO6	35 06
203	GTO6	22 06	019	RTN	24	065	2	02
204	R↓	-31	020	*LBL3	21 03	066	4	04
205	3	03	021	1	01	067	÷	-24
206	6	06	022	6	06	068	+	-55
207	0	00	023	GTO1	22 01	069	P⇄S	16-51
208	-	-45	024	*LBL4	21 04	070	RCL0	36 00
209	→HMS	16 35	025	2	02	071	P⇄S	16-51
210	PRTX	-14	026	2	02	072	-	-45
211	RTN	24	027	*LBL1	21 01	073	1	01
212	*LBL6	21 06	028	STOI	35 46	074	6	06
213	R↓	-31	029	R↓	-31	075	÷	-24
214	GTOb	22 16 12	030	ENT↑	-21	076	STO5	35 05
215	*LBLa	21 16 11	031	ENT↑	-21	077	P⇄S	16-51
216	HMS→	16 36	032	P⇄S	16-51	078	RTN	24
217	P⇄S	16-51	033	RCLi	36 45	079	*LBLC	21 13
218	STO1	35 01	034	x	-35	080	P⇄S	16-51
219	P⇄S	16-51	035	DSZI	16 25 46	081	STO0	35 00
220	RTN	24	036	RCLi	36 45	082	P⇄S	16-51
221	*LBLa	21 16 11	037	+	-55	083	RTN	24
222	RTN	24	038	x	-35	084	*LBLC	21 13
223	*LBLa	21 16 11	039	DSZI	16 25 46	085	+	-55
224	RTN	24	040	RCLi	36 45	086	P⇄S	16-51
			041	+	-55	087	STO0	35 00
			042	x	-35	088	P⇄S	16-51
			043	DSZI	16 25 46	089	RTN	24
			044	RCLi	36 45	090	*LBLC	21 13
			045	+	-55	091	+	-55
			046	x	-35	092	P⇄S	16-51

400

093	STO0	35 00	139	P⇄S	16-51	001	*LBLα	21 16 11
094	P⇄S	16-51	140	2	02	002	DSP0	-63 00
095	RTN	24	141	4	04	003	F0?	16 23 00
096	*LBLD	21 14	142	X≤Y?	16-35	004	GTO0	22 00
097	P⇄S	16-51	143	GSB8	23 08	005	0	00
098	STO1	35 01	144	P⇄S	16-51	006	SF0	16 21 00
099	P⇄S	16-51	145	RCL7	36 07	007	RTN	24
100	RTN	24	146	P⇄S	16-51	008	*LBL0	21 00
101	*LBLE	21 15	147	→HMS	16 35	009	1	01
102	HMS→	16 36	148	PRTX	-14	010	CF0	16 22 00
103	P⇄S	16-51	149	SPC	16-11	011	RTN	24
104	STO3	35 03	150	RTN	24	012	*LBLA	21 11
105	P⇄S	16-51	151	*LBL2	21 02	013	HMS→	16 36
106	X<0?	16-45	152	P⇄S	16-51	014	STOC	35 13
107	GSB2	23 02	153	RCL3	36 03	015	R↓	-31
108	RCL8	36 08	154	3	03	016	HMS→	16 36
109	-	-45	155	6	06	017	STO0	35 00
110	1	01	156	0	00	018	RTN	24
111	→R	44	157	+	-55	019	*LBLB	21 12
112	→P	34	158	P⇄S	16-51	020	STOD	35 14
113	X⇄Y	-41	159	RTN	24	021	X⇄Y	-41
114	X<0?	16-45	160	*LBL9	21 09	022	STOI	35 46
115	GSB9	23 09	161	3	03	023	3	03
116	P⇄S	16-51	162	6	06	024	0	00
117	STO4	35 04	163	0	00	025	5	05
118	RCL1	36 01	164	+	-55	026	6	06
119	RCL0	36 00	165	RTN	24	027	%	55
120	P⇄S	16-51	166	*LBL8	21 08	028	INT	16 34
121	SIN	41	167	P⇄S	16-51	029	R↑	16-31
122	×	-35	168	RCL7	36 07	030	STOE	35 15
123	6	06	169	P⇄S	16-51	031	R↓	-31
124	0	00	170	2	02	032	RCLD	36 14
125	÷	-24	171	4	04	033	+	-55
126	1	01	172	-	-45	034	STOD	35 14
127	5	05	173	P⇄S	16-51	035	RCL4	36 04
128	+	-55	174	STO7	35 07	036	3	03
129	P⇄S	16-51	175	P⇄S	16-51	037	X>Y?	16-34
130	RCL4	36 04	176	RTN	24	038	1	01
131	P⇄S	16-51				039	RCL5	36 05
132	X⇄Y	-41				040	4	04
133	÷	-24				041	÷	-24
134	RCLE	36 15				042	FRC	16 44
135	HMS→	16 36				043	+	-55
136	+	-55				044	1	01
137	P⇄S	16-51				045	X⇄Y	-41
138	STO7	35 07				046	X=Y?	16-33

047	2	02	093	RCLC	36 13	139	0	00
048	RCLD	36 14	094	-	-45	140	x	-35
049	-	-45	095	STOE	35 15	141	GSBb	23 16 12
050	CHS	-22	096	STOC	35 13	142	GSBb	23 16 12
051	STOI	35 46	097	RTN	24	143	3	03
052	F3?	16 23 03	098	*LBLE	21 15	144	0	00
053	GTO0	22 00	099	SF2	16 21 02	145	x	-35
054	6	06	100	*LBLD	21 14	146	3	03
055	CHS	-22	101	CF3	16 22 03	147	4	04
056	SIN	41	102	GSBB	23 12	148	7	07
057	X⇄Y	-41	103	RCLI	36 46	149	+	-55
058	2	02	104	1	01	150	X⇄Y	-41
059	0	00	105	5	05	151	INT	16 34
060	-	-45	106	÷	-24	152	RCLI	36 46
061	COS	42	107	1	01	153	STOC	35 13
062	2	02	108	2	02	154	+	-55
063	3	03	109	+	-55	155	RCLI	36 46
064	.	-62	110	→HMS	16 35	156	+	-55
065	3	03	111	DSP2	-63 02	157	2	02
066	x	-35	112	PRTX	-14	158	-	-45
067	CHS	-22	113	*LBLC	21 13	159	STOD	35 14
068	STOE	35 15	114	HMS→	16 36	160	6	06
069	SIN	41	115	1	01	161	x	-35
070	RCL0	36 00	116	5	05	162	-	-45
071	SIN	41	117	x	-35	163	DSP0	-63 00
072	x	-35	118	RCLC	36 13	164	RND	16 24
073	-	-45	119	+	-55	165	RCLE	36 15
074	RCL0	36 00	120	STOE	35 15	166	+	-55
075	COS	42	121	2	02	167	X⇄Y	-41
076	÷	-24	122	1	01	168	INT	16 34
077	RCLE	36 15	123	STOI	35 46	169	COS	42
078	COS	42	124	*LBL7	21 07	170	SIN⁻¹	16 41
079	÷	-24	125	RCLi	36 45	171	RCL0	36 00
080	COS⁻¹	16 42	126	FRC	16 44	172	X⇄Y	-41
081	RCLC	36 13	127	GSBe	23 16 15	173	1	01
082	X⇄Y	-41	128	RCLi	36 45	174	→R	44
083	F2?	16 23 02	129	INT	16 34	175	R↑	16-31
084	CHS	-22	130	EEX	-23	176	X⇄Y	-41
085	-	-45	131	5	05	177	→R	44
086	*LBL0	21 00	132	÷	-24	178	R↑	16-31
087	X⇄I	16-41	133	GSBe	23 16 15	179	STOI	35 46
088	7	07	134	DSZI	16 25 46	180	X⇄Y	-41
089	2	02	135	GTO7	22 07	181	→R	44
090	.	-62	136	RTN	24	182	X⇄I	16-41
091	2	02	137	*LBLe	21 16 15	183	R↑	16-31
092	+	-55	138	1	01	184	→R	44

185	X≠I	16-41
186	+	-55
187	X≠I	16-41
188	-	-45
189	→P	34
190	R↓	-31
191	1	01
192	8	08
193	0	00
194	+	-55
195	RCLC	36 13
196	X≠I	16-41
197	SIN⁻	16 41
198	5	05
199	X≤Y?	16-35
200	GSB0	23 00
201	RTN	24
202	*LBL0	21 00
203	SPC	16-11
204	CLX	-51
205	RCLD	36 14
206	GSB5	23 05
207	DSP2	-63 02
208	→HMS	16 35
209	GSB5	23 05
210	DSP1	-63 01
211	*LBL5	21 05
212	PRTX	-14
213	F0?	16 23 00
214	R/S	51
215	R↓	-31
216	RTN	24
217	*LBLb	21 16 12
218	1	01
219	8	08
220	x	-35
221	FRC	16 44
222	LSTX	16-63
223	X≠Y	-41
224	RTN	24

403

001	*LBLA	21 11	047	P⇄S	16-51	093	ST÷6	35-24 06
002	HMS→	16 36	048	STO3	35 03	094	ST÷7	35-24 07
003	STOB	35 12	049	P⇄S	16-51	095	ST÷8	35-24 08
004	R↓	-31	050	GSB3	23 03	096	ST÷9	35-24 09
005	HMS→	16 36	051	STO3	35 03	097	P⇄S	16-51
006	STOA	35 11	052	GSB4	23 04	098	GSB0	23 00
007	RTN	24	053	STO6	35 06	099	RTN	24
008	*LBLB	21 12	054	GSB5	23 05	100	*LBL0	21 00
009	HMS→	16 36	055	STO9	35 09	101	RCLE	36 15
010	STOD	35 14	056	RCL0	36 00	102	RCLI	36 46
011	R↓	-31	057	COS	42	103	RCLC	36 13
012	HMS→	16 36	058	P⇄S	16-51	104	RCLD	36 14
013	STOC	35 13	059	RCL2	36 02	105	STOI	35 46
014	RTN	24	060	COS	42	106	R↓	-31
015	*LBLC	21 13	061	RCL3	36 03	107	STOE	35 15
016	HMS→	16 36	062	COS	42	108	R↓	-31
017	STOI	35 46	063	X	-35	109	RCLA	36 11
018	R↓	-31	064	-	-45	110	RCLB	36 12
019	HMS→	16 36	065	RCL2	36 02	111	STOD	35 14
020	STOE	35 15	066	SIN	41	112	R↓	-31
021	3	03	067	RCL3	36 03	113	STOC	35 13
022	7	07	068	SIN	41	114	R↓	-31
023	1	01	069	X	-35	115	STOB	35 12
024	STO8	35 08	070	÷	-24	116	R↓	-31
025	P⇄S	16-51	071	COS⁻¹	16 42	117	STOA	35 11
026	GSB1	23 01	072	STO9	35 09	118	RTN	24
027	STO0	35 00	073	RCLE	36 15	119	*LBL1	21 01
028	GSB3	23 03	074	SIN	41	120	RCLD	36 14
029	STO1	35 01	075	P⇄S	16-51	121	RCLC	36 13
030	GSB4	23 04	076	RCL7	36 07	122	*LBL2	21 02
031	STO4	35 04	077	X	-35	123	COS	42
032	GSB5	23 05	078	RCLC	36 13	124	LSTX	16-63
033	STO7	35 07	079	SIN	41	125	SIN	41
034	GSB0	23 00	080	RCL8	36 08	126	RCLA	36 11
035	GSB1	23 01	081	X	-35	127	SIN	41
036	P⇄S	16-51	082	+	-55	128	X	-35
037	STO2	35 02	083	RCLA	36 11	129	RCLB	36 12
038	P⇄S	16-51	084	SIN	41	130	R↑	16-31
039	GSB3	23 03	085	RCL9	36 09	131	-	-45
040	STO2	35 02	086	X	-35	132	COS	42
041	GSB4	23 04	087	+	-55	133	RCLA	36 11
042	STO5	35 05	088	ST÷1	35-24 01	134	COS	42
043	GSB5	23 05	089	ST÷2	35-24 02	135	R↑	16-31
044	STO8	35 08	090	ST÷3	35-24 03	136	X	-35
045	GSB0	23 00	091	ST÷4	35-24 04	137	X	-35
046	GSB1	23 01	092	ST÷5	35-24 05	138	+	-55

139	COS⁻¹	16 42	185	RCLI	36 46	001	*LBLA	21 1
140	RTN	24	186	SIN	41	002	RCL4	36 0
141	*LBL3	21 03	187	RCLD	36 14	003	-	-4
142	RCLE	36 15	188	COS	42	004	RCL8	36 0
143	COS	42	189	X	-35	005	÷	-2
144	RCLI	36 46	190	-	-45	006	STOA	35 1
145	SIN	41	191	RCLE	36 15	007	RTN	2
146	RCLC	36 13	192	COS	42	008	*LBLB	21 1
147	SIN	41	193	X	-35	009	RCL5	36 0
148	X	-35	194	RCLC	36 13	010	-	-4
149	X	-35	195	COS	42	011	RCL8	36 0
150	RCLE	36 15	196	X	-35	012	÷	-2
151	SIN	41	197	RTN	24	013	STOB	35 1
152	RCLC	36 13	198	*LBLE	21 15	014	RCLA	36 1
153	COS	42	199	STO5	35 05	015	COS	4
154	RCLD	36 14	200	R↓	-31	016	RCL2	36 0
155	SIN	41	201	STO4	35 04	017	COS	4
156	X	-35	202	R↓	-31	018	-	-4
157	X	-35	203	HMS→	16 36	019	RCL2	36 0
158	-	-45	204	STO7	35 07	020	SIN	4
159	RTN	24	205	R↓	-31	021	÷	-2
160	*LBL4	21 04	206	HMS→	16 36	022	STOC	35 1
161	RCLE	36 15	207	STO6	35 06	023	RCLA	36 1
162	SIN	41	208	GSB6	23 06	024	SIN	41
163	RCLC	36 13	209	ST+4	35-55 04	025	RCL2	36 0
164	COS	42	210	ST+5	35-55 05	026	SIN	41
165	RCLD	36 14	211	GSB6	23 06	027	÷	-24
166	COS	42	212	ST-5	35-45 05	028	STOD	35 14
167	X	-35	213	GSB6	23 06	029	RCLB	36 12
168	X	-35	214	ST-4	35-45 04	030	COS	42
169	RCLE	36 15	215	WDTA	16-61	031	RCL3	36 03
170	COS	42	216	RTN	24	032	COS	42
171	RCLI	36 46	217	*LBL6	21 06	033	-	-45
172	COS	42	218	GSB0	23 00	034	RCL3	36 03
173	RCLC	36 13	219	RCL7	36 07	035	SIN	41
174	SIN	41	220	RCL6	36 06	036	÷	-24
175	X	-35	221	GSB2	23 02	037	STOI	35 46
176	X	-35	222	RCL8	36 08	038	RCLB	36 12
177	-	-45	223	X	-35	039	SIN	41
178	RTN	24	224	RTN	24	040	RCL3	36 03
179	*LBL5	21 05				041	SIN	41
180	RCLI	36 46				042	÷	-24
181	COS	42				043	STO0	35 00
182	RCLD	36 14				044	RCLI	36 46
183	SIN	41				045	RCLD	36 14
184	X	-35				046	X	-35

047	RCLC	36 13	093	RCLB	36 12	139	PRTX	-14
048	RCL0	36 00	094	x	-35	140	RTN	24
049	x	-35	095	+	-55	141	*LBL0	21 00
050	-	-45	096	+	-55	142	RCLI	36 46
051	STO0	35 00	097	STOD	35 14	143	X²	53
052	RCLC	36 13	098	RCL4	36 04	144	RCL1	36 01
053	RCL9	36 09	099	RCLA	36 11	145	X²	53
054	COS	42	100	x	-35	146	+	-55
055	x	-35	101	RCL5	36 05	147	RCL0	36 00
056	RCLI	36 46	102	RCLC	36 13	148	X²	53
057	-	-45	103	x	-35	149	-	-45
058	STOI	35 46	104	RCL6	36 06	150	√X	54
059	RCLC	36 13	105	RCLB	36 12	151	x	-35
060	RCL9	36 09	106	x	-35	152	RCLI	36 46
061	SIN	41	107	+	-55	153	RCL0	36 00
062	x	-35	108	+	-55	154	x	-35
063	STO1	35 01	109	STOI	35 46	155	+	-55
064	GSB0	23 00	110	RCL7	36 07	156	RCLI	36 46
065	RCL1	36 01	111	RCLA	36 11	157	X²	53
066	CHS	-22	112	x	-35	158	RCL1	36 01
067	GSB0	23 00	113	RCL8	36 08	159	X²	53
068	X>Y?	16-34	114	RCLC	36 13	160	+	-55
069	X⇆Y	-41	115	x	-35	161	÷	-24
070	F0?	16 23 00	116	RCL9	36 09	162	RCLD	36 14
071	X⇆Y	-41	117	RCLB	36 12	163	+	-55
072	STO1	35 01	118	x	-35	164	RCLC	36 13
073	RCLA	36 11	119	+	-55	165	X⇆Y	-41
074	+	-55	120	+	-55	166	÷	-24
075	COS	42	121	P⇆S	16-51	167	TAN⁻¹	16 43
076	STOA	35 11	122	STO0	35 00	168	X>0?	16-44
077	RCL1	36 01	123	RCLI	36 46	169	RTN	24
078	RCLB	36 12	124	RCLD	36 14	170	1	01
079	+	-55	125	→P	34	171	8	08
080	COS	42	126	R↓	-31	172	0	00
081	STOB	35 12	127	STOB	35 12	173	+	-55
082	RCL1	36 01	128	SIN	41	174	RTN	24
083	COS	42	129	RCL0	36 00	175	*LBLC	21 13
084	STOC	35 13	130	x	-35	176	HMS→	16 36
085	P⇆S	16-51	131	RCLI	36 46	177	STO7	35 07
086	RCL1	36 01	132	÷	-24	178	R↓	-31
087	RCLA	36 11	133	TAN⁻¹	16 43	179	HMS→	16 36
088	x	-35	134	STOA	35 11	180	STO6	35 06
089	RCL2	36 02	135	→HMS	16 35	181	RTN	24
090	RCLC	36 13	136	PRTX	-14	182	*LBLD	21 14
091	x	-35	137	RCLB	36 12	183	RCLA	36 11
092	RCL3	36 03	138	→HMS	16 35	184	STO6	35 06

185	RCLB	36 12	001	*LBLa	21 16 11	047	CHS	-22
186	STO7	35 07	002	STOE	35 15	048	HMS+	16-55
187	WDTA	16-61	003	RTN	24	049	HMS→	16 36
188	RTN	24	004	*LBLb	21 16 12	050	x	-35
189	*LBLE	21 15	005	STOC	35 13	051	CHS	-22
190	RCLA	36 11	006	RTN	24	052	STO6	35 06
191	RCL6	36 06	007	*LBLA	21 11	053	RCL7	36 07
192	+	-55	008	RCLE	36 15	054	→P	34
193	2	02	009	+	-55	055	STO9	35 09
194	÷	-24	010	RCLC	36 13	056	X⇄Y	-41
195	COS	42	011	+	-55	057	STOD	35 14
196	RCL7	36 07	012	STO2	35 02	058	RTN	24
197	RCLB	36 12	013	RCLA	36 11	059	*LBLc	21 16 13
198	-	-45	014	→HMS	16 35	060	HMS→	16 36
199	x	-35	015	STOA	35 11	061	P⇄S	16-51
200	RCLA	36 11	016	RCLB	36 12	062	STO3	35 03
201	RCL6	36 06	017	→HMS	16 35	063	P⇄S	16-51
202	-	-45	018	STOB	35 12	064	RTN	24
203	→P	34	019	RCL2	36 02	065	*LBLC	21 13
204	6	06	020	RTN	24	066	HMS→	16 36
205	0	00	021	*LBLA	21 11	067	P⇄S	16-51
206	x	-35	022	STO3	35 03	068	STO2	35 02
207	PRTX	-14	023	RTN	24	069	P⇄S	16-51
208	X⇄Y	-41	024	*LBLB	21 12	070	RTN	24
209	X<0?	16-45	025	STO0	35 00	071	*LBLD	21 14
210	GTO5	22 05	026	RTN	24	072	P⇄S	16-51
211	PRTX	-14	027	*LBLB	21 12	073	RCL3	36 03
212	RTN	24	028	STO1	35 01	074	RCL2	36 02
213	*LBL5	21 05	029	X⇄Y	-41	075	-	-45
214	3	03	030	RCLA	36 11	076	STO6	35 06
215	6	06	031	X⇄Y	-41	077	P⇄S	16-51
216	0	00	032	CHS	-22	078	RCL9	36 09
217	+	-55	033	HMS+	16-55	079	X⇄Y	-41
218	PRTX	-14	034	HMS→	16 36	080	÷	-24
219	RTN	24	035	STO7	35 07	081	6	06
220	R/S	51	036	2	02	082	0	00
			037	÷	-24	083	x	-35
			038	RCL0	36 00	084	STO9	35 09
			039	HMS→	16 36	085	PRTX	-14
			040	+	-55	086	RCLD	36 14
			041	COS	42	087	GSB0	23 00
			042	P⇄S	16-51	088	PRTX	-14
			043	STO4	35 04	089	RCL2	36 02
			044	P⇄S	16-51	090	RCL3	36 03
			045	RCLB	36 12	091	P⇄S	16-51
			046	RCL1	36 01	092	RCL6	36 06

093	P⇄S	16-51	139	0	00	001	*LBLa	21 16 11
094	x	-35	140	ST04	35 04	002	P⇄S	16-51
095	6	06	141	ST05	35 05	003	ST02	35 02
096	0	00	142	ST07	35 07	004	R↓	-31
097	÷	-24	143	ST09	35 09	005	ST03	35 03
098	→R	44	144	RCL3	36 03	006	P⇄S	16-51
099	ST-7	35-45 07	145	RCL2	36 02	007	RTN	24
100	X⇄Y	-41	146	P⇄S	16-51	008	*LBLA	21 11
101	ST-6	35-45 06	147	ST04	35 04	009	STOE	35 15
102	RCL6	36 06	148	R↓	-31	010	RTN	24
103	RCL7	36 07	149	ST05	35 05	011	*LBLA	21 11
104	→P	34	150	RCL6	36 06	012	STOD	35 14
105	6	06	151	P⇄S	16-51	013	RTN	24
106	0	00	152	RTN	24	014	*LBLA	21 11
107	x	-35	153	*LBL0	21 00	015	STOI	35 46
108	P⇄S	16-51	154	3	03	016	RTN	24
109	RCL6	36 06	155	6	06	017	*LBLB	21 12
110	÷	-24	156	0	00	018	STOC	35 13
111	P⇄S	16-51	157	→R	44	019	RTN	24
112	ST05	35 05	158	→P	34	020	*LBLd	21 16 14
113	PRTX	-14	159	X⇄Y	-41	021	P⇄S	16-51
114	X⇄Y	-41	160	X<0?	16-45	022	ST00	35 00
115	GSB0	23 00	161	+	-55	023	RTN	24
116	ST04	35 04	162	RTN	24	024	*LBLd	21 16 14
117	PRTX	-14	163	*LBLE	21 15	025	ST01	35 01
118	RCLA	36 11	164	CLRG	16-53	026	P⇄S	16-51
119	ST00	35 00	165	P⇄S	16-51	027	RTN	24
120	P⇄S	16-51	166	CLRG	16-53	028	*LBLb	21 16 12
121	ST00	35 00	167	P⇄S	16-51	029	HMS→	16 36
122	P⇄S	16-51	168	CLX	-51	030	ST00	35 00
123	RCLB	36 12	169	RTN	24	031	RTN	24
124	ST01	35 01	170	*LBLd	21 16 14	032	*LBLb	21 16 12
125	P⇄S	16-51	171	STOI	35 46	033	HMS→	16 36
126	ST01	35 01	172	RCLi	36 45	034	RCL0	36 00
127	P⇄S	16-51	173	ISZI	16 26 46	035	-	-45
128	RCL4	36 04	174	RCLi	36 45	036	ST04	35 04
129	RCL5	36 05	175	RTN	24	037	RTN	24
130	P⇄S	16-51	176	*LBLe	21 16 15	038	*LBLc	21 16 13
131	ST07	35 07	177	ST03	35 03	039	P⇄S	16-51
132	R↓	-31	178	R↓	-31	040	RCL2	36 02
133	ST06	35 06	179	ST02	35 02	041	RCL3	36 03
134	0	00	180	RTN	24	042	STO1	35 01
135	ST09	35 09	181	R/S	51	043	R↓	-31
136	RCL4	36 04				044	ST00	35 00
137	STOD	35 14				045	P⇄S	16-51
138	P⇄S	16-51						

046	RTN	24
047	*LBLC	21 13
048	STO2	35 02
049	RTN	24
050	*LBLC	21 13
051	STO3	35 03
052	RTN	24
053	*LBLD	21 14
054	P⇄S	16-51
055	RCL0	36 00
056	RCL1	36 01
057	RCL2	36 02
058	RCL3	36 03
059	GSB0	23 00
060	PRTX	-14
061	STO4	35 04
062	X⇄Y	-41
063	GSB2	23 02
064	PRTX	-14
065	STO5	35 05
066	P⇄S	16-51
067	RCL4	36 04
068	P⇄S	16-51
069	RCL4	36 04
070	P⇄S	16-51
071	X⇄Y	-41
072	÷	-24
073	STO5	35 05
074	RCLE	36 15
075	GSB3	23 03
076	RCLC	36 13
077	P⇄S	16-51
078	RCL5	36 05
079	P⇄S	16-51
080	RCL5	36 05
081	GSB0	23 00
082	STOB	35 12
083	PRTX	-14
084	X⇄Y	-41
085	GSB2	23 02
086	PRTX	-14
087	STOA	35 11
088	P⇄S	16-51
089	RCL2	36 02
090	RCL3	36 03
091	P⇄S	16-51
092	RCL2	36 02
093	RCL3	36 03
094	GSB0	23 00
095	STO8	35 08
096	X⇄Y	-41
097	GSB2	23 02
098	STO9	35 09
099	RCLA	36 11
100	RTN	24
101	*LBLe	21 16 15
102	RCL9	36 09
103	RCLA	36 11
104	-	-45
105	SIN	41
106	RCLB	36 12
107	×	-35
108	RCLC	36 13
109	÷	-24
110	SIN^{-1}	16 41
111	RCL9	36 09
112	+	-55
113	GSB2	23 02
114	P⇄S	16-51
115	STO8	35 08
116	P⇄S	16-51
117	RCLD	36 14
118	-	-45
119	RCLI	36 46
120	-	-45
121	GSB2	23 02
122	STOE	35 15
123	PRTX	-14
124	P⇄S	16-51
125	RCL8	36 08
126	P⇄S	16-51
127	RCLC	36 13
128	RCLA	36 11
129	RCLB	36 12
130	GSB1	23 01
131	PRTX	-14
132	P⇄S	16-51
133	STO6	35 06
134	P⇄S	16-51
135	RCL8	36 08
136	X⇄Y	-41
137	÷	-24
138	→HMS	16 35
139	DSP4	-63 04
140	PRTX	-14
141	PSE	16 51
142	RTN	24
143	*LBLE	21 15
144	RCLE	36 15
145	GSB3	23 03
146	RCLC	36 13
147	RCLA	36 11
148	RCLB	36 12
149	GSB1	23 01
150	P⇄S	16-51
151	STO7	35 07
152	X⇄Y	-41
153	RCL7	36 07
154	P⇄S	16-51
155	RCL4	36 04
156	×	-35
157	P⇄S	16-51
158	RCL2	36 02
159	RCL3	36 03
160	GSB1	23 01
161	STO3	35 03
162	X⇄Y	-41
163	STO2	35 02
164	RCL3	36 03
165	P⇄S	16-51
166	RCL2	36 02
167	RCL3	36 03
168	GSB0	23 00
169	STO8	35 08
170	PRTX	-14
171	X⇄Y	-41
172	GSB2	23 02
173	STO9	35 09
174	PRTX	-14
175	RTN	24
176	*LBL0	21 00
177	→R	44
178	R↓	-31
179	R↓	-31
180	→R	44

181	X⇄Y	-41	001	*LBLA	21 11	046	x	-35
182	R↓	-31	002	RCL4	36 04	047	RCLC	36 13
183	-	-45	003	-	-45	048	RCL0	36 00
184	R↓	-31	004	RCL8	36 08	049	x	-35
185	X⇄Y	-41	005	÷	-24	050	-	-45
186	-	-45	006	STOA	35 11	051	STO0	35 00
187	R↑	16-31	007	RTN	24	052	RCLC	36 13
188	→P	34	008	*LBLB	21 12	053	RCL9	36 09
189	RTN	24	009	RCL5	36 05	054	COS	42
190	*LBL1	21 01	010	-	-45	055	x	-35
191	→R	44	011	RCL8	36 08	056	RCLI	36 46
192	R↓	-31	012	÷	-24	057	-	-45
193	R↓	-31	013	STOB	35 12	058	STOI	35 46
194	→R	44	014	RCLA	36 11	059	RCLC	36 13
195	X⇄Y	-41	015	COS	42	060	RCL9	36 09
196	R↓	-31	016	RCL2	36 02	061	SIN	41
197	+	-55	017	COS	42	062	x	-35
198	R↓	-31	018	-	-45	063	STO1	35 01
199	+	-55	019	RCL2	36 02	064	GSB0	23 00
200	R↑	16-31	020	SIN	41	065	RCL1	36 01
201	→P	34	021	÷	-24	066	CHS	-22
202	RTN	24	022	STOC	35 13	067	GSB0	23 00
203	*LBL2	21 02	023	RCLA	36 11	068	X>Y?	16-34
204	3	03	024	SIN	41	069	X⇄Y	-41
205	6	06	025	RCL2	36 02	070	F0?	16 23 00
206	0	00	026	SIN	41	071	X⇄Y	-41
207	→R	44	027	÷	-24	072	STO1	35 01
208	→P	34	028	STOD	35 14	073	RCLA	36 11
209	X⇄Y	-41	029	RCLB	36 12	074	+	-55
210	X<0?	16-45	030	COS	42	075	COS	42
211	+	-55	031	RCL3	36 03	076	STOA	35 11
212	RTN	24	032	COS	42	077	RCL1	36 01
213	*LBL3	21 03	033	-	-45	078	RCLB	36 12
214	RCLD	36 14	034	RCL3	36 03	079	+	-55
215	+	-55	035	SIN	41	080	COS	42
216	RCLI	36 46	036	÷	-24	081	STOB	35 12
217	+	-55	037	STOI	35 46	082	RCL1	36 01
218	RTN	24	038	RCLB	36 12	083	COS	42
219	R/S	51	039	SIN	41	084	STOC	35 13
			040	RCL3	36 03	085	P⇄S	16-51
			041	SIN	41	086	RCL1	36 01
			042	÷	-24	087	RCLA	36 11
			043	STO0	35 00	088	x	-35
			044	RCLI	36 46	089	RCL2	36 02
			045	RCLD	36 14	090	RCLC	36 13

(CONTINUED)

091	x	-35	136	PRTX	-14	181	RCLB	36 12
092	RCL3	36 03	137	RCLB	36 12	182	RCLA	36 11
093	RCLB	36 12	138	→HMS	16 35	183	GSB6	23 06
094	x	-35	139	PRTX	-14	184	STO6	35 06
095	+	-55	140	RTN	24	185	RCLD	36 14
096	+	-55	141	*LBL0	21 00	186	RCLC	36 13
097	STOD	35 14	142	RCLI	36 46	187	GSB6	23 06
098	RCL4	36 04	143	X²	53	188	STO7	35 07
099	RCLA	36 11	144	RCL1	36 01	189	RCLI	36 46
100	x	-35	145	X²	53	190	RCLE	36 15
101	RCL5	36 05	146	+	-55	191	GSB6	23 06
102	RCLC	36 13	147	RCL0	36 00	192	ST-7	35-45 07
103	x	-35	148	X²	53	193	ST-6	35-45 06
104	RCL6	36 06	149	-	-45	194	RCL6	36 06
105	RCLB	36 12	150	√X	54	195	RCL4	36 04
106	x	-35	151	x	-35	196	+	-55
107	+	-55	152	RCLI	36 46	197	PRTX	-14
108	+	-55	153	RCL0	36 00	198	RCL7	36 07
109	STOI	35 46	154	x	-35	199	RCL5	36 05
110	RCL7	36 07	155	+	-55	200	+	-55
111	RCLA	36 11	156	RCLI	36 46	201	PRTX	-14
112	x	-35	157	X²	53	202	RTN	24
113	RCL8	36 08	158	RCL1	36 01	203	*LBL6	21 06
114	RCLC	36 13	159	X²	53	204	COS	42
115	x	-35	160	+	-55	205	LSTX	16-63
116	RCL9	36 09	161	÷	-24	206	SIN	41
117	RCLB	36 12	162	RCLD	36 14	207	RCL0	36 00
118	x	-35	163	+	-55	208	SIN	41
119	+	-55	164	RCLC	36 13	209	x	-35
120	+	-55	165	X⇄Y	-41	210	RCL1	36 01
121	P⇄S	16-51	166	÷	-24	211	R↑	16-31
122	STO0	35 00	167	TAN⁻	16 43	212	-	-45
123	RCLI	36 46	168	X>0?	16-44	213	COS	42
124	RCLD	36 14	169	RTN	24	214	RCL0	36 00
125	→P	34	170	1	01	215	COS	42
126	R↓	-31	171	8	08	216	R↑	16-31
127	STOB	35 12	172	0	00	217	x	-35
128	SIN	41	173	+	-55	218	x	-35
129	RCL0	36 00	174	RTN	24	219	+	-55
130	x	-35	175	*LBLE	21 15	220	COS⁻	16 42
131	RCLI	36 46	176	HMS→	16 36	221	RCL8	36 08
132	÷	-24	177	STO1	35 01	222	x	-35
133	TAN⁻	16 43	178	X⇄Y	-41	223	RTN	24
134	STOA	35 11	179	HMS→	16 36			
135	→HMS	16 35	180	STO0	35 00			

Index

[*For each major topic, routines are listed under a separate heading following the subject entries.*]

Adler, Alan J., 157
Almanac for Computers (Doggett, Kaplan, and Seidelmann), 8, 227, 230–31, 234, 261–62
  Stellar Tables in, 231, 262
altitudes of celestial objects
  regression methods and, 4, 9, 228–29, 241–42
  see also local apparent noon
anemometers, 153
  heel angle's effect on, 155–56
apparent wind, 153, 154, 156, 160
  leeway and, 157–58, 176
  racing and, 176
Aries, GHA of, 8, 256
  data cards for, 230, 233
average speed, determination of, 34–35
averaging of bearings, 5, 19–23
  see also regression
azimuth, calculation of, 4, 9, 236–40
  see also sight reduction

Barco-Navigation, 14, 312
bearing error, defined, 18
bearing regression, *see* linear regression; regression running fix
beat to windward
  in cruising, 158–71
  defined, 173
  in racing, 172–97
beat to windward, routines: (HP-67/97) 189–90; (SR-52) 168–70, 196
"Best Course to Windward, The," (Adler), 157
"Bowditch"—*American Practical Navigator*, vol. 1 (Defense Mapping Agency Hydrographic Center), 228, 265
buoys and floating aids, updating position of, 90–91

calculator navigation
  accuracy of, 5, 7
  convenience of, 4
  intended users of, 5–6
  objectives of, 3–5
calculators, 3–14
  external memory of, 3–4
  use of, in marine environment, 14
  see also specific calculators
celestial linear regression, routine: (HP-67/97) 229
celestial navigation, 8–9, 13, 226–62
  abbreviations in routines of, 226
  introduction to, 227–28
  magnetic-card memory used in, 3, 4, 227, 230–35
  observations at local apparent noon in, 243–55

prerecorded almanac data cards in, 230–35, 311–12
  regression for accuracy improvement in, 227, 228–29
  sight reduction in, 8–9, 227, 230–43
  star observations planned in, 256–62
  tenths of minutes in, 91
celestial navigation, routines: (HP-67/97) 229, 232–35, 237–40, 251–53, 255, 257–59
  see also specific routines
chart factor
  calculation of, 87, 92*n*
  defined, 19, 87
chart-factor method
  estimated position by, 104–5
  fixing by, 87, 122–26, 133–37, 138, 139–43
  planning by, 96, 97, 98–99, 281
  set and drift by, 126–27, 134–35
  tracking by, 104, 105–7, 111–15
chart plotting, 4, 227, 243
charts, 19, 243
  as source of co-ordinates for prerecording, 90
  updating of, 91
Coastal Navigation (Williams), 24*n*
Coast Guard, U.S., 90
coastwise navigation, 4–5, 16–150, 228, 243
  abbreviations in routines of, 16
  defined, 17
  using distances and bearings, 17, 18, 28–86
  HP-65 in, 3
  introduction to, 17–18
  using latitude and longitude, 7–8, 17, 18, 87–150
  latitude and longitude vs. distance and bearing in, 18
  magnetic-card memory used in, 3, 4, 7–8
commercial mariners, calculator navigation for, 5, 6
compass, magnetic, variation and deviation of, 4–5, 9, 24
correction and uncorrection, 25–27, 157–58
  defined, 25
course and speed made good, 17
  in cruising, 158–60
  leeway and, 24–25
  in loran navigation, 282–85
  in racing, *see* downwind sailing; optimum speed to windward
  from two fixes, 80–86, 138, 149–50
course and speed made good, routines
  using distances and bearings: (HP-67/97) 81–82, 193–94, 282–84; (SR-52) 83–85, 169–70
  using latitude and longitude: (SR-52) 149–50
  loran navigation: (HP-67/97) 282–84
  see also course made good, routines

413

course made good
  regression used for, 61, 76–79
  from three bearings, 61, 62, 76–80
  see also course and speed made good
course made good, routines: (HP-67/97) 77;
  (SR-52) 79
  see also course and speed made good, routines
course to steer, see planning
crab angle, defined, 25
cruise sailing, 153, 158–71
cruise sailing, routines: (HP-67/97) 162–63;
  (SR-52) 168–71
current
  tacking and, 153
  wind combined with, 153–54
  see also set and drift
current wind, 153
curve fitting, routines: (HP-67/97) 181–84;
  (SR-52) 185–87, 202–3

data cards
  celestial, use of on HP-41C, 311–12
  duplication of, 14, 91
  prerecorded almanac, 230–35
  prerecorded latitude and longitude, 90–95,
    310
  purchase of, 14, 312
  for star planning, 256–59, 311
data cards, routines
  GHA Aries: (HP-67/97) 233
  latitude and longitude: (HP-41C) 310; (HP-
    67/97) 92–93; (SR-52) 94–95
  moon: (HP-67/97) 233–34
  planet: (HP-67/97) 232–33
  star: (HP-67/97) 232, 235
  star planning: (HP-41C) 311; (HP-67/97)
    257
Defense Mapping Agency Hydrographic Center, 228, 265
deviation, see variation and deviation
distances and bearings, 18, 28–86
  coastwise navigation using, 17, 18, 28–86
  course and speed made good by, 80–86
  estimated position by, 31–32, 42–46, 53–60
  fixing by, 28–30, 32–37, 39, 45, 47–50, 52–53
  in loran navigation, 279, 282–90
  planning by, 30–31, 37–41, 50–53
  set and drift by, 32, 46, 80, 81–82, 85–86
  tracking by, 56–60
Doggett, LeRoy E., 227n
downwind sailing, 197–224
  direct, 197–216
  direct, current present, 209, 210, 215–16
  direct, no current, 211–15
  Fourier-series coefficients and, 204, 205–10,
    211, 222–23
  polar performance curves and, 197–214
  tacking, 8, 153, 215–24
downwind sailing, routines
  direct: (HP-67/97) 213–14; (SR-52) 224
  exponential curve fit: (HP-67/97) 183;
    (SR-52) 202
  Fourier series: (HP-67/97) 207; (SR-52) 208
  logarithmic curve fit: (HP-67/97) 184;
    (SR-52) 203

power curve fit: (HP-67/97) 182–83; (SR-52)
  186–87
tacking: (HP-67/197) 218–19; (SR-52) 196
downwind-speed curve, 200
downwind tacking, 8, 153, 215–24
  current present, 215, 217, 221
  desirable circumstances for, 172, 173,
    197–99
  direct-downwind sailing compared to, 220–21, 222
  no current, 219–20
downwind tacking, routines, see downwind
  sailing, routines
downwind tacking sector, routines: (HP-
  67/97) 183; (SR-52) 202
due-downwind speed, routines: (HP-67/97)
  182–83; (SR-52) 186–87
Dutton's Navigation and Piloting, 265

estimated position, 17, 265
  defined, 42
  using distances and bearings, 31–32, 42–46,
    53–60
  using latitude and longitude, 87, 104–8, 114,
    116–22
  leeway and, 25
  in loran navigation, 283–90
  multiple legs, 54–56, 116–22
  see also tracking
estimated position, routines
  using chart-factor method: (HP-67/97) 105
  using distances and bearings: (HP-67/97)
    31–32, 57–58, 283–84; (SR-52) 54
  using latitude and longitude: (HP-67/97)
    105–10, 118–20; (SR-52) 121–22
  in loran navigation: (HP-67/97) 283–84
  using mid-latitude method: (HP-67/97) 108,
    118–20; (SR-52) 121–22
  multiple legs in: (HP-67/97) 32, 58, 106–7,
    120, 283–84; (SR-52) 54, 122
  tracking of, see tracking, routines
exponential curve fit, routines: (HP-67/97)
  183; (SR-52) 202
external memory
  advantage of, 3
  latitude and longitude method facilitated by,
    87–90
  two forms of, 3–4

fishing, 6
fixing, 5–6, 7–8, 17
  in celestial navigation, 227, 230, 240–43,
    250, 252–53
  in determining course and speed made good,
    80–86
  using distances and bearings, 27–30, 32–41,
    44–53, 61–75
  using latitude and longitude, 87, 90, 122–26,
    128–31, 133–48
  leeway and, 25
  linear regression in, 7, 20–22, 33, 61–69
  in loran navigation, 9–10, 268, 273–79
  loran vs. celestial navigation for, 272
  from moving vessel, 27–28
  planning combined with, 39–41, 50–53,
    133–34
  see also fix on two objects; regression run-

414

416